Merchants of SPEED

Paul D. Smith

Foreword by Barney Navarro

motorbooks

DEDICATION

To Ed Iskenderian and John Athan . . .
without their support, this book would never have been written.

First published in 2009 by Motorbooks, an imprint of MBI Publishing Company, 400 First Avenue North, Suite 300, Minneapolis, MN 55401 USA

Motorbooks titles are also available at discounts in bulk quantity for industrial or sales-promotional use. For details write to Special Sales Manager at MBI Publishing Company, 400 First Avenue North, Suite 300, Minneapolis, MN 55401 USA.

To find out more about our books, visit us online at www.motorbooks.com.

Library of Congress Cataloging-in-Publication Data

Smith, Paul D., 1946-
  Merchants of speed : the men who built America's performance industry / Paul D. Smith.
    p. cm.
  Includes index.
  ISBN 978-0-7603-3567-3 (hb w/ jkt)
  1. Automobile engineers–United States–Biography. 2. Hot rods–United States–History. 3. Automobiles–Performance–United States–History. 4. Automobile supplies industry–United States–History. I. Title.
  TL139.S65 2009
  629.228'6092273–dc22

                                                            2009009939

Front Cover: *Photo courtesy Peter Vincent*

Title page: The Evans tank gets a push start at El Mirage from the well-known customized '40 coupe of Gil Ayala. *Courtesy Gene Ohly*

Acquisitions Editor: Dennis Pernu
Content Editor: Peter Bodensteiner
Design Manager: Kou Lor
Designer: Simon Larkin

Printed in China

Contents

Foreword

The achievements presented in this book needed to be preserved truthfully without creating myths, and I feel that Paul Smith has accomplished this task. Having been a published writer for a while myself, I know the tedium involved in attaining accuracy. The stories written here were put forth, as much as possible, from quotations taken directly from recorded interviews, seemingly forsaking any urge to indulge in further embellishments.

The dry lakes racers opened a door of opportunity. They were the inspiration for small entrepreneurs to try their hands at manufacturing what they knew best: speed equipment, but for sale to the public. Being one of this group myself, I know the dedication and focus it required to be successful. When I was discharged from the U.S. Army Air Corps, I had already put into action my plans to design and produce the equipment I believed to be winners.

It's been an arduous ride, always challenging. The memorable associations and incidences along the trek give me hours of entertainment in recall. All in all it's been good. My hope is that the reader will be able to come along for the ride, place himself in this recounted history, and feel the beginning and continuation of a great sport.

—B. J. Navarro

The author, right, with Barney Navarro, 2003. *Author photo*

Introduction

Since the early 1920s, the Mojave Desert of Southern California has provided a playground for hot rodders to run whatever the imaginations and wallets could conjure up. These dry lakes, plus warm winters, early speed equipment manufacturers, and speed-hungry teenagers helped create what is often referred to as the "cradle of hot rodding."

With the end of World War II, there erupted a phenomenal growth of motorsports throughout the United States. In Southern California, attendance and participation in all types of racing dramatically increased. The California Roadster Association was created to give those who wanted to participate on circle tracks places to race. Organizations like the Southern California Timing Association and the Russetta Timing Association provided safe racing venues at the dry lakes for speed trials. The introduction of hot rod shows allowed kids to display their hopped-up cars, and the founding of *Hot Rod* magazine in 1948 was the direct result of one such hot rod show. This publication spread Southern California's hot rodding trends across the country, thus creating a demand for specialty equipment and saving many small-parts manufacturers from falling into obscurity. Who knows—if it

hadn't been for *Hot Rod*, the National Hot Rod Association, under the skillful leadership of Wally Parks, may never have been formed. By 1950, the specialty speed equipment business, centered in Southern California, had grown to a $12-million-a-year industry.

History is not always exact or even true, but the following accounts come as close as possible to recording the facts without taking liberties to fill in the blank spaces. By 1953, basically everything that needed to be known was, and those who followed needed only to reinvent. This book originally intended to begin with Ed Winfield and finish with Harvey Crane Jr., and report on as many individuals as possible within that time frame. Unfortunately, a book can contain only so much, and the stories of Harmon & Collins, Clay Smith, Ed Meyer, Ed Winfield, and others had to be left out due to a lack of space or a lack of photographs.

The merchants mentioned herein are but a fraction of the speed-equipment manufacturers who have come and gone over years of racing history, but this group and their peers played a huge role in the history of hot rodding as we know it today.

—*Paul D. Smith*

CHAPTER 1

Ansen Automotive

LOU SENTER

Without a doubt, the most prolific manufacturer in the speed equipment business during the 1940s, 1950s, and 1960s was Louis Senter, cofounder of Ansen Automotive. There was little in the specialty automotive business that the Ansen shop didn't design, manufacture, warehouse, or sell. The Senter influence in automotive products stretched from coast to coast.

His competitive and entrepreneurial spirit evolved early in life, beginning with soapbox derbies. It was nurtured through his teenage years by building speed parts in his backyard garage, honed by automotive racing, and finally matured by building a successful, internationally recognized manufacturing and marketing company.

FIRST TROPHY

Lou Senter was born in Los Angeles and, like a lot of youngsters who were fortunate enough to grow up in this cradle of hot rodding, his interest in cars developed early in life. His first introduction to four wheels occurred during his last year of grammar school and resulted from a promotional stunt put on by a local race car track.

Besides being in the petroleum business, Earl B. Gilmore was the owner and promoter of the famed Gilmore Stadium, a quarter-mile dirt race car track that saw some of the finest midget racing in the country. Over time, Earl realized that he needed something to keep his fans entertained during intermissions and came up with the idea of having a contest in which kids pushed their homemade soapbox karts around the track. It appealed to Lou's competitive nature when he heard about the event, being a fast runner and in pretty fair condition from participating in a variety of school sports.

After laying out a rough plan for a racer, he scrounged together enough parts to put the project together. A natural propensity toward mechanics began to surface as he built the kart using stuff he found. A borrowed metal sign became the hand-formed body, a length of pipe was the exhaust, wheels were procured from a wagon, and it was finished off with handpainted flames on the hood, making the racer look as close to a real midget as was possible. It was no contest on race day. With his younger brother Bobby steering, Lou pushed the kart around the track in front of a stadium of cheering fans to win his first race, and today that same first-place trophy that he won so many years ago sits alongside a lifetime of mementos on a shelf in Lou's den.

LAYING THE FOUNDATION

Although he was deeply involved with track and field sports at Fremont High in Los Angeles, Lou couldn't stay away from the lure of hot rods. He'd chosen Fremont because of the great machine and auto shop courses, with future plans of becoming a machinist. After collecting enough parts and pieces, he put together a stripped-down T roadster powered by a Model A engine with a Rajo head.

Lou's natural aptitude for mechanics soon had him working on friends' cars in his parents' backyard. His father preferred that Lou was constructive with his time rather than hanging around on the streets, and he encouraged his son to set up a small shop in the family's two-car

Opposite: The first car to break the 150-mile-per-hour barrier in the quarter-mile on gasoline was Ansen's A/G dragster powered by a Packard 435-ci V-8 outfitted with a GMC blower and Hilborn injectors. *Courtesy Lou Senter*

The car that started it all. Lou sits proudly in the push cart that he built to enter a contest held during an intermission at Gilmore Stadium. He pushed his younger brother around the dirt quarter-mile track to take the first-place trophy. *Courtesy Lou Senter*

garage that was eventually equipped with a small metal lathe, welder, drill press, and assorted hand tools. At the age of 16, Lou ventured into his first business on a part-time basis, performing engine repairs, splitting manifolds, and doing whatever else he was capable of doing on his friend's cars. He even hand cast the aluminum plaques for the Idlers car club, of which he was a member.

Though it wasn't a moneymaker, his business established his love of working with cars, and a lot of trial and error in experimenting with different ideas became the catalyst of success. "I held the belief that if you tried it and it didn't work, try it again," Lou said. "Find a way to make it work." The makeshift garage machine shop was the genesis of a keen interest and desire for making speed parts and laid the foundation for things to come.

PART-TIME JOB

Even while participating in high school sports and working in his garage shop, Lou found time for a part-time job at the Alexander Company, which manufactured gas-powered, tethered, model race cars. A fad of the day was racing these tethered miniature race cars on small, wooden, oval tracks. The idea originated during the 1930s in Southern California and eventually spread across the country. Lou recalled going to a track on Santa Monica Boulevard and watching these cars racing two at time, tethered on wires and held onto the track with a small guide that fit in a slot—an early version of the slot-car craze of the 1960s.

These little speed demons consisted of a miniature cast-aluminum body powered by a model airplane engine. The Alexander Company manufactured a car that used an Olson gas engine. Lou's job was assembling the miniature working-drive assembly of the race car's chassis.

The Alexander Company also manufactured an overhead-valve conversion assembly for the 21-stud Ford flathead V-8. Later, when Lou raced at the dry lakes, he outfitted his '32 roadster with a set of Alexander OHV heads and managed 112 miles per hour at Muroc.

RACE CAR DRIVER

Back in the 1930s, an ex-heavyweight bare-knuckle prize fighter named Jim Jeffries trained fighters and held informal fights in the barn on his ranch in the San Fernando Valley. The Jeffries ranch also contained a dirt half-mile race track where amateur drivers honed their racing skills. Around 1936 or 1937, Lou Senter and schoolmate Jimmy Miller drove their roadsters up to the ranch to watch the races. It was a "run whacha' brung" style of racing, and it took very little persuading to get the two youths to strip their cars of nonessentials and get into the fray. Lou became more or less a regular at the track, and to help with expenses, one of the racers would walk through the crowd of spectators with a crash helmet in hand, collecting donations that'd be used as prize money for the drivers. The Jeffries ranch was a track where novices could go have some fun and get a little racing experience, and it spawned several great drivers, including the fabulous Frank "Wildman" McGurk.

Upon graduating from Fremont High in 1939, Lou got a job with the Byron Jackson Oil Tool Company as an apprentice machinist. During the late 1930s, the Midget Auto Racing Association (MARA) was riding high in popularity at tracks such as Gilmore and Balboa, and it didn't take much prodding for Lou to jump into the action.

He even found time to be a reporter for a short-lived racing magazine called *Throttle* and penned a column about midget racing entitled "Speedway Highlights." Unfortunately, poor timing spelled an early demise for the racing paper, which was first published in January 1941 and folded with the advent of World War II (Lou's brother Sidney was also a writer for the magazine).

BOARD-TRACK RACING

Once America entered into World War II, Lou enlisted in the navy, where he spent his military tour as a first-class machinist. Four years later, when he was honorably discharged, his naval uniform sleeve displayed the stripes of a chief machinist. It was only a matter of time before Lou was again caught up in racing, picking up where he'd left off four years earlier. The postwar growth in auto racing was nothing short of amazing. The West Coast had every description of race track, including wooden tracks like the one at the Los Angeles Coliseum.

This board track began as the Nutley Bowl in New York State, but after several racing fatalities, the track was shut down and sold. Bill White, a promoter and owner of a bar on Slauson Avenue in Los Angeles, purchased the outfit and installed it at the coliseum for midget racing. An estimated 70,000 spectators came out to watch the grand-opening race.

To promote the grand opening, White offered substantial appearance money to make sure there'd be plenty of midgets for the show. Lou received a phone call from White offering Lou, who had just finished building his midget racer, $500 in appearance money for opening night. Lou hired Marty Kline to drive the car, but as luck would have it, Marty got ill just before the race, so Lou decided he would drive the midget himself. (Kline would later become an employee of Ansen Automotive.)

In 1935, Lou and his brothers Harold and Sid built this hot rod using a T body with a hand-formed engine hood, a chrome spare-wheel cover on the rear, and a chrome bar grille in front of a T radiator shell, topped off with a skull radiator cap (similar to the one on the Iskenderian roadster today). Power came from a Rajo OHV Model A. That's Sid with two lady passengers. *Courtesy Lou Senter*

The majority of the midgets were running the 105 Offenhauser engine that was designed especially for that class, while fellows like Lou, who were on a tight budget, used the little Ford V8-60 flathead on alcohol.

When race day arrived, all the cars had already qualified by the time Lou got to the track, and the starter, Dominic Distarce, told Lou that he had 15 minutes to get on the track and try to qualify for the race. This added pressure didn't help his nerves any. After running 10 or 15 warmup laps, he'd calmed down enough to feel pretty comfortable on the wood track. Once he was back in the pits, Lou was told that he had just bumped Duke Nalon to take over the pole position for the feature. Feeling more than a bit apprehensive, Lou said, "I don't want to start up here. I have no experience. Put me in the back."

Joe Garson, a local midget driver, replied, "Don't worry, Senter, we'll help you through." Lou wasn't quite sure what Joe meant by that and started at the rear of the pack anyway.

Once the race was under way, Lou gradually moved up through the ranks, being cautious not to spin out and cause an accident. Averaging 103 miles per hour in 11-second laps around the board track, he moved up enough to finish sixth overall and collected close to $2,500 in winnings.

"It felt so darn good," Lou said. "Racing on the board track just came natural to me. The sides of the track were banked to the point where you couldn't walk up them. In the pits, there was a length of white linoleum, and as you came off the track, you had to drive down it. If your car was leaking anything—water, oil, or fuel—you were out of racing for the day. The last thing the promoter wanted was a leaky car to make the wooden track any more slippery than it already was. Running on the narrow tread tires of those days didn't help the handling either.

"How the hell do you keep a V8-60 from leaking? My secret was to place an inch-thick felt pad on top of the belly pan just under the engine. It would never leak."

"It was smart, and it wasn't smart. In one race, the engine was leaking alcohol, and I didn't notice it. Finally, the alky was set ablaze by a leaky exhaust header. As soon as my feet started to burn, I knew that I had problems [alcohol burns clear]. The whole belly pan was on fire. I pulled off the track into the pits and dove out of the cockpit. Fortunately, I just singed my feet."

Only six races were held on the board track at the coliseum before it was closed down.

Always in search of something that'd give him an edge over the competition, Lou outfitted his V8-60 midget with dual exhaust pipes along the side of the car, while everyone else was running a single pipe. "It sounded better, if nothing else," Lou said.

Another idea that resulted from racing the midget was a water-cooled manifold that bolted to the sides of the V8-60 or a V8-85 block. Lou would later market this product when he cofounded Ansen Automotive. It was called the Eskimo Dual Water Pump and could either be driven directly off the front end of the crankshaft or by a chain drive.

RACING SECRETS

Conventional motorsport wisdom says that there are no magic potions for increasing automotive performance, just the ability to out-think your opponent on the track and in the shop. No doubt standing in the right spot looking over your opponent's shoulder without his knowledge also helps.

In the postwar era, one of the top-running midgets racing in Southern California belonged to Vic Edelbrock Sr. Vic and Lou ran similar V8-60s in their midgets, and though the race cars looked similar, Lou's was never quite able to overpower the Edelbrock car. Vic's midget could easily pull away from the rest of the pack coming out of the corners.

Vic and Lou were pretty good friends on and off the track, and occasionally Lou would stop in at Vic's shop after work for a little bull session and a drink. On one particular visit, fortune was riding with Lou; walking by Vic's dynamometer, he noticed the midget engine partially covered with a tarp, but not enough to prevent Lou from seeing an Edelbrock speed secret—Vic was running a flywheel. Midgets didn't normally have flywheels, as they used a magneto ignition and an in-out gearbox (no clutch or transmission), and they were push started. They had no explicit need for a heavy standard flywheel or starter, but the flywheel no doubt helped Edelbrock's engine maintain its momentum and accelerate more easily when getting back on the gas out of a corner. At the next race date, Lou's midget was able to run almost side by side with the surprised Edelbrock. Though Lou had installed a flywheel behind his own V8-60 engine, the Edelbrock midget still had a little extra speed. It eventually came to light that Vic was running nitromethane fuel—with propylene oxide to hide the distinct smell of the nitro—and a two-speed Casale quick-change rearend. "After adding that stuff to nitro it smells like shoe polish, and the nitro would add maybe 15 to 20 horsepower in the little V8-60," Lou said. He also found out later that the Edelbrock engine ran a very lightweight crankshaft. The combination of nitro, a lightweight crank, a two-speed rearend, and a flywheel made the Edelbrock midget unbeatable—most of the time.

Ed Winfield was the first to use flywheels in his race cars back in the 1920s. Winfield believed the flywheel helped the engine use as much of its kinetic energy as possible when coming out of the corners.

SENTER ENGINEERING

Following his discharge from the navy in 1945, Lou went to work for the Eddie Meyer Company as a machinist. The company had been manufacturing performance V-8 heads and intakes since before the war and was well known for its V8-60 equipment in powerboat and midget racing. Lou's job was to build any specialty tooling needed for the company's daily operation, but as time wore on, he thought more and more about starting his own business and began to buy used machinery. After about eight months at Meyer, he had enough equipment to open his own machine shop.

Lou built his V8-60–powered midget on a rail frame while still in high school. He raced at tracks in the area with varying degrees of success. This photo was taken at Balboa Stadium's dirt track in San Diego in 1940. *Courtesy Lou Senter*

The newly opened Senter Engineering consisted of a used metal lathe, milling machine, drill press, hand tools, and his brother, Sol, who stayed with Lou until 1950. On Crocker Street in Los Angeles, they shared space in a building with their brother-in-law, who manufactured chrome kitchen tables and chairs. It was his brother-in-law's metal tube bender that helped establish Lou's relationship with famed race car builder Frank Kurtis.

One day, while Lou was in the Kurtis shop, he noticed that tubular items, such as nerf bars for midget and sprint cars, were being fabricated by hand. With a keen eye for a business opportunity, Lou proposed to Frank that he could save the Kurtis shop countless man-hours of expensive labor if he contracted these items out to him. That contract to bend nerf bars, bumpers, and smaller tubular items for Kurtis race cars was one of Senter Engineering's first, and it was the one that paid the rent.

Ernie Casale was another early customer who supplied enough work to help get the fledgling business over the hump. Casale manufactured quick-change rearends for race cars and contracted Senter Engineering to machine the center sections.

Three-Piece Wheel

It was in 1946 when Lou first met Max Rose. Rose Tire was located just across the street from Senter Engineering on Jefferson Boulevard and manufactured racing tires for midgets. The company was looking for a solution to mounting a racing tire on a rim without tearing the tire bead. When Max approached Lou with this problem, Lou was working on a project of spinning steel wheels on an engine lathe, and after giving Rose's dilemma some consideration, he came up with a spun three-piece steel wheel.

"The wheel consisted of a lip that bolted on a bead lock," Lou said. "It was the only way you could mount the midget tires then; it was a ring that was bolted onto the outside of the rim to hold the tire on after it was installed onto the wheel."

Full-Race Flatheads for Sale

In those days, the fairly isolated stretch of Lincoln Boulevard in the Mines Field area (now Los Angeles International Airport) was one of the popular spots for street racing.

Lou participated in these runoffs and got to be known for having the roadster to beat. That reputation helped pay the rent when times were thin. He would assemble three or four full-race flatheads, install one in the roadster, and go racing, looking for a potential customer. After beating the competition, someone in the crowd would offer to buy his hot engine. In went another engine, and Lou was off to find another customer. He said that the rent was paid numerous times using this method.

Lou's wife, Betty, remembers times in 1946 and 1947: "I'd come out of my office [at Senter Engineering] and wonder where everyone went. It was almost a daily occurrence that someone would show up at the shop with a race car in tow, wanting a runoff with Lou. The racing was held out on Rodeo Road, with Lou usually winning, taking the fifty-dollar bet. Numerous times, the loser or a bystander would inquire about buying that engine out of his roadster."

SENTER ENGINEERING SPEED SHOP

In between general machine shop business and modifying engines, Lou still found time to compete on the midget circuit. Over time, he began to find he was left with a lot of used speed parts sitting idle on the shelves that were too decent to junk. He decided to set aside a small area in the main shop. After bringing in several lines of speed equipment mixed with his own used parts, he had himself a speed shop. The new and used racing equipment soon became a very profitable sideline and, in due time, Lou was buying in bulk from speed manufacturers.

Senter Engineering and Lewie Shell of Shell Auto Parts were perhaps the first two dealers in the L.A. area who would take used speed equipment in trade for new parts. Lou also took in speed parts on consignment sales; being able to trade used parts when upgrading their equipment was a bonus for many budget-minded hot rodders. It wasn't long until the sales from the speed shop outweighed what the machine shop was bringing in, giving a strong indication in which direction Lou should expand his business.

ANSEN AUTOMOTIVE

Ansen Automotive was founded after Lou met Jack Andrews. Lou knew that this guy had just the right attributes to make a successful business partnership. "Jack was a brilliant engineer and had a lot of good ideas," Lou said. "We thought along the same lines." Both fellows agreed that the time was right to open a well-equipped speed shop that could supply just about everything to the automotive enthusiast. The name "Ansen" was derived by combining their last names, and Jack stayed with the company until about 1950, when he decided to move on to other business interests.

By 1951, Ansen had already outgrown its old Jefferson shop. A larger building was leased at 6317 South Normandie Avenue in Los Angeles. Seven employees were on the payroll, working in the machine shop, at the parts counter, or in the mailroom. Ansen was one of the first speed shops to go mail order, offering a parts-filled catalog for 25 cents. "We had a retired fellow who would spend the day just opening letters containing 25-cent pieces, filling a bucket by the end of the day, and the sale of those catalogs paid our rent," Lou said. Bob Johnson was one of the new employees hired at this time. He would later become Lou's right hand and manager of the entire operation.

Ansen Auto did very good business selling custom-built engines, with the majority being Ford-Mercury V-8s, but including a considerable number of modified Ford four-cylinders, GM and Chrysler products, and everything from semi-race motors to all-out racing jobs. "A full-race flathead would go for around $1,500 to $2,500 complete, and we sold lots of them," Lou said. "I figure that we built and sold more hot V-8s than anyone else, and that the races on the beach at Daytona were a very good market for our engines. We shipped a lot of these engines east. Honest Charley [Speed Shop] bought them and sold them to bootleggers and cops, and then to the NASCAR racers." Honest Charley was the first to order the Ansen 1/8-x-1/8 racing engine for its own stock car. Lou said that Charley would race the full season with the engine and then ship it back to Ansen at the end of the season to have it freshened up for the following year.

One of the more colorful customers for Ansen racing engines was the Jack Daniels whiskey company, which sponsored stock cars. "They told Betty that if the engines were shipped on time, there'd be a case of Jack Daniels delivered to her door. When the truck arrived to pick up the engines, the case of liquor arrived with it."

Ansen was always aggressive with innovative ideas and would promote these ideas to high-performance aficionados. One rather novel idea was to demonstrate the effectiveness and importance of engine balancing. The actual field test was held at the Saugus drag strip and involved a completely street-stock Ford. Initially, the car turned 69 miles per hour in the quarter-mile. At the Ansen shop, the flathead was disassembled and given a complete balancing job, and again it was sent down the quarter-mile, this time turning 74 miles per hour—a gain of 5 miles per hour just from a balancing job.

In the early 1950s, Ansen and Bell Auto Parts were probably the two largest speed shops in the Los Angeles area. It was only a matter of time before Ansen had outgrown its premises. Lou decided to build a much larger, up-to-date facility in nearby Gardena. A writeup about the new facility in the May 2, 1964, issue of *Drag News* reported on the company's modern 22,000-square-foot building at 13715 South Western Avenue that contained offices, a retail outlet, a service shop, manufacturing, and warehousing all under one roof.

BIG-BORE GASKETS

The infallible Ford flathead was to hot rodding as an ice cold beer is to a hot summer day, and whatever one can imagine that can be done to an engine has probably been done to the flathead. Without exotic turbos, nitrous-oxide systems, and the like, one of

The Ansen display at the first *Hot Rod* show held at the L.A. Armory in 1948. He shared the display with Iskenderian Racing Cams and Nordon Steering. From left to right are Jack Andrews (Lou's partner), Charlie Nordon, and Ed Iskenderian. Note the eight carbs sitting on a high-rise Tattersfield-Baron four-carb manifold at the top of the center display. *Courtesy Lou Senter*

A mid-1950s photo of the Ansen Auto Center at South Normandie Avenue, with Lou standing at far left and his wife, Betty, next to him. An Anscraft quarter-midget is pictured in front of them. As the advertising on the wall said, the shop did everything from engine tune-ups, brakes, and engine rebuilding to selling speed equipment. *Courtesy Lou Senter*

the surest ways to get some more horsepower out of an engine was to give it more cubic inches. With the flathead, a problem arose when the engine bore was made larger than the diameter of the stock head gasket. Lou said, "The trick was to shave off any part of the piston that came in contact with the gasket. It was not really performance enhancing but necessary because the stock gaskets were all there was available."

Lou knew that there was a way around this problem, but at a considerable expense. It was a gamble and a hefty investment (he was running Senter Engineering at the time) to have a set of specialty gasket dies made, but these two dies allowed him to manufacture a big-bore, double-layer, copper head gasket, plus a big-port intake manifold gasket. The big-port gasket allowed the builder to use it as a template when port matching the manifold and block.

The response was enormous, and Lou sold thousands of the big-bore gaskets at $3 to $4 each. The Fel-Pro Company was under license to manufacture the gaskets and, in the early 1950s, made a proposal to purchase the rights for the dies for $5,000 and allow Ansen to purchase all the gaskets it needed at cost. Unfortunately for Lou, he accepted the offer. Later on, he learned that Fel-Pro sold shiploads of these gaskets—they were real money makers.

HYDRAULIC BRAKES

The one item that had a major influence on the direction the company came from a dry lakes race car owned by a couple of high school students.

A sponsor for one of Lou's midgets was the Junior Dudes Bubble Bath Company, which was located next door to the Ansen shop on Jefferson Boulevard. The company manufactured

children's bubble bath soap and was owned by Steve Riley. Riley's son, Dale, was a high school chum of Bob Morton, who worked for Ansen part-time.

As part of its sponsorship duties, Junior Dudes Bubble displayed the Ansen midget on its float in a local parade. Lou recalled that it was a real crowd pleaser, with a bubble-making machine inside the float that was rigged to blow bubbles out the race car's exhaust pipes.

Dale Riley and Bob Morton were partners in a roadster that ran at the lakes. When the two teenagers first bought the car, the previous owner had already modified the backing plates to accept hydraulic brakes, which gave Lou and Jack the idea to offer hydraulic-brake conversion kits.

The first time Ansen ran an advertisement for the brake conversion job in a local newspaper (in 1948), the phone rang off the wall. All vehicles up to 1939, and some into the late 1940s, were equipped with mechanical brakes, and at the time of the newspaper ad, there were still lots of these older cars on the road. "We had to stay open Saturdays and Sundays," Lou said. "Customers were literally lined up; this kit got us up and running."

The shop could handle only so many brake jobs in a week. That's when Lou came up with the idea of the brake conversion in a kit form, advertising that most backyard mechanics with simple hand tools could do this conversion on their own vehicle in three to four hours.

The kit included four backing plates with wheel cylinders and brakes, a master cylinder, a swing-pedal (brake) setup that mounted on the firewall, 20 feet of copper tubing, and enough miscellaneous bits and pieces to do the job—all for the sum of $75. It was a very successful business venture, and it made Lou realize there was a huge potential market for such products.

SPEED EQUIPMENT

Lou Senter is responsible for the introduction and manufacturing of many automotive speed products that remain on the market today. He was instrumental in producing the first aftermarket engine mounts, floorshift kits, explosion-proof bell housings, hydraulic brake conversions, big-bore gaskets, three-piece racing wheels, a wheel-testing machine, and on and on. Lou figured that he had developed hundreds of items related to the speed business, but he never had sufficient funds to develop any one product to its fullest capacity. He also didn't stay with any one item very long, usually heading off on a different tangent once the job was done.

"A lot of my ideas for hot rod equipment came from discussing ideas and problems with other fellows in the same situation and coming up with the solution, or at least making an attempt to solve the problem," Lou said. "My philosophy on that subject is to try it. If it works, fine; if not, try again. Keep trying until it's solved."

In the days when the flathead still held its place at the head of the line, Ansen employees Lou Baney and Bob Morton spent a considerable amount of time experimenting with pop-up pistons in the side-valve engine. "When we started to play around with pop-up pistons, that's when we started going fast," Lou said. "We went 7/16ths of an inch up into the head with high compression. The flathead Ford was a great engine, but it couldn't breathe; when you popped the piston up, it opened up the whole chamber and allowed the engine to breathe. That's when the flathead Ford started to run good." (The origin of this pop-up technology is credited to Frank Baron and Tommy Thickstun, who collaborated on the dynamics of airflow in the flathead, making this practice feasible.)

Aside from its substantial list of flathead parts and a longer list of four-cylinder stuff, Ansen manufactured other products that could fill a book. These included everything from forged chrome-moly steel connecting rods, forged-aluminum rods, forged-aluminum pistons, carburetor adaptors, valvetrain components, traction bars under the names of Traction Master and Ground Grabber, and so on. The shop also catered to the custom car crowd with a louver-cutting machine, charging 20 cents per louver.

The Ansen Posi-Cap was introduced in the early 1960s. This one-piece, high-tensile aluminum, bearing-cap girdle replaced all the main bearing caps to keep the crankshaft from exiting the bottom of the block. Ansen also offered four-bolt steel main caps and crankshaft straps for racers on a budget, and was the first to offer a forged offset rod. Lou said that he noticed a European auto manufacturer using that type of rod and decided to manufacture a similar item. The Ansen pistons were formally known as Jahns Pistons. Ansen was the first to come out with a sprint car kit, and offered a complete car kit less engine, selling 10 kits the first year they were available.

ENGINE SWAPPING

Another popular item from Ansen Automotive was its engine conversion kit. Ansen manufactured over 140 different chassis conversion kits for engines and transmissions, and even offered these engine swaps as an in-house service at its shop. In the early 1950s,

the Cadillac V-8 was a pretty popular choice for engine swapping into a Ford chassis.

CRANKSHAFTS

Ansen became well known for its one-piece, half-inch stroker crankshafts. Ansen also was well known for its very lightweight flathead crankshafts, but it wasn't until after Lou received help from Vic Edelbrock Sr. that Ansen had one that worked. Lou's first attempts to lighten a crank by cutting a good portion off the counterweights produced nothing but scrap metal, and after numerous tries, he got in touch with the Edelbrock shop. Vic said to bring it over and he'd balance it. After a significant amount of time and effort, the balancing job was successful, and once one was done, the rest were easy.

"The counterweights were cut down to the point where these cranks would run 500 rpm faster than any other on the market," Lou said. Anywhere from 14 to 20 pounds were removed from a stock 75-pound crankshaft. He said that a cutting torch was used originally to remove the counterweight material until the company purchased a metal-cutting band saw, which made the job much easier.

FLOORSHIFTS

Trends often come back to repeat themselves, including the floorshift. The column shift was originally developed to replace the floor model, making the vehicle's interior roomier and more convenient for its occupants. Later, aftermarket companies brought floorshifters back.

Like other types of specialty items, a variety of floorshifts were available during the late 1950s, including Ansen's patented Posi-Shift Floor Shifter. Lou came up with a design and, after many hours refining the prototype, had it patented and put into production. But there was a fly in the ointment. It happened that one of his employees had a father who was a lawyer, whom Lou hired to place a patent on the shifter. Not being mechanically inclined, the lawyer was not familiar with, and did not understand, the aspects

In 1958 the *SanChez, Kamboor & Ansen Special* 1953 Studebaker became the first full-sized stock-appearing car to break the 200-mile-per-hour barrier at Bonneville. The successful results are shown here. *Courtesy Lou Senter*

The first Ansen sprint car kit built by Lou and Walt Rieff (chief designer and engineer at Ansen) in 1963. The car featured many new innovations which are still used today, including power steering, torsion bars, adjustable rear sway bar, and roll cage. It was sold to Eagle Auto in Seattle. *Courtesy Lou Senter*

of the shifter that needed patent protection. Lou got his patent, but what was left out of the patent was the most important feature of the shifter: the firing pin.

"In changing gears, the pin would pick up the other arm to go into second gear," Lou said. "The firing pin was the key to the whole shifter."

Not realizing this fatal error in the patent, the shifter was put into production in 1958. A car magazine doing an article on Lou's muffler hoist decided to include an article on the installation of his new floorshifter. One of the spectators watching this installation got a good look at the shifter and, after some research, realized that the part that made this shifter great wasn't included under the patent. Lou said that particular person came out with his own shifter and went on to become quite a famous floorshift manufacturer.

ANSEN FIRE SUIT

About the most horrific accident that can befall a race car driver is being trapped in a burning wreck. Since the dawn of racing, countless drivers have either lost their lives or have been permanently disfigured due to fires. As unfortunate burn victims in the early days of drag racing quickly discovered, an open-face helmet and T-shirt offered nothing in the way of fire protection. Fortunately, this all changed when the fire suit was introduced.

In 1964, Ansen came out with an aluminized fire suit that was approved by the NHRA, AHRA, SEMA, and other racing organizations. The idea came to Lou when he saw how the American Optical Company produced fireproof suits for the U.S. military and airport firefighters. Over his many years in racing, Lou had seen enough fire-related accidents to realize that these fireproof suits were needed in auto racing, and with a suit that American Optical custom manufactured to his specifications, Ansen put on a demonstration to show how well the suit was capable of protecting one from a fire. Lou personally donned the suit, was doused with gasoline, and ignited. Obviously, he didn't sustain any injuries,

and various race car sanctioning bodies quickly endorsed the Ansen fire suit. Lou mentioned that even though the suit worked, it was pretty warm to wear for any length of time. The suit also came with a fireproof hood with air filters and gloves.

BELL HOUSINGS

In the days when the standard transmission still ruled drag racing, the sight of an exploding clutch was not uncommon at the strip. In certain classes, it was mandatory to use a steel shield around the stock bell housing with hopes of retaining the shrapnel of an exploding clutch, which was detrimental to both car and driver. Regrettably, those shields were not always bulletproof, and mishaps still occurred, sometimes with disastrous results.

When Ansen got into the business of manufacturing safety housings, Lou felt it was imperative that the organizations that sanctioned the races be aware of the destructive power behind an exploding clutch, and how his shield could retain such a force. After a bit of brainstorming, he came up with a demonstration machine. The unit comprised a large explosion-proof steel box mounted on a trailer. Inside the box was a modified crankshaft hub that a clutch could be bolted to. An externally mounted Corvair car engine drove this clutch assembly. In order to get the clutch to explode, the flywheel was cut in with a hacksaw to the point that it would self-destruct at around 5,500 to 6,000 rpm. Lou towed the test machine out to a local drag strip and performed the demonstration for some NHRA officials. The results were so convincing that the NHRA made that particular type of safety bell housing compulsory in certain classes.

Even this recommended safety shield didn't always prevent an accident. In one such case, the shield held the clutch pieces, but the explosion destroyed the rear of the engine block, sending bits of shrapnel toward the front of the fast-moving car, cutting a front tire and causing the car to lose control and flip.

Lou ran into this same problem when he was testing prototype housing designs on a mule engine; occasionally, he'd end up with a broken block. After losing several engines, he came up with the idea to use a 3/16-inch steel deflector plate to cover the back side of the engine block and prevent any flying metal from escaping forward.

At the time when Ansen introduced its two-piece, cast-steel, safety bell housing, it weighed around 65 pounds. In 1970, Lou came out with a hydraulically formed, quarter-inch thick, high-tensile steel, 360-degree scatter shield. The combined weight of this one-piece shield and the deflector plate was a lightweight 44 pounds.

ANSCRAFT QUARTER-MIDGETS

Similar to go karts but equipped with an Indy-style body, the Anscraft miniature race cars were very popular among 1950s parents who wanted to give their kids their first taste of racing. For some youngsters, it was a way to develop driving skills that would pave the way into auto racing.

Quarter-midgets were scaled-down versions of midget race cars. They were powered by a 2.5-horsepower Continental engine and could be safely handled by most youngsters. A quarter-midget consisted of a tubular frame, wheelbarrow-type wheels, a midget-type fiberglass body, and the engine. Some of the manufacturers produced a very realistic-looking race car, offering everything from ready-to-run jobs to a line of engine performance parts.

With a daughter at the right age to go racing and an eye on a business opportunity, Lou and a partner produced quarter-midgets under the Anscraft name. Lou's young daughter, Marsha, followed her father's racing footsteps, winning her share of races driving an Anscraft quarter-midget.

Anscraft manufactured about 400 of these tiny racers, which became so popular that the Yeakel Cadillac dealership in Los Angeles gave one away free with the purchase of every new Caddy. In a 1958 advertisement, the Anscraft quarter-midget listed at $375 for the base model and $445 for the deluxe model, which included a factory-painted body, upholstery, a Continental engine, and chrome parts. Optional full-competition engines were available from $125 to $150 (2- and 3-horsepower Continental engines).

Bill Smith of Speedway Motors in Lincoln, Nebraska, has a beautifully restored example of this quarter-midget in his automotive museum. It is one of the few Anscraft models left in existence.

PACKARD V-8 ENGINES

Lou was always receptive to a new idea, business venture, or a good deal that came his way. A shipping container of 50 brand-new 1956 Packard V-8 engines, which was initially destined for an overseas customer, ended up in a warehouse in Los Angeles. Although he wasn't sure what to do with 50 engines of mediocre popularity, Lou bought the entire lot. One thing the Packard V-8 had going for it was a fairly decent 352-ci displacement, but it weighed a hefty 810 pounds.

Meanwhile, Ansen Auto had plans to race a dragster as part of its advertising agenda. The venture would also provide a good excuse to give the Packard a try. The displacement was increased to 435 ci after boring and stroking, and the engine was topped off with six carburetors on a Weiand manifold. A streamlined body was added to the chassis, both of which were built by Joe Itow.

The dragster turned a respectable 138 miles per hour on its first run down the strip and was up into the 140s after some fine-tuning. To up the ante, the six carburetors were replaced with a blower after Lou fabricated a chain-drive setup for the GMC. He topped it off with Enderle injectors.

The talented Leonard Harris (Lou's cousin) was the first to drive the *Ansen Special* A/G Dragster, but he moved on to the Albertson Olds fuel car, allowing Tommy Dyer to take over. Later, famed tennis player Poncho Gonzales drove it to a new NHRA record of 151 miles per hour on gasoline. That record helped sell off the remaining stock of Packard V-8s.

MORE DRAGSTERS

In 1961, famed chassis builder Kent Fuller built a dragster chassis for Rod Stuckey. In March of that year, Stuckey was badly burned after an engine explosion. He put the car up for sale in order to pay his mounting medical bills, and Lou bought the dragster to add to his stable of race cars. In early 1962, Lou and Ed Pink made a deal with Stuckey, who'd recuperated from his injuries, to drive that same dragster. The trio went on to win the AHRA Winter Championship, setting the low elapsed time of 8.51 seconds at 188.66 miles per hour.

Lou was now the proud owner of two midgets, two dragsters, a Bonneville car, and a race boat. This collection was too much, and he sold the race-ready Kent Fuller dragster to Tommy Greer for $5,000. Greer had Fuller update the chassis, and with partner Keith Black and driver Don Prudhomme, the car became the famous Greer, Black, and Prudhomme dragster. That legendary GB&P dragster recorded 236 wins out of 243 races, and today the totally restored dragster is owned by Bruce Myers and is on display at the Petersen Automotive Museum in Los Angeles.

One of the more unusual cars that came out of the Ansen shop was a fuel-injected, nitro-burning, Chrysler dragster. It certainly wasn't the first fuel-injected Hemi on rails, but what really made this car totally unique were its experimental aluminum Hemi heads and aluminum crankshaft. The Harvey Aluminum Company had donated a newly formulated aluminum-stock material to Ansen Automotive for testing. It wanted to see just how well this product would hold up under rigorous use, and what better test than in a fuel dragster. The experimental aluminum heads and crankshaft were machined on a CNC lathe.

Once the parts were bolted in place, the car was taken to Bakersfield for its maiden shakedown voyage. Over the course of the day, the mix was bumped up to 98 percent nitro and 2 percent alcohol, putting out enough horsepower to win the meet. Driver Jim Kamboor got about 10 runs out of the extremely high-revving engine before breaking the crank on the final run, yet winning Top Fuel Eliminator.

SAUGUS

The Santa Ana drag strip opened on July 2, 1950, and was an overnight success; it didn't take long for others to follow suit. With Lou Baney as his partner, Senter leased a runway for $300 a month at the Six-S Air Park at Saugus, located just north of Los Angeles. Senter had noticed this little-used airstrip on his way to Bonneville and figured that it would be an ideal spot to hold races. With a $500 loan from his brother and Baney borrowing $500 from his father, they incorporated the drag strip operation under the name Sports Events Inc. and opened the country's second organized drag strip several months after Santa Ana. Having a growing business to contend with, Senter went into this venture as a silent partner, leaving Baney to oversee the strip's operation.

The entrance fee was 99 cents, keeping below the $1 mark so the business didn't get involved with the government in having to collect taxes on anything $1 and over. The strip was getting anywhere from 1,000 to 1,200 spectators attending the weekly races. Saugus was the first strip to give out cash prizes, offering the eliminator winners the choice between a war bond and cash. Top Eliminator would receive a $25 bond or $18.75 in cash, and for a big meet it would be a $100 bond or $75 cash. Lou said that he couldn't remember anyone ever taking a bond. Saugus also started up a points system for the racers.

Occasionally, a good idea is the result of an act of necessity, which was the case with the nation's first nighttime drag racing event. The eliminations were running late one Sunday, and it was nearing nightfall. The track officials called for all the spectators to line their cars up along the length of the strip with the headlights on so the racers could finish the runoffs. This presented Baney with the idea of holding night drags on Saturday nights, allowing the competitors to run elsewhere on Sunday. Large aircraft searchlights were mounted on a platform behind the starting line that lit up the entire length of the strip. The downside was that the drivers had to wear sunglasses on the return road to the pits.

One notable drawback to the strip was a public road that ran close to the end of the short runoff at the end of the strip. After several near mishaps with traffic, a flagman was posted at the end of the runoff to warn any oncoming vehicles of a runaway race car and allow it to safely cross the public road.

The Saugus drag strip enjoyed a successful five years in operation, closing its doors in 1955 because of stiff competition from other strips much closer to Los Angeles.

BONNEVILLE

Since the opening of Bonneville in 1949, a race car either sponsored or owned by Ansen Automotive has competed on the salt flats every year.

In 1958, the *SanChez, Kamboor & Ansen Special* was the first full-sized, stock-appearing vehicle that clocked in at over 200 miles per hour at Bonneville and set a two-way record at 184 miles per hour. The '53 Studebaker hit 210 miles per hour for a one-way record and was on its record verification run when its rearend failed.

BAJA

The allure of race driving never quite leaves one's system, and many years after his short-lived midget career, Lou had a chance to co-drive in a race and satisfy any desire that he had left for the sport. The enticement of a wide-open, pedal-to-the-metal race through the rugged desert terrain of the Baja was enough to put Lou back in the driver's seat.

Competing with a heavily modified Chevy pickup truck, he and co-driver Bill Pendleton of JE Pistons entered the 1971 Baja 1000 that was put on by the National Off-Road Race Association (NORRA). The duo competed in the bone-shaking race against the likes of Mickey Thompson, Bill Stroppe, Parnelli Jones, and Rick Mears. Lou was the oldest driver in the race, but that didn't prevent him and Bill from coming in third in their class.

In the garage at the Ansen shop in Gardena, Lou and Biff Caruso used this particular car to develop sprint car kits never offered on the market. *Courtesy Lou Senter*

With Walt Rieff driving the Ansen sprint car at El Centro Speedway, their newly designed roll cage proved its worth as the car plowed through the wood retaining wall, rolled, and landed on all four wheels with little damage. *Courtesy Lou Senter*

Over the years Lou saw so many racing accidents involving fire that he finally decided to provide the driver with a fighting chance. In the 1960s he came out with the Ansen fire suit. He is seen here demonstrating the fire suit as an assistant pours gasoline on his arm and ignites it. *Courtesy Lou Senter*

INDIANAPOLIS

The grand reopening of the Brickyard in 1946 was the first time Lou had ever been to the track, and he went as member of a race car team, not as a spectator. To be able to compete in the legendary Indy 500, even if only as a pit-crew member, was every racing aficionado's fantasy, and that opportunity arrived on Lou's front door in the form of Louis Bromme, a Californian garage owner and race car builder.

Bromme and Senter laid out plans to enter Bromme's homemade sprint car in the 500. All the chassis and engine preparations were done in the Senter Engineering shop; without access to a corporate sponsor with deep pockets, the team was tapped out by the time the car was ready to go. Lou personally raised the $5,000 needed to take the team to Indianapolis and to cover the expenses of fielding a car in the race.

The low-budget racing team hauled its race car on an open trailer behind a '34 Ford all the way to Indiana. Bill Sheffler was hired to take care of the driving chores and, after starting in 25th spot, he was running 4th when a leaky gas tank caused several lengthy pit stops. The team finished a respectable 9th place after completing 139 laps of the 200-lap race.

From that first experience with the Bromme car, Lou attended the Speedway annually as a spectator for the next 20 years, until the 1966 Memorial Day Classic when he arrived as a car owner. He'd bought the *Halibrand Shrike*, which Lloyd Ruby drove to a 11th-place finish in the 1965 race. He entered the car under the dual sponsorship of Tipton Motors (of San Diego) and Ansen Automotive, but the car failed to qualify.

That old Halibrand race car still sits in a corner of Lou's warehouse today, waiting for a new owner. The Indy 270 Offenhauser engine was removed, detuned, and installed in Lou's street-driven '23 T roadster, which is usually on display in the Justice Brothers' fabulous racing museum in Duarte, California.

MR. FOUR-BARREL

The engines that have stirred up the most dust on the dry lakes of Southern California have got to be the revered Ford four-cylinders—models T, A, B, and C, respectively. The number of manufacturers who developed speed equipment just for those engines was in the hundreds. It all ended when the mighty little engine was displaced by the V-8, spelling the end for many of the manufacturers and leaving only the intransigent diehards.

Lou took up the call of the orphaned four-cylinder in the late 1940s and became known as "Mr. Four-Barrel" due to the prolific amount of speed equipment Ansen Automotive manufactured and supplied for the Model A engines. The "Mr. Four-Barrel" moniker has stuck with Lou into modern times.

When GM introduced the Chevy II, with its economical little four-cylinder, it wasn't very long before manufacturers were tooling up speed equipment as the displaced four-cylinder found its way onto the race track. By the early 1960s, Ansen was one of the main manufacturers of performance parts for the Chevy II engine, and its parts catalog listed about everything needed to turn the thrifty four into a potent, high-revving midget powerplant. The list included stroker kits, forged-steel rods and aluminum pistons, valve and timing gear covers, steel main caps, oversize valves, and an eight-port aluminum head. Lou was very proud of the qualities of his eight-port head—better heat dispersion, spark plug location moved for better burning of gases, replaceable cast-iron valve guides, larger runners in the valves, and eight individual ports.

SEMA

SEMA, the automotive aftermarket organization, began in 1958 when some equipment manufacturers got together to form an alliance. The Speed Equipment Manufacturing Credit Association (SEMCA) was founded by Lou Senter of Ansen, Els Lohn of EELCO, Fred Offenhauser of Offenhauser Equipment, Harry Weber of Weber Cams, Roy Ritcher of Cragar, Phil Weiand, and several other manufacturers. The purpose was to allow each manufacturer to share information regarding credit abuse from speed shop owners.

Around 1960, the Revell Toy Company approached the group and suggested that it form an association that would represent them all, making it easier for outfits such as Revell to deal with them as one group rather than individually. Revell was looking to use miniature decals of some of these companies on its model car kits and needed their permission. As well, the speed equipment industry realized that such an organization would be to its benefit in setting standards and guidelines for aftermarket manufacturers and keeping their products safe.

Ansen developed the first "real" knock-off wheel spinner for street use. The kit bolted onto early-model Corvette wheels. It was about to be marketed but an unexpected incident with a similar spinner forced them to scrap the project. *Courtesy Lou Senter*

The Ansen crew prepares for the next race with Lou holding the bow of the boat. The Ansen 266 class hydroplane was powered by a small-block Chevy V-8 and won a 1969 championship with Bud Meyer behind the steering wheel. *Courtesy Lou Senter*

At the start, there were a dozen or so representatives who banded together to form what was called the Speed Equipment Manufacturers Association. These original members included Phil Weiand, Ed Iskenderian, Jim Deist, Howard Douglas, Lou Senter, Dean Moon, Vic Edelbrock Jr., Bob Hedman, Al Segal, John Barlett, Roy Ritcher, and several others. As the organization grew, it became a conglomeration of manufacturers and distributors and changed its name to the Specialty Equipment Manufacturing Association in 1967, and again in 1979 to the Specialty Equipment Market Association to better reflect its membership. Lou Senter was inducted into the SEMA Hall of Fame in 1978.

BARRIS KUSTOMS

In his teenage years in the Jefferson Boulevard area of east Los Angeles, Lou became well acquainted with the Barris brothers, long before George became internationally known as "King of the Kustomizers." The two talked about combining George's auto body expertise with Lou's mechanical skills in a business partnership, but it never transpired. Many years later, his old friend George asked Lou to build engines and equipment for many of his custom movie and TV vehicles. Lou's shop built an engine for the coffin car used in the *Munsters* TV series, as well as custom wheels made to fit the irregular-shaped, Barris-made *Batmobile* body. These special 10-inch wheels had to be offset 6 inches so that they tucked under the body.

WHEELS

Lou never had any intentions of entering the world of wheels until he got into sprint car racing. As a race car owner, he was forever replacing wheels. He felt that the Halibrand magnesium wheels were far too expensive for the average car owner, and he saw a need for a good, inexpensive racing wheel.

In the mid-1960s, Lou spent two years studying wheel design before he entered the market. His first wheel was less than successful, but when he introduced his Top Eliminator and Sprint series wheels, he was on the right track. *Hot Rod* ran an article

on the Ansen wheel, and it became an overnight success story. These wheels were manufactured with a one-piece permanent mold and later were die cast. Though more expensive than the sand-cast method, the die-cast method ensured superior strength and consistency in the casting. The wheels were designed with a bolt-on wheel adapter that allowed the wheel to be used on a variety of vehicles.

Ansen sold a true knock-off spinner to be used with its wheels. The kit included a knock-off adapter and spinner that looked and operated just like what would be seen on a race car or some pricey European sports car. Ansen also manufactured a line of chrome steel wheels and a complete line of steering wheels from custom to competition use.

In 1969, Ansen was sold to the Whittaker Corporation, with Lou remaining at the head of Ansen Division. With the financial backing of Whittaker, he purchased the world's largest, state-of-the-art, 12,000-ton, die-casting machine, making Ansen the largest specialty wheel manufacturer in the business. Ansen invested $30,000 in an engine lathe that could machine the two sides of a wheel simultaneously and complete the total operation in less than five minutes.

The huge investment in machinery spawned the Sprint II series of wheels that incorporated a revolutionary new multipattern design. Interchangeable, tapered, lug-bolt inserts allowed the wheel to be changed with a variety of car makes. The Sprint II was the first one-piece die-cast wheel to meet and surpass SEMA specifications.

ROLL CAGES

Lou recalled that the small roll bars in some early midgets were designed to protect the bodywork, not the driver, whose only protection was a Cromwell helmet and seat belt. Lou is credited with being the first car owner to install a full roll cage on a sprint car, not to be confused with Vince Conze's down-tube car.

ANSEN EMPLOYEE BOB MORTON

Bob Morton was one of Ansen Automotive's earliest employees and is still a close friend of the Senter family. During his first year of high school, Bob and Dale Riley pooled their resources together and bought a roadster. Both young lads had little mechanical knowledge at the time and farmed out the modifications to Lou, who installed a Clay Smith cam, dual Offenhauser intake manifold, and milled the 21-stud stock heads for their street rod engine. Bob reported that the Model A roadster was never beaten in a street race.

The roadster only whetted Bob's appetite to learn more about high performance. He began to hang out at Lou's shop whenever he had time; he was there often enough that Lou figured he might as well put him to work and offered Bob a part-time job.

Street racing was okay, but what Bob really wanted to try was dry lakes racing. Dale's father didn't want his son to get involved, and the racing partnership ended. Bob sold the roadster's engine to Lou's brother, Bob Senter, for $325 to help finance a new engine—a big 296-ci full-race job that he'd personally built in Lou's shop.

In 1971, Lou and Bill Pendleton (JE Pistons) entered this pickup in the Baja 1000, competing against Parnelli Jones, Mickey Thompson, Rick Mears, and other hot drivers. Although they didn't win their class, Lou had the distinction of being the oldest driver at the event. *Courtesy Lou Senter*

His first and last adventure with the roadster was at a Rosamond Dry Lake meet held on a Sunday in May 1948. Disaster struck on the very first trip down the lakebed when he hit a soft spot and the left rear wheel split, causing the car to flip end over end, destroying the roadster.

"Luckily, I had a good seat belt and helmet," Bob said. "There were no roll bars; the seat broke its mounting bolts and flew out of the car, and I fell backward under the trunk deck as the car ended upside down. When help came, they couldn't find me, and they were afraid to turn the wreck over. I was still in the mangled wreck, stretched out half in the cockpit and half in the trunk, held in by the seat belt." Bob was extremely fortunate to have escaped with only numerous bruises, cuts, and a fair bump on the head.

Frank Baron and Bob Tattersfield were having problems with their own engine and wondered if they could use Bob's engine in their belly tank. After getting the mangled wreck back to the Ansen shop, the engine was pulled, and the Weiand heads and dual intake manifold were replaced with Tattersfield-Baron heads and a four-carburetor intake. That following Sunday, B&T took the belly tank to a Russetta meet and set a new streamliner record of 134 miles per hour on gas and later on ran 151 on straight alcohol. An article later appeared in *Hot Rod* about the Baron and Tattersfield streamliner. It mentioned that the record was set on a borrowed engine but neglected to give any credit to Bob Morton.

After destroying his roadster, Bob teamed up with George Rubio to build a lakes car, as neither lad had sufficient funds to go it alone. George had a '29 street roadster on a '32 frame, and Bob had his record-setting Mercury engine—the same engine that the Baron and Tattersfield belly tank had set the record with. Each Friday night, they'd meet at Lou's shop, remove George's street engine, install the hot Merc engine, and after a weekend of dry lakes racing, they'd repeat the engine swap on

Sunday night. The roadster was run as the *Ansen Special*, as Lou sponsored the duo.

During an SCTA meet at El Mirage in 1950, Bob set the C/Roadster class record at 145 miles per hour. Later that day, a friend named Bob Robinson asked if he could take the roadster for a run down the lake. Robinson was well acquainted with dry lakes racing, but sadly, it would be his last run. He drove the *Ansen Special* to an all-time record high speed of 151 miles per hour, but after completing the clocked run, he didn't slow down and angled off course, hitting a low sand dune. The roadster was totally destroyed, and Bob Robinson was killed. It was the second fatality during an SCTA sanctioned meet since the organization's founding in 1937.

Eventually, Bob's days of racing on the dusty lakes were put aside for marriage and the responsibilities of raising a family, but the hot rodding spirit never dies. With the kids grown and out the door, Bob returned to his roots. His latest creation was featured in the March 2003 issue of *American Rodder*—a stunning, retro '29 Brookville steel-body roadster powered by an Oldsmobile Aurora V-8.

THE SENTER LEGACY

In the world of speed merchants, Lou Senter was among the most creative manufacturers. Most outfits specialized in one or a handful of types of automotive parts. Lou made a little bit of everything, or at least tried to.

He and Lou Baney made the front cover of the 1955 Fawcett Books publication *How to Build Hot Rods*, showing Lou lowering a modified flathead V-8 by a chain hoist as Baney directed the engine into the chassis of a roadster. Another Fawcett publication titled *Hot Rod Handbook*, published in 1958, had Lou and his Ansen shop heavily featured throughout the book. Countless other publications and articles helped make Ansen Automotive an authority in the performance world during the 1950s and 1960s. Although the Ansen company no longer exists in name, Lou can be credited in taking an obscure machine shop and turning it into a major player in the specialty marketplace.

Today, when he isn't involved in his grandson's midget car racing career, Lou can be found in the small machine shop in the back of his garage where he fabricates custom parts for his buddies when needed and makes old-style, hand-operated, fuel pressure pumps in small quantities for nostalgic race car buffs.

A promo shot of Ansen's popular Sprint II mag wheels, safety bell housing, and Ground Grabber traction bars. The Sprint series wheels proved very popular with car enthusiasts for many years. *Courtesy Lou Senter*

CHAPTER 2

Tom Thickstun, Frank Baron, and Bob Tattersfield

This is the story of three young automotive enthusiasts whose love of mechanical performance developed into lasting friendships as well as successful business ventures. Tommy Thickstun, Bob Tattersfield, and Frank Baron were individualists whose personal strengths melded together over time to form a successful line of high-speed racing equipment.

The unfortunate aspect of their business was similar to outfits such as Evans and Navarro, who specialized mainly in the Ford/Mercury V-8 flathead. These companies eventually fell by the wayside when the Ford Motor Company's faithful old engine became obsolete in the presence of the overhead valve.

THOMAS T. THICKSTUN

The first, and probably the most important, member in this trio was Tommy Thickstun. He was born in 1912, raised in Los Angeles, and, while attending L.A. High, developed an interest in hot rodding. But unlike his peers who wanted to drive fast, Tommy's interest lay in understanding the theory that made the cars go fast. In high school, he took pattern-making and sand-casting shops, and in 1930 designed his first two-carburetor intake manifold—for a Chrysler straight-eight engine. In the early 1930s, he made a dual-carburetor adapter that bolted directly onto the stock Ford V-8 manifold. Tommy was intuitive enough to see that there was potential in Henry's V-8. Finding an easy way to increase the engine's output could possibly develop into a money-making business.

After gaining enough practical working experience, he started up the Thickstun Manufacturing Company in El Segundo, California. This small company manufactured a dual-intake manifold for the flathead V-8, which was one of the first aftermarket manifolds that had a 180-degree firing order. It was also designed as a high rise, allowing the generator to be mounted in its stock position.

Along with the intake manifold, Tommy added a cast-aluminum air breather and high-compression, nonfinned heads with optional marine cast-aluminum splash covers for powerboat usage. Thickstun equipment was sold through automotive supply shops, engine repair shops, and Ford dealers across the country. All the equipment came in Thickstun Red enamel.

THICKSTUN DUAL-INTAKE MANIFOLD

Unfortunately for Tommy, as clever an engineer as he was, the drawback of his high-rise intake manifold was a poor design of the interior runners. The sharp angles of the manifold's runners where they entered the engine ports impeded the natural flow of the fuel mixture. This design flaw eventually led one of his friends to develop an intake manifold that would be the basis for an extremely successful aftermarket business.

When Frank Baron opened an automotive repair shop in 1937, his shop and Vic Edelbrock's shop were two local facilities where Thickstun equipment was installed on vehicles. By 1939, Edelbrock had gained enough practical experience in racing and modifying engines that he'd developed his

Opposite: The beautiful movie starlet Colleen Townsend looks on thoughtfully as Bob Tattersfield adjusts the four-carb setup on the Tattersfield-Baron belly tank. *Courtesy Tony Baron*

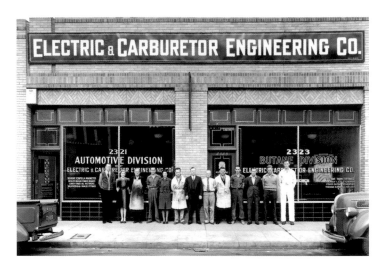

Above: A prewar photo of the Tattersfield building shows a lineup of employees, with Ernest Tattersfield standing ay far left. *Courtesy Tony Baron*

Right: Frank Baron works on a modified four-cylinder engine in his shop at Highland and Venice Boulevard in Los Angeles around 1940. *Courtesy Tony Baron*

own theories on manifold design. No doubt Vic suggested that Tommy make changes to the Thickstun manifold runners, but for unknown reasons, Vic's ideas went unheeded, leaving him no choice but to manufacture his own manifold.

THICKSTUN MARINE HEADS

As the popularity of Ford's V-8 engine spread among the public and racers, so did its many uses. It became a popular and inexpensive powerplant for marine conversions and also became a favorite among the powerboat racing crowd. It wasn't long after the engine's introduction that there were racing classes expressly for the flathead V-8 and V8-60. About the only real problem using the flathead engine in a boat was the location of the spark plugs, which made them prone to shorting out if exposed to spray.

Frank Baron, Tommy, Bob Tattersfield, and friends often spent weekends at Frank's cottage on Lake Elsinore. Frank had always been a boating enthusiast, and when he became involved in boat racing he experienced the spark plugs shorting out. Tommy also noticed the problem and came up with the foolproof, cast-aluminum splash cover that was bolted on top of an aluminum high-compression head, giving the appearance of Ardun-style head.

Tommy also introduced a marine, tear-shaped, cast-aluminum, spark arrestor–type air breather to fit his dual-intake manifold. This combination was rather lavish, and it didn't take long for those who could afford it to install this custom package in their boats and street rods. One prewar boating magazine described the Thickstun marine heads, covers, dual-carburetor manifold, and air breather as: "Accessories that finish off the discriminating boater's engine; functional yet tasteful."

The Tickstun Manufacturing Company was like many small outfits—it lacked capital and the business savvy to move forward. That's when Ernest Tattersfield came to the rescue.

THE ELECTRIC & CARBURETOR ENGINEERING COMPANY

The Electric & Carburetor Engineering Company of Los Angeles dealt in automotive, marine, and aircraft products, and was founded by Ernest Tattersfield, an astute and successful businessman. In 1939, when war broke out in Europe, Ernest knew it was only a matter of time before America would become involved. He figured that there'd possibly be a good future in butane as a gasoline replacement for cars and trucks if there were fuel shortages due to the war. To get into the butane conversion kit business, he would need butane manifolds. Ernest met Tommy Thickstun through his son, Bob, and knew that Tommy was a brilliant engineer whose talents would benefit the Electric & Carburetor Engineering Company. Thickstun had a proven product line with national outlets, and Tattersfield had the financial and business experience to make the collaboration work. After negotiations were finalized in 1941, Ernest acquired the Thickstun outfit, changing the name to the Thickstun Manifold Division of the Electric & Carburetor Engineering Company, and keeping Tommy on as supervisor of the newly formed division.

Besides continuing on with the existing line of Thickstun engine manifolds, the company introduced a new line of gasoline and butane manifolds for Ford, Chevrolet, and Chrysler products, as well as most of the truck lines. There was an announcement of this business venture in the 1941 January issue of *Throttle* magazine: "The Thickstun Manifold Company, formerly

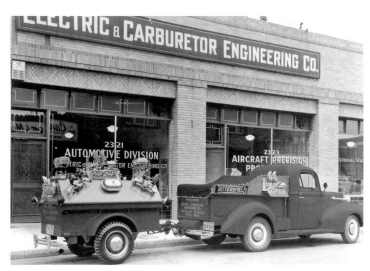

Bob Tattersfield arrived at the 1947 Indy 500 with this traveling display to promote his line of speed equipment. The complete package was pulled by a red 1940 Ford pickup. *Courtesy Tony Baron*

of 2002 West Washington Street in L.A., has merged with the Electric & Carburetor Engineering Company and will be known as Thickstun Manifold Division of E&CEC. Thomas T. Thickstun will be chief engineer and in complete charge of the department; the department will manufacture a complete line of butane manifolds as well as the popular Thickstun dual gas manifolds."

Tommy's reign as head of Thickstun Manifold Division was short-lived due to the United States' entrance into the war after the bombing of Pearl Harbor. Any work that the division was involved in, unless it was related to the war effort, was shelved for a future date. Due to medical reasons, Tommy was deferred from active military duty, but his engineering qualifications landed him an assignment to North American Aviation. He resumed his position as head of the Thickstun Manifold Division once the hostilities ended.

It may have been the success that Vic Edelbrock had with his slingshot manifold and its matched-port design, but for whatever reason, Tommy decided it was time to upgrade his intake manifold. The new postwar version was called the Thickstun PM-7, and Frank Baron's son, Tony Baron, explained that the initials stood for the seventh production model made. The new design was advertised as a manifold that produced more miles per gallon of gasoline, more horsepower, more top speed, and faster acceleration, and like all Thickstun products, the intake was painted in Thickstun Red enamel.

Later on, the PM-7 manifold pattern was acquired by another company, which marketed it under the name of SAE Manifolds. The prewar Thickstun manifold pattern was sold to Lee Chapel, who reissued the manifold under the Tornado brand.

THICKSTUN SUPERCHARGER

As head of the Thickstun Manifold Division, Tommy had the assets and facilities to work on projects that had been shelved due to the war, and it wasn't just the manifold line he wanted to develop;

there was also a Roots-type supercharger of his own design. Once a working model of this blower had been completed, Tommy installed it on his own roadster for road testing. Tony Baron recalled that his dad would on occasion drive Tommy's supercharged roadster along Venice Boulevard well beyond the speed limit with Tommy sitting beside him, busily checking various vacuum and pressure gauges. Unfortunately, Tommy died before the blower had reached its final stage of development, and the one and only time it was ever used was on the Tattersfield-Baron streamliner when the belly tank was taken for a trial run down Wendover's main street.

With the availability, outstanding performance, and low cost of the GMC Roots blower, there was little incentive to continue to develop a better mousetrap when there already was a working one. Tommy's supercharger faded out of existence, and when the assets of the Thickstun Manifold Division were sold off, the blower ended up stored under a workbench in the Ansen Automotive shop. As far as Lou Senter could remember, it was probably thrown out into the scrap-metal bin.

ILL FORTUNE AT LAKE ELSINORE

Frank Baron's enthusiasm for boating eventually led him to purchase a cottage on Lake Elsinore, east of Los Angeles. On numerous occasions, Frank and his friends would gather at the cottage on weekends to enjoy some boating and the serenity of the lake. On a weekend in 1946, the gang traveled to the cottage, where tragedy struck. Unfortunately, Tommy suffered from heart disease, and it finally caught up with him that ill-fated weekend at lake, where he died at the age of 34 years old. Sadly, Tommy's friends were at the cottage to celebrate his marriage, which was scheduled for the following week.

TATTERSFIELD MANIFOLD DIVISION

Between the war and his early death, Tommy spent little more than a year in his position as head of the Thickstun Manifold Division. Bob Tattersfield filled the unexpectedly vacant position.

Bob wanted to update and expand the product line, and one of his first moves after taking over the department was to change the product name to "Tattersfield." Next, he dropped the costly cast-aluminum marine splash covers for the Thickstun heads and, by adding cooling fins, made the existing heads more appealing and affordable to the average car enthusiast. A new cast-aluminum, finned, box-style, oil bath air breather was introduced to complement the dual-carburetor manifold, and a V8-60 two-carburetor racing manifold was added for those who raced midgets and powerboats. This particular intake had a patented balance tube and was advertised as the only manifold without backpressure: "the only manifold that is scientifically heat relieved." The unique characteristic of this manifold was that there were three carburetor mounting bases, allowing the engine tuner to run one or two carburetors to suit the style of racing.

In addition to the Ford and Mercury products, Tattersfield offered a line of two- and three-carburetor intakes and a high-compression head for the Ford six, intakes for the less popular six-cylinder Mopars and Chevys, as well as an intake for the almost-obsolete Model A four. The company boasted in its advertising that Tattersfield equipment was being used by truck operators, police and highway patrol cars, race cars, and hop-up enthusiasts.

TATTERSFIELD SPECIAL OF 1947

Possessing a natural flair for advertising, Bob wanted to promote the Tattersfield name and had the resources to do it. He felt that the best way to get the company's name out to the public quickly was to get involved in the greatest show on earth: the Indianapolis 500. Realizing that it'd be chancy at best to enter a flathead V-8–powered car against the formidable Offenhauser, he sponsored Bill White's prewar Alfa Romeo as the *Tattersfield Special*, which Cy Marshall drove to an eighth-place finish in the 1947 race. Even though the Alfa didn't carry any of the company's equipment, the Tattersfield outfit didn't go unnoticed, as Bob showed up at the gala affair with a highly visible advertising gimmick. He arrived at the Speedway driving a new Ford pickup truck pulling an open trailer; both truck and trailer were decked out with a very elaborate display of Tattersfield products. The trailer was outfitted with slanted display sides covered with a variety of manifolds and air breathers that were either chrome plated, brightly polished aluminum, or gold-color plated. The pickup truck and trailer were given a bright Thickstun Red paint job.

TATTERSFIELD-BARON COLLABORATION

By the late 1940s, the spectacular growth of specialized equipment manufacturing in Southern California had mushroomed (by 1950, it'd become a $12 million a year industry), and Bob realized that to be competitive and own a share of the market he'd need a product that appealed to the hop-up enthusiast. The Indy-sponsored race car was a one-shot deal, and although new manifold designs were in the works, he knew that it'd take something really special to get the Tattersfield name in lights. That's when the creative Frank Baron was called upon to enter into a partnership. Bob had hung

out at Baron's Automotive Shop and sat in on enough of the endless discussions between Tommy and Frank concerning airflow theories to know Frank had the expertise to design the equipment Tattersfield Manifold Division needed. Under the Tattersfield-Baron Frank was called on to develop something totally different from what was already available on the market, and within a year the pair was ready with some pretty radical material for that time period.

TATTERSFIELD-BARON RACING EQUIPMENT

The Tattersfield-Baron racing equipment was a coordinated package consisting of heads modified to accept 7/16-inch pop-up pistons custom manufactured by JE Pistons and a four-carburetor intake manifold that was perfected by Frank. The package was ready by the early summer of 1948 and launched with an advertisement in the April issue of *Hot Rod*. The full-page ad introduced to the public a four-carburetor manifold; in those days, three carburetors seemed more than adequate and four carbs on a flathead V-8 was quite radical. The ad showed the manifold as a high-rise unit, the first and last time it was shown in that configuration; it was produced as a high-rise model in very limited quantities and is today scarce as hen's teeth.

To help the public understand the theory behind the pop-up system, Bob wrote a technical article in *Hot Rod*'s May 1948 issue titled, "Pistons and Designs." The article went into detail to explain the advantages of the pop-up piston, head, and four-carburetor manifold combination and why the components work well together.

The Electric & Carburetor Engineering Company handled the sales end and machining of the equipment, which left Frank time to continue with his automotive repair business. Although this venture with Bob wasn't a full-time job, Frank did attend auto shows and other functions to help promote the products. He also attended dry lakes meets, not as a driver, but as the chief mechanic on the Tattersfield-Baron belly tank. One of the perks of

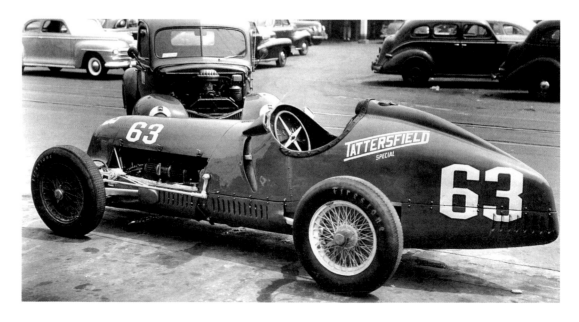

The *Tattersfield Special* that showed up at the 1947 Indy 500 was a prewar Alfa Romeo owned by Bill White and driven by Cy Marshall. The car placed a respectable eighth. *Courtesy Tony Baron*

the business partnership was that it involved Baron's Automotive Shop as the garage that installed Tattersfield-Baron equipment on customer's vehicles, providing a profitable sideline for Frank.

TATTERSFIELD-BARON MANIFOLD

Although it wasn't the first flathead V-8 four-carburetor manifold to be put on the market, it was the first commercially successful one. In the days when three carburetors seemed extravagant, using four intimidated many would-be customers, and in order to increase sales of the manifold, the company had to show that it could be used for more than all-out competition. The intake was advertised as having the flexibility to run four carburetors for full-race competition or two for street use. The company said that with two carburetors the manifold could be used primarily for performance in power and economy, while using four carburetors was for high-speed performance only. The Tattersfield-Baron Blue enameled manifold came with two flange plates for the option of blocking off two carburetor bases. This manifold was also available in a 5-1/2-inch high-rise model.

TATTERSFIELD-BARON HEADS

The piston, head, and intake manifold designs that Bob and Frank manufactured were products of the accumulated theories derived from the long hours of discussions between Frank and Tommy Thickstun regarding airflow in the flathead V-8. Their theories, combined with the financial backing of Tattersfield's company, produced the first viable pop-up piston, special heads, and four-carburetor intake manifold package for the Ford-Mercury engine. Although the pop-up theory had been around for some time and

Tommy Thickstun and Ernest Tattersfield point to various gauges to show the performance of Tommy's supercharger as it is tested. *Courtesy Tony Baron*

Tattersfield and Baron obviously were not pioneers, they were the first to commercially offer a complete pop-up system that worked. Since the conception of Henry Ford's V-8 back in 1932, the criteria for upping horsepower in the flathead had followed along the same basic line of modifications, but the workable pop-up piston opened up new avenues in the search for more power. The Tattersfield-Baron piston design protruded an extremely long 7/16 inch above the surface of the block deck into a specially manufactured head, allowing the protrusion into the head to open up a transfer area that was never possible before. This design in turn allowed the use of much larger valves, increasing the airflow to the point that the engine could easily handle the output of a four-carburetor manifold.

Tony Baron said, "At the first *Hot Rod* [magazine] show held in Los Angeles, my father had their racing equipment set up at the Tattersfield display booth. People couldn't figure out the theory behind the pop-up piston or how it worked, and Dad would try to explain how it worked. At the same show, Dad gave away a four-carburetor intake manifold as a drawing prize, and Don Ferguson won it. In 1974, I met Ferguson and was told the story of him winning the manifold, and the irony of the story was that when he won it, he couldn't afford carburetors for the intake."

COMPANY RACE CAR

Bob possessed a great ability to promote a product, and he knew that if the Tattersfield-Baron equipment were going to sell, it'd first have to be proven under actual race conditions. The partners needed a Tatersfield-Baron-equipped vehicle that could set records; it had to be something flashy, something that would attract attention whether it was racing or just sitting still. What he needed was a vehicle that'd appeal to their main customers—hot rodders—and at that time, the dry lakes seemed to offer the best solution.

At that time, long-distance fuel tanks made for World War II aircraft were beginning to show up at the dry lakes as race cars, thanks to the innovative thinking of Bill Burke. He first noticed these streamlined, pod-like "belly tanks" while in the South Pacific, and after the war, he introduced the belly tank to dry lakes racing by shoe-horning a flathead V-8 into the cramped quarters of a surplus tank.

Bob contacted Burke in 1948 to build a belly tank streamliner, but just not a run-of-the-mill tank. After Bill completed the interior frame and mechanical workings on the inside of the vehicle, he handed it over to the Electric & Carburetor shop, which specialized in aircraft work. The final product was a rolling showpiece. The exterior was painted in Tattersfield-Baron hammer-tone blue, the cockpit was furnished in leather with an aircraft-style windscreen, the body sported a streamlined rounded tailfin, and the engine compartment was covered in as much chrome plating as possible. The vehicle had a Buck Rogers spaceship look about it. Bob got what he was looking for in a high-profile race car to promote Tattersfield-Baron, a show car with race car qualities that was no doubt the envy of many dry lakes racers who didn't have deep pockets.

Any question of the car's performance was quickly answered, as it was completed just in time to set the A/Streamliner record at

Tommy Thickstun's supercharger was mounted in the Tattersfield company pickup for road testing. The V-belt-driven blower was outfitted with two carbs. Unfortunately the performance results are unknown. *Courtesy Tony Baron*

137 miles per hour at the 1948 Russetta Timing Association Finals held on El Mirage Dry Lake. Bob belonged to the Revs car club which enabled him to enter RTA-sanctioned meets, and he also belonged to the Road Runners, allowing him to run at Southern California Timing Association meets. In 1949, he set the record in C/Streamliner at 145.16 miles per hour during an SCTA meet and ran B/Streamliner at an RTA meet, taking the record with 136.37 miles per hour.

Besides driving the belly tank, Bob owned a coupe that he periodically raced at RTA meets, running in the A/Coupe class. He also owned a very beautiful fenderless '32 Ford roadster street rod that sported a black-lacquer paint job, loads of chrome, white interior, louvered engine hood, and a full-race Tatterfield-Baron–equipped V-8—it was one gorgeous show car.

In 1949, the SCTA had finalized a deal with the authorities in Utah to hold speed trials on the wide-open salt flats of Bonneville. This endless racecourse offered the ideal opportunity to display the total performance of the Tattersfield-Baron tank; it would also spell the beginning of the end of the Tattersfield-Baron business relationship.

BONNEVILLE NATIONALS 1949

Bob and his crew towed the tank up to Bonneville, while Frank declined the offer to attend the weeklong event, as he couldn't take the time away from his automotive shop. Tony Baron said, "My dad was the quiet engine builder behind the scenes and never cared to drive the belly tank. The Tattersfield crew was a more flamboyant

group who didn't really take the racing seriously." Unfortunately, there was too much truth in that statement, and the crew's casual attitude about racing and safety would be the reason that Bob and Frank's business venture ended.

The race meet at Bonneville was set up by the authorities as a trial run for the SCTA in its bid to have access to the salt flats, and the SCTA wanted to make a good impression for the Utah state officials who had made it all possible. The Tattersfield crew had rented several motel rooms in the small border town of Wendover, Nevada, a stone's throw west of the salt flats. Tired from the long trip, Bob had checked into his room for the night, leaving his crewmembers to their own devices. Among the boxes of spare parts that accompanied the Tattersfield caravan was Tommy Thickstun's supercharger, which Bob had considered trying out after they'd made some runs with a normally aspirated engine. Unfortunately, the crew spotted the supercharger, and it wasn't long before they'd hacked away the tank's engine cowl to make room for the blower. Once installed, it was time for a demonstration run, and by that time it was into the wee hours of the night. No doubt the consumption of alcoholic beverages encouraged the boys to fire up the car and go for a wild ride down the main street of Wendover, open exhausts blasting away. It would have made a great scene in *American Graffiti*. Needless to say, their actions didn't go over well with the SCTA officials or Wendover's town fathers.

The next morning, when Bob came out of his motel room, he found an empty space in the parking lot where the tank had been, as the rambunctious crew had already left for the salt flats to see just how fast it really was. High school student, part-time Ansen Automotive employee, and dry lakes racer Bob Morton was on hand to see the action. Bob said, "Tattersfield almost got kicked out of the SCTA because of what his crew did at Bonneville when they chopped the belly tank body up to install the blower, and then drove the tank through Wendover at night with the open exhausts singing their tune. In the morning, when Tattersfield came out of his motel room, his tank and crew were gone. All that remained in the parking lot were the pieces of metal they'd chopped out of the top of the tank. The crew had already gone out to the salt flats to try it out. The carburetors sat high up on the blower and were rigged up with a hand-operated throttle. Fortunately for the driver, the starting officials prevented them from taking the car down the course."

After the hullabaloo was smoothed over and the blower removed, the tank was allowed to run, but no speed records were achieved during the meet. The only highlight for the Tattersfield outfit at Bonneville was when John Browning's Tattersfield-Baron-equipped '29 roadster set the fastest speed for a roadster that year, with a speed of 140 miles per hour, taking the C/Roadster class.

LOU BANEY

Of all the racers using Tattersfield-Baron equipment, Lou Baney drew more attention to the actual performance qualities of the Tattersfield-Baron equipment than anyone else. Lou was on the RTA governing board, an avid competitor on the dry lakes, a top engine builder at Ansen Automotive, and, being a good friend of Frank's, it was only natural that he'd be involved with Tattersfield-Baron products.

At the RTA Finals in 1948, Baney's chopped and fenderless '32 Ford coupe set a new class record in B/Coupe and had the fastest time for that body style with a 123-mile-per-hour run. For the 1949 season, Lou ran the car in C class and again held the record for the fastest coupe, competing in 11 meets, winning 10 firsts and 1 third place. It was the first coupe to break the 125-, 130-, and 135-mile-per-hour marks at RTA meets and had an unofficial 137-mile-per-hour run to make it the fastest coupe of that time.

In a magazine article that covered one of the RTA meets, Charles Camp reported that Lou's consistency in improving speeds was accounted for by the sheer brute horsepower of his car's Tattersfield-Baron-equipped engine. The article went on to say that the 296-ci flathead put out 225 horsepower on straight methanol, peeking at 5,200 rpm. Camp described the unusual pop-up pistons that extended 7/16 inch up into the heads, compared to other manufacturers whose pop-up pistons traveled only 1/4 inch into the head. He also mentioned that the four-carburetor manifold didn't cause overcarburetion due to the clean-breathing characteristics of the rest of the induction system. Camp went on to say that the lack of aerodynamics of Baney's coupe was even more convincing of the engine's efficiency. In another article, Baney is quoted as crediting Frank Baron for the successful development of the "seven-sixteenths kick-up piston design."

MORTON AND RUBIO

In 1948, Bob Morton first became acquainted with Bob Tattersfield and Frank Baron when he crashed his roadster at a dry lakes meet. After Morton's accident, Frank and Bob were having engine problems and had contacted Lou Senter at Ansen Automotive, where Morton was employed, to ask to borrow the engine out of Morton's wrecked roadster. In order to assess the condition of the engine, Tattersfield picked up Bob Morton at his house, drove up to the dry lake where the destroyed roadster was, and brought the remains back to the Ansen shop. The 296-ci Mercury V-8 was unhurt, and the men struck a deal in which Tattersfield-Baron equipment would be installed on the engine to run it in the belly tank. In the December 1948 issue of *Hot Rod*, there was a writeup on the results of the RTA's final meet for the season with a picture of the Tattersfield tank speeding to a 136-mile-per-hour record. The article only mentions that the record was set with a borrowed engine.

Eventually, Morton got his engine back and, with his racing partner, George Rubio, used the engine to set numerous records on the dry lakes and at the drag strip. In 1950, the two installed the Tattersfield-Baron-equipped engine in a '29 roadster known as the *Ansen Special*, which went on to be the first roadster to top 150 miles per hour at an SCTA dry lakes meet. Regrettably, the record run was marred by a fatal freak accident. The day of the accident, the car had turned a qualifying run of 145 miles per hour, but a second run down the lakebed wasn't high enough to break the existing record. Nearing the end of the day, Bob

This view of the highly detailed engine compartment of the Tattersfield Ford pickup truck shows the experimental radiators mounted inside each fender and the custom grille designed to deflect the air flow. *Courtesy Tony Baron*

Robinson asked Morton and Rubio if he could try for the record driving their roadster. Robinson, an experienced dry lakes racer, was clocked at 151 miles per hour as he passed through the timing traps, but for reasons never uncovered, the car veered off on an angle at high speed and hit a low sand dune, causing the roadster to disintegrate. The only conclusion that the SCTA officials could come up with was that wind-blown dust at the end of the course obscured Robinson's line of vision, causing him to take the wrong course. The car was totally destroyed, leaving only the engine and quick-change rearend. It was the second racing fatality that had occurred at a sanctioned SCTA event since the organization began in 1937.

That same year, members of the SCTA and the American Motorcycle Association (AMA) collaborated to put on a drag race demonstration at an unused blimp base near Santa Ana. The main event of the meet was a final runoff between four of the fastest cars and four of the fastest motorcycles. The top speed and quickest elapsed time for a roadster was set by the Morton and Rubio *Ansen Special* roadster at 10.83 seconds ET with a speed of 114.79 miles per hour. They'd installed the Tattersfield-Baron-equipped Merc in a '27 T borrowed from renowned hot rodder Ak Miller.

THE BEGINNING OF THE END

After the Bonneville fiasco, anytime Frank would take the belly tank to a dry lakes event, he blocked out the Tattersfield name and ran it under the Baron name only. He'd had enough and wanted to disassociate himself from the Tattersfield name, which had become a bit controversial among the racing crowd. It seems that the apple of discord was the Tattersfield-Baron belly tank. Since it first arrived on the scene, it had stirred up nothing but friction between the two partners. Bob had grown up in a rather affluent environment and chummed around with a Hollywood-type crowd. Although this lifestyle didn't distract him from his ability to run a successful business, his playboy lifestyle was quite different from that of his more subdued partner. And although Bob loved racing, sometimes he didn't take it all that seriously, and safety was one of the things that caused problems between the partners.

Frank Baron, on the other hand, was a highly skilled hands-on engine builder, was serious about racing, and winning was his foremost goal, but not at the expense of safety. Tony Baron recalled a time his dad took the belly tank to a dry lakes meet, and only after making several runs did Frank discover that the front wheels could easily have come off, all due to negligence. Bob's crew had run the car last, and someone had forgotten to replace the cotter keys that held the rims onto the axle hubs. When confronted with the mishap, the Tattersfield bunch found it humorous, as no one had been injured. Frank, however, wasn't amused. Tony also recalled an embarrassing incident that occurred when the Tattersfield group was at a dry lakes meet. Someone had connected the gas pedal linkage improperly and, when the engine started, the throttle was instantly wide open. The belly tank was being push started in the pit area, and it instantly took off at full throttle into a low sand dune, causing sufficient damage that put the tank out of commission.

Maybe the projected sales weren't as anticipated and the partners were losing money. Maybe Bob lost interest in manufacturing speed equipment and facing stiff competition from other manufacturers. But more likely, it was the Korean War that had a strong influence on the demise of the Tattersfield Manifold Division in 1952. With the outbreak of the war, the Electric & Carburetor Engineering Company focused its attention on aircraft production and military contracts, and Bob went on to become

very successful in that line of the business. The manifold line was dropped and the assets were sold off to various companies such as Ansen Automotive, which purchased a good portion of the equipment and kept the Tatterfield brand available for several more years.

The good-looking Tattersfield belly tank was sold off only to meet a sad end. It was last seen in 1952 performing at a local drag strip, and the engine had been relocated to the front of the tank.

FRANK BARON

The third party in this trio of speed merchants was Frank Baron, who was born in Akron, Ohio, in 1911. When he was nine years old, Frank and his family moved to Los Angeles, where his father opened a barber shop on Pico Boulevard, west of La Brea. Tony Baron said that his dad spoke of the times when the great Harry Miller frequented the shop for a haircut and gave young Frank tickets for the car races. With enthusiasm built up by watching races at the old Legion Ascot track, 12-year-old Frank bought his first car, a vintage Model T. He eventually modified the body and installed a Rajo overhead-valve conversion on the engine.

After graduating second in his class from Beverly Hills High School in 1928, Frank began work as an automotive mechanic at Mark Bloom's service station in Los Angeles, eventually going to the Fahy Ford dealership, where he met Tommy Thickstun. The two hot rod enthusiasts shared similar beliefs on engine modification, especially on how to improve the fuel flow and breathing characteristics of the flathead engine.

By 1936, Frank had picked up enough practical mechanical know-how to open Baron's Automotive Shop on West Eighth Street in Los Angeles, offering general auto repairs. He began to do a fair amount of engine hop-up work, and over time the shop became

The Tattersfield-Baron belly tank at the 1949 *Hot Rod* show in Los Angeles. The rear body panel is elevated to show the engine compartment's accessibility. Notice all the louvers in the rear panel. *Courtesy Tony Baron*

a hangout spot for hot rodders, including Tommy Thickstun and Bob Tattersfield. It was there, in Frank's service shop, that a strong friendship developed between the three speed enthusiasts. With Thickstun manufacturing manifolds, Frank did a fair amount of business installing Tommy's speed equipment on customer's cars.

Frank and Tommy had similar thoughts on engine performance, and the two pooled their knowledge and hand-fabricated a four-carburetor manifold to run on one of Bob Estes' roadsters at the dry lakes. The two also did a lot of engine developmental work in Frank's shop. Tony Baron said, "My dad felt that Tommy Thickstun was the driving force behind many of their technical achievements. When Tommy was talking, everyone was listening."

Just prior to the outbreak of World War II, Frank got involved in racing 135 Hydro class powerboats at Marine Stadium in Long Beach, where he ran against stiff competition from the likes of Eddie Meyer and Richard Hallett.

BARON MANIFOLD

After the 1949 Bonneville fiasco and several other minor, yet justifiable incidents, the business arrangement between Frank and Bob began to wear thin. In 1950, the Tattersfield-Baron partnership came to an amicable parting of the ways, and, although the partnership was over, Frank continued manufacturing the four-carburetor manifold under the Baron banner. There were two models of the Baron intake: one was cast with the generator mounting bracket, and the other was a race-only model without the bracket. These manifolds were made available into the early 1950s, until the demand for flathead speed equipment declined to the point that it was no longer a profitable venture.

BOAT RACING

With the humiliation at Bonneville, the lackadaisical attitude of the Tattersfield crew toward the safe running condition of the belly tank, and the reputation the crew had garnered, Frank's desire to race at the dry lakes began to wane. He eventually edged himself out of the dusty hot conditions of the dry lakes, and from 1949 to 1951 was back into powerboat racing, competing in the popular crackerbox class.

The two-man, flat-bottomed boats were fast, dangerous, unpredictable, and beloved by racing fans. Frank's boat was named *Let's Go*, and Frank usually had Lou Baney or George Baldie as his riding mechanic. It soon became obvious where Frank's niche in racing lay. In the first year of competition, he won the main feature the first time out for the season opener, won the Labor Day Perpetual Trophy, won the crackerbox class club trophy for the season, and, to top it off, won the Hell Divers Trophy when he flipped his boat in the final race of the season.

Tony Baron said, "One of the rules for this class stated that there could only be one carburetor venturi per two cylinders, so my father ran four one-barrel Zeniths on a four-carb manifold. The little 239-cubic-inch flathead put out a healthy 235 horsepower at 5,300 rpm on straight alcohol and was clocked at a record-setting 73 miles per hour in the Kilo at Marine Stadium in Long Beach in 1950."

MOVING ON

With the Tattersfield-Baron venture behind him, Frank focused all his attention on operating his high-end automotive repair business, which specialized in Cadillac repairs. When his son, Tony, was old enough to join the business, Tony and three business associates formed a partnership with Frank that included two automotive repair shops: the Studio City Shop and the Miracle Mile Service Shop.

Old habits are hard to bury, and in the early 1960s, Frank became involved in developing a Paxton supercharger kit. He installed one of the Paxton blowers in a '63 Jaguar XKE coupe, and in 1965, the Paxton-motivated six-cylinder Jag ran an impressive 115 miles per hour at 13.50 seconds at the San Fernando Drag Strip.

In 1971, Tony began to collect Tattersfield-Baron speed equipment, and in doing so, he was fortunate enough to come across the original casting-mold patterns for the heads. With his father's help, the heads were updated and put into production on a limited basis under the Baron name, and it wasn't long before flathead enthusiasts were placing their orders. Not only was there a resurgence of the flathead V-8 for use in street rods, but there was an increasing demand from the hard-core racing crowd that competed in nostalgic classes at the dry lakes, Bonneville, and drag strips. Tony developed an updated version of the Tattersfield-Baron pop-up piston head for those who needed all-out power.

Even though the legendary engine went out of production more than 50 years ago, the renaissance of the Ford flathead has put a strain on the old, well-worn speed parts that are still kicking about. Specialty companies are dusting off their old molds and recasting new equipment to meet the demand, and today Baron Racing Equipment is busy filling orders for everything from street rods to Bonneville flyers. The company has been in business almost 30 years, and Frank was no doubt proud of Tony for bringing back a part of Frank's life that had ended so many years earlier. Frank Baron retired in the mid-1960s and passed away on April 2, 1991, at the age of 88.

After the fiasco with the blower at the 1949 Bonneville Nationals, any time Frank took the belly tank to a dry lake meet, the Tattersfield name was blocked out. Frank (looking at camera) is helping push the tank. *Courtesy Tony Baron*

CHAPTER 3

Braje Equipment

NICK BRAJEVICH

When one contemplates high-performance equipment for an automobile engine, it usually centers around parts for a big-block, a Hemi, nitrous oxide for the wife's Honda—anything but racing stuff for a 26.5-horsepower miniature four-cylinder—unless your name is Nick Brajevich. Of all the automobile engines to choose from, Nick picked the least conspicuous of the litter—an engine that was originally designed to power auxiliary equipment for the military during World War II—and transformed it into the heartbeat for an economy micro car and used it as an outboard motor. Nick built his manufacturing company around the Crosley car engine.

Nick Brajevich was born and raised in Los Angeles, and while attending Freemont High School, he developed an interest in cars. As a teenager, he looked up to the dirt-track racing exploits of his cousin, Johnny Pasco, who introduced Nick firsthand to the world of race cars. It was Nick's job to sit in Pasco's sprint car and steer as it was flat towed by a piece of rope to the races. Those early memories held mixed emotions for Nick, for he remembered his longing to race but also heartbreak after an accident.

In 1934, Johnny Pasco was killed during a sprint car race at the old Jeffries Ranch half-mile dirt oval. "Gentleman" Jim Jeffries was an old-time bare-knuckles boxing champion who taught boxing and held amateur events in a barn on his ranch. Jim also had a passion for automobile racing and had a half-mile dirt track built on his ranch in the San Fernando Valley.

The death of his much-admired cousin Johnny had a long-term effect on Nick. It kept him from racing and influenced the design of his street rod. Nick said, "My mother made me promise that I'd never race while she was still alive after my cousin Johnny was killed in the racing accident; it was very hard on the family." Later on, outside of the occasional runoff with his hot rod on deserted streets, Nick only raced at the dry lakes, where he managed to get a Chevy hot rod up to a 105 miles per hour. He said that his mother didn't consider runs at the dry lakes to be actual racing.

Upon graduating from Freemont High in 1935, Nick got a job with the fire department at the Todd Shipbuilding Yards in San Pedro, where he remained as an engineer for 14 years.

HOT ROD SPRINT CAR

Although his first two cars were rather nondescript vehicles—a Briscoe and a Model T—his third one meant something to him. In 1936, Nick came up with a design for his first real hot rod, fashioned after a sprint car in memory of his cousin, Johnny Pasco. The basis for the street rod/sprint car was a '25 Chevrolet roadster minus the fenders and other unnecessary parts. Nick hand-fabricated its sprint-style front end out of sheet metal. The hot setup for a Chevy four-cylinder in those days was installing a three-port Oldsmobile head, Durant rods, oil pump modifications, and an SR Winfield carburetor. Nick fondly remembered the little roadster as being pretty perky for its day and mentioned that the local constabulary would on occasion stop him out of curiosity to question him about the body and engine modifications.

Opposite: Nick Brajevich's just-completed CRA track roadster and the fellows who helped build the car. From left to right are Bill Morrisetto, John Meyer, unknown, Al Goety, unknown, Leroy Snooks (driver's seat), and Nick (on the rear tire). Snooks was one of the few black drivers on the CRA circuit. *Courtesy Nick Brajevich*

TRACK ROADSTERS

Nick was true to his word to his beloved mother and did not follow in his cousin's footsteps as long as she was alive. It was only after her passing, just prior to the outbreak of World War II, that he finally ventured onto the track. His first race car was a combined partnership with Bill Barnes, and Nick quickly realized that he just didn't have what it took to be a competitive driver. Nick's forte was in maintaining the car while Barnes took care of the driving chores. Their car was based on a T roadster and powered by a modified Ford flathead six-cylinder, an odd engine choice.

In 1940, the two fellows competed in the Western Racing Association (WRA) races held on the dirt ovals of Culver City Speedway and Gardena Bowl Speedway. The duo consistently ran with the pack, not up front or bringing up the rear, and with the outbreak of the war, the tracks closed and the partnership ended.

In the postwar era, the popularity of automobile racing in America mushroomed, and in Southern California a group of car enthusiasts were busy organizing what would become known as the California Roadster Association (CRA). The organization began with a bunch of fellows who, after removing fenders, windshields, and the like, would tear around a dirt track in their stripped-down roadsters. But within a year, these street rods morphed into full–race track roadsters. The CRA quickly attracted a multitude of drivers and race car owners, and became the proving ground for many rooky drivers who would later become famous in other avenues of auto racing.

Once back in civilian life, Nick had the desire to go racing, but this time it'd be on his own. His new car was based on a '27 T roadster with a brilliant gold paint job, and, as with his previous racer, his didn't follow the majority of his peers by going with a flathead V-8. Nick was very good friends with Wayne Horning, who had just completed the development of a 12-port head for the Chevrolet six. This aftermarket head had six intake ports on one side and six exhaust ports on the other and was designed to breathe life into the otherwise-underpowered six-cylinder. Nick's roadster was one of the first to run the Horning 12-port head. The alcohol-burning '41 Chevy six was originally outfitted with dual Riley carburetors, then with a three-carburetor setup, and lastly with Stuart Hilborn's fuel injectors when they became available.

The Brajevich roadster's list of drivers reads like a who's-who in track racing: Leroy Nooks (one of the few black drivers of the era and a great driver) was the first to drive it, followed by Harry Stockman, Frank McGurk, Jim Rigsby, Lou Tio, Pat Flaherty, Andy Linden, Ed Haddad, and others. Nick mentioned that many of the track roadster drivers honed their driving skills on the CRA circuit and eventually went on to Indy and other prestigious racing venues.

In addition to owning a good-looking track roadster that would have done well in any custom car show, Nick was also pretty proud of his tow car. He built up a sleeper '28 Model A sedan with hydraulic brakes and a highly modified Mercury V-8 that surprised many a Sunday driver, as he shot by with the race car in tow.

Nick stands behind the track roadster in which he and Bill Barnes were partners. Jack Bayliss is in the driver's seat. Motivation for the racer was a Ford flathead six-cylinder rather than the standard flathead V-8. *Courtesy Nick Brajevich*

LITTLE 500

In 1948, the CRA elected to imitate the Indy 500 with its own Little Indianapolis 500, held at Carrell Speedway in Gardena; it was to be the CRA's longest race and largest winning purse up to that time. The 250-mile, 500-lap race was held on Memorial Day weekend and, like the big Indy, there were 33 cars competing on the half-mile dirt track. Reportedly, there were over 17,000 race fans watching the excitement that day.

Nick's roadster qualified up near the front, with the talented Andy Linden in the driver seat. Once the race started, Linden rapidly moved to the front of the pack, and it looked like he might have run away with the race had it not been for a situation that could have been avoided. Prior to the race, Nick instructed Andy to be careful when he drove into the infield for a pit stop, as there were numerous low guard posts sticking out of the ground, and Nick had seen what they could do to a car in previous races at the track. Regrettably, when Andy pulled in for fuel he drove right over a guard post, destroying the oil pan and damaging the undercarriage. Nick felt that they stood a good chance of winning that race had it not been for that guard post.

Meanwhile, back on the race track, a relatively unknown driver named Dempsey Wilson took over the lead on lap 208 and held on to win. Wilson had started in 17th, worked his way up through the field, was one of the few drivers who drove the entire race himself, pitting twice for fuel. Dempsey was one of those drivers who would eventually end up at Indy, and he opened a successful camshaft business.

Andy Linden's driving abilities would also move him quickly up the ranks, and in 1951, he was running at Indianapolis.

CROSLEY

The Crosley Automotive Company first appeared on the scene in 1939, as its founder Powel Crosley Jr. introduced to the American public his economical form of transportation. Powel had made his

Nick sits in the unfinished CRA track roadster, no doubt dreaming of the many victories to come. *Courtesy Nick Brajevich*

fortunes through numerous successful business ventures including the Crosley Radio Corporation, and like Preston Tucker, Powel wanted to build his own car. The prewar version of Crosley's novel subcompact car was powered a petite, 12-horsepower, air-cooled, Waukesha two-cylinder engine.

The next-generation engine that powered a Crosley vehicle was the brainchild of Lloyd Taylor from San Francisco. The Taylor engine was a dependable, tiny, lightweight engine used by the military in World War II as a power source for lighting. When Crosley unveiled a revised version of its car in 1946, it came with this beautifully engineered 44-ci single-overhead-cam (SOHC) four-cylinder; in comparison, the Harley-Davidson Motorcycle Company shoe-horned an elephant-sized 74-ci two-cylinder engine into its motorcycle frame.

The early Crosley engines were manufactured with welded, stamped-steel head and block assemblies, making them prone to internal leakage and warping problems, but these problems were overcome in 1949, when Crosley came out with a cast-iron block with an integral head. For a tiny engine, as compared to the behemoth Olds and Caddy V-8s of the day, the four-cylinder ran a shaft-gear-driven single-overhead camshaft and a crankshaft supported by five main bearings. It produced 26.5 horsepower at 5,400 rpm from 44 cubic inches and weighed less than 150 pounds. It was probably the most technology advanced engine design put out by any of the competing American automobile manufacturers in the late 1940s postwar era.

It didn't take long for the powerboating fraternity and midget racers to take notice of the charming little Crosley engine, and it quickly found its way into powering three-quarter midgets and 48 Hydro–class boats. Sonny Meyer, the son of three-time Indy winner Lou Meyer and nephew of speed equipment manufacturer Eddie Meyer, was quick to set the record in the 48 Hydro class with a Crosley engine.

BRAJE EQUIPMENT

An acquaintance of Nick's who worked for Service Motors in Los Angeles, which was the regional Crosley dealer, knew that Nick had a lot of success building and racing track roadsters. He wanted Nick's opinion on the potential of this minuscule engine. Nick's first impression of the engine was that it could probably make good horsepower for the size of it, but it would need work in the carburetion area and possibly other things once he'd inspected the internal workings. After dismantling and carefully studying the individual engine pieces, Nick drew up a list of recommendations to strengthen and improve this amazing little engine. At that point, he saw a potential market to supply performance equipment for an engine that everyone else seemed to have neglected.

Nick decided to take a gamble and manufacture some specialty equipment on a part-time basis. He opened his business venture under the name Braje Equipment and ran it out of the garage behind his house on 422 West Eighty-third Street in Los Angeles. "Braje" was a nickname given to him years earlier by his longtime friend, Wayne Horning.

The first item on the agenda was the factory stamped-steel camshaft cover, which was noisy and had a bad habit of leaking oil. He had a friend make a wooden pattern for a new cover that would be a plain, square-sided, cast-aluminum unit (it was later redesigned to be a finned cover). The next item on the list was the faulty stock intake manifold system. The factory manifold contained a design flaw that resulted in air/fuel mixture problems with the center two cylinders. The siamesed intake ports were the primary cause of this condition, and Nick's one- and two-carburetor model intakes were designed to eliminate this condition. From the intake, he moved to the oil pan. The factory 2-quart pan proved adequate for a stock job, but the Braje 4-quart oil pan was more than sufficient to keep the oil cool under any racing conditions. Next, Nick created a cast-aluminum finned side plate to reduce internal engine noise and provide a decorative look, and the modification list continued to grow.

Nick pretty well had the marketplace for Crosley performance products sewn up, excluding camshafts, which buyers could purchase from several different cam grinders. There were no specialty pistons available at the time, so he used motorcycle pistons and reworked the skirts to clear the crankshaft. These pistons were sufficient until demand warranted custom-made sand-cast pistons from Frank Venolia, and eventually Nick had Frank design a permanent piston mold. Nick said a young fellow named Nick Arias, later of Arias Pistons fame, machined the pistons for him in Wayne Horning's machine shop.

Along with a steady increase in equipment sales, Nick received constant inquiries from customers wanting to know where they could purchase custom-built performance engines. At the time, Crosley enthusiasts were left to their own devices when it came to modifying the engine—easy for some, but confusing for those who had never had experience with an overhead-cam job. It was only natural that the next step in Nick's business would be modifying engines for his customers.

It soon became apparent that Braje had the Crosley specialty market to itself and, by 1948, the demand for parts and custom engines was great enough that Nick left the fire department to operate Braje Equipment on a full-time basis. About the same time, the Harbor Freeway Commission was expanding its services with a freeway that went right through Nick's house, leaving him no choice but to relocate to his present address on 130th Street in Gardena.

Nick received one of the first 12-port Chevrolet heads and three-carburetor manifolds for his CRA track roadster from old friend Wayne Horning. *Courtesy Nick Brajevich*

BRAJE BOMB

Nick put aside the time-consuming, high-maintenance, track roadster due to the pressures of business, but in 1950, when C. J. Hart and his two partners opened a drag strip in Santa Ana, it caught Nick's attention. It took a while for the idea to mature, but a Crosley-powered race car began to take shape. Besides providing some fun, it would be a testbed for his products, and the exposure would be good for business. Looking over the variety of car classifications at Santa Ana, Nick found the O class maximum 91-ci engine displacement to be the only one suitable for the tiny 44-ci Crosley. It was evident that anything he built would have to be as light as possible, as there were no trophies given for dragging extra weight down the strip. He came up with a superlight, 460-pound dragster, motor included; two strong people could easily pick up the car.

Nick bored out the engine to 48 ci and ran all Braje equipment, except for the camshaft that he bought from Iskenderian Racing Cams. The Braje dragster was about as simplistic a car as anyone could build, but it proved to be a winner on the strip. Don Turner and Johnny Meyer helped in the construction of the vehicle, while the driver position was filled by Sonny Meyer, who was the lightest guy they could find for the job. The flyweight dragster hit a top speed of 97.8 miles per hour on straight methanol, putting a lot of cars with much larger engines on the sidelines. Sonny Meyer was well known in the powerboat circles and held numerous speed-boat records.

In an effort to get to get the maximum potential out of his car, Nick collaborated with Frank McGurk on a design for a streamlined body. But by time the aluminum body panels were completed, pressing business matters had to be taken care of, leaving no time to play with the mini-dragster, which was sold to someone out east; the streamlined body was never tried out at the strip.

Nick was correct in assuming that the car would invite attention, and *Hot Rod* did a full-coverage story on the *Braje Bomb* in its June 1953 issue.

SPORTS CAR

When Crosley first introduced its new compact Hot Shot roadster sports car with the hopes of making its small automobile more appealing to the buying public, it worked on Nick. He liked what he saw, but he felt that the company hadn't gone far enough with the design and decided to add his own personal touch to the roadster by practically redesigning the entire exterior. Nick handmade custom doors and used MG sports car door hinges. He mounted Studebaker rear taillights in Cadillac-style rear fins. A Studebaker windshield was molded into the front cowl, headlights were set into the front fenders and extended forward, a custom grille was added, and the car was finally topped off with four, custom, stainless-steel spun hubcaps. Nick and an assistant did all the lead bodywork on the car in the Braje shop.

The car hadn't been on the road long when the upper management of the Crosley Company contacted Nick about licensing his design modifications into their own production line. But some things were not meant to be. He was in the middle of negotiations with Crosley when the ill-timed news came out about its manufacturing plant closure. He was to receive $25 per fiberglass body that was reproduced from a mold taken off his customized Hot Shot—that was 1952 dollars, and it would have turned into a tidy sum of money for him.

While the contract negotiations were taking place, Nick was working on developing a twin overhead-cam head for the Crosley engine in the hopes the company would take it over. The head castings had already been completed and were ready to be machined, but after the plant closure, Nick let everything go by the wayside.

DYNAMOMETER

After the plant closure, Crosley was sold to the Aerojet General Corporation, which was only interested in the four-cylinder engine and sent the remains of the car manufacturer to the scrap heap. Aerojet had a contract with the U.S. government to supply 1,000 of the small, dependable, lightweight engines monthly to be used to drive portable generator units, water pumps, and so on, much like World War II. One of the stipulations in the government contract was that Aerojet had to submit performance specifications on the engine and, lacking its own dynamometer facilities to run the tests, Aerojet contacted Nick. They figured that since Braje was the main manufacturer of aftermarket parts for the engine, it might also have a dyno. When he was contacted about a dynamometer, Nick said that at the moment Braje didn't have one, but he was certain that he could come up with a suitable unit within several weeks. He was given three weeks to complete the job, as Aerojet had to meet its contract deadline.

Due to the small size of the Crosley engine, Nick had a hard time finding a dyno suitable for the job, so he decided to build his own with the assistance of Johnny Junkins, a repair shop owner and longtime dry lakes competitor. The pair purchased a homemade water absorption unit from Vic Hubbard that was small enough for the Crosley engine to operate, and the remainder of the dyno was fabricated in Braje's shop. The water wheel was installed on a steel-channel frame outfitted with wheels and designed to be self-contained to allow engine testing to be done outdoors. Nick's dynamometer got the job done for Aerojet, and Nick contracted out the dyno to test different anti-knock gasoline additives for the Ethyl Corporation using a Crosley mule test engine. *Hot Rod* did a very good article on the Braje dynamometer in its October 1953 issue.

PERFORMANCE CAMSHAFTS

As the feisty little Crosley engine found its way into more and more racing venues, the demand for speed equipment increased accordingly. Braje Equipment was the only manufacturer to offer Crosley engine enthusiasts a complete performance package. The only item that Nick didn't manufacture or stock was a high-performance camshaft.

Just after World War II, race car driver Frank McGurk retired from competition to open an automotive repair shop specializing in Chevrolets. McGurk's business quickly evolved from general auto repairs into the number-one Chevrolet and GMC speed equipment manufacturer in the country, and McGurk become known as "Mr. Chevrolet." The rapid expansion of his manufacturing business, which also included grinding camshafts, was too much for his Inglewood shop, and he made plans to relocate to Gardena. Frank asked Nick if he could set up his two cam grinders in the Braje shop until he moved into his new quarters, not wanting to lose out on any camshaft sales if the grinders were out of commission. He made a deal with Nick's two sons, Mike and Blaz, to grind McGurk camshafts, and after training them to operate the machines, the brothers worked after school and on weekends to fill orders for McGurk cams.

Once he understood how a camshaft grinder worked from watching his sons operate the grinders, Nick decided to grind his own Braje cams for the Crosley. He enlisted McGurk's know-how in laying out the designs for the cam masters, and the new Braje performance camshafts ranged from a 3/4 regrind to a steel-billet, full-race job.

Nick said that he found the new shop for McGurk on Halldale Avenue, several blocks from the Braje facility. (Frank's new neighbor was Howard Moore, who was heavily involved in racing, building track and dragster engines, and noted for his Cadillac and Olds engine swaps.) Once McGurk Engineering was up and running again, it passed a lot of subcontract work over to Nick's machine shop.

44 CUBIC INCHES OF POWER

The Crosley engine eventually found its way into three-quarter midgets, powerboats, sport cars, hot street setups, and the strip. For the output that this pint-sized powerhouse produced, it

Nick's 1941 Chevy six-cylinder outfitted with a Wayne 12-port head, three carbs atop a Wayne manifold, Wayne cast exhaust system, and Spalding ignition and camshaft. Originally Nick ran the Chevy with two Riley side-draft carbs. *Courtesy Nick Brajevich*

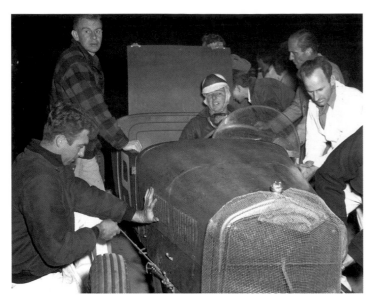

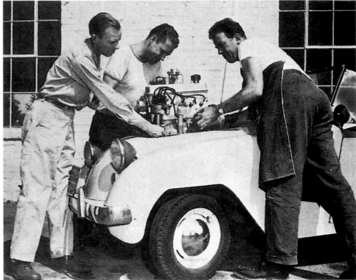

Pit action at Carrell Speedway during the CRA's 1948 Little 500. Andy Linden is driving Nick's roadster, with co-driver Carl Myday standing on the left side with hands on the door. On the lower left, adjusting engine hood strap, is Bill Morrisetto. *Courtesy Nick Brajevich*

Sometimes an engine hoist is not necessary—like when removing an engine from a Crosley. Nick is on the right side of the Crosley Hot Shot, assisting two fellows in literally hand-lifting the tiny four-cylinder out of the sports car. *Courtesy Nick Brajevich*

proved that it had no equal. Across the country, there were several outfits that supplied Crosley engine equipment, but the number one in the business was Braje Equipment. By the mid-1950s, Braje carried camshafts, pistons, side plates, cam covers, cast-iron exhaust headers, intake manifolds, oil pans, 9-pound aluminum flywheels, and more, solely for the little Crosley. Nick even designed special main cap straps to eliminate crankshaft whip.

Customer demand pushed Nick into the engine-building business. The shop offered everything from mild to wild alcohol burners—whatever a customer wanted—and many Braje engines were shipped to racers out east.

One of the engines that Nick remembered coming out of the Braje shop was a bored and stroked racing job equipped with two motorcycle carburetors, a Vertex mag, a Weber stroker crankshaft, and headers. Nick said, "I was able to get fifty-five horsepower at eight thousand rpm out of that engine, and there was another full-race version with a fifty-three-cubic-inch displacement that delivered sixty horsepower on alcohol."

The all-time high was a Scott Roots-type supercharged Crosley that churned out 75 horsepower at a screaming 10,000 rpm. Nick said, "The engine's short stroke enabled it from coming apart at such high rpm. Fuel injection was tried out on the engine, but I felt that carburetors gave equal performance with less tuning problems."

Although the Crosley Automotive Company terminated business in 1952, the engine was kept in production until around 1971. It's been used for inboard boat engines, water pumps, Homelite and Fisher-Pierce Bearcat 55-horsepower outboard motors, generators, homebuilt aircraft engines, and even refrigeration units on transport trucks. After Crosley was sold to Aerojet,

a division of the General Tire and Rubber Company, it was sold to the Fageol Company and then to Crofton Marine.

VINTAGE AUTO RACING ASSOCIATION

Fifty-two years after he promised his mother he wouldn't get behind the wheel of a race car, Nick felt that he had kept his promise long enough and it was time to go racing. (He does not count his attempt to drive a track roadster in 1940.) Nick had discovered the remnants of a race car hidden away among some heavy underbrush in Palos Verdes. All that remained was the body and a frozen engine, but once he got the wreck back to the shop for a closer look, Nick realized it was Don Miller's No. 1 H/Modified race car. Miller was renowned for the modified Crosley Super Sport he raced in the H/Modified class during the 1950s. Unfortunately, the sports car's state of disrepair didn't warrant the time it would take to restore it to its former glory, so Nick acquired a '51 Crosley Super Sport in much better condition for what he had in mind.

In 1986, Nick joined the Vintage Auto Racing Association (VARA), a collection of racers who enjoyed having a good time with their vintage cars. This group raced for the sheer pleasure of the sport, and with no prize money to race for, it provided a relatively safe atmosphere for amateur enthusiasts. Nick's H/Mod class Crosley Super Sport had more than enough power to give him plenty of thrills and enjoyment in the Laguna Seca Vintage Races. Nick said, "Vintage racing has given me an opportunity to get into racing after all these years."

CAR STUFF

In all his years in business, Nick said that the strangest request he'd ever received for an engine was for one that was going to be installed

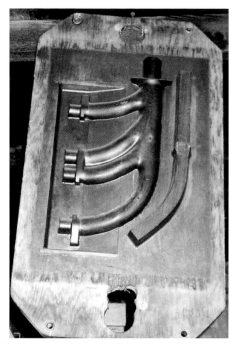

Nick kept all aspects of his manufacturing business close at hand, including the wooden molds used to produce engine parts. Shown is the half-mold for the Braje cast exhaust manifold. *Author photo*

in a helicopter. A company in the Los Angeles area was attempting to build a one man helicopter and needed a small, lightweight, yet powerful motor for its prototype. Nick was contracted to supply them with a Crosley modified to their specifications. The last he'd heard of the experimental helicopter was that when it attempted to take off it tipped over while still on the tarmac, sadly killing the test pilot with the rotating blades.

Nick ventured into a few non-Crosley pursuits, one of which was for the Nash Metropolitan. He had a friend who was drag racing one of these subcompact two-seaters, and, after a look under the hood, Nick decided that he would manufacture speed equipment for the car. Regrettably, this venture didn't get off the ground. After investing a considerable amount of money into having an intake, valve cover, and oil pan molds made for the Austin 840 engine, the Nash-Rambler Company upgraded the Metropolitan engine the following year to the larger 850 series. He'd already spent too much time and money to start the process all over again and instead shelved the project.

Nick felt that his long-standing relationship with the automobile sort of came naturally. "It's in the blood," he said, reflecting on the early exploits of his cousin, Johnny Pasco, and his relation to the great race car designer Frank Kurtis. Frank was a distant relative of his father, and Nick remembered Kurtis before he'd become a world-famous race car builder. Nick and his buddy Frank McGurk each owned one of the fabulous Kurtis Kraft 500 sports cars; Nick's was powered by a nailhead Buick V-8.

There are those speed aficionados who love nothing better than the powerful testosterone-filled V-8 wonders of Detroit, and there are a number who are more inclined to search for something a little different and a little less ostentatious, such as a Crosley, a Nash Metropolitan, or even a Beetle. In keeping with his love affair with compact automobiles, Nick worked on a VW Bug after the ill-fated Nash. Although the VW offered great fuel economy, it was about as plain and unassuming as the Crosley and left lots of room for improvement. After studying the exterior, Nick felt the easiest and most economical change he could make to the Bug—outside of a custom paint job—was to replace the bland factory wheels with something that had a bit of style. Investing in a pattern mold, he had a foundry cast some aluminum wheels, finishing the raw castings in his shop and marketing them under the name Braje Wheels.

OVER THE YEARS

After years of being involved with race cars and manufacturing, Nick had developed a good friendship with Vince and Andy Conze, who lived not far from his own home. In those days, before heavy industrial growth took over the area, Vince and Andy could be seen riding the trails in the surrounding vacant land and on occasion would ride over to Nick's for a visit. Mrs. Conze had bought a horse for her two sons, who kept the animal in a makeshift corral behind their home. As time went on, Andy and Vince became too busy with their machine shop to care for the horse, and the neighborhood riding trails were slowly being overtaken with the spread of urban growth. Mrs. Conze offered the 27-year-old horse to Nick as a gift, as she knew that he had the room for it at his hobby ranch and had two teenage sons who loved to ride.

There are small cactuses, and there are big cactuses; in Nick Brajevich's backyard, there is no doubt the world's largest cactus. This monstrosity of a plant is almost as old as Nick. He first planted it when he was a very young child, and everywhere the family moved, the cactus was dug up and moved along with them. Today, that cactus has grown to the point that it has to be supported by an adjacent building with a chain to keep it from toppling over. It is a living testament of sorts to the man who spent the better part of his life giving it nourishment.

Today, the Braje Equipment Company is alive and well, operating for over 50 years out of the same machine shop behind Nick's home. Now, Nick's youngest son, Blaz, runs the company, and in place of speed equipment it manufactures truck brake-line components and related items. Although he has been retired for some time, Nick retained his office, where he is often found answering inquiries for Braje speed equipment, and he will still manufacture small runs of Crosley parts if demand warrants it. Stored in several outbuildings are his collection of outboard motors using the Crosley engine, his beautiful little H/Modified Super Sport racer, and shelves of all the Crosley engines manufactured from 1946 to 1952.

The Crosley engine found favor with many racing buffs and saw service in numerous fields of racing, but without the efforts of Nick Brajevich in producing a complete line of speed equipment and engine development, the odd little four-cylinder may never have seen the amount of interest that it received.

CRANE ENGINEERING 77 SPECIAL

CRANE CAMS
HALLANDALE, FLORIDA

CHAPTER 4

Crane Cams

HARVEY J. CRANE JR.

Not all of the notable speed merchants were located on the West Coast, as was the case of Crane Cams. The founder of this very successful company was probably the last of the early merchants of speed to break new ground in building his business. Harvey J. Crane Jr. began like so many of his peers, although he didn't have to make the grinder that set him up in the camshaft business. In 1953, he ventured into the performance cam trade after the Storm-Vulcan Company introduced an affordable camshaft grinder that was directed toward the engine-rebuilding industry. By the time Harvey had hung a shingle over the door and fired up his cam grinder, the path was almost completed by individuals like him, for newcomers had only to follow in their footsteps in the business of manufacturing speed equipment—the hard stuff was pretty well taken care of.

EARLY YEARS

In 1915, Harvey Crane's grandfather opened one of the first machine shops in the Miami, Florida, area, and 10 years later, Harvey's father relocated that shop 25 miles north to the small town of Hallandale, where Harvey Jr. was born in 1931. The Crane enterprise was situated on the Old Dixie Highway and catered mainly to the local farming community. As a sideline venture, Harvey Sr. manufactured small economical farm tractors that were a hit with farmers who were trying to scratch out a living during the Depression era.

Old cars supplied the basis for the Crane tractor. After the car body was removed, the chassis was shortened up, and a second transmission was installed backward and mated up to the existing transmission. This design provided the needed gear reduction for true lugging power. To keep the costs within reason, he made an adapter to use a dual rear tire setup rather than expensive tractor tires. Farmers could add tire chains if they deemed it necessary. With several further modifications, Crane Sr. had produced an affordable farm tractor that was capable of performing most jobs around the farm. Harvey Jr. first learned to drive by practicing on those homebuilt tractors in his parents' backyard. Crane's manufacturing wasn't limited to homemade tractors, as he also delved into producing electric lawn mowers, no doubt well ahead of his time with that product.

Life was pretty relaxed in those carefree days, and Harvey recalled the time his father bought a 1929 Model A Tudor for $50 and gave it to him and his two younger brothers to use. Although he was only 12 years old and not old enough to have a driver's license, Harvey was allowed to drive the Model A to school, where it soon became known as *Crane's Cozy Cabana* because the boys stuffed so many of their friends into the car. In remembrance of those lighthearted days some 60-odd years ago, Harvey kept a duplicate of the *Cozy Cabana* until the early 2000s, when he finally sold it to a neighbor.

THE APPRENTICE

Growing up in a family that operated its own business came with certain responsibilities. Beginning at the age of 12, Harvey Jr. was taught how to run the milling machine, lathe, and other machine tools, and Crane Sr. stressed adamantly to his son the importance of accuracy in all his measuring and machine work.

Opposite: Frank Smith, one of Harvey Crane's earliest employees, used his 1934 Ford coupe to test and promote Crane cams at the drag races. Frank later raced a roadster and eventually moved into the dragster classes. *Author collection*

Inset: The first Crane Engineering decal, drawn by Bill Kniffin. It came out in the 1950s. *Author collection*

When the hostilities of World War II ended, the general public attempted to pick up the pieces and get back to a normal existence. For the most part, everything was how they had left it; everything, that is, except auto racing—it was taking the country by storm. Even for a 14-year-old, Harvey Jr. took notice of the increased number of street rods and the overwhelming interest in stock car racing in the area. What little he knew about automobile engines and how they operated was more than enough to spark his entrepreneurial spirit. He figured that these speed machines needed performance parts and he could possibly make some extra money by taking advantage of the family machine shop. Harvey got his dad to show him how to mill and re-dome Ford flathead V-8 heads, and his father went one step further by making him the doming and fly-cutting tools to do the complete operation. Harvey Jr.'s first jobs involved milling and fly cutting Ford cast-iron heads for $12 a set. Then, seeing another untapped opportunity, he began buying early stock aluminum V-8 heads from scrap-metal dealers that he then milled and resold. Crane Sr. knew how to weld aluminum and would assist in repairs on the heads when needed. Harvey Jr. next added chopping stock flywheels to his little business venture, completing his work in between attending high school and working in his dad's machine shop. To teach his son the life lesson that what you use you pay for, Harvey Sr. charged Harvey Jr. a nominal 10 cents an hour to use the shop facilities when doming heads or cutting flywheels.

Eventually, Harvey looked beyond flywheels and cylinder heads to see that the real money was in building engines, as there was a ready market with the phenomenal growth of stock car racing. Considering it was all done on a part-time basis, engine sales were good, and Harvey Jr. used profits from the engine sales to buy tools that the shop didn't have, such as a boring bar and valve grinder. Occasionally, Harvey Jr. would farm out specialty work that couldn't be performed in the shop to local engine rebuilders.

In 1948, Harvey read his first issue of *Hot Rod* and saw what thousands of other hungry young car enthusiasts across the country wanted to see: the California hot rod scene. Magazines such as *Hot Rod* became the mail-order Sears catalog for hot rodders everywhere, enabling them to buy speed equipment directly from the specialty manufacturers in California. Like countless other speed-hungry aficionados, Harvey sent for speed equipment from a variety of Los Angeles companies and eventually got himself into the camshaft business.

HOT RODS

A fellow named Jim Wynne from Miami was instrumental in sparking Harvey Jr.'s original interest in street rods. Wynne had gone off to California, and when he returned home, he was driving a genuine Californian '32 Ford hot rod equipped with all the latest speed goodies. It didn't take Wynne very long to show the local hot dogs that he had the fastest car in town. As a note of interest, years later Jim Wynne patented the inboard/outboard drive for powerboats, selling Volvo a license to manufacture the unit. Later still, he was involved in designing the famous Donzi powerboat hull.

Seeing Wynne's Californian roadster and those early issues of *Hot Rod* was enough to make Harvey want his own hot rod, and knew where he could get one. His grandfather had the remnants of a tired, old Dort automobile stored away in a barn, and all that remained was the frame, running gear, and a pile of parts, but that was good enough for Harvey. He convinced his grandmother to let him have the relic, and after dragging it home, he dismantled it even further. The finished product was a rather crude-looking, fenderless two-seater with an aluminum Indy-style body, running lights, and an early stock Ford flathead V-8. It may not have been pretty, or even similar to a West Coast job, but as far as Harvey was concerned he had a hot rod and drove it to school.

Harvey's second and more successful hot rod was a 1932 Plymouth coupe body mounted on '32 Ford frame rails. Harvey wanted a Ford body but couldn't find one at the time and located the Plymouth body, which was free if he hauled it away. To give it the California look, he installed a suicide front end on the Z'd frame, which resulted in the rod sitting as low as possible. To motivate the Plymouth, he installed a modified 1936 Ford V-8 equipped with an Iskenderian No. 44 grind cam, a Navarro dual-carburetor intake manifold, and cast-iron heads that he milled himself. He remembered buying the camshaft from an Isky dealer in Miami Beach. Harvey said, "The guy was selling cams out of his mother's house. The inventory was stored under his bed. In those days, you bought your speed equipment where you found it."

Harvey's engine-building shop prior to 1953. He is seen boring the cylinder of a flathead V-8 while his first employee, Bill Polhe (kneeling), helps rebuild a metal lathe Harvey bought from a junkyard for $50. *Courtesy Harvey Crane*

THE FIRST CRANE CAMSHAFT

The first camshaft that Harvey Crane Jr. endeavored to grind belonged to old-time track racer Bud Swanson from Ojus, Florida. Bud was building a new midget racer to replace his old one and decided it would be a good idea to upgrade his engine at the same time. He replaced the Ford V8-60 in favor of a much lighter, Henderson four-cylinder, inline motorcycle engine. Occasionally, Harvey would stop in at Bud's shop on the way home from school to check on the progress of the race car, and one day he learned about Bud's predicament. Bud wanted to modify the timing on the engine, and as there were no known racing cams available for the Henderson, Bud was looking for someone who could regrind the camshaft. He'd already drawn up a timing diagram that he felt would make the engine perform well, and Harvey offered to grind the cam at his dad's machine shop, figuring that it was just a matter of transferring the specs over to the camshaft.

Harvey set up the camshaft in a cylindrical grinder and made a degree wheel that he could follow and began to grind away. Unfortunately, having no prior experience in camshaft grinding or knowledge of the intricacies of the process, Harvey ruined the cam by misinterpreting the timing specifications. Luckily, Bud had a spare, and the second time Harvey ground it to what Bud wanted. Harvey mentioned that after all his hard work in grinding the cam, Swanson didn't use the motorcycle engine after all, but reinstalled the V8-60 and went on to win his fare share of trophies.

Harvey tossed that first failed cam-grinding attempt in 1946 into his toolbox and all but forgot it, until many years later when one of his employees found the cam still in the toolbox. After having it gold-plated and mounted, the employee presented the "first Crane cam" to Harvey as a reminder of his humble beginnings.

CAR RACING

Upon graduating from Miami Edison High, 18-year-old Harvey and a couple buddies decided to go stock car racing. They'd heard that up in Iowa there was racing seven times a week, from Tuesday night to Saturday night and twice on Sunday. The testosterone-filled trio figured that they could go up there and show the locals what racing was all about while cleaning up on the prize money. The fellows figured that they'd have a much better chance running with two cars and that Harvey's experience in modifying engines would be a definite aid to their cause.

They converted a pair of '37 Ford two-door sedans into stock cars in accordance with the track rules in Iowa. The rulebook stated cars had to use an open rearend and run a completely stock Ford flathead V-8. Harvey's friend Harold Wilcox knew V-8s inside and out, and Harvey had him build the two engines by combining the best factory parts to get all the performance that they could hope for from a stock engine. With his two friends doing the driving and Harvey keeping the cars in top running condition, the guys had quite a successful summer. Bud Swanson had taught Harvey how to wedge the cars to make them handle and had the chassis tuned so they were carrying the left front tire coming out of the corners. Numerous times, they were accused of running locked rearends.

Not only did the trio have a successful season of racing but Harvey got married over the summer months to Mildred, and the newlyweds returned home to Hallandale driving a 1939 Ford coupe with a spare flathead V-8 engine in the trunk.

The following year, Harvey decided to try his hand at driving on some of the tracks in southern Florida with a '34 Ford two-door sedan, and he managed to win $50 in 50-cent pieces in one event. However, oval-track racing could be more than a little hazardous, and Harvey decided that driving just wasn't his forte. But where he did shine was in drag racing, and with the help of the little '39 Ford coupe, he built up quite a reputation for making engines run fast. He'd picked up a Canadian Ford V-8block from his friend Ralph Moody, as the Canadian engines were reputed to have a little more metal in places where it was needed when going all out on the flathead V-8.

To get the most out of the engine, he bored it to 3 7/16 inches with the biggest stroker he could find (4 1/8 inches) to give him a 306-ci flathead, which was considered fairly big for a flathead in those days. A combination of skilled driving and a powerful engine provided Harvey with a profitable little business of building engines for others. After a successful Saturday night of runoffs, the phone would be busy the rest of the week with calls for souped-up engines. They say there's a double for everything in the universe, and maybe so, as across the country in Southern California, Lou Senter was doing the same thing to make money.

The last time Harvey ventured into any form of auto racing was in 1957, when his friend Bill Kniffin built a B/G Dragster powered by a Crane-modified Olds V-8. The car was entered in the South Florida Timing Association's NHRA Regional Drag Championship races held in Sebring, Florida, where Harvey drove Kniffin's dragster to a class win. That one race was all it took to satisfy his curiosity about drag racing, and Harvey went back to grinding camshafts.

KARTS

Although he'd tried his hand at stock car, street, and drag racing, and he really had no desire to pursue them any further, karting did tweak Harvey's interest. After the little speed demons first made an appearance on the West Coast, they quickly took the country by storm, and when they arrived in Florida, Harvey wanted to give them a try, but he is by no means a small man. Standing 6 feet 6 inches tall and weighing in well over 200 pounds, Harvey needed an edge, and the only thing he could come up with was to use the largest McCullough chainsaw engine available to be competitive with the drivers who weighed much less. After about six months of competitive karting, he decided that with the long hours spent racing and maintaining the kart, and with several permanent scars on his legs, karting wasn't worth the time spent away from his burgeoning speed equipment business.

CRANE ENGINEERING 1953

After a summer of racing stock cars in Iowa, Harvey returned to building and selling performance engines out of his dad's shop. It'd take about a week to do an average engine with roughly $200 in

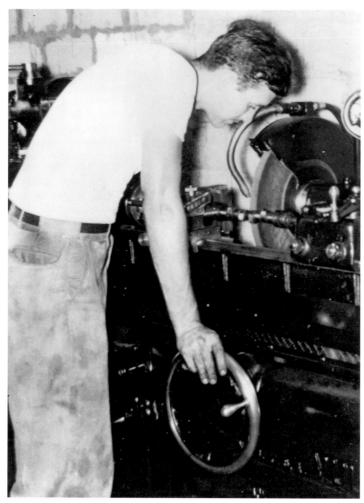

In 1953 Harvey bought his first cam grinder. He is seen here studiously grinding a camshaft. *Courtesy Harvey Crane*

parts and labor invested, and he could retail it for around $400. The engines proved to be a nice little cash-producing business that ran from 1950 to 1952. While building the engines, it never crossed his mind to go into the camshaft-grinding business, but a West Coast cam grinder and a machine manufacturer put the idea in his head.

Harvey began to notice a discrepancy in the quality of camshafts from his usual supplier in California, and he remembered the time he'd bought five reground flathead cams, all with the same profile. Every time he attempted to degree one of the cams in an engine, it came out differently. He phoned the camshaft manufacturer about the discrepancy and was told, "Kid, you don't know what you're talking about. Stop degreeing my cams; just put them in and set the lash." Harvey had learned how to degree a camshaft when he was 14 and held strong views on the importance of correct timing when building a performance engine.

The only thing he could do about the cam situation was to switch to another manufacturer, but in January 1953, while attending a trade show in Miami, he saw the solution before him: a Storm-Vulcan camshaft grinder. Harvey knew the California cam

grinder was unable to supply accurately ground cams and figured he could do a better job of it himself if he had the chance, and now the opportunity was right in front of him.

After only a brief conversation with the sales rep, Harvey went gung-ho and purchased a brand-new Storm-Vulcan camshaft grinder with a down payment of $800—all he had in his bank account. The down payment would get the grinder in his shop, and then he would have to make $600 monthly payments. The payments were high, but Harvey had confidence in himself and could see how the market was rapidly growing. In the spring of 1953, the young 22-year-old entrepreneur opened the doors of Crane Engineering in a small, 500-square-foot shed that was attached to his father's machine shop. Harvey Crane Sr. had at one time built an addition onto the end of his machine shop with the idea of using the space to build a sailboat. Next to the sailboat shop, he'd added a small shop to rent out to his son for engine building.

The cashflow was nearly nonexistent at Crane Engineering after Harvey emptied out his account for the down payment. The day the camshaft grinder arrived by freight, the shipping charges amounted to $800, which had to be paid before the truck driver would unload the machine. Harvey said that he had to go next door and borrow the money from his dad. The factory representative from Storm-Vulcan showed up about a week later and instructed Harvey on how to operate the grinder; this particular machine was unique because of its copying device attachment that enabled the operator to make a master cam off any existing camshaft. The grinder was originally designed for the engine-rebuilding trade so rebuilders could refurbish the worn camshaft when rebuilding an engine.

It seems that most of the early novice cam grinders chose a revised version of an Ed Winfield profile to start their businesses, but Harvey based his first camshaft on a modified version of a Howards Cams grind that performed not too badly for his initial attempt at cam design. No sooner was Crane Engineering up and running than it was time for military duty. Being newly married, Harvey figured it'd be a lot easier to enlist in the national guard and still be able to support his wife with his fledgling business rather than to get drafted. Unfortunately, Harvey was drafted anyway, as the Korean War needed more bodies, but luckily he was stationed at Fort Benning, Georgia, for the duration of his military tour. The base was close enough that he could drive home when time allowed it, and on the occasions he did get home, he spent his time either in front of the grinder or working on a new lobe profile. He would take a competitor's camshaft and build up a lobe with brass weld and hand-file it to a profile that hopefully would be an improvement over the original grind. This was a slow self-learning process, but it was the only way to learn first-hand about the complexities of camshaft design.

Harvey's friend Dave Smith, who later became a Crane employee, raced a '34 Ford competition coupe at the local drag strips that became the rolling testbed for Harvey's latest grind. When Dave won at the drags and his competitor complained about not being able to get a special cam like Dave was running, they'd pull the cam out of the engine and sell it to the disgruntled racer right there on the spot—anything to sell a cam!

In due time, Dave moved into a modified T roadster known as the *Crane Cam Special*, powered by a flathead that was eventually replaced with a more potent Lincoln V-8. Several years later, Dave replaced the roadster with a fuel-injected Chevy V-8–powered B/Dragster also known as the *Crane Cam Special*.

Looking to increase camshaft sales, Harvey brought his company's products up into the state of Georgia. After spending the weekend grinding cams, he'd return to Fort Benning with a trunk full of reground cams to sell to local hot rodders, track racers, and those individuals who wanted to keep ahead of revenue agents. The performance of his perky '39 Ford coupe proved very useful in demonstrating the power of a Crane cam.

Harvey's wife, Mildred, was the glue that kept Crane Engineering together for those two long years that Harvey spent with Uncle Sam. Although they'd hired several employees to build racing rearends and perform lathe work and engine porting, Mildred was responsible for keeping the business afloat, taking care of the accounts and counter sales, and even running the cam grinder. After being honorably discharged in 1955, Harvey returned to cam grinding, allowing Mildred never to set foot in the shop again, as she'd finally enough of that camshaft grinder. Business was growing, and it wasn't long before Harvey had to hire someone to operate the grinder so he could concentrate on the business end of the shop. The rapid growth in stock car and drag racing in the region created a strong demand for Crane-modified engines, full-floating rearends, custom machine work, and camshafts. Even though his employees worked on various components of an engine, Harvey was the only one in the shop who performed the final assembly; with his insistence on minute details and measurements, he preferred to do the job himself.

By 1956, the Crane work force had increased to 10 employees, and the cam business had grown so much that Harvey purchased a used Storm-Vulcan grinder to help fill the back orders. Around that time, Harvey realized the future in performance camshafts held a much greater financial reward than did modifying engines. Also, the growth of the company reached the point that he could finally draw a $100 weekly paycheck for himself. Harvey said that his father had mixed opinions on his son's cam business, saying, "I don't know what that kid is doing over there. He seems to be doing all right, but he never has any money."

As Crane Engineering outgrew the original 500-square-foot shop, Harvey took over the space of the sailboat shop. Before long, the shop had grown to 35 employees and was renting a total of 3,500 square feet of manufacturing space from Harvey Sr., and it wasn't long until the premises proved inadequate. With no more room to expand, Crane Engineering had to relocate and built a new, 15,000-square-foot factory in Hallandale that was later increased to 45,000 square feet. Over time, the Crane employment force increased to nearly 200, and in 1986, the company moved to a much larger facility in Daytona Beach, Florida.

TURNING POINT

The incident that made Crane Engineering a contender in the camshaft marketplace occurred at the 1961 NHRA Nationals. A

Harvey served Uncle Sam in the National Guard from September 1953 to September 1955. He's seen here at boot camp in Fort Jackson, North Carolina.
Courtesy Harvey Crane

relatively unknown drag racer out of Atlanta named Pete Robinson won Top Eliminator with his super-lightweight Chevy-powered dragster running a combination of a Crane camshaft and Crane-modified cylinder heads. This unexpected win prompted Harvey to run a 1-inch ad in *Hot Rod* that resulted in approximately 900 inquires—about 800 more than he could send catalogs to. Prior to that ad in *Hot Rod*, Crane Engineering's advertising was mainly in the form of mimeographed flyers handed out at race meets throughout Florida and word-of-mouth from satisfied customers throughout the southern states. Crane Engineering's ability to produce winning camshafts was reinforced the following year when Jim Nelson took Top Eliminator at the 1962 NHRA Winternationals driving the Crane-equipped *Dragmaster Dart*.

Harvey said that what really made the company grow in sales was directly related to two fellows he knew from drag racing. Jim Davis and Monk Reynolds had started up a magazine called *Super Stock*, and Crane Engineering bought the rear cover on a monthly basis for the first three or four years running. This continued exposure, at a time when drag racing was growing at a phenomenal rate, kept Crane Engineering in the limelight.

DYNAMOMETERS

The only way to know the actual amount of power an engine can produce is to stick it on a dynamometer and crank it open. And anyone who is seriously into manufacturing performance-enhancing equipment will need one of these instruments to find out if his or her stuff is doing the job or not. The first dynamometer that Crane Engineering used in its business was an old Clayton model with a rev limit of 5,000 rpm that Harvey borrowed from "Shorty" Johns of Miami. Harvey had mounted the dyno on wheels so it could be rolled outside when testing engines, keeping the noise and exhaust out of the shop. One day, it ran past 5,000 rpm and Harvey realized that he was pushing it beyond reason and, before his luck ran out, returned it to Shorty.

In the early 1960s, Crane Engineering imported the second English-made, Heenan & Froude, 1,000-horsepower dynamometer into the country; Holman & Moody had imported the first unit. This dyno was guaranteed not to explode up to 14,000 rpm, although several engines, including Pete Robinson's SOHC 427 Ford and the Moser four-valve engine, came close to meeting the maximum rpm of the dynamometer.

LOGO

Every speed equipment manufacturer had some sort of logo/decal to advertise to the onlooker that a particular vehicle used a certain product, and if the car were a winner, it'd be evident at the sales counter. Some of those company's logos ran from unimaginative to very creative and colorful to attract the eye.

The first Crane Engineering logo design was drawn up by Bill Kniffin and pictured a determined-looking cartoon crane wearing a crash helmet and driving a dragster. The logo that is used today was derived from a design by a sign-painter friend of "Dyno" Don Nicholson. The painter happened to be hand-lettering Don's race car, and when it was time to paint "Crane Cams" on the fenders, he came up with the original big "C" Crane Cams design. The company modified the typeface slightly and uses that logo today.

GROWING

In some fields of manufacturing, control over the quality, pricing, and availability of material from suppliers has a direct influence on the growth of the business. At times, it makes economic sense to absorb satellite suppliers, and in the case of Crane Cams, Harvey realized that in order to expand the confines of his existing business, he had to acquire new product lines. Crane could best control a product if it owned the company that manufactured that particular item, and Harvey began to acquire the small businesses that manufactured related valvetrain components for Crane. And so began the expansion of Crane Cams, which would eventually become the leader in the specialty camshaft market.

In the 1970s, Crane Cams West opened its doors in California to offer immediate delivery of Crane products to its western customers. This mega-warehouse in the Los Angeles area was established to cut down the time-delay in shipping from the factory in Florida and provided Crane Cams a spot inside the West Coast marketplace.

Gotha

The Gotha Company started back in the early 1950s, specializing mainly in cast-iron products that included rocker arms, split manifold exhaust fittings, cast carburetor-riser kits for the home builder to make a dual- or triple-intake manifold, cast-aluminum engine degree wheels, and even thin copper head gaskets to raise engine compression. Gotha was located about 5 miles south of Chicago in Harvey, Illinois, and though small in size, it produced a

quality line of cast rocker arms that was carried by a variety of the larger specialty manufacturers.

The one Gotha product that interested Harvey was the cast-iron high-lift rocker arm, as he and other camshaft companies had been buying them for years. By the 1960s, the sale of those rocker arms was keeping Gotha afloat, and Harvey felt that he'd better purchase the company before it went under. After finalizing the sale, he drove up to Harvey, Illinois, towing a U-Haul trailer behind his Lincoln to get what was left of the company. Gotha had done little in-house machine work, mostly farming out what needed to be done, and most of the company's patterns were sitting in machine and foundry shops that were holding on to them until they were paid for outstanding debts. Fortunately, Harvey was successful in getting the Gotha rocker-arm patterns with the homemade rocker-arm machining jig and some other related items that were eventually merged into the Crane catalog.

Other Acquisitions

As his business grew in strength, Harvey was able to absorb smaller companies that complemented Crane Cams. One of these acquisitions was the legendary Harman & Collins Cam Company, which once upon a time was the largest specialty camshaft manufacturer in the country. Through a partnership breakup and declining interest from Cliff Collins for the business, Crane purchased the company and retained Cliff's services on a short-term contract. Several divisions of Harman & Collins had already been liquidated before Harvey got the company. He pulled in the aspects of the business that would be useful to Crane Cams and sold the remainder to Dema Elgin of Elgin Cams in Redwood City, California.

Any aftermarket camshaft company has to purchase new cast-iron cores from a camshaft manufacturer and steel-billet roller camshaft cores, which are less expensive to buy than make from scratch. But there weren't too many raw camshaft manufacturers in the county, and most cam grinders bought from the same outfit. In 1974, Crane bought the Universal Camshaft Company of Muskegon, Michigan. Universal was the only manufacturer of SAE 8620 steel-billet roller camshafts, and about 80 percent of Universal's business consisted of stock cast cams for Detroit's automobile companies. This latest acquisition put Crane Cams in direct involvement with the major auto manufacturers, supplying them with stock and performance camshafts. The prototype-design end of the Universal Camshaft Company was relocated to the Hallandale shop in Florida where Harvey could have personal control over it.

During the 1970s, Crane Cams acquired JE Pistons in Los Angeles. Crane Cams ran it for about three years before selling it off, as it didn't really suit the business plans.

PRODUCT

Since the company's inception in 1953, Harvey purchased all valvetrain components from outside sources, and it wasn't until 1962 that the company began to manufacture its first noncamshaft product: valve spring retainers. A year later, Harvey designed and patented a drop-in, self-locking roller tappet, and he was the fifth person in the

United States to ever patent a roller tappet, just five years after Ed Iskenderian had taken out a patent on a self-locking roller lifter. Later on, Harvey introduced hydraulic roller lifters with the intention of producing a hydraulic roller camshaft for street use, utilizing the advantages of both the roller and hydraulic lifter. Some executives of his company didn't feel that the idea would fly, but as Harvey said, "The results speak for themselves." Unfortunately for Harvey, Detroit didn't offer hydraulic roller lifters in its production engines until after his 17-year-old patent had expired—the remuneration in royalties would have been staggering. In 1972, Crane Cams manufactured the first hydraulic roller camshaft at its Hallandale operation for General Motors. The design for the cam package was from GM's blueprints and to be used in its Chevrolet V-8 engine.

Harvey also said that Crane Cams was the first to grind private-label cams for the large specialty-automotive warehouse distributors, as no one had done it before, and he saw the opportunity to fill a large, untapped market.

HORSEPOWER SALES SPEED SHOPS

Horsepower Sales Speed Shops originated out of necessity, as the front office employees at Crane were continuously interrupted by walk-in customers who wanted to purchase merchandise. It seemed economically plausible to offer a one-stop store where a racer could buy the total camshaft package plus other related performance items. The first speed shop opened at the main factory and proved to be very successful, so Harvey added new stores until there were 11 Horsepower Sales outlets throughout southern and central Florida. Although the speed shops were a viable asset, they didn't really fall into Crane's business agenda for the future, and

Harvey sold them off in order to concentrate on the camshaft and related manufacturing business.

COMPUTER CAMSHAFT DESIGNS

The process of developing a new cam profile normally meant long hours of intensive labor using a desktop calculator to plot a multitude of complicated mathematical equations on graph paper. In 1965, Harvey heard about J. H. Nourse, a fellow in Michigan who was using a mainframe computer to assist in camshaft design. Possessing a strong desire to be on the cutting edge of technology, Harvey paid Nourse a visit. Harvey was so impressed with the computer's capabilities to decrease the time spent in developing new camshaft designs that Crane Cams took out a license with Jesse Nourse to design profiles in a time-share computer company called ComShare in Ann Arbor, Michigan. This license enabled Crane to have direct access to the computer through a Teletype machine.

In 1967, Harvey made his first computer-generated camshaft design using a computer program written for him by J. H. Nourse. By connecting the Teletype terminal in his office directly to the ComShare computer by way of a telephone line, the results of lobe profiles could be formulated at speeds impossible to conceive of in earlier times. Information was received by the Teletype at Crane and fed into another machine that produced a perforated tape, which in turn was fed into a Moore numerically controlled automatic grinder to produce a prototype camshaft lobe profile. The Moore numerically controlled grinder had a resolution of "ten millionths of an inch."

Harvey felt that in 1971 he'd come up with a winning computer-generated profile with a .466-inch high-lift camshaft called the

This photo, circa 1954–1955, shows the interior of Crane Engineering. Harvey's wife, Mildred, is seated at the desk while the shop cat stretches out on the floor. Note the master cams for the Storm-Vulcan grinder hanging on the back wall. *Courtesy Harvey Crane*

Outgrowing his original location, Harvey had this 15,000-square-foot shop built in Hallandale in 1965. It was later tripled in size before eventually moving to much larger facilities in Daytona Beach. *Courtesy Harvey Crane*

Compu-Cam. It was the first extra-high-lift profile that produced the results he was searching for. Harvey said, "Others in the business said that it'd never work, but by 1972, this cam design became the standard of the drag racing industry. Practically every drag race car, especially the late Chrysler Hemi, had one of my cams in it. This cam was the turning point when Crane Cams made their mark in the marketplace." The .446-inch lift combined with the 1.5 rocker-arm ratio produced .669-inch lift at the valve. The late Hemi had a little more lift due to its rocker ratio and ended up with a .700-inch lift at the valve. And with 288 degrees duration at .050-inch valve lift, Harvey said that this particular camshaft grind was groundbreaking for that time.

COPYING

Harvey said that copying other company's designs was common practice in the early days and many cam grinders would make a modified version of a competitor's successful camshaft in the hopes of producing something a little bit better. One of the most blatant copiers that Harvey ever came across was a cam grinder in Mexico who was copying Crane cams. This grinder phoned one day to inquire about the possibility of Crane Cams grinding 16 different profiles on one camshaft. That one camshaft never got ground, but you've got to give the guy credit for trying!

CAMSHAFT WITH A TWIST

About the strangest request for a camshaft design came from a very successful drag racer that Harvey happened to be sponsoring at the time. Bill "Grumpy" Jenkins wanted Harvey to grind a cam that had a built-in twist, as Jenkins felt that when he wound the engine up to around 8,000 rpm, the camshaft developed a twist in it. He theorized that once the engine was up in the higher-rpm range, a built-in twist would offset any effect of the cam twisting. Harvey didn't agree with Grumpy about this theory, saying the cam doesn't twist and that he wouldn't grind the camshaft.

To prove that he was right, Harvey and "Sneaky" Pete Robinson installed a degree wheel at both ends of a camshaft in Pete's SOHC Ford V-8. With the use of a strobe light and degree wheels, they proved that a cam doesn't twist at speed, but while performing this experiment, they found the chain that drove the cams would snake at high speed, causing the left cam to retard itself as the rpm went up. As a result of this discovery, Harvey and Pete learned how much to retard or advance one camshaft versus the other to gain more performance out of the SOHC engine.

Besides being a good friend, Harvey had a lot of respect for Pete's superb mechanical abilities: "Robinson's success as a drag racer was due to the way that he intelligently studied and analyzed everything before putting it into practice."

BERCO CAMSHAFT GRINDERS

Harvey bought his first Storm-Vulcan camshaft grinder in 1953 and eventually purchased three more as the workload increased. In the early 1960s, Crane purchased a precision Van Norman camshaft grinder, eventually replacing all the Storm-Vulcans with Van Normans, as Harvey didn't think too highly of those early camshaft grinders. In his opinion, they were not built for precision production work, and he sold his to a competing cam company.

A deal of a lifetime occurred when Harvey heard about 20 well-used Norton automatic-production cam grinders sitting in a scrap yard in Detroit. The units had been used in one of GM's engine production lines and were for sale at $1,000 apiece. This type of high-speed precision grinder would allow Crane to economically mass-produce quality camshafts. The grinders were purchased and, after being completely refurbished, were put into production. Crane Cams was the first specialty cam company to have fully automatic cam grinders that could grind a camshaft in seven to eight minutes (today's modern camshaft grinders can do the same job in about two minutes).

Always searching for a better mousetrap, in 1972 Harvey conceived the idea of the Berco camshaft grinder. The Italian Berco Manufacturing Company developed a cam grinder to Harvey's design and specifications, which he had based on Berco's existing crankshaft grinder. He traveled to Italy annually for five years before Berco fully finished assembling the grinder to his satisfaction. The first Berco camshaft grinder cost less than $20,000; now, that same machine costs about $100,000. Crane Cams purchased the first Berco grinder that was imported into the United States, and Harvey mentioned that he never received royalties or monies for his personal input into the project.

MOSER FOUR-VALVE

Since the dawn of the combustion engine, engineers and backyard innovators have created a wide variety of cylinder-head and valve-train designs in attempts to find the perfect combination for the task at hand, whatever that might be. Some North American automobile manufacturers had slowly migrated from the side-valve to the overhead; others had started off with the overhead layout. Whatever the case, the overhead-valve design won out, proving to be very adequate and economical for the average passenger car.

Richard Moser could see the superior advantages of an overhead camshaft in relation to the overhead-valve engines pumped out by Detroit's automobile manufacturers. Through lengthy research and development, Moser came up with a double overhead-cam conversion for the Chevrolet V-8 engine, but without corporate backing, he struggled to complete the development on his brainchild and, although almost finished, there were still some bugs to work out. Harvey caught wind of Moser's engine and could see the potential in the conversion, and he became instrumental in completing the venture.

Moser's enterprise was relocated to the facilities of Crane Cams West in Los Angeles, where financial and technical support hastened the completion of the project. But regrettably, the partnership was damaged after Richard decided to enter his unproven engine in the country's most prestigious race, the Indianapolis 500. With orders for some 40-odd engines, Harvey felt that it was more advantageous to fill the orders, seeing that there was still a lot of developmental work to do in the dyno room before even thinking about entering Moser's creation into competition. The partnership split, and Moser failed to qualify for the Indy race; not long afterward, the whole project was shut down and disbanded. Harvey retained the head patterns, many spare parts, and all the original blueprints for the Moser four-valve engine, which are tucked away in storage. Periodically, he receives inquiries for replacement parts, as the pair had produced and sold 28 of the twin-cam conversion kits prior to the shutdown. The Moser engine appeared on the front cover of *Hot Rod*'s August 1971 issue with an article about what Richard and Harvey were attempting to do.

LIFE AFTER CRANE CAMS

In the grand scheme of things, just because a man spends countless years of his life building a successful business up from literally nothing there is no guarantee that he will reap its rewards at the end, and such was Harvey's case. In 1989, Harvey found himself without a job after the company that he created let him go. Through the voting power of ESCOT, an executive committee of 10 major shareholders, he was forced into early retirement. Unfortunately, he had allowed himself the fatal error of parting with too many of his company's shares, eventually owning only 17 percent of the shares in the company that he'd created and labored untold, long, hard hours to develop.

Much too young to hang out a "gone fishin'" sign, he contemplated in what direction to take his career, as his second love was the computer. Since the days when Crane Cams had first been involved with ComShare, he held a fascination with the little marvel of electronic technology. He considered opening a computer retail outlet, but he felt there was much to be done in the area of camshafts, and he wanted to be a part of it. He still had ideas and theories on camshaft design that he wanted to formulate.

Once that decision was made, it didn't long to set up shop. Harvey Crane Inc. was opened in 1990 and included CamDesign and Harvey Crane's Design School. Through CamDesign, he

Harvey and the highly accurate camshaft-measuring machine that he designed. The machine is so sensitive that it has inflatable airbags to lift itself off the cement floor when measuring a camshaft. *Author photo*

offered consultant services in the camshaft field that also extended the use of a precision camshaft-measurement machine. This highly sensitive piece of equipment has an extremely accurate resolution of 0.02 microns with an angular resolution of 1.67 arc seconds. Harvey Crane's Design School is held on the premises of his shop and offers either one-on-one or small-group sessions in which the students are taught just about everything there is to know about camshaft design. There's a bit of irony attached with this business venture, as Harvey now draws on personal expertise gathered from many years devoted to making his own company the leader in the industry to assist camshaft companies that were once his competitors.

For a while, to break up the tedium of his shop, Harvey and his second wife, Maxine, whom he married in 1973, could be found traveling throughout the country in their fully equipped motorhome, visiting gatherings such as the Bonneville Nationals and making personal consultant visits to various cam outfits. Sadly, their 34-year relationship ended with Maxine's passing in February 2007.

In 1988, Harvey was elected as a Fellow of the Society of Automotive Engineers.

CHAPTER 5

Edelbrock

VIC EDELBROCK SR.

What has developed into the nation's leading specialty automotive-parts manufacturing corporation can follow its roots back to a small town in the heartland. A business that would become a corporate dynasty under second-generation leadership began in 1913 with the birth of Victor Edelbrock in Eudora, Kansas.

In 1927, fire destroyed the family grocery store, leaving Vic no choice but to help out financially by finishing school at the age of 14 to become an apprentice mechanic. After four years working for several automotive repair garages, and under the devastating economic effects of the Great Depression, Vic and his brother Karl moved out to California in 1931, where they hoped the grass was greener. Their middle brother Ross had already established himself in Los Angeles and was working for the Bank of America.

VIC'S GARAGES

Even though it was a time of high unemployment, Vic landed a job at an automotive shop earning $2 a day. Within two years (at the age of 20), he'd saved enough money to get married and, with his brother-in-law, he opened a garage on Wilshire Boulevard in Beverly Hills. After a year in business, the partnership wasn't working, so Vic ventured out on his own, leasing a service station on the corner of Hoover Street and Venice Boulevard in Los Angeles; between the three gas pumps and one repair bay, Vic was busy enough to hire his first employee, a teenager by the name of Bobby Meeks. As business increased, Vic outgrew the one-bay shop and moved to 4204 Venice Boulevard. Around 1940, he again relocated to Vic Edelbrock's Breawood Garage on 363 North La Brea, near Hollywood.

In the beginning, work consisted mainly of general auto repairs, but once the garage got involved in dry lakes and midget racing, the shop's engine-building activities increased to the point where the name "Edelbrock" became well known. To help supplement the garage business and to assist in his own racing expenses, Vic started a little sideline offering speed equipment, advertising his engine building in Southern California Timing Association (SCTA) newsletters and that he carried Thickstun manifolds. The speed equipment part of his business began to grow and, by 1941, the Breawood Garage was advertising, in racing programs such as the SCTA newsletter and *Throttle* magazine, that it carried a full line of dual ignitions, high-altitude heads, reground camshafts, and—the item that would make Edelbrock a household name among performance enthusiasts—the "slingshot" manifold.

Even in those early days, Vic knew the power of advertising.

DRY LAKES

Back in the 1930s, the Model A ruled the lakes and for good reason. Just about anything that could be done to an engine was done to this Ford's engine. It was the Chevy V-8 of the 1930s until its V-8 big brother made an appearance on the scene. At first, the V-8 was accepted with limited enthusiasm, but some could see the engine's potential and were willing to develop it. Vic became one of those believers in 1938 after buying a V-8-powered '32 roadster that became a dual-purpose machine as the family vehicle and a dry lakes racer.

Opposite: Vic Edelbrock Sr. and the Edelbrock V8-60-powered midget. Note how meticulous the car is—what wasn't painted was chromed. *Courtesy Edelbrock Corporation*

A group gathered at Vic's garage on Venice and Crenshaw around 1939 discusses the attributes of a manifold. Left to right are Duke Harding, Pee Wee Gallant, Wes Collins, Vic, Tommy Thickstun, and Ray Haven. That's Thickstun's high-rise manifold on the stool. *Courtesy Edelbrock Corporation*

The 21-stud V-8 ran modified cast-iron Arco milled and filled Denver heads, a Winfield camshaft, a Thickstun manifold, Sandy's headers, and dual ignition. Originally, Vic ran a Davies dual-carburetor manifold that was highly recognizable due to the two inverted high-rise V-runners with two carburetors positioned side by side on a flat mounting plate. This design allowed for the generator to be installed in the stock position.

When Vic began to sell speed equipment from his garage, he took on the Thickstun line. It was with this manifold that the roadster started making a name on the lake beds. The fastest roadster at the lakes was usually a tossup between Eddie Meyer (speed equipment manufacturer), Karl Orr, and Vic. As Edelbrock and Meyer were members of the Road Runners car club, there no doubt was a fair amount of camaraderie despite the competition. Speed shop owner Karl Orr was always a threat to the two racers, running just slightly under their speeds.

In the days before the speed equipment market developed, rodders had to rely on their own ingenuity and that of friends. Obviously, those who were leading the pack were getting more power from their engines, and Vic was in that group.

"When Vic had his shop (service station) on Highland Avenue," related Bud Meyer of Eddie Meyer's shop, "he came down to our shop one time with a set of cast iron heads to have them milled. We had this old milling machine that had a long horizontal travel on it, about 28 inches. He wanted the heads milled on an angle—60 thousandths over the valves and ninety thousandths over the pistons—so he could gain some compression and still keep some valve clearance."

After several years of competing on the lakes and building engines, Vic began to fully understand the importance of fuel induction with the flathead. Although he'd had great success with Thickstun's manifold, he could see ample room for improvement. By 1940, he had developed his own dual-carburetor intake and was setting records at the lakes, finishing up the season in third place in SCTA points. The following year, he set a record at 121.42 miles per hour at a Rosamond Dry Lake meet and finished off the '41 season at the top of the SCTA points standings.

After the war, Vic became heavily involved with the speed equipment business and circle-track racing. There was no longer time for lakes racing, and the roadster was sold. That car led a charmed life, as it remained intact for years, long enough for Vic Jr. to purchase it back many years later. After a complete frame-off restoration, the superbly restored '32 was displayed in the Edelbrock Museum at Vic's Garage.

THE SLINGSHOT MANIFOLD

The slingshot manifold is "the piece" of speed equipment that launched a worldwide aftermarket-parts manufacturing conglomerate.

When Vic Edelbrock first went up to the dry lakes to race, his engine was outfitted with a Davies dual intake that only produced mediocre results. After switching to a Thickstun intake, Vic's car became a contender for top speed at the lakes meets. Vic appreciated that Tommy Thickstun incorporated the 180-degree runner design in his manifold, but he didn't really care for how the manifold's runners entered the block obliquely. He attempted to get Tommy to change the runner design. What transpired in their conversation is anyone's guess, but the end result was that Vic felt he could make an intake that would work the way he wanted it to. He came up with a rather unique two-carburetor job that incorporated 180-degree firing order, ports that were in smooth alignment with the block, a plenum chamber, and a built-in exhaust heat riser that allowed for a faster warmup and smoother running (like a stock manifold). The intake itself consisted of two pieces with a Y-shaped high-rise adapter that bolted onto the top of the plenum chamber of the manifold body. The high-offset design allowed for the generator to be used in its stock position and kept the manifold's runners equal in length. It was a well-planned design that even had an optional single-carburetor adapter available for cars competing in classes that allowed only one.

The manifold derived its name from the shape of its design, and it became an instant success on the dry lakes. Not that many were made, however (reportedly around 100 were produced), as war was declared, ending any further production of the manifold. It was reintroduced after the war, but the labor-intensive slingshot design was replaced with a more economical one-piece unit.

WAR

The outbreak of World War II resulted in a shortage of skilled labor in many sectors of manufacturing. With an abundance of available job opportunities, Vic closed the garage and went to work for Len Sauter's Machine Shop, where he manufactured aircraft components. He also worked the night shift at the shipyards in San Pedro Harbor as a welder.

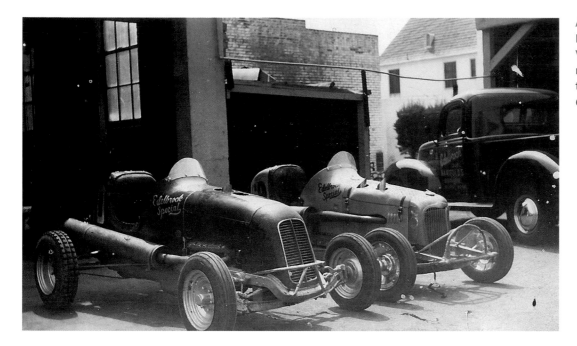

A prewar shot shows two Edelbrock midgets parked at Vic's Breawood Garage. One midget is running a V8-60 while the other has a four-cylinder. *Courtesy Edelbrock Corporation*

Near the end of the war, people were returning their thoughts to peacetime activities, and Vic was convinced that there would be a surge in the growth of auto racing and a strong demand for speed equipment. He began to buy up machinery so when the war ended he'd be ready to go into production.

EDELBROCK POWER AND SPEED EQUIPMENT

As the hostilities ended, Vic opened up an automotive repair–machine shop combination in a five bay garage at 1200 North Highland in Hollywood, with the idea that auto repairs and machine work would cover the operating costs, while the speed equipment line would run as a secondary business. The slingshot manifold was put back into production but was quickly replaced with two new very popular styles of dual-carburetor manifolds: the "regular" for street and the "super" for racing.

The speed equipment business was brisk, and more items were added to the inventory list. Edelbrock aluminum high-compression heads were introduced in two series: the "R" for racing, which were thicker, higher compression, and held more coolant, and the "S" series for street use. Al Sharp of SP Pattern recalled the time when a set of Vic's heads was brought into his shop by an eastern auto-parts supplier who wanted a set of duplicate patterns made but with his own company's name on them. Barney Navarro commented that he had similar problems with this same eastern outfit.

It only took a year of phenomenal growth for the company to issue its first parts catalog called "Edelbrock Power and Speed Equipment." It listed Edelbrock heads and intakes as well as pistons, steering wheels, and crankshafts for the Ford/Mercury V-8 flathead and V8-60 engines. Vic decided early on that if he was going to be in the specialty business, he was going to be aggressive about it, which meant putting the profits back into the

business in the form of advertising. Edelbrock was one of the first manufacturers to supply a product catalog. Vic Jr. remembered his dad "sitting at the kitchen table in our little two-bedroom home after supper, drawing charts with a French curve to show the performance gains by installing his equipment. These graphs were the result of many hours spent testing engines on the dyno." Being an astute businessman, Vic knew well in advance that it was going to take long hours of hard work and sacrifice to make his company successful.

In 1948, the Edelbrock shop was one of the first aftermarket manufacturers to have its own dynamometer. The 200-horsepower Clayton absorption unit eventually proved inadequate for advances in engine performance and was replaced with a more powerful English-made Heenan & Froude dynamometer. By 1949, the company had outgrown its premises and relocated to a larger facility at 4921 West Jefferson Boulevard, where there was 5,000

A father's pride. A prewar photo of Vic Sr. and his young son in front of the family roadster that also raced on the dry lakes. *Courtesy Edelbrock Corporation*

The speed part that started a dynasty: the Edelbrock "slingshot" dual-intake manifold. Note how the Y casting is bolted to the main body and can be removed to run a single carb. *Courtesy Edelbrock Corporation*

square feet of space. One side of the building was for machine shop production, while the other was for automotive tune-ups, parts installation, and the dynamometer facility. Edelbrock's first non-Ford product was a dual intake manifold for the Chevrolet six-cylinder engine.

After six short years in business, Edelbrock Equipment was one of the largest specialty manufacturers in the country and in due time became the largest producer of Ford flathead speed equipment. However, unlike some aftermarket manufacturers who specialized solely in the flathead stuff, Vic was ready to meet the arrival of the overhead-valve engine head on.

When the Ford Motor Company put the faithful but outdated flathead into the annals of history with the introduc-

tion of its 272 overhead-valve Y-block, Vic was ready with a three-carburetor manifold for the engine. The Edelbrock reputation didn't go unnoticed by the other Detroit auto companies; before GM introduced its revolutionary new 265 V-8, it had already sent three engines to Edelbrock for developmental work, enabling Vic to be the first aftermarket manufacturer to offer a multiple-carburetor (three-carb) manifold for the Chevy. He repeated the feat with the Dodge V-8 Hemi.

Vic's crew spent a great deal of time testing a wide variety of manifold designs on the company's dynamometer, which led to an amicable relationship with Iskenderian Racing Cams, which had moved in across the street from the Edelbrock shop. Numerous times during dynamometer testing, an engine needed a particular camshaft grind for the job, and Isky was called upon for that profile. Whether it was one cam or a half dozen, Isky would supply Vic with whatever cam grind he asked for. The shops often worked together on projects that benefited both parties, such as in 1958 when Vic and Isky collaborated to perform 30 different tests on the newly released Ford 352-ci V-8. The tests were performed in the Edelbrock dynamometer facility and incorporated a variety of Edelbrock manifolds and Iskenderian camshafts. The complete program was well documented by *Hot Rod*'s technical editor Ray Brock.

OVAL-TRACK RACING

Even though Vic realized that he didn't have what it'd take to compete on the track in midget racing, it didn't quench his interest, as he enjoyed the competitiveness of the sport, and the advertising opportunity of being involved in the popular sport was good for business. The first *Edelbrock Special* midget was a used job that

Vic and the family roadster. This car made him a legend on the dry lakes. The restored roadster now resides in the "Vic's Garage" museum in Torrance, California. The photo was taken during World War II, as the license plate has a "V" for victory where the year would normally have been. *Courtesy Edelbrock Corporation*

became a regular contender at the local tracks after Vic installed a modified V8-60 in the chassis and hired a driver. Before war was declared in 1941, two of the little screaming race cars were running under the Edelbrock banner.

Once the war was over, Vic found himself totally immersed with his new business venture. He had no time for the dry lakes but still held a fascination for the midget race car. In 1946, he purchased his third midget, which was built by D. W. McCully of Los Angeles. Later that same year, he bought the seventh midget to come out of Frank Kurtis' shop. The Kurtis midget was painted blue with an orange stripe and carried No. 63 for a short time, until both Edelbrock midgets were painted white with different-colored front cowls. Power for the midgets came from a race-bred Offenhauser and an underrated V8-60. The Offenhauser-powered McCully car ran a blue front cowl, while the V8-60 Kurtis had a red front cowl. Both cars were outfitted with No. 27, which was to become the lucky Edelbrock number. With Bobby Meeks tuning the cars, the Edelbrock midgets toured the local circuit, racing up to six nights a week with such notable drivers as Perry Grimm, Walt Faulkner, Billy Vukovich, and Rodger Ward taking care of the driving chores.

For the 1950 racing season, Vic had two highly talented racers driving for him: Rodger Ward in the seat of the V8-60 midget, and Perry Grimm in the Offenhauser midget. Rodger and the underestimated V8-60 made the pages of midget racing history in August 1950.

"That midget driven by Rodger Ward had a special two-speed rearend," Lou Senter said. "After a race, it'd be running at 180 degrees while everyone else's engines were out of water. Vic had discovered that you could run 30 to 40 pounds of pressure in the radiator and it wouldn't overheat. The rest of the racers just pumped the water out into an overflow tank. There was no way to get it back into the engine, and by the end of the race, [their cars were] close to overheating."

One thing that was noticeable immediately about the Edelbrock team when it arrived at a track was its air of professionalism. They were there to race. Vic's belief in operating a first-class business even showed in his race cars, as he was adamant about the cars being kept in top-notch running condition and squeaky clean. At the end of every racing season, the race cars were completely rebuilt from the frame up, new chrome and paint were applied, and the engines were updated.

With the increasing demands of a burgeoning business, he retired from active midget racing in 1952.

NITROMETHANE

The Dooling brothers of Culver City, who manufactured model airplane motors that powered tethered slot cars, had developed a mixture of nitromethane and methanol to fuel their tiny powerplants. Edelbrock employees Bobby Meeks, Don Towle, and Fran Hernandez lived in Culver City and got to know the Doolings and their use of nitro.

Vic Jr. was there the day that his father and the Edelbrock crew ran nitro for the first time in a test V8-60 engine on the dynamometer. "They made up a mixture of ten percent nitro in methanol, but didn't know that they had to run a different spark plug and richen up the carburetors by putting in larger jets," Vic Jr. said. "They just ran the same setup as they did with alky. The engine was on the 200-horsepower Clayton dyno that had the sliding beam scale. Once the engine was fired up and given a full pull, it overrevved so quick that it almost broke the beam as a result of the large, instant increase in horsepower. Dad held the throttle long enough to settle the beam to get a reading. After getting their reading, an attempt was made to shut the engine down, but by this time the spark plugs were so hot that they were acting like glow plugs, and the V8-60 ran till it expired."

From extensive testing on the dynamometer, Vic's crew knew that the V8-60 produced 40 percent more horsepower on nitro than the Offenhauser did on straight methanol. Vic tuned the V8-60 so it could run as high as 20 percent nitro/alcohol mixture safely.

Nitro was the secret ingredient that helped Fran Hernandez defeat Tom Cobb in April 1949 in a grudge runoff at the first-ever recognized drag race. The Santa Barbara Acceleration Association held the race on an airport service road near Goleta. (Fran later left Edelbrock to work for Lincoln-Mercury as its performance division manager.) Once the secret of this potent fuel additive was out, Vic marketed a methanol and nitromethane conversion kit for the Stromberg carburetor.

MIDGET RACE CAR HISTORY

Before August 1950, you needed an Offenhauser midget engine under the hood if you wanted to win a midget race. The little engine was a jewel of engineering perfection and was designed specifically for midget race cars. The origins of this particular Offy four-cylinder go back to prewar days, when Earl B. Gilmore (the oil magnate and race-track owner) put a request into Fred Offenhauser for an engine design to fit into a midget chassis. The results went much further than either gentleman had dreamed, as the engine dominated midget racing. The cost of this handmade engine wasn't cheap, leaving many racers to find an alternative power source. The Ford Motor Company's tiny V8-60 fit the bill due to its physical dimensions, weight, horsepower capabilities, and cubic-inch displacement. For a production-run engine that was built with

Both Edelbrock Kurtis-Kraft midgets are shown in close competition. Note each car ran the number 27 and had a different colored nose shell. *Courtesy Edelbrock Corporation*

An interior shot of the busy Edelbrock machine shop on West Jefferson Boulevard. *Courtesy Edelbrock Corporation*

DRY LAKES AND BONNEVILLE RACING

Once he'd reopened the garage business in 1945, the mounting pressures of business didn't allow Vic the luxury to personally run at the lakes. The two midgets consumed any spare time he had, but that didn't prevent the shop from giving support to a wide variety of track, drag, powerboat, and dry lakes racers.

At the inaugural 1949 Bonneville National Speed Trials, the top speed of the meet was set by the Edelbrock Ford V-8-powered *So-Cal Special* streamliner of Dean Batchelor and Alex Xydias, making it the fastest car in America. Vic had loaned Alex and Dean the souped-up flathead along with the expertise of Fran Hernandez. At Bonneville, the streamliner ran 193 miles per hour one way with a 189-mile-per-hour two-way average. During the same meet, it ran 156 miles per hour with an Edelbrock-equipped V8-60 engine. Bobby Meeks and an Edelbrock V-8 accompanied the *So-Cal Special* to Bonneville the following year, where it ran a two-way average of 208 miles per hour and a one-way speed of 210 to retain the title of the fastest car in the country. The same engine was in the C class car when it was co-sponsored by *Hot Rod* and Sta-Lube for the 1951 Speed Week at Daytona Beach, Florida.

Many Edelbrock employees were quite active in racing. Fran Hernandez raced his '32 coupe in C class at the lakes; Bobby Meeks teamed up with Fran to win the C/Roadster class at Bonneville in 1950; Don Towle, Bill Likes, and Don Waite also competed on the dry lakes.

Waite earned a nickname early on at the dry lakes. Before tying up with Vic, Don received the moniker "dumb kid" while competing with an unconventional yet well-designed rear-engined roadster. The nickname came from Paul Schiefer (Schiefer clutches). Harold Daigh and his brother Chuck were serious competitors at the lakes. Harold recalled, "I was telling Paul that I was going to build a car for circle-track racing. Paul said that he wanted the record that I owned, but I told him that he'd never get it because [pointing over to Don Waite's roadster] he's going to get the record. That rear-engined car has too much of an advantage on us; you can't race against him with a front-engined car. Schiefer said, 'That dumb kid!' And that's where he got his name from." Harold was correct in his assumption that the ultra-slippery design of Don's roadster would become a record holder—with assistance from the Edelbrock garage.

The Edelbrock company also sponsored notables such as the Pierson brothers and their famous chopped coupe, which has become a show piece and a reminder of those early days; Jazzy Nelson's Fiat coupe, which ran an unheard-of 10.90-second elapsed time (ET) at the 1955 National Hot Rod Association (NHRA) Nationals with a nitro-induced flathead; the So-Cal tank; the Kenz & Leslie record-setting streamliner; and many, many more.

EDELBROCK X1 RAM

Before the modern high-performance four-barrel carburetor came into existence, and excluding fuel injection, the answer for inducing loads of fuel into a normally aspirated engine was to add as many dual-throated carburetors as the engine could possibly handle, which usually amounted to six or eight Strombergs.

economy in mind, the little V8-60 found its way into many race cars and powerboats, but it was never considered a threat to a well-tuned, race-bred, methanol-burning Offenhauser.

It was during an American Automobile Association–sanctioned midget race at the Gilmore Stadium on August 10, 1950, that the Edelbrock cars qualified first and second for the feature. Rodger Ward, driving the V8-60, won the trophy dash and led the field to an outstanding win in the 50-lap feature. It was the first time that a V8-60 defeated the once-unbeatable Offenhauser engine. The following day at the San Bernardino Orange Bowl Raceway, Rodger repeated the feat by trouncing the mighty Offenhausers once again in the 40-lap feature, disproving any doubters that thought the previous night's win at Gilmore was merely a stroke of luck. *

"At the Gilmore track, they ran an inverted start for the slow heat, which meant that the fast cars were in the back and the slow cars were in the front," Vic Jr. said. "Ward won the slow heat that put him on the pole for the main feature. Allan Heath was on the outside pole with racers like Bill Vukovich, Sam Hanks, Walt Faulkner, et cetera—all the guys who just came back from running at the Indy 500, who were West Coast boys who raced at Gilmore Stadium on a regular basis. The V8-60 had super-quick acceleration as a result of dad's ultra-light crankshaft and the 20 percent nitro mix in the tank.

"Starting on the pole allowed Rodger to set the pace at the green flag, and he knew that by slowing the pace the Offys would bog and sputter. Twice Heath jumped the gun, and the officials told Allan that the next time he'd be put at the rear of the pack. The third time Heath jumped the start again but Ward pushed the accelerator down, got on the outside of the track, and led the entire race for 50 laps to end up as the only flathead V8-60–powered midget ever to beat the formidable Offenhausers."

*Note: The race results compiled here were partially contributed by Don Weaver, who is a former midget racer and now a Gilmore historian.

Edelbrock introduced the X1 Ram six-carburetor manifold in 1958. It was designed especially for competition engines, and Edelbrock was so confident in the increase in horsepower ratings that the company guaranteed it would outperform any other six-carburetor manifold on the market. The crossram design came about after numerous runner and plenum changes and countless hours of dynamometer testing. The manifold's runners tapered in toward the engine ports as the fuel left the plenum chamber. This design allowed the mixture to accelerate at a steady rate rather than having maximum velocity as soon as the mixture entered the runners, as when a runner has a common diameter throughout its entire length. This particular manifold produced a whopping 37 horsepower gain over an older design.

The X1 manifold was used to test Vic Jr.'s Chevrolet-powered ski-boat engine in 1961. The 283 was enlarged to 339 inches and with six 97 Strombergs squirting gasoline into the engine, and it made 364 horsepower on the dyno. The following year over at Iskenderian Racing Cams, the X1 managed to pull 375 horsepower out of a 283 Chevy while testing out a new Polydyne profile camshaft.

Outside of the original slingshot dual intake, the high-performing crossram X1 manifold proved to be Vic Sr.'s most significant manifold design for ultimate horsepower output. *Hot Rod* did a full cover story on the X1 in its April 1961 issue.

DUAL FOUR-BARREL CROSSRAM MANIFOLD

When Vic Sr. designed the X1 Crossram in the late 1950s, the manifold proved to be a very strong performer. Years later, Vic Jr. and his crew were working on a dual four-barrel crossram manifold that was similar to the X1, only designed with rounded corners. After many futile attempts to get more horsepower out of the design, Vic Jr. remembered his dad's six-carburetor intake. Vic Jr. said, "We began by blocking off the four outside carburetor mounting bases and enlarging the center two by welding adapter plates to mount the four-barrel carburetors. As soon as we fired it up, it became apparent that the rounded corners of the intake were allowing ultrasonic pulses to bounce back up from the valve area to the carburetors, disrupting the intake flow of the fuel. Dad's square-cornered design cancelled out these pulses when they reached the corners; he'd spent a great deal of time studying all the literature he could find on internal combustion flow and the effects of ram-type manifolds and came up with what he felt would work for his needs."

BOAT RACING

To compete in the SK class powerboat racing held at Marine Stadium in Long Beach over the 1958–1959 seasons, Bobby Meeks and Don Towle went into partnership on a Stevens flat-bottomed hull powered by a Pontiac V-8 engine. The SK class was limited to engines with a maximum displacement of 400 ci, and the popular choice of power for the day was the Chrysler 392 Hemi.

Although their Pontiac was structurally strong, it wasn't able to really rev and produce enough horsepower to run against the Hemi and win races. Both Vic Sr. and Vic Jr. helped out with the dyno testing on the engine, but no one could come up with a reason why the Pontiac just wouldn't put out the power. Vic Jr. said, "The problem was between the camshaft, piston, and combustion chamber design. After making the changes to Dad's specifications, the Pontiac came alive with the horsepower that had been eluding them. He just had a natural ability to be able to solve mechanical problems."

Keith Black, as well as other fellows who were involved in the speed business, would often stop in for a visit to hash out their latest mechanical problems, bouncing ideas off each other and hoping someone might have the answer. Keith had about six or seven SK boat deals underway for local racers, and all were equipped with the Chrysler 392 V-8. The problem he and others were having was that the Hemi peaked around 400 horsepower—it was a wall that no one could breach with the engine rules that they had to compete under.

Dick Jones (a Champion Spark Plug performance rep) was another occasional visitor to the Edelbrock shop. He was also running the Hemi in his SK boat and had similar troubles. Jones even had taken the engine to his friends who owned Traco Engineering and had it tested to the limit before destroying it on the dyno.

Vic Sr. had just finished manufacturing a six-carburetor crossram intake for the Chrysler Hemi and outfitted all of Black's SK engines with the manifold. It wasn't long before Black had returned them, saying that they didn't do the job; but Vic disagreed and said he could prove it. He had Meeks and Towle visit the local auto wreckers and pick up two Chrysler 392 engines. After checking out the combustion chamber, Vic realized that it was not a true hemispherical design. "It was a semi-hemi with a flatter dome," Vic Jr. said. "All of Keith's engines were running pistons manu-

Bobby Meeks was a driving force behind the scenes at Edelbrock. Meeks proved to be one of the best flathead V-8 men in his day.
Courtesy Edelbrock Corporation

The X-1 Ram Log six-carb manifold came out in 1958. Of all the manifolds designed by Vic Sr., it produced the most horsepower, getting 284 horsepower from a 283-ci Chevy V-8. *Courtesy Edelbrock Corporation*

factured by the same company that made the pistons for the almighty Offenhausers. They had the same deflector built into the Chrysler pistons as they used on the Offys." The Offenhauser had a true hemispherical head with a tall combustion chamber. Vic said that the pistons were blocking everything off (similar to what he'd found in the Towle Pontiac). He went to JE Pistons and had a set of pistons made with the crowns unmachined, as he wanted to finish them with a design that he thought would work in the Chrysler engine. Next, he walked across the street to Iskenderian Racing Cams and gave Isky the particulars on what he wanted done to the camshaft. Vic Jr. said of his dad's working relationship with Ed Iskenderian, "My dad could tell Ed to grind the camshaft upside down and it'd be done."

After the Chrysler engine was completed and installed on the dyno (Bill Stroppe had sold Edelbrock a surplus military tank dynamometer that had an actual horsepower readout gauge on it), Vic pulled the throttle handle and it went well past 400—up to 425, and then to 430 horsepower (on gasoline), much to the joy of the Edelbrock crew. But on the second run, the engine let go. The crew discovered that one piston had destroyed itself, leaving

behind the rod, piston pin, and little bits of what was left of the piston. "Dad figured that the Hemi had a harmonic in it and that the harmonic [vibration] destroyed the piston."

Vic went to Art Sparks at ForgeTrue Pistons and ordered a set of pistons, telling Art not to machine the deflector, and that he would finish machining the pistons on his own lathe. "Once these were installed, the engine could run all day on the dyno producing 435 to 440 horsepower on gasoline," Vic Jr. said. "Dad invited Dick Jones over and asked him if he wanted to see it run. Dick just about fell on the ground with a heart attack." Vic had his crew build Dick a similar engine for his SK boat for the upcoming Fourth of July race at Marine Stadium. It was one of the biggest boat races held on the West Coast, and the SK class was the big thing at the time.

Just prior to the race, Vic was diagnosed with cancer and was to be hospitalized a week after the boat race. "Dad sat up in the back of a pickup truck to watch the races," Vic Jr. said. "He saw Don Towle go out in the first race and beat all comers, and Dick Jones ran second. In the second heat, Jones ran first and Towle in second place. It was the most gratifying moment for my father in the latter part of his illness, knowing that he had the mind and the ability to overcome any obstacle that lay in his way."

BUSINESS SAVVY AND SKILLED HELP

Any type of leader, whether a businessman, general, politician—anyone who has been successful in his endeavors—has gotten there with help. Vic Edelbrock Sr. was no different; he had the business savvy to surround himself with employees who were skilled and dedicated to their trades. Over the years, these employees developed lasting, lifelong friendships with their boss.

Bobby Meeks was a neighborhood kid hired on to help out at Vic's first shop, the service station at Hoover and Venice. After serving in the navy during World War II, he returned to the Edelbrock shop to become one of the top engine tuners and builders in the business, with an amazing ability to build a bulletproof flathead. Meeks also has the distinction of being Edelbrock's longest-serving employee. He retired in 1993 after almost 60 years on the job.

"Jazzy" Jim Nelson's fuel-burning Topolino coupe powered by an Edelbrock-equipped flathead V-8. The record-setting car put many OHV race cars on the trailer. *Courtesy Edelbrock Corporation*

Other key employees from the early 1950s were Don Towle, Fran Hernandez, Don Waite (vice president of Edelbrock Engineering), and Harvey Hartman (pattern-maker; today, Hartman's two sons, Mark and Randy, work as pattern-makers for Edelbrock Company). Many of these longtime employees were there to help Vic's son take over the reigns of the company after his father's passing in 1962.

Regardless of his lack of a secondary education, Vic Sr. studied all he could find about the combustion engine and took a very methodical approach to any mechanical problem that he encountered. Made obvious by the phenomenal rate of growth and success of his company, Vic had an inherent sense for business. And like Ed Iskenderian, Vic was not afraid to break the budget on advertising, knowing full well that if your name is not constantly out there, they'll soon forget who you are.

"I would dyno test engines at the Edelbrock shop," Harold Daigh said, "and while there, if I needed to know anything or ask a question, Vic, like Clay Smith, would always take time and give you a straight answer to the best of his knowledge."

GENERATIONAL CHANGE

In November 1962, Victor Edelbrock Sr. died of cancer at the age of 49. "My father was very conservative with his finances and had $250,000 cash in the bank, and the business was all paid for," Vic Jr. said. "He wanted the money in the bank rather than to invest it in real estate or stocks, like many of his peers who lived through the hard times of the Depression era."

At the time of his father's death, Vic Jr. was only 24 years old and had some very large shoes to fill. He was faced with a multitude of decisions about what direction the company should travel and how best it should do so.

In 1962, the Edelbrock Company was doing about $500,000 worth of business annually with a staff of approximately 10 employees. By 1967, the company had outgrown its previous facilities and moved to a modern 27,000-square-foot building in El Segundo. Outgrowing those facilities again, it later moved to Torrance. The company became the world's largest specialty automotive manufacturer, became a corporation, built two ultra-modern aluminum foundries, and was at one time listed on the NASDAQ stock exchange, although it has since returned to private ownership. Vic Jr. was one of the original speed equipment manufacturers who got together to form the Specialty Equipment Market Association (SEMA).

"Vic Jr., like his dad, is a very intelligent man," Lou Senter said. "After taking over the family business, he advertised, whereas his competition didn't spend the same amount of money. Edelbrock also had a large research and development lab and was a very aggressive company."

Vic Jr. feels that his father's greatest achievement was the success he had with the small-block Chevy in 1958, when the Edelbrock X1–equipped 265-ci V-8 made 284 horsepower on the dynamometer—more than 1 horsepower per cubic inch, running on gasoline. Even though the Ford flathead put the Edelbrock name on the map, the introduction of GM's 265 V-8 in 1955 gave the Edelbrock Company (as well as others) the final push to become successful in the speed equipment market. Vic Jr. said that the Chevrolet V-8 really got things in motion for the performance industry. "It made horsepower with about every modification done to it and was very receptive to modification."

Both of Vic's midgets ran with the magical No. 27. The number has been very lucky for the Edelbrock clan, and is retained today in the company's street address, phone numbers, and elsewhere. That lucky number could trace its origins back to 1927, when the Edelbrock family business in Eudora, Kansas, was destroyed by fire, helping prompt Vic to relocate to Los Angeles.

REMEMBERING VIC

As a tribute to the memory of his father and to the company his father founded, Vic Jr. built a classy car museum. There are at least 23 cars, 1 powerboat, and 5 motorcycles, plus displays of various intake manifolds and related items. These gorgeous vehicles demonstrate how an automobile should be restored and include the original Edelbrock family 1932 roadster, the original V8-60-powered Kurtis midget that made history when it defeated the mighty Offenhausers, and a fantastic collection of sports cars, muscle cars, and race cars, most painted either "Edelbrock red" or black.

The display of Vic Sr.'s original small metal toolbox, complete with hand tools, brings one back to reality after viewing these high-dollar vehicles. The sight of those simple hand tools makes one realize that the person responsible for these beautiful surroundings got there by hard work and more hard work, starting at the bottom and working his way to the top.

The master and the student. This picture of father and son was taken in 1960. It wasn't long after this photo that Vic Jr. took over the reigns of the family business. *Courtesy Edelbrock Corporation*

CHAPTER 6

Engle Racing Cams

JACK ENGLE

Engle Racing Cams is the longest-running performance camshaft manufacturer. From the company's meager beginnings back in 1941, Engle outlasted its fellow prewar cam grinding competitors, such as Winfield, Riley, Harman, and Bertrand. Jack Engle took his company from a part-time business run out of his parents' garage to one with highly respected products that have been used worldwide in some of the most prestigious race cars. It has weathered competition from modern-day corporate giants of the mass-production age by producing viable racing components that work for the customer.

Engle Racing Cams can trace its roots back to the Canadian city of Regina, Saskatchewan, where Jack was born in 1921. His father was in the construction trades and sought employment where he could find it, and in those days it happened to be in Saskatchewan. Anyone involved in construction usually found himself unemployed during the cold winter months as work ground to a halt. The idea of living in a climate where there was year-round employment in the trades was enough for the Engle family to pack up and head south, settling in Santa Monica, California.

STREET ROD

By the 1930s, the seemingly endless expanse of the dry lakes of Southern California had become a mecca for teenagers and their hopped-up jalopies. The lure of smooth, hard surfaces of dried-up ancient lakebeds offered speed enthusiasts unrestricted freedom. Over time, organized racing developed into a more or less regular event.

In 1937, while attending Venice High, Jack Engle purchased his first automobile, a '26 Chevrolet coupe powered by a rather sedate four-cylinder engine. It wasn't long before he was under the engine hood, trying to squeeze a little extra out of the docile four. The most common method used in those days to get a little extra out of an underpowered Chevy was to replace the stock head with a three-port Oldsmobile. That additional port provided better breathing and could be bolted on to a Chevy block without too much difficulty, making the small gain in horsepower well worth the effort. At a time when speed equipment was a scarce commodity for GM's bowtie four-cylinder, an Oldsmobile head was an inexpensive hop-up item that could usually be picked up at a salvage yard.

DRY LAKES RACING

Jack and some friends had heard about the racing at the lakes, and driving up to have a look was all it took to get him hooked. To compete at most of these sanctioned meets, a driver had to belong to an organized car club, making for a more stable meet than if it were just a horde of disorganized individual racers attending a race. Living in Santa Monica, the closest car club was the Low Flyers, whose membership roll had some pretty ambitious racers, including Phil Remington, Stu Hilborn (who joined after World War II), Frank Coons and Jim Travers (Traco Engineering), Tom Cobb, Howard Wilson (who broke the 150-mile-per-hour barrier in Hilborn's streamliner), and many others.

Jack had worked long enough on his car to know that it just wouldn't cut it at the lakes. He needed to replace the old Chevy with something that had a little more grunt under hood. Looking

Opposite: In this late-1950s photo, Jack Engle (left) watches employee Mort Smith make adjustments to their new camshaft grinder. *Courtesy Jack Engle*

Inset: Jack never was one to advertise to the extent of his competitor, Ed Iskenderian. This early ad simply stated what he offered and made no promises regarding performance and winning. *Courtesy Jack Engle*

In the days when most everyone at the dry lakes was running carburetion, Jack was one of the few who chose to try something different, installing a McCulloch supercharger on his Model A engine. Note how the belt-driven blower and side-draft Winfield carburetor are mounted on the left side to pump pressurized fuel mixture over the head via tubing into a homemade intake manifold on the right side. Also, a large machined and crank-driven pulley drives the generator, water pump, and supercharger. *Courtesy Jack Engle*

around, he located a '27 T roadster parts car that was more suitable for the job. After stripping the body down to the bare bones, it was mounted on a Model A chassis. In those days, the Ford four-cylinder was still king of the lakes and very affordable, and there was an abundance of used speed equipment available for it.

At the time, nearly all of the cars competing at the lakes were running normally aspirated engines, but Jack's Model A engine was outfitted with a Winfield side-draft carburetor feeding fuel into a belt-driven McCulloch supercharger that was mounted on the opposite side of the engine into a homemade intake manifold. Although he's not quite sure what camshaft he first ran in the engine—probably a Winfield, seeing that it was one of Ed's cams that Jack used as a model for his first camshaft master—it didn't stay in the engine long, as the roadster set its class record in late 1941 using an Engle cam in the engine.

This backyard-built engine revealed Jack's natural insight into mechanics, his willingness to experiment, and it no doubt sparked his curiosity concerning the relationship between camshafts and engine breathing.

ENGLE CAMS 1941

Upon graduating from Santa Monica College as a machinist in 1940, Jack went to work for the North American Aircraft Company. With a conscientious work attitude, it didn't take long for Jack to work his way up through the ranks to the position of an experimental machinist, where he was involved in such projects as the P-51 fighter and the formidable B-25 bomber.

Even with the threat of war clouds looming on America's distant horizon, dry lakes racing events were still drawing a large showing of competitors and spectators alike, and Jack labored away on the roadster in attempts to find a few extra horsepower. He felt that he'd gone as far as possible with about everything on the engine, excluding the valvetrain, where he knew there was still room for improvement. As for cam grinders in prewar Southern California, there were Winfield, Bertrand, Cannon, Riley, Harman, and several lesser-known fellows. Those were the days before precision factory camshaft grinders were readily available, so cams were ground by the hand of a skillful craftsman on a converted grinder of sometimes-questionable accuracy.

Jack had been over to Pierre Bertrand's place on occasion and had observed Pierre's homemade (converted lawnmower sharpener) camshaft grinder in operation. The idea of experimenting with camshaft timing intrigued Jack, and he figured that the only affordable way to do it was to grind his own camshafts. So, using Bertrand's grinder as a guide, Jack fashioned a cam grinder by rigging up a rocking table to an old bench lathe. But, unlike Bertrand, Jack installed an electric motor to drive his grinder. Bertrand had the nickname "Popeye" due to his muscular left arm, developed from years of cranking the rocking table by hand as he ground camshafts. Pierre's protégé was the legendary Clay Smith, who eventually took over Bertrand's operation and continued to grind cams by hand for some time, just as he'd been taught by his mentor.

For his first prototype camshaft, Jack made a master off of a modified Winfield cam. After a bit of trial and error, he came up with a workable cam that put his roadster in the record books. On November 30, 1939, during a Russetta Timing Association (RTA) meet at El Mirage, he ran 113.92 miles per hour and had a clocked time of 7.90 seconds for the measured flying quarter-mile.

After his record-setting feat, other racers began to inquire about getting Jack to grind them a cam. Jack could see that there was a market for racing camshafts and figured he could make a little extra cash regrinding them, but he wasn't about to give up his day job. With a full-time job at North American and living with his parents in Venice, Engle Racing Cams opened for business on a workbench in the family garage. Jack even remembers that his first cash-paying customer was Fred Zimmer, who bought a full-race Engle regrind for a Cragar-equipped Model A Ford engine.

WAR YEARS

With the outbreak of World War II, Jack's employment at North American was deemed essential to the war effort until 1943, when his deferment finally ran out. Once he knew he was going to be called up for duty, Jack chose to enlist in the U.S. Navy. With his machinist background, he was transferred to the 36th Squadron and enrolled in the Packard Engine Repair School. Upon graduation, Jack and his classmates found themselves being shipped out to the South Pacific, posted in the Philippines under the 7th Fleet Command and assigned to maintain PT boat engines.

These high-performance craft were propelled by three 1,500-horsepower, 2,500-ci Packard V-12s, and Jack remembers his part in keeping the PTs in top running condition. "Get it done quickly and back in service, which usually meant the replacement of the problem (parts) with new parts, rather than doing the repairs," Jack said. "Many in the service considered the PT boat assignment as a good duty, referring to the small and casual nature of the repair crews. I enjoyed this posting, but it wasn't quite on the same level as that TV sitcom show, *McHale's Navy*."

When the war finally came to a close, Jack found himself stationed in Borneo. Like everyone else, the fellows were more than anxious to get home. An order that came down the line to his squadron was short and precise: "Lighten the load to get home quicker." He says that it was a hard thing to do and disheartening to see, but over the side went many brand-new, ready-to-run, Packard marine engines that had never been uncrated, truckloads of boxes containing new engine parts, and who knows what else. Being a true hot rodder at heart, Jack managed to save a V-12 Packard magneto from entering the salty depths with the hopes of adapting it to a car once he was back in California.

ENGLE MACHINE SHOP 1947

Upon returning to civilian life in 1945, Jack returned to his old job at North American with plans of only working there until he saved up enough money to open up a machine shop. In the meantime, he pulled the old roadster from storage and returned to the dry lakes, along with hundreds of other hot rodders eager to make up for lost time. It wasn't long before he began to receive inquiries for racing

camshafts, and, again working out of his parents' garage, he fired up the cam grinder to supply cams for friends and for two local speed shops in Santa Monica.

As the demand grew for cams, and the more he experimented with the profiles, Jack began to come up with some fairly decent grinds. His part-time cam business started to grow. He recalled spending many long hours sitting at the kitchen table calculating the amount of lift in relation to the degrees of rotation and plotting it out on graph paper—no computers or calculators in those days. It was a laborious, time-consuming job that involved a multitude of mathematical equations to come up with a camshaft lobe that hopefully would perform the way he wanted it to. He had set up the bench-mounted grinder to produce Model A and B cams and the increasingly popular flathead V-8 camshaft.

"In those early days," Jack said, "used cam cores were all that was available. The odd one was so worn that it was a challenge even to try to grind it."

More than half a century later, that original homemade cam grinder is still in use. With the rocking-table apparatus removed and tucked away in Jack's artifact cupboard, the old grinder is used as a fixture to hold freshly ground camshafts so a coating of protective molycote can be applied to the cam lobes prior to shipping.

By 1947, Jack had saved enough money and purchased sufficient used machinery to leave North American and start his own business. The Engle Machine Shop opened its doors at the corner of 14th and Montana in Santa Monica, situated in the back part of the building where his father ran a radio sales and service business.

His father had a small addition built onto the side of the main building for Jack, and in the beginning Jack was the sole employee. "I figured that if I could make $20 before lunch, I was going to

This is where it all began. In 1941, Engle Racing Cams was founded in Jack's parents' garage, where Jack set up his homemade grinder to supply racing camshafts for four-bangers and flatheads. *Courtesy Jack Engle*

have a great day," Jack said. "At first, I didn't do proprietary work, just automotive and general machine work."

It didn't take long before the shop had developed a decent reputation for milling cylinder heads, boring blocks, chopping flywheels, building full-race engines, and regrinding cams. By the latter part of that same year, the camshaft-grinding end of the business had increased to the point that a more accurate grinder was necessary. Jack bought a used cylindrical grinder from a machinery dealer in downtown Los Angeles. Once it had been converted over to a camshaft grinder, this machine became known as "Grungus," and subsequently the output of performance camshafts began to grow. He mentioned with a bit of pride that old Grungus is still alive and in use today, relieving cams (grinding away the metal in between cam lobes). In 1953, the Storm-Vulcan Company introduced a commercial camshaft grinder that came with a built-in cam master generator. The timing couldn't have been better for Jack, as business in camshafts was brisk and he needed something that could handle the workload efficiently.

DYNAMOMETER

The late "Shorty" Don McKenzie, a dirt-track stock car racer of the old school, once said, "It doesn't have to be new, shiny, and expensive to win races—just perform like hell." That describes the dynamometer facilities at Engle Racing Cams.

The Engle dynamometer is the perfect combination of parts that were on hand when it was first conceived and of the mechanical astuteness of its builder. The water brake itself originally belonged to Eddie Edmunds of Edmunds Speed Equipment and was purchased by the partnership trio of Jack, Tom Cobb,

Rated at 300-horsepower, the Engle dynamometer represents a collection of stuff: a water brake from Eddie Edmunds; an aircraft oxygen tank mounted on the wall for fuel; a 1922 Cadillac pressure pump in the lower right corner; a large marine transmission between engine and water wheel; a step-on scale in the background for torque readings; and a bunch of other items making up a facility that had seen more experimentation than most could imagine. *Author photo*

and Stuart Hilborn. The dynamometer was constructed from a collection of odd parts, ranging from vintage automotive to vintage aircraft. An oxygen bottle from a World War–II era B-17 bomber serves as a fuel tank, which is pressurized by a 1919 Cadillac hand-operated, fuel-priming pump. Four 55-gallon barrels located just outside the dynamometer room are connected to a circulating pump to supply cool water to the water turbine.

One time, Jack was attempting to test an Offenhauser midget motor, but the little engine just didn't have enough torque to work the water pump properly and get an accurate horsepower reading, so a marine 2:1 transmission solved any future problems. Numerous dents in the corrugated metal walls testify that not every engine survived its torturous ride on the dyno.

The dynamometer may not be or look high-tech compared to today's standards, but the work that has been performed on that dyno over the years is equal to any. "That dyno has seen well over 800 horsepower (in very short bursts) at times," Jack said, "and it is still in regular use today, giving the same accurate readings as one would find with any new high-priced dynamometer."

OHC CADILLAC

Jack's oddest request came in 1955, when the Jeffries Boat Company of Venice, California, hired him to make an overhead cam engine. Dale and Dan Jeffries, two brothers who were into high-performance boats and cars, came up with the idea of turning a 331-ci Cadillac V-8 into an overhead camshaft engine. A rather unique approach to this project was the system employed to drive the camshafts. The standard practice of the day was to use either a chain or gear drive. The Jeffries wanted to try a Gilmer timing belt. This type of drive belt was relatively new on the scene and didn't have a track record to prove itself as being durable enough to withstand the rigors of driving an engine camshaft. "When I first saw the belts, I didn't think that it would work and called it the rubber-band drive."

Cast-aluminum camshaft tower housings were made to attach directly onto the tops of the engine's existing stock cast-iron heads. This setup proved to be a relatively simple solution and saved considerable expense over having to redesign a completely new head. Another innovative feature was the use of clear plastic valve-cover tops, enabling an observer to see the cams in motion and make sure that oil was reaching the upper camshaft bearings. Jack spent countless hours with mathematical equations before coming up with a camshaft design suitable for this hybrid Cadillac. When the engine was finally assembled, it was first tried out with a four-carburetor setup and later switched over to Hilborn fuel injectors.

"When you have a rocker arm ratio, you gain valve motion considerably because of the multiplication." Jack explained. "With an overhead cam motion, it's a direct action on the valves, and even though I had put a severe grind on the cams, it didn't show any improvement at the valves. It didn't make any more power than if they'd just modified the stock Caddy."

The overhead-cammed Cadillac was run in the Taby brothers' dragster but fell short of expectations due to the lack of time spent on the engine. Because the engine was never taken to the next level of development, it fell into obscurity. At last report, the over-head-cam Cadillac engine was installed in a sports car that was used in competition. Jack believed that the engine conversion idea was Dan Jeffries' personal experiment to see what the outcome would produce with such a drive system, and he never bothered to pursue the venture further.

OLDSMOBILES

During the early 1950s, Engle Cams was known for its Olds racing cams. With a touch of modesty, Jack revealed, "I feel that I happened to fall onto a grind that worked in the early Oldsmobile V-8." Whether it was luck or just long hours spent toiling in the dyno room, when the Oldsmobile engine was considered to be a top contender in drag racing, a large majority of the winning Olds-powered cars were triggered by Engle camshafts. The top engine tuners of the day could make those early Olds V-8s outrun the mighty Chrysler Hemi, and one of the best examples was the Albertson-Olds dragster team of Scrima, Adams, and Harris. This winning car was driven by the talented Leonard Harris, who was reputed by many to be the best dragster pilot of the day. With Leonard driving, the Albertson-Olds took 10 straight wins in 10 consecutive weeks at Long Beach and went on to win the 1960 NHRA Nationals. Several other top names that dominated the competition with Engle-equipped Oldsmobile engines were K. S. Pittman with his Willys, the C/Gas of Pittman and Edwards, and the record-holding A/Altered of Ratican, Jackson, and Stevens. Probably the most famous drag car to ever run in the ranks of the gas class was the fabulous Engle-equipped Willys coupe of Stone, Woods, and Cook.

DESTINY

Mark Engle, the younger of Jack's two sons, began as an apprentice employee with the company at the tender age of seven. Looking back over the years, Mark came up with the phrase, "A lot of destiny," to describe some of the events that occurred under the Engle Racing Cams roof. It might also have been called good fortune, being in the right place at the right time, or providence. This "destiny" expression Mark used best describes how his dad hired two employees who would leave a profound imprint on the Engle business.

One time, Jack was out back in the shop, struggling with a newly acquired screw machine. The machinery had a few mechanical bugs that even Jack was having a difficult time trying to solve. A customer by the name of Wes Cerney appeared on the scene. Wes was a drag racer from back east and had dropped by the Engle shop to purchase some parts for his 392 Chrysler-powered dragster. From the other side of the parts counter, he stood there for a while watching Jack's predicament—more out of curiosity than anything—before finally coming to Jack's aid.

Wes said, "I used to run these at the sewing machine factory back in Pennsylvania." Jack replied, "Well, come on back around here and if you can run this machine, you're hired." Wes Cerney played an important part as an Engle employee for many years, adding his extensive racing experience to the company.

John Peters sets up a blown Chevy for some dyno time. Peters began working for Jack in 1961 and for many years performed everything from cam grinding and machine work to R&D in the dyno room. Peters was also partners with Nye Frank in the much-feared twin-engine dragster *Freight Train. Courtesy Jack Engle*

"Cerney was always a little ahead of his time in tuning and solving engine problems," Mark said. "He was instrumental in the development of the three-inch fuel lines and in the big-diameter Engle camshafts (that other companies copied)." In 1991, Mark said, Wes teamed up with Dale Armstrong to work on the *Hawaiian Punch* Funny Car. Wes introduced the large fuel pump and some radical Engle cam designs, and with Armstrong's expertise on the ignitions, the team got the car up and running strong, but it was too late in the season to make it in the points standings.

Then there was the day Don Moody and Jimmy Nix walked through the door. These two drag racers came to Southern California from Oklahoma to compete against the West Coast boys. Don originally stopped into Engle's for some engine parts but ended up staying there from 1960 to 1980. He and Wes Cerney ran the front end of the Engle shop, allowing Jack the time to develop new valvetrain components and spend time in the dyno room testing his theories.

Mark mentioned that his introduction to the world of speed equipment manufacturing took place under the tutelage of these two outstanding gentlemen. It was to be a great learning

The Engle-cammed, twin-V-8 *Freight Train* won more than its share of Top Gas Eliminators. Co-owned by Engle employee John Peters and Nye Frank, the car was driven mainly by Bob Muravez. *Courtesy Jack Engle*

experience that would pave the way for his eventual takeover as general manager of Engle Racing Cams.

Don Moody, known as the "Weekend Warrior," made a name for himself in the 1960s, winning Top Fuel 18 times during the 1963 and 1964 seasons. Piloting a front-engined fuel dragster wasn't without its share of danger; in 1965, good fortune was riding with him when he survived a horrific crash at Lions that destroyed his ride.

The Moody-Cerney duo fielded a fuel dragster that dominated the 1971–1972 series in Top Fuel racing on the West Coast. Some of the other racers at the time accused the duo of receiving special parts (because of their employment at Engle) that were not available to everyone. The story starts when a disgruntled racer approached Moody at the strip, accusing him of running a special camshaft. Don replied, "I'll sell you that so-called special cam for $200 providing that you help Wes remove it from the engine, 'cause it's still hot and I don't want to get my hands dirty." The happy fellow walked away with a well-used "special" cam that cost him about $50 more than if he'd bought the identical one from the Engle catalog. Moody's response to this unforeseen but profitable sale was: "You are in serious trouble next week, 'cause I'm gonna grind me a new, faster cam."

Don, along with Mike Snively, broke into the five-second bracket together, tying as the second racers to do so, on November 17, 1972. Don's 5.91 elapsed-time run was the lowest ever recorded at the time and was set while winning the 1972 NHRA Supernationals at Ontario, California, with a speed of 231.95 miles per hour. That same year, the partnership of Walton, Cerney, and Moody won the Professional Racers Association National Challenge held at Tulsa, Oklahoma.

After many years of being one of Jack's right-hand men, Don retired from Engle Cams as general manager, and from drag racing altogether, and was last known to be living with his family in Thailand.

Maybe not as influential as Cerney and Moody in the daily operation of the shop, but well known across the country in drag racing circles, was another Engle employee, John Peters. John was heavily involved in racing and best known for his partnership with Nye Frank in a series of infamous record-setting twin-engine dragsters all named *Freight Train*.

VW CAMSHAFTS

Before these cars became popular with certain racing groups, Engle Racing Cams was approached by the Volkswagen Company (U.S. Division) to design and manufacture performance camshafts. Moody's attitude to the request wasn't favorable at first. Mark said that Don's idea of grinding cams, if he could've gotten away with it, was to "grind nothing but top fueler cams." Regardless of what type of engine the request was for, the company was in the business of selling racing camshafts and there were bills to pay.

After studying the layout of the Volkswagen's valvetrain, Jack decided to try one of the company's winning Chrysler Hemi profiles on the VW cam as an experiment. After running engine tests on the dynamometer, the choice proved an instant success. The Volkswagen Company liked what it saw and placed orders for hundreds of these camshafts. Jack said that although Engle Racing Cams was not readily prepared to supply cams in those numbers, it soon geared up to meet the quotas. He mentioned that other camshaft companies at that time weren't really interested in grinding VW cams, as the popularity of the engine hadn't caught on yet. For several years after that, Engle Cams was one of the few sources of high-performance VW cams.

Today, Engle Racing Cams still produces more VW racing cams than any other outfit. They are sold either under the Engle name, in small-quantity orders under specialty custom-house brands, or for large warehouse suppliers who sell cams under their own labels.

300-MPH CAMSHAFT

When a record is broken, it can translate into sales for the companies who have their advertising decals stuck on the sides of that record-breaking vehicle. Mark Engle told the story of setting a world speed record, and not being able to cash in on it, with the first car to break the 300-mile-per-hour barrier in the quarter-mile.

It began when Dale Armstrong went to work on Kenny Bernstein's Budweiser Top Fuel dragster. Taking the same Cerney-Armstrong engine package that was developed during the Hawaiian Punch experience, Dale helped Kenny run 301 miles per hour at Gainesville, Florida, in 1992.

"We couldn't afford to put the Engle decal on the Budweiser dragster, which now resides in the Smithsonian Institution," Mark said. "If all the parts of the car were left as original from its 300 mile run, and if you pull the cam out and check the back of it (that's where they stamp them), you'll see the Engle name."

In the Engle Machine Shop, they keep one camshaft grinder permanently equipped with a specially calibrated, Engle-designed index plate. This grinder produces those 300-plus-mile-per-hour cams.

CAM WARS

One of Jack's favorite and more amusing memories of his many years in the cam-grinding business is of the "Cam Wars." This war in advertising no doubt originated on the Iskenderian side of the street, as Isky was notorious for his advertising campaigns. By the mid-1950s, many specialty manufacturers were placing a heavy emphasis on advertising the virtues of their products and the successes of their sponsored cars. Technological advances in valvetrain components raised performance levels, which showed up on the race tracks. As the performance of the cars improved, so did many cam grinders' claims of superiority. Various weekly and monthly racing newspapers and magazines became the focal point for such claims, and the rivalries between certain competing cars became almost soap opera-like. Well-known racers such as Stone, Woods, and Cook took on Big John Mazmanian, K. S. Pittman was pitted against Junior Thompson, and a host of others played their parts in this advertising war game. The cam-war advertising was associated with cars that competed mainly in the highly visible categories, where high speeds and low elapsed times were the cause of much ballyhoo.

Look back at some of the 1950s and 1960s vintage hot rod magazine advertising and you'll see how each issue presented a new set of winners and speculative claims by their supporting companies. It provided controversy for the readers and, as Jack said, "It provided a very good business for the cam grinders."

INVERSE-LOBE CAMSHAFT

In a very competitive high-performance marketplace, where large conglomerates have the financial resources to fill the advertising pages of today's automotive magazines, Engle Racing Cams still holds its share of the rock. Where the Engle team differs from others is its handle on the technical development of the inverse-flank camshaft. This particular lobe design has been around for many years. The theory behind it is very sound, but to get it to work efficiently is another question. The inverse camshaft (concave flank on both sides of the cam lobe) will produce more power and torque in midrange rpm than its counterparts. It opens quicker, holds the valve longer, and closes it quicker. The downside to this design is the severe valve action. If not properly designed to be compatible with the complete valvetrain, engine destruction is inevitable. At Engle, one camshaft grinder is equipped with a special 8-inch grinding wheel just for inverse cams.

Jack gives credit to the late Dick Jones for developing the inverse flank into a viable camshaft design. Jones was the performance supervisor at Champion Spark Plug in Long Beach.

"I became acquainted with Dick through the times I'd bought racing spark plugs from Champion," Jack said. "Jones said that he had faith in the inverse cam design and that it could be made to work. He approached me for my assistance in grinding some experimental camshafts.

After testing many cams through trial and error, we began to get a handle on the nature of the inverse flank." Between the two men, they developed this unique camshaft into a viable product, and today, Engle Cams is one of the few companies that can supply an inverse cam in which the buyer can be confident.

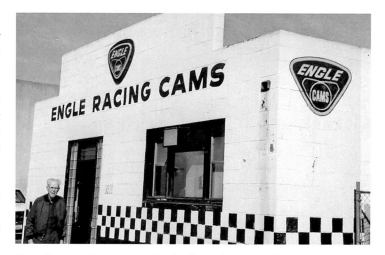

Even though his two sons basically took over the business, Jack continued to work in the back on his own projects. Here, Jack stands in front of the Engle Racing Cams shop that he made synonymous with speed. *Author photo*

LOGO

About the same time (1960) that Jack relocated the camshaft business to its present-day facilities, he contacted Noel Carpenter to design a logo for his burgeoning company. Stickers on race cars were free advertising, and that sticky little piece of paper turned out to be a very effective sales tool when seen on a winning car. Carpenter came up with a highly visible and distinctive bright yellow and black cam lobe–shaped logo that has decorated many of the country's fastest and quickest race cars in all forms of competition.

OVER THE YEARS

By not getting caught up in the mass production of racing camshafts, Jack's company has carved out a niche for itself in the performance market. Engle offers a catalog with a large selection of cam grinds, but it also offers personalized service and can supply the engine builder with a custom-ground cam to suit whatever application may be needed. It's a far cry from the days when Jack operated out of his parents' garage, cranking out regrinds on a homemade grinder with only three different cam grinds to choose from.

Although remaining relatively small in size, Engle Racing Cams has produced more than its fair share of winners throughout the years. The likes of Jerry Ruth, Mike Sorokin, The Surfers, Kenny Safford, Danny Ongais, Tom McEwen, Don Prudhomme, Jimmy Nix, the Frantic 4, the *Freight Train*, Stone, Woods, and Cook, Keith Black, Dave Zeuschel, and Traco Engineering are some who have used Engle products.

Even when he was semiretired for some time, Jack Engle could be found out in the back shop with a project on the go. His two sons, Mark (general manager) and Doug (shop manager), continue to run Engle Racing Cams with the same attitude with which their father built the business, making the Engle name synonymous with horsepower.

Jack Engle passed away in 2008 at the age of 87.

CHAPTER 7

Evans Speed Equipment

EARL EVANS

When the Ford Motor Company retired its long-running flathead V-8, it not only put the faithful old girl to rest, but also spelled the end for several manufacturers who specialized in speed equipment for that engine. Evans Speed Equipment was one manufacturer with its business centered around the flathead. Earl Evans never really ventured outside of the V-8 flathead, although in prewar days he produced a dual intake manifold for the Ford four-cylinder engine. In the mid-1950s, he made a half-hearted attempt to venture into the domain of the overhead-valve V-8 engine by making a three-carburetor intake for the Oldsmobile engine.

The business was turned into a machine shop and only returned to manufacturing specialized equipment when the quarter-midget craze hit Southern California in the 1950s. The Evans shop began producing and marketing a variety of performance engine parts for these very popular little race cars.

PREWAR DAYS

Growing up in east Los Angeles, Earl took up the foundry and pattern-making trade like his father. It was this direct insight into how patterns were designed and functioned, along with a first-rate knowledge of mechanics, that would lead to a career in specialty automotive manufacturing.

As a speed-enthused teenager in 1923, Earl took up dirt-track racing, competing in an organization called the Outlaw Circuit, named for its breakaway from the American Automobile Association (AAA) sanctioning body.

Evans' first attempt in the performance market was in the late 1930s, when he manufactured a dual-carburetor intake manifold for the popular Model A and B engines, operating a small pattern business out of the garage shop behind his home on Via Corona in Montebello, California. His client list was quite impressive; he made patterns for Model A head conversions for outfits such as George Riley and Cragar.

Because he did not own a milling machine, Earl would take a batch of raw manifold castings over to the backyard machine shop of his old school chum, Mendel "Cookie" Ledington, to finish them off. Mendel would eventually open Cook's Machine Works and manufacture his own line of Cyclone speed equipment.

EVANS & TRIBOLETT

With World War II over, Earl had just reopened his small pattern shop when an opportunity came knocking. A guy by the name of Tribolett, who was a successful tomato producer with the nickname "Tomato King," was interested in producing speed equipment. Being a perceptive businessman, he had observed how quickly the aftermarket parts business was growing. Tribolett looked at it solely as a financial investment opportunity. Without any knowledge of foundries and the accessory business, Tribolett approached Earl with a business plan that would be beneficial to both parties. Earl was the ideal partner, being well acquainted with racing equipment, and he knew the foundry-pattern business inside and out.

Opposite: Earl Evans in his belly tank at the dry lakes with his wife, Catherine, no doubt asking him where he thinks he's going. *Courtesy Gene Ohly*

Above: A very young-looking Earl on military duty in the navy in the early 1930s. *Courtesy Gene Ohly*

Right: In the 1930s Earl drove a sprint car on the Outlaw circuit. Results of his driving ventures are unknown. *Courtesy Gene Ohly*

After the war had ground to a halt, the Los Angeles area had its share of underutilized machine shops and foundries. It wasn't hard to locate a foundry for the right price in the city of El Monte. The pair opened up under the name of Evans & Tribolett, with a well-equipped, small aluminum foundry and all the machinery necessary to manufacture heads and intake manifolds. Earl hired his father, who was a foundry man by trade, to run the casting end of the new business.

It was like a bit of providence when two of Earl's acquaintances—Johnny Ryan and Nelson "Nellie" Taylor—walked through the door looking for work. Nellie was put in the machine shop, while John went to work in the molding room and helped out in the foundry when needed.

On his first day at work, John recalled Earl's father asking him, "Do you have any experience in foundry work?" John replied, "I took it in high school shop classes." Evans Sr. responded, "Oh, then you don't know anything about it." Evans Sr. was of the old school, where practical hands-on experience and years of apprenticeship were the only teachers.

It didn't take John and Nellie long to realize they weren't exactly cut out for foundry work. Being hot rodders at heart, they left Earl to try their hand at engine building. In the future, it would be Earl who asked his two friends for a favor.

The partnership between Earl and the Tomato King didn't last very long, and by late 1947, they'd parted ways and the El Monte shop was closed down.

EVANS SPEED EQUIPMENT

With the breakup of the partnership, Earl found himself back where he started, as it was Tribolett's money that bankrolled the now-defunct business. Earl owned the patterns for the equipment, which he still had orders for, but he lacked the resources to rent a machine shop. Luckily, he was rescued by his two former employees, Nellie and John. The two fellows had opened Taylor & Ryan Engine Building in a building owned by Ak Miller's brother at 2667 Whittier Boulevard in the city of Whittier. Originally, John and Nellie started off manufacturing engine stands. Their first sale was to Clay Smith. Ryan said, "We didn't make too many stands and went into the engine business."

The boys gave Earl the use of a small area that had an entrance off the alleyway. It consisted mainly of a sales counter and a small display area for his speed equipment. The casting of the heads and manifolds was farmed out to a foundry, and a machine shop owned by the two Kasperoff brothers in Montebello machined the raw castings. Earl had a large sign painted across the front of the building that read "Speed & Power Equipment." Local truck drivers having lunch at the coffee shop next door would occasionally pop their heads into the shop and jokingly inquire, "Who's Speed, and who's Power?"

Evans was never known to be an astute businessman, but he did design and manufacture some of the best products in the industry. Johnny Ryan says, "A customer came into the shop to purchase a set of Evans high-compression heads for a flathead. Earl was out at the time, so I sold the guy a set. Later, when Earl returned and I handed him the money from the sale, he asked what it was for. Earl's response was, 'I never sold anything for that price in my life.' He rarely sold his equipment for the advertised price. He wasn't a very good businessman, and one of his problems was that he was probably the first or second nicest guy in the world. He was so easy-going that he often got taken advantage of."

Taylor & Ryan Engine Rebuilding grew to the point that it was shipping performance engines nationwide. The company always used Evans equipment on its flathead V-8s, Ryan said, "because his stuff worked best for us, and you could depend on the quality." This company built the potent flathead that propelled Calvin Rice's dragster to Top Eliminator at NHRA's first National Meet in Great Bend, Kansas, in 1955. After the death of Nellie Taylor, the business became known as Ryan Engine Rebuilders. It was this shop that performed the step-by-step rebuild seen in "The Modern Flathead" series done by *Rod & Custom* in 1969 and 1970.

By 1949, Earl was back on his feet financially and moved the operation over to 545 South Greenleaf in Whittier. An ad in *Hot Rod* showed that he was manufacturing Ford 21- and 24-stud heads, intakes for the V-8 flathead, dual intakes for Model A and Bs, heads and dual intakes for the little V8-60, and even a high-compression aluminum head for the Studebaker six-cylinder. The fast growth in business soon caused him to relocate to a larger shop at 4135 East Union Pacific in Los Angeles.

In 1951, the Evans Speed Equipment was captured on film for a fleeting moment when the front of the shop was used in a short documentary entitled *Road Runners*. This short film on the dangers of street racing, directed by George de Normand and released in 1952, featured a typical outlaw teenager who ends up being saved from his wayward ways by organized drag racing. The leading teen actor in this drama (Earl's stepson, Melvin Potts)

was shown coming out of Earl's shop after buying some speed parts. Later, he appears wearing a helmet decked out with flames with the name "EVANS" painted across the front, just above the visor, which was no doubt loaned to the actor by Earl. The car club involved in the movie was the Road Runners, hence the name of the movie. As Earl was a member of that car club, it was only fitting that his shop and helmet appeared in the movie.

As a note of interest, the sign over the entrance of Earl's shop in the movie read, "Evans Speed Shop, Custom Engine Rebuilding, Reboring, Valve Refacing." It did not mention that he manufactured heads and manifolds.

The shop was involved in everything from machine work to building custom engines. Because of its reputation of putting out quality work, Evans had the contract to hand-polish crankshafts for Chick Wilson's Crank Grinding Service of Pomona. Wilson was the first to offer stroked Mercury crankshafts on a quantity basis. It was reputed to have taken approximately six hours to skillfully hand-polish a flathead crankshaft.

Business again warranted a larger shop, and this time Earl decided on something permanent. In 1952, he purchased a vacant parcel of land at 2550 North Seaman Avenue in South El Monte and had a suitable cement-block building erected on site. The original intention was to build an aluminum foundry on the property, but Earl ended up with a complete in-house machine shop for engine rebuilding and speed equipment manufacturing, while contracting the casting out to a foundry. This

Earl (left) holds a dual-intake manifold while Nellie Taylor displays an Evans high-compression head. One of Earl's original dual-carb intake manifold is between them. *Courtesy Gene Ohly*

building has been expanded several times and is still operating as Evans Speed Equipment some 50-odd years later under the guidance of Gene Ohly.

Over the years, numerous employees of the Evans shop would move on to become quite successful in their own ventures, including Fred Carrillo of Carrillo Rods, Joe Reath of Reath Automotive, Nelson Taylor and Johnny Ryan of Taylor & Ryan, and Al Teague, owner-builder-driver of the world's fastest single-engine streamliner.

SPEED EQUIPMENT

Although he wasn't officially in the racing parts business prior to World War II, Earl Evans did dabble with a dual-carburetor intake for the Model A, but it was in the postwar era that he made a name for himself as a speed equipment manufacturer. Like Barney Navarro, Earl based his business largely on the V-8 flathead. When this antiquated engine was finally pushed aside, so went the demand for flathead equipment, and so went Earl's business.

But what the business lacked in direction and resources, it made up for in excellent workmanship. Evans' heads were cast of quality aluminum, had plenty of material were it was needed, and contained large water jackets. Evans knew how to design and manufacture a quality product and finish the product off with an attractive appearance. It has even been reputed that he manufactured cylinder heads for Clay Smith when Clay and his partner operated Smith & Jones.

Earl was always progressive with ideas when it came to the flathead. In 1950, he introduced a new head for the Ford/Mercury V-8. This head's design was ideal for an engine builder who wanted to experiment with combustion chamber shapes. The area above

This photo was taken out the front window of the Evans pickup as it was push-starting George Bentley down the beach at Daytona in 1951 for the NASCAR Speed Week. The head of an inquisitive reporter can be seen just above the truck's hood. The journalist was straddling the belly tank and about to get a very quick ride down the racecourse. *Courtesy Gene Ohly*

the combustion chamber was thick enough to accommodate re-doming the chamber and to allow the use of pop-up pistons. These heads were made from 40-E aluminum alloy that was originally developed for the military to be used on equipment where extra strength was needed.

For the powerboat racing crowd, Earl introduced flathead marine heads. These had three water outlets located along the upper edge of the head, and the combustion chambers contained enough material that they could be run in a pop-up piston configuration. Earl also gave his cylinder heads a little extra eye appeal by polishing the fins and sides.

In 1948, Tattersfield & Baron was the first to introduce a commercially successful four-carburetor flathead manifold, which was used in conjunction with pop-up heads and special pistons. It took a while before the notion of equipping a flathead with four carburetors caught on, as the popular three-carb intake seemed quite adequate for most jobs. Only when Al Sharp introduced his four-carburetor in 1952 did other manufacturers follow suit. Earl introduced his version that same year. Gene Ohly recalled that Earl once told him that he got the idea for the Evans four-carburetor manifold design from the gas manifold in the stove in his kitchen. After studying it, he came up with a similar design for the intake manifold.

The only Evans manifold ever designed for an overhead-valve V-8 engine was for the Oldsmobile. In 1956, Earl introduced a three-carburetor, dual-throated manifold. Gene figured that possibly only three of these intakes were ever cast. The original wood pattern still remains in Ohly's storage shed, along with many of Earl's flathead patterns. Another rare piece of Evans equipment was the cast-aluminum gas pedal that was popularized by Al Sharp.

DRY LAKES RACING

To run at a dry lakes meet put on by one of the sanctioning organizations, a racer had to belong to a recognized car club that followed the guidelines of that particular sanctioning body. Among the organizations that held races on the lakebeds, the RTA and SCTA were the most prominent. The SCTA had classes for roadsters and lakesters only, while the RTA also included hardtops (coupes/sedans).

Being in the speed equipment business and a lakes competitor, it made business sense for Earl to belong to both major organizations. He joined the Road Runners car club to run SCTA and the Hutters club to run RTA. To get the biggest advertising bang for his buck, Earl chose to compete with a belly-tank lakester to draw the most attention to his speed equipment. The akester used a surplus aircraft fuel tank that was outfitted with wheels and had the driver and engine stuffed into the small confines of the egg-shaped, metal body. He had the lakester painted a color called "Burple," created by Bill Burke, who first came up with the idea of using the streamlined tanks to make racers. Burke combined purple paint with a mystery mix to produce the flamboyant color. Earl's tank had a white body with flowing Burple flames on the nose section, resulting in a rather distinctive lakester.

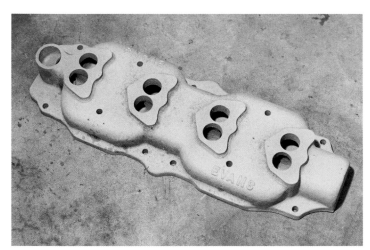

Earl conceived the Evans four-carburetor intake manifold introduced in 1952 after studying the plumbing of the gas stove in his kitchen. *Courtesy Gene Ohly*

Gene Ohly holds an unmachined Evans four-carb manifold that was misplaced about fifty years ago and recently found in the Evans' storage shed. *Author photo*

The Evans tank proved quite formidable at the lakes, consistently finishing first or close to the top and setting the record for its class on numerous occasions. The car was piloted mainly by two drivers, Bob Ward and George Bentley. The majority of the driving was done by George, who later on teamed up with the Sadd brothers and Al Teague to capture records of their own with a high-speed roadster on the salt flats of Bonneville.

The Evans car was a regular competitor during the early days of Bonneville and was there for the inaugural meet of 1949, when it set the class record for C/Streamliner at 166 miles per hour. The following year, Ward was clocked at 175.76 miles per hour to set the speed record for belly tanks. At the 1951 Speed Week, Bob again was behind the wheel of the tank as Earl experimented with two different flathead engine combinations for the same class. It captured C/Lakester with a 180-mile-per-hour two-way average. One run reached a blistering 188 miles per hour down the salt bed, which was outstanding for a normally aspirated (carbureted) flathead.

The Evans tank also was successful on the dry lakes. During the SCTA's 1950 Finals, the C class car set high speed for the meet with a run of 166 miles per hour. Under the RTA banner, Earl's tank was classified as a B/Streamliner and set a fast time of 161 miles per hour. During the 1950 RTA season finals, he installed the Mercury V-8 from the belly tank into Fred Carrillo's 1927 rear-engined roadster, where it set the second fastest time of the meet at 156 miles per hour.

Leslie Long said that he recalled an engine that Doug Hartelt and Chuck Potvin souped up to run in the Evans lakester. At El Mirage in 1950, the car set the record for its class with a run of 172.74 miles per hour on straight methanol, tossing a rod while achieving the record. At that time, this run was the fastest time ever recorded by the SCTA on the dry lakes.

The following year, the Evans car achieved fast time at a RTA meet, setting B class at a very quick 177.33 miles per hour, which also was the fastest time ever recorded at a RTA-sanctioned meet. In the SCTA division, Earl's streamliner did even better in 1951 with Johnny Dahm in the driver's seat, setting a record of 181.08 miles per hour that was also the all-time high-speed record for the 1.3-mile course at El Mirage.

In 1952, NASCAR invited five cars to Daytona Speed Week for the annual Time Trials that were held on the flat, hard surface of the beach. The group included Earl and his driver, George Bentley, with the Evans tank, Ak Miller with his T roadster, the So-Cal streamliner (which flipped), a roadster from Texas, and one other car. Gene can't remember who the last car belonged to, but he does recall Bentley taking a pesky reporter for a fast trip down the beach, straddling the rear of the tank like a wild bronco rider.

No doubt one of the last times Earl was at the dry lakes was the RTA meet at El Mirage in 1960. Gene Ohly and Harry Mardon had built a formable C/FR class 1929 roadster for Bonneville and the dry lakes, with the Evans shop as one of their main sponsors. Earl was there to assist the two fellows with their blown Chevy-powered roadster, which set the class record at 189 miles per hour.

DRAG RACING

Earl was a dry lakes racer at heart, but when organized drag racing showed its head in Southern California, like everyone else, he had to have a look and see what the commotion was all about. In 1950, members of the SCTA and the AMA collaborated to put on an event at the old navy blimp base near Santa Ana. It was to be a drag race demonstration with motorcycles and hot rods competing in runoffs over a measured quarter-mile course. The main feature of the meet was a final runoff between four of the fastest cars against four of the fastest motorcycles.

There were two dry lakes belly tanks on hand to run for exhibition purposes, and the Evans tank was one of them. The tank ran a direct-drive system without a clutch or transmission, so Bob

The Evans display at a *Hot Rod* magazine show with Earl standing behind a fully loaded and highly polished flathead. *Courtesy Gene Ohly*

QUARTER-MIDGETS

Before the go kart craze sprouted up in Southern California and spread across the continent, there were quarter-midgets. These pint-sized little speedsters were miniature copies of sprint cars. Their rapid growth in popularity spawned a variety of companies that manufactured everything from engine accessories to complete ready-to-race jobs. Quarter-midgets were an ideal and affordable way to introduce kids to the world of auto racing and for the dad who, for one reason or another, never got to race a car to get his son (or daughter) involved in the sport.

No doubt Earl also saw a profitable business in producing custom speed parts with little capital investment for these little racers. His original product in 1956 was a high-compression head for the small, Continental Red Seal AU-7 two-horsepower engine. After a favorable response to the head, Earl came out with a complete line of performance parts that included everything from a cast-aluminum heavy-duty gearbox, sump pan, modified distributor, ball bearing–equipped crankcase side plates, and even miniature cast-aluminum throttle pedals. Not having the machinery to grind camshafts, he had Gus Garnat (who learned camshaft grinding from Pierre Bertrand) grind performance cams for the Continental engines. The Evans line of quarter-midget products was so successful that it was soon copied by other manufacturers. These quarter-midget items were probably the last products that Earl manufactured with the Evans name cast on them.

GENE OHLY

The shop that Earl built back in 1952 on Seaman Ave in South El Monte is still in operation as Evans Speed Equipment under its present-day owner, Gene Ohly, who was one of Earl's early employees. Gene was hired on at the Evans shop as part-time help during the summer months of 1952 and 1953 and was assigned to drilling head bolt patterns on the 24-stud head. He also learned how to polish the edges and tops of the fins to highlight the heads—an Evans trademark. Later on, Earl's son-in-law, Edmund Potts, taught Gene how to bore blocks and install exhaust seats in them.

Upon graduating from high school, Gene had his sights on dentistry and enrolled in a predental college course. Instead of returning to Earl's shop for that summer, he landed a job as a ready-mix truck driver for a rock and sand outfit. The sheer enjoyment and freedom of working outdoors was enough to distract him from any future plans of attending dentistry school.

While Gene was in the navy in 1962, Earl passed away due to complications from a blood clot. Once back in civilian life, Gene was approached by Catherine Evans to see if he would be interested in taking over the business. Earl had mentioned to her before his death that of all the people who had worked for him, Gene might be the most interested in buying the business.

After purchasing the machine shop from Catherine, Gene hired his first employee, Al Teague, the future world speed record-holder for a single-engine streamliner. Al worked at the Evans shop for 15 years.

Ward had to use a rolling start off the line, yet he posted the top overall speed of the meet at 120.96 miles per hour.

POP OR PAPPY?

There is some misconception regarding the nickname "Pop" when referring to Earl Evans. Being older than most of the fellows at the dry lakes meets, Earl no doubt received a nickname such as "Pappy" or "Pop" from his friends, but he wasn't the first "Pop" Evans to appear on the Southern California racing scene. A prewar track racer by the name of C. D. "Pop" Evans moved from Texas to California in the early days of racing, when the race cars were powered by Model T engines. This "Pop" Evans was also in the manufacturing business, offering a high-performance head for the Model A Ford known as the Pop Evans high turbulence head, which had a re-entrance baffle that was angular rather than straight across like most others. According to Barney Navarro, the first "Pop" Evans was a colorful character with a distinctive handlebar mustache.

By 1941, C. D. "Pop" Evans was the chief track engineer for the American Racing Association, and he and his crew would travel throughout California preparing various tracks for upcoming races. He was 91 years old when he passed away in 1967 in Glendale, California.

The Evans reputation for producing fine engine machine work grew steadily over the years. Today, the shop does a large cross-section of custom engine work that encompasses everything from replacing valve seats in the flathead V-8 to precision line boring of Rolls-Royce and Allison aircraft engine blocks. Gene and his shop foreman, Jaime Gonzalez, do a fair amount of line boring for Frontier Aviation of Dallas. Gene says engine builder Dave Zeuschel got him into machine work on aircraft engines. A large portion of Evans' work consists of custom machining for engine builders of race cars, antiques, and so on.

Years ago, Gene partnered with Harry Mardon in a fuel-burning roadster that ran at Bonneville and the lakes. The pair belonged to the Rod Riders car club, which originally ran under the RTA and later with SCTA. Gene was not normally behind the steering wheel at these high-speed meets, but he did manage to make a 195-mile-per-hour pass at Bonneville. The record-holding duo took on another partner—George Bentley—and continued to set records in the C/FR class. Gene still has the proud, old, Ohly-Mardon-Bentley roadster stored under a tarpaulin, waiting to be restored to its former record-setting glory.

Both Earl and Gene have been inducted into the Dry Lakes Hall of Fame.

FRED CARRILLO

In the early 1950s, a young hot rod enthusiast by the name of Fred Carrillo got a job at the Evans shop. He recalled that one of his tasks at the Seaman Avenue shop was building custom engines. He mentioned that many of these full race V-8s were sold to the likes of Junior Johnson and other notable moonshine transporters back east, where speed was an important factor.

Hot Rod featured Fred's bright yellow '27 T roadster as the Hot Rod of the Month in its July 1952 issue, with a beautiful color shot of the car on the front cover. The photo of the Evans Custom Engines–sponsored rear-engined roadster with the trunk lid removed showed just how immaculate and well engineered the car was. Its construction was a collaboration between Fred and his brother-in-law, Robert Betz (an automotive paint specialist). The Evans-equipped 296-inch Mercury was a product of Earl's shop. The car set the fastest time for a roadster at the 1951 Bonneville Nationals, with a speed of 178 miles per hour.

Carrillo recalled that, while working at Evans, a young local hot rodder named Mickey Thompson hung around the shop. Mickey ran one of Evans' full-race V-8s in a record-setting '36 Ford coupe. It was said that Mickey sold several engines out of that coupe after setting the record, and that each engine was reputed to be "the one" that set the record.

After his success with the Ford coupe, Mickey got into the record books again using Earl's equipment. At the 1952 Bonneville meet, Mickey ran a rather unique dual-engine Bantam coupe. The Liqui Moly–sponsored D/Competition coupe was powered by two inline, normally aspirated, Ford V-8s equipped with Evans heads and intake manifolds. Mickey ran 194 miles per hour for a two-way average and had one amazing run of 198 miles per hour.

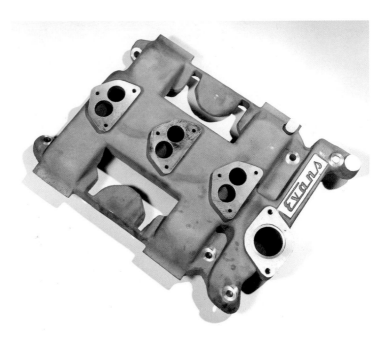

The only piece of speed equipment manufactured by Earl that wasn't for a Ford product, outside of a head for the Studebaker flathead six, was this three-carburetor Oldsmobile manifold unveiled in 1956. According to Gene Ohly, only three were ever produced. *Courtesy Gene Ohly*

Many years later, Fred built a radically designed stream-liner for Bonneville—the infamous *United Auto Special*. He was traveling an estimated 250 miles per hour when the car began to drift from the black line, crashed, and was destroyed, although Carrillo survived. Leaving the dangers of high speeds for others, Fred went on to develop the world-famous Carrillo Rods.

MORE THAN A MANUFACTURER

From all indications, Earl Evans was a soft-spoken, unassuming fellow who let his speed equipment and mechanical talent speak for themselves. Those who remember Earl from the old days cannot express enough kindness toward this quiet, humble gentleman.

It's obvious from the outstanding performance of the Evans streamliner on the salt flats of Bonneville and the lakebed of El Mirage that Earl was far more than just a speed equipment manufacturer. A considerable amount of mechanical talent was required to design and manufacture engine components, complete the casting and machining, and to build a record-setting race car, modify the engine to motivate that car, tune it for a variety of running conditions, and so on. He possessed very similar qualities to Barney Navarro—an intelligent and formidable force tied up in one man.

EVANS EPILOGUE

In 2007, Gene's shop foreman, Jaime Gonzalez, took over Evans. A nostalgia enthusiast, Gonzalez plans to reintroduce Evans speed equipment.

CHAPTER 8

Herbert Racing Cams

CHET HERBERT

Like Henry's Model T, which was offered in any color so long as it was black, in the postwar era of hot rodding, a performance-minded engine builder could purchase any aftermarket racing camshaft . . . as long as it was a flat-tappet model. Chet Herbert was convinced of the benefits of the roller camshaft and set about to prove it.

Growing up in Southern California wasn't a guarantee that summer vacations would be spent on the beaches, surfing, and taking in the wildlife. Some high school students had jobs, especially if they wanted cars and motorcycles. Chet was one who wanted his toys, and he spent several summers with his buddy Jay Burgess slugging hefty sacks of sugar at the Clark Sugar Mill in Santa Ana. Upon graduating from Santa Ana High in 1945, Chet saw an opportunity to get into the trucking business and landed a government contract to haul sugar throughout Southern California.

STREET RODS AND MOTORCYCLES

His first car was a run-of-the-mill '36 Ford coupe, but his second car was a jet-black 1939 Mercury convertible with a padded, nonfolding, Carson-style top. The Carson top was popular at the time and Chet, being industrious, figured that he could make his own. Hours of labor were spent modifying the top, wrenching on the engine, and spraying on a polished black-lacquer paint job. Chet sold the street rod so he could go on to other projects. Unfortunately, the car met an unglorious end when the new owner lost control on a canyon road and rolled it over an embankment with three passengers in the vehicle. The Merc was totaled, while the youths only sustained minor cuts and bruises, saved no doubt by Chet's top, which remained intact during the rollover.

In 1946, he made the transition from four to two wheels with a 61-ci Harley-Davidson. Not content with the bike's performance, he studied the engine and it appeared that the valvetrain was the weak link and could be improved upon. He modified the cam timing and spent hours hand-filing and reshaping the cam before coming up with a workable profile that actually did improve the bike's performance. Although he knew very little about the complexities of camshaft design, when all was said and done, Chet owned one of the fastest bikes in the area. It was while attempting to alter the motorcycle's valve timing that he first became aware of camshaft design, its function, and the roller tappet. Harley used the roller in its engines, and it was this device that would provide the cornerstone for the future Herbert Cams.

ALLISON V-6

Surplus aircraft engines were plentiful after the war, and, outside of powerboat racing, there wasn't much demand for the monstrous relics. Gene Ellis remembered that Allison V-12 aircraft engines in new condition could be purchased very reasonably from the surplus stores and could be had with or without a supercharger.

Chet's first encounter with these engines occurred when he happened to stop in at an oil-drilling outfit and noticed a stack of them in the yard. He asked a worker about the engines and was told that they were either going to be installed in heavy-duty trucks or converted to power some oil-drilling machinery. Chet watched as they tried unsuccessfully to start one of these behemoths. Thinking he

Opposite: Chet Herbert and driver Art Chrisman in front of the *Beast III* at the 1952 Bonneville Nationals, with the crewmembers behind the streamliner. Art drove the D class streamliner to a record of 235.99 miles per hour, making it the fastest single-engine car in America. *Courtesy Chet Herbert*

Wanting something different for a street rod, Chet cut an Allison V-12 in half to make one powerful V-6 engine. Unfortunately he didn't know about the reverse rotation on some of these monsters and never got the project up and running. Note the Model B carburetor on the fabricated manifold camshaft, and that cover is off the right bank of the engine—no doubt, Chet was trying to figure out the timing. *Courtesy Chet Herbert*

could do better than a bunch of oil workers, he offered to give it a try. Lucky or not, Chet got the engine to fire, which impressed the owner enough that he was offered a job.

The experience with the Allison tweaked Chet's interest enough that he bought five of the surplus V-12s. He could visualize one of these exotic engines in a hot rod. Realizing the weight and dimensions would be prohibitive in a vehicle, he decided to cut the engine in half. This one-of-a-kind V-6 was to be installed in a Buick frame with a custom-built aluminum body.

He had Red's Welding Shop in Anaheim slice the Allison in half and complete the welding and fabrication work on the engine. Gene Ellis contributed a Model B carburetor for the engine's homemade manifold. A modified automotive distributor was adapted to the engine, and a radiator was hooked up to cool the engine via a water pump driven by an electric motor. The half-block Allison was bolted down to a wooden frame for testing, and when it came time to fire it up, it wouldn't. Chet said that everything that could be thought of was done to that engine, but it never fired.

Chet said, "I never got the engine running. The problem was that I didn't know P-38s had right- and left-hand rotation engines in them, and those were left-hand rotating engines. I was trying to run it as a right-hand rotation engine. Later, somebody asked me if I knew that there were right- and left-rotation Allisons. I checked the cams, and sure enough they were left-hand rotation; the cams were all ground to run the other way. I only cut the one engine and sold the remaining engines to a guy who raced hydroplanes."

Later on, he experimented with the Allison's camshaft profile ground onto an automotive cam that produced some degree of interest.

The motorcycle that started Herbert Racing Cams. The Beast was a highly modified, nitro-burning 80-inch Harley-Davidson that was the scourge of the Santa Ana drag strip. From 1950 to 1951, Chet's bike usually set fast time of the day at the strip. *Leslie Long collection, courtesy Chet Herbert*

POLIO AND A CAREER CHANGE

Poliomyelitis was a feared disease that afflicted scores of young people the world over until a vaccine was finally developed to eradicate the virus. Unfortunately for Chet, in 1948, he came down with the disease. After being hospitalized for eight months, he was left confined to a wheelchair. The 20-year-old was now confronted with the fact that his life was forever changed, and he had to rethink his future. His options were limited, but whatever he was going to do, it had to be involved in the performance field.

In early 1949, Chet figured that he could start a business producing performance Harley-Davidson camshafts using what experience he already had. Realizing that there was no way he could possibly reshape the bike cams by hand, he needed some sort of grinding machine After a bit of searching, he settled on a Sears, Roebuck bench-top metal lathe. A grinding-wheel mechanism was attached to the lathe bed so it rolled onto the camshaft that was positioned in the head and tail stock.

Chet rented some space in Ernie Backman's automotive repair shop in a Quonset hut on 2049 South Main Street in Santa Ana, and he was in business.

THE BEAST

Although Chet built a number of Bonneville cars called *The Beast*, the original was a nitromethane-addicted 1948 Harley-Davidson 80-ci motorcycle. The fact that he wouldn't be able to ride was of little concern; he wanted the challenge of modifying a motorcycle to see what she'd do at the dry lakes and on the drag strip. Plus, he needed a fast billboard for his fledgling camshaft business.

The bike was stripped down to the barest necessities, while the engine had the cam reground, valvetrain worked over, modified pistons installed, and two floatless Offenhauser midget carburetors set up to burn a mixture of alcohol and nitro.

Gene Ellis made the pistons by building up the tops of the stock pistons with aluminum welding rod in order to achieve the right compression ratio. The pistons were then hand-ground to fit the modified combustion chamber, and the skirts were cut back to keep the weight in check. Gene said, "There was never a problem with those pistons while they raced the bike, burning very decent loads of nitro." The clutch and brake controls were moved to the rear footpegs, and the handlebars were lowered to the point where the rider was in an almost prone position. *The Beast* was also one of the first motorcycles to run a drag slick that was made by cutting off the rounded shoulder of a re-tread oval-track racing tire.

Gene recalled the time he took *The Beast* out for a test run down Harbor Boulevard in Anaheim: "It was quite uninhabited in those days, so a ride down the road at full speed with open exhausts wasn't too much to be concerned with, unless the local constabulary happened to appear on the scene. I rode the bike in the 'flaked-out' position, lying straight out on the bike." Flaking out on motorcycles was eventually outlawed by racing organizations, requiring the riders keep their feet on the footpegs. The bike was such a handful to control under full power that the name "Beast" seemed only fitting.

At the second drag race meet held at Orange County Airport (Santa Ana) on July 16, 1950, Al Keyes rode *The Beast* on a 103-mile-per-hour run for the fastest time of the day and took home Top Eliminator. Later that summer, the bike won the "fastest-thing-on-wheels" honors, clocking in at 119.20 miles per hour. *The Beast* all but ruled the first season of racing at Santa Ana. By 1951, the bike had upped the strip record to an incredible 138 miles per hour. Four-wheeled competitors were complaining that motorcycles had an unfair advantage and should be disqualified from Top Eliminator. That same year, *The Beast* was filmed at the drag strip for a movie called *Sportlight*, produced by Grantland Rice.

Gene said they could compete in several races in one day if they hurried. "Chet, Al Keyes, and I hitched up the motorcycle trailer behind Chet's '39 Mercury sedan. After topping off the crankcase with Union 76 purple oil (it burned and leaked oil at an incredible rate), we headed for a meet at Rosamond Dry Lake. At the lake, Keyes won the fast time of the day (158 miles per hour), and then it was a hurried 110-mile drive back to Santa Ana, where the bike took Top Eliminator."

The Beast and nine other top motorcycles, members of the AMA, were invited to participate at the 1951 Bonneville Nationals. Unfortunately, a poorly designed streamlined fairing had been installed on *The Beast* that unbalanced it to the point where the team couldn't get a complete run out of bike and cancelled any further attempts.

It took the combined talents of Chet, Gene Ellis, and Roy Felkner to build the record-breaking motorcycle and the skills and nerve of drivers Al Keyes, Johnny Hutton, and Ted Lorio to power the thing down the quarter-mile.

As business demands grew and other projects were developed, there was no time for *The Beast*, so the bike was sold to a party in Chicago. Rumor has it that *The Beast* eventually ended up in Florida.

Don Turner (McGurk employee and early drag racer) recalled, "I was standing at the start line at Santa Ana and watching *The Beast* take off from the line with flames of excess nitro burning as it overflowed out of the two floatless carburetors." It seems that this was a common occurrence.

In the early days at Santa Ana, C. J. Hart would have a "fastest-car-of-the-day" race at the end of the day. It usually would be between a motorcycle and a car. The drag bikes had the fast ETs, but the cars had it on the top end because of the horsepower difference. Two very formidable motorcycle opponents at that time were Bud Hare, with his twin 40-ci Triumph bike called *Double Trouble*, and Chet's infamous Harley-Davidson. Usually, one of

Chet's *Beast III* at Bonneville in 1952. Chet is in the wheelchair just behind the streamliner, talking to the starter. The D/Streamliner set the class record at 235.99 miles per hour and became the fastest single-engine car in America. *Leslie Long collection, courtesy Chet Herbert*

these two bikes would be the contender for the runoff trophy if they didn't explode in nitromethane flames racing each other.

Ollie Morris was another drag racer who ran at the Orange County Airport strip with his famous *White Owl* flathead dragster that sat in the winner's circle more than most. "I remember seeing both bikes just explode in flames coming off the line," Ollie said. "The majority of the time, it was the *White Owl* racing one of these two bikes. My car was damn quick off the line, and Bud Hare was damn sharp off the line. Al Keyes was pretty damn good, and *The Beast* usually ran a better time than Hare, but the rider was so [expletive] busy to keep from setting himself on fire that he couldn't always concentrate on the race."

CHEVY SIX ROLLER

The final push into the automotive cam business came about from a partnership with Gene Ellis to build a CRA track roadster. Chet's engine preference was the 270-ci GMC truck six-cylinder, as he recognized the benefits of an overhead-valve configuration over the customary flathead V-8. From the experience of modifying Harleys with roller-tappet camshafts, he felt that a roller provided timing, lift, and speed beyond that of a flat tappet. Because he had no luck getting one of the established camshaft companies to grind him a roller cam for the GMC, he decided to grind his own. He chose a Chevrolet forged-steel camshaft core to grind because it could withstand the wearing characteristics of a roller tappet and it was interchangeable with the 270 GMC.

The mechanical process of grinding the Chevy cam was similar to that of grinding a motorcycle cam. After he had what he wanted for lift and duration transferred onto a master cam, Chet ground his first automotive roller-tappet camshaft. He used brass sleeve guides in the engine's lifter bosses to keep the rollers running in line with the cam lobes.

The methanol-burning GMC was set up with six Riley midget side-draft floatless carburetors on a custom-made intake manifold, a Spalding ignition, a Wayne Horning 12-port head, Venolia pistons, and Chet's roller camshaft. Gene's part in this deal was to build the '24 T track roadster and be its driver.

Once completed, it was off to Carrell Speedway for some shake-down runs before entering it in the races that same night. Once on the track, Gene said that he increased the speed with each lap until he set a new track record. During a race later that day, the carburetors leaned out and caused internal damage to the engine. Floatless carburetors were bears to tune at the best of times, and the duo replaced them with a more reliable Hilborn injection system. It soon became apparent to other car owners that the Herbert-Ellis roadster was pulling very strong for a six, and they started to get curious about this newfangled roller cam. Chet knew he'd found his niche in the automotive field.

1949

The prospect of grinding automotive roller cams looked promising, but if Chet were going to venture into that market, he'd need something a little more substantial than a converted Sears, Roebuck lathe. Its replacement was a piston grinder that was purchased from Santa Ana Motor Parts and converted into a cam grinder. To make it convenient to operate, Chet mounted all his master-cam templates directly to the grinder. All he had to do was move the duplicating wheel over to the desired master cam that was to be ground onto the camshaft.

The Harley roller Chet had been using was perfect for motorcycle engines but not for the high horsepower and abuse of an automobile engine, so it was replaced with an improved steel roller-tappet body.

The potential of Chet's roller cam was authenticated in 1950, when Dagwood Johnson ran a Champ Car powered by a Herbert-built, bored and stroked 270 Chevy with a Wayne 12-port head and Hilborn injection. The car was even featured in racing scenes from the movie *To Please a Lady*, starring Clark Gable and

Barbara Stanwyck. While some of the racing scenes for the movie were being filmed at the one-mile Arlington Downs dirt track in Texas, the Johnson car also ran in a championship race held at the track during the filming. Spec Frieden drove the Chevy-powered car and qualified second fastest for the 30-lap main against the feisty Offenhausers, only to run out of fuel during the race.

Soon, the cam business outgrew Backman's garage. In 1951, Herbert Cams moved to Tony Capanna's Wilcap shop on South San Pedro Street in Los Angeles. Tony had a dynamometer, which greatly influenced Chet's cam development.

Initially, Chet specialized in grinding cams for Harleys, Chevrolet/GMC six-cylinders, and Buick straight eights. Being the only cam grinder specializing in performance roller camshafts, inquiries from owners of Chrysler, Cadillac, and Olds V-8 engines led him to introduce a line of engineered steel-billet roller cams for those engines. Although he was partial to overhead-valve engines, especially the Chevrolet, Chet did grind roller cams for Ford flatheads that were equipped with Ardun overhead-valve conversions.

Herbert Cams began its business based solely on the roller tappet, but over time Chet realized that the company was missing a sizeable market of racing classes that were restricted to flat-tappet usage only, so he began to offer flat-tappet cams in 1964.

MOVING

By 1953, the facilities at Wilcap proved inadequate for his needs. Chet moved to a corner-lot building on East Firestone in South Gate, which lasted about a year before he relocated to Anaheim. This larger facility had more than enough room for his camshaft business. Being the entrepreneurial sort, Chet also opened the Herbert Muffler Shop. It was during this time that Chet hired his neighbor's 13-year-old kid, Zane Shubert, to do part-time cleanup and gofer duties around the place. Then the day came when Chet's shop was designated as part of the Santa Ana Freeway (later renamed Manchester). This time, the journey to a new shop was just across the highway, to where he's been located for the last 50-plus years, just a stone's throw from Disneyland.

'32 HOT ROD

Chet had not had a personal hot rod since the Carson-topped '39 Merc, and around 1950, he decided it was time to build another one. This new one wasn't a traditional street rod for those days. It was based on a chopped and channeled '32 Ford four-door sedan with all its fenders removed, a dropped axle, air brakes, 25 coats of black lacquer, and a GMC sitting between the frame rails. A 1950 Buick Dynaflow automatic transmission was mated to the hopped-up 270 GMC converted to run on butane, supplying two Century side-draft carburetors with a butane tank mounted in the rear seating area. It had a 12-volt starting system, while a 6-volt system ran the lights. Hand levers for the gas and brakes enabled Chet to drive the car.

The sedan saw little street time, as the engine was in constant demand for dry lakes racing. For racing, the butane outfit was removed in favor of a more aggressive Hilborn injector system. At Bonneville in 1951, the engine powered the DuBont-Herbert *Beast*

The twin-engine *Beast V* at the 1954 Bonneville Nationals. Note the open cockpit and the magnetos sticking up through the body panels. *Courtesy Chet Herbert*

II, a modified Crosley, to a C/Modified record of 149 miles per hour with a one-way run of 154. The GMC also pushed Ed Pink's 1936 Ford coupe to a 133-mile-per-hour class B/Coupe record at the dry lakes. At one Bonneville meet, Chet's engine set three different class records running on six, four, and three cylinders. He simply removed two and then three of the spark plugs and re-directed the individual injector fuel lines back to the fuel tank.

Hot Rod featured the car as the Hot Rod of the Month in its March 1952 issue. It was advertised for sale in the April issue, complete with the 275-horsepower butane-burning GMC. In 1955, the sedan surfaced in a magazine article equipped with a modified V-8 flathead in place of the Jimmy six.

INDY

Due to his knowledge of nitro as an alternative fuel, Chet was asked by car owner Ernie Ruiz to crew his Travelon Trailer–sponsored race car for the 1953 Indy race. Chet accompanied Gene Ellis and Gene's father in their pickup truck to Indianapolis. Jim Rathmann replaced the injured Troy Ruttman and, after qualifying the car to start 25th, fought his way up to finish in 7th place.

For the 1954 race, Chet was hired to convert a stock Chrysler Hemi V-8 into an SOHC racing engine. The owners of the *Shouse Motors Special* felt this might just be the engine to defeat the mighty Offenhauser. Chet designed a set of cast cam towers that attached to the top side of the stock Hemi heads. A gear attached to the engine's stock camshaft was used to drive two shafts that ran up through the engine's heat risers to drive the overhead cams. When the valve covers were in place, the Chrysler looked just like a stock overhead-valve engine. The converted SOHC Hemi performed up to its expectations on the Wilcap dynamometer and then was installed in a race car and taken to Indy for trial runs with driver Pat Flaherty.

The main bearings went out during warmup laps. After the crank was reground and installed with new bearings, the engine suffered the same failure. By time the problem was finally resolved, it was too late to qualify for the 500. The full potential of this cammer engine was never realized, as the owners set it aside for the more reliable Offy.

BONNEVILLE

In keeping with the name, *Beast II* was a team effort of Chet and Jim DuBont of DuBont Motors in South Figeroa in Los Angeles. Their C/Modified Sedan Crosley used the 270 GMC out of Chet's '32 hot rod to set a record during the 1951 Bonneville Nationals with a two-way average of 149.26 miles per hour and a top speed of 154.37 for the class win.

The following year, Chet created *Beast III* and had Schapel Engineering of Inglewood, California, develop the design and plans for the construction of the streamliner body. A one-tenth scale model was wind tested and proven to be stable at high speeds. Chet mentioned that it was one of the first such wind-tunnel tests conducted in the United States for a land-speed vehicle. The custom tubular frame was originally designed around the Franklin engine, but when it self-destructed on the dynamometer stand,

Preparing to leave for the AHRA's seventh annual championship drags in Green Valley, Texas, in 1961. Left to right are Zane Shubert, Chet, Don Brown, and Dave Cole. Zane's 454-ci, fuel-injected Chevy twin-V-8 dragster is loaded behind Chet's Pontiac convertible. *Courtesy Zane Shubert*

a more powerful Chrysler V-8 was used to fill the vacancy. This Hemi was loaned by Dana Fuller, whose new Chrysler Imperial happened to be in Chet's shop having a roller cam installed. A factory stock Dodge truck clutch and an early 1940s Chrysler flywheel were bolted up to the Hemi, which proved to be the weak link. Later on at Bonneville, the clutch package developed serious slippage problems. The clutch disc had to be bolted directly to the flywheel in order to make the record runs.

The company manufacturing the two-piece fiberglass stream-liner body was behind schedule and finally delivered it to Chet's shop midweek during the Bonneville Nationals. The pieces of the body were taken over to Chrisman & Sons Garage in Compton, where the body was assembled with the assistance of Art, Lloyd, and their father. After a 700-mile trip, the unpainted streamliner arrived at Bonneville that Friday with only two days left for testing and serious running.

George Bentley drove the maiden run to a speed of 182 miles per hour, with two followup runs at 197 and 211 miles per hour. Art Chrisman took over the controls and ran 219, 224, and 230, with a top speed of 235.99 miles per hour to set the class D/Streamliner record. This run established *Beast III* as the fastest single-engine car in America.

Chet came up with a very unusual engine for the 1953 Bonneville trials. An old-timer who'd been around racing for years told Chet about a rather strange-looking engine sitting in a local scrap yard. This radical Wehr engine was the brainchild of a man of the same name who had designed it to compete in the 1932 Indianapolis 500. The engine was a 183-ci, two-cycle, rotary-valve four-cylinder. A straight rotary-valve tube extended all the way through the engine head and used piston rings to separate the ports, but because of a lack of efficient sealing material, the rotary valves would freeze up when the rings expanded. Chet came up with the idea of using hydraulic-assisted tapered cones to replace the rings. With a compression ratio of 14:1 and with the

The foil of many Hemi-powered dragsters was the ultralight *Herbert Cam* Chevy piloted by Zane Shubert, which won more Top Eliminators than any other Chevy-powered dragster in drag racing history. The car mainly ran on straight alcohol while the Hemis suffered under large dosages of nitro. *Courtesy Zane Shubert*

installation of a GMC blower, theoretically the engine should have developed more than 400 horsepower. The supercharged Wehr was hooked up to Tony Capanna's dyno, and just as it was beginning to produce loads of power, the engine self-destructed. Once again, Chet found himself going back to a more conventional engine for Bonneville with another Chrysler Hemi.

Chet contracted George Barris to build an aluminum streamliner body for *Beast IV* that was completed in three weeks of concentrated work just prior to the opening of the 1953 Nationals. During the fabrication of the body, the Wehr engine died and modifications had to be made to accommodate the much larger Chrysler. *Hot Rod* ran a picture of Chet welding the streamliner's chassis on the front cover of its December 1952 issue, and an article on building the car appeared in *Rod & Custom's* January 1954 issue.

Following 1954 Bonneville Nationals, AAA officials held a week-long event in conjunction with the Federation Internationale de l'Automobile (FIA) for cars wishing to compete for international speed records. Leroy Neumayer set six speed records with *Beast V*, taking the B/International class 5-mile and 10-kilometer records with a two-way speed of 233 miles per hour. He set four records in D class. Overall, Neumayer set a one-way high-speed record run of 246 miles per hour, making the Herbert streamliner the fastest single-engine car in America once more.

The following year, a new *Beast VI* streamliner set top time at the flats with a one-way, 256-mile-per-hour run. This *Beast* was a four-wheel-drive E/Streamliner powered by two Dodge Hemi V-8s. The front drive of the car was a modified Jeep unit. When one of the axles broke during a warmup run, the streamliner was estimated to have been running in excess of 260 miles per hour. The broken front end prevented any further speed runs for the 1955 meet.

The next visit to the salt flats was in 1958, when Chet arrived with an E/Streamliner that had three Chevy V-8s connected inline and Dave Ryder handling the driving chores. The car had to

settle for the second-highest one-way speed of 272, next to Mickey Thompson's phenomenal one-way run at 294 miles per hour, after a fire destroyed Chet's middle engine.

LEFTY AND THE *HERBERT CAM SPECIAL*

Chet considered running a dragster to be the best testbed for his products. He used drag racing to get first-hand knowledge of how his camshafts were performing and to try out specific engine modifications. He'd sponsored single-engine dragsters, but the twins really held his interest.

The first successful partnership for a Herbert twin-engine car was around 1958 with chassis builder Allen "Lefty" Mudersbach. Lefty's original lightweight dragster ran an odd combination of two tandem-mounted Herbert Chevrolet V-8s. One engine was 331 ci while the other was punched out to 351. Each was equipped with six Stromberg 97 carburetors and "zoomie" headers. Eventually, the engines were enlarged to 402 ci each and Hilborn fuel injection replaced the 12 carbs.

In 1961, Herbert Cams introduced the Pulsation camshaft. Using Lefty's dragster as a rolling testbed under documented conditions, the camshaft added 14 miles per hour to Mudersbach's top-end speed and set a strip record of 184.42 miles per hour on gasoline at Long Beach.

THE BEARD

The most well-known and successful relationship Chet had with any of his drivers was with Zane Shubert. In the late 1950s while still in school, Zane grew a beard, which eventually earned him the nickname "The Beard." He started drag racing while still in high school, going through several different classes and graduating to dragsters by the time he turned 20. Zane had just built his first dragster and hadn't yet decided what kind of engine he was going to run when Chet noticed the chassis and offered him an engine. The only condition was that Zane had to keep up the maintenance and return the engine when he was finished with it.

Zane Shubert at Lions in the Herbert Cam fuel-injected Olds twin-aluminum-V-8 dragster. Mickey Thompson is second from the right, giving the car a thoughtful going over. Mickey later came out with a similar car. Note the plywood for streamlining purposes. The car originally ran fuel injection; later, when GMC blowers were added, it set record ETs on pump gasoline. *Courtesy Zane Shubert*

The engine was a supercharged Chevy V-8 out of Lefty Mudersbach's old single-engine dragster. It had been bored out to 300 ci with a square Enderle injector sitting on top of a 4:71 GMC blower and a Herbert roller. The water passages in the engine block were filled solid, but the engine ran with water-cooled heads.

"Back in those days, guys used to try to burn me on the line," Zane said. "I could sit there forever. We started off running C/Gas because we couldn't afford to buy fuel. If I had $10 when I came home from racing, I was doing good.

"We ran the orange-painted car for about eight months and then built the twin fuel-injected car. Chet offered to supply two engines if I'd build the chassis . . . it'd be a rolling experimental lab for Chet, who wasn't too fond of blowers. The twin injected engines would make up the difference of a blown engine. We went on to win the AHRA Winternationals with Don Brown and Dave Cole as pit crew members."

In 1961, the 21-year-old was piloting the Shubert-Herbert twin Chevy-powered AA/F dragster that was one of the longest-wheelbase dragsters running at the time. It had two experimental Chevrolet engine blocks given to Chet by General Motors' chief engineer, Zora Arkus-Duntov. The 4.25 stroke by 4.125 bore engines had a displacement of 454 ci, adding up to 908 inches total. The chassis was designed with a removable suspension system, as Chet felt that an adjustable, sprung rear axle might help out on rough track surfaces. This suspension consisted of two containers holding three valve springs each, which allowed the rear axle about an inch of travel and was adjustable depending on track conditions. Zane said that the mechanism was heavy and was only used on a particularly rough strip in Texas.

The business arrangement between Zane and Chet was that Zane's wages would be half of whatever prize money they won. This worked out fine, as the team was taking Top Eliminator on a regular basis. Only once did the arrangement work against Shubert—the American Hot Rod Association (AHRA) 7th Annual Championship Drags held at Green Valley, Texas, in 1961. They'd hauled the AA/F dragster behind Chet's '60 Pontiac convertible, with Don Brown and Dave Cole as pit crew, and Lefty Mudersbach accompanying them with his AA/G dragster.

The final runoff for Overall Top Eliminator was between Zane and Ed Garlits. As Zane was being pushed down the side road to start the car, he noticed that there was no oil pressure in the front engine.

"I pointed to Dave to go back and ask Chet if he wanted me to run or not." Zane said Dave came back and pointed, "Go!"

When Don Garlits, who was staging his brother, saw Zane's predicament, he kept Ed from staging as long as possible. Mudersbach, who was helping stage the Shubert car, picked up on what was going on. He promptly grabbed the removable push bar from Zane's car and moved toward Don with intent; Ed was quickly staged.

"The flagman saw what was going on, and as soon as Garlits was staged, he jerked the green flag and I was gone," Zane said. "Halfway down, the front engine blew with flames blowing back, but I kept my foot in it 'til the end."

Zane took Top Eliminator, turning in a winning speed of 179.28. Lefty won the AA/G dragster class, and although he was beat out by Ed Garlits in an A/G dragster for Top Gas Eliminator, it was a pretty good showing for the Herbert Cams–sponsored cars. Instead of a cash prize, Top Eliminator was awarded a new Pontiac Tempest convertible. Zane couldn't afford to buy Chet's half of the prize, and Chet already had a new car, so Zane's parents bought out Chet's interest. "All I got out of the deal was the publicity from winning the race," Zane said.

ULTRALIGHT DRAGSTERS

The Shubert-Herbert ultralight cars didn't run the popular Chrysler rearend (which had a low pinion takeoff), as did most dragsters in those days. The S-H cars used a Championship quick-change, with the pinion coming out of the center and a 5-inch magnesium driveshaft that allowed the nose of the engine to be tilted down as low as possible to keep the weight off the front of the car. At first, the crankshaft-driven blower pulley was barely off the ground, but later a steel skid plate was installed below the new pulley. Even with a cast-iron Chevrolet block, the S-H cars weighed less than 1,000 pounds.

"One chassis I built didn't have any uprights between the tube rails, and it really flexed," Zane said. "The front axle was welded to the frame. It had no wishbones on it, no suspension at all. The rules of the day said that you had to have suspension on the front end, so I made it look as if there was suspension. The chassis was .035-inch wall thickness. In those days, if you could get it off the trailer, it was legal.

"When I first made the chassis, we did a trial run on the street in front of my shop, and the whole car collapsed. The frame bent down, so we took it back to the shop and put a block of wood under the frame rails, heated them up with a torch, bent the front wheels back down, and welded a little piece of plate in the side to give it a little more strength.

"This car didn't have any rear motor mounts," Zane added. "Each side of the Chevrolet engine has three holes where the motor mount goes on. I put one 3/8-inch bolt in each side, and that was the only thing that held the motor in the car. There was no rear mount in it at all. The weight of the back of the engine was sitting on the rearend. To keep the engine aligned, there were two tubes attached from the rear axles to the bell housing.

"We ran an open-tube rearend in the dragster with a brake only on one side. The Halibrand banjo-type rearend had bearings mounted on the frame rails for the axle supports. It'd move around a lot, and the cars would shake so much.

"The most nitro that I would ever run was 20 percent, but most times I'd just run straight alcohol and beat the nitro-burning Hemis for Top Fuel," Zane said. "The Chryslers were famous for blower explosions on nitro, but not so with the Chevys.

"The slicks available in those days were good enough for the horsepower produced by my ultralight Chevy dragster, but they wouldn't hold the horsepower made by the Hemis. The Chrysler owners would have to de-tune their cars to get the tires to work."

Shubert said that he ran the Chevys rather than the more

The Herbert Cam twin aluminum Olds V-8 AA/G dragster that had the blowers driven off a common drive belt between the engines. This dragster set an unbelievable low ET record on 8.19 at San Gabriel Drag Strip on pump gas in 1963. *Courtesy Zane Shubert*

popular Hemi engines because of the costs of running a fast Chrysler. They were going to run a Hemi after the Chrysler drivers finally found out how to put all their horsepower to work, but it never materialized, although Chet did get involved with Connie Swingle's Chrysler-powered dragster.

Shubert won Top Eliminator for 12 consecutive weeks at Long Beach in a car that weighed slightly over 900 pounds. From 1963 to 1965, Zane drove a single-blown-Chevy fuel dragster that won more races than any other Chevrolet-powered car in drag racing history. In 1964, Zane set the NHRA ET record for AA/F dragster at Riverside with an elapsed time of 7.91. At the 1965 Winternationals, he was the only Chevy dragster to qualify for Top Eliminator.

F85 OLDSMOBILES

In 1963, another super lightweight dual-engine dragster came out of the Herbert Cams shop. This one came in under 1,000 pounds, which was pretty remarkable for a twin-engine car. Its tandem-mounted F85 Oldsmobile V-8 aluminum engines were each given a 1-inch stroke to produce 300 ci; 600 ci was unusually small for a Herbert twin. To save weight, the exhaust pipes were even made out of aluminum tubing and were welded directly to the aluminum heads. A sheet of plywood was installed in the front for streamlining, and Hilborn fuel injectors distributed the gasoline. "The welded-on headers were really good for picking the motors up," Zane said.

To get a little more speed out of the car, superchargers were added and the engines were switched over to run on fuel. The GMC blowers were joined together by a common flex coupling to act as one unit and were driven off the rear engine's crankshaft pulley, a unique weight-saving arrangement. In an attempt to get better traction, dual slicks were tried out, but they created too much air resistance and placed too much strain on the car's axles from the excessive tire bite.

Jeep Hampshire and Roy Steen campaigned a similar twin-aluminum Oldsmobile-powered dragster that was sponsored by Herbert Cams.

V-16 CHEVROLET

Staying with the dual-engine theme, in 1970 Chet brought out another radical twin-engine car, an experimental V-16 Chevrolet-powered dragster. The engine was made from two Chevy 402-ci V-8s lined up facing each other and bolted together. The crankshafts were welded into one long, solid unit, with one long, custom-made 16-quart oil pan. The camshaft for the front engine had to be ground with a reverse firing order because it rotated backward, and both camshafts were driven by a custom-made center drive. The fuel-induction system was made from two Offenhauser tunnel-ram intake manifolds fitted with injector jets and connected by an extended Herbert bug catcher.

Individually, the engines put out 800 horsepower on the dynamometer, but when joined together, the horsepower rating went down to 1,200. After some investigation, the problem was traced back to crossfiring in the distributors. The vibration between the two engines caused the ignition points to bounce, which was rectified by placing pieces of foam rubber behind the points. At the strip, Lee LaBarron got the V-16-powered dragster up to 209 miles per hour with 90 percent nitro in the tank, but regrettably, the car didn't see much, if any, competition.

TWIN SIDEWINDER

The idea of mounting an engine sideways in a chassis has been around since Creighton Hunter's infamous *Piece of Pie* dragster of 1955, and possibly earlier. This type of drive configuration usually powers the rear wheels by means of a chain drive. Several successful race cars have run this style of setup.

In 1961, Chet came up with a radical new approach for a sidewinder rear-mounted, twin-engine dragster that took him and Zane eight months to construct. Chet stroked out two 327s to 450 ci and fed them with Hilborn injectors. The drive system consisted of a set of spider gears in a tube containing the axles and 52 small clutch discs that were activated by a truck air brake cylinder. The driver's foot pedal disengaged the clutch system, assisted by 300 pounds of CO_2 pressure. The system used three flywheels. Two flywheels ran off the engines and drove the center flywheel, which turned the driveshaft. The result was a very complicated drive system that had a tendency to flex.

With the engines positioned behind the driver, there was little weight on the front end. With a short, 120-inch wheelbase, the front end was quick to lift. "There was nothing you could do to steer that thing," Zane said. "You were all over the place. About the fastest I ever got out of the car was about 168 miles per hour . . . backward through the lights at Bakersfield."

ZOOMIES

Around 1959, the fellows at Herbert Cams were spending a fair amount of time testing a variety of engine programs on the dynamometer and at the track. The zoomie header evolved as a result of needing a quick and easy header for dyno testing.

Chet had bought a dynamometer from Ron Hammel and installed it in Shubert's shop, which at the time was located in his mother's backyard. Zane could pull the engine out of his dragster and put it right onto the dyno and vice versa. The hydraulic dyno needed lots of water to function properly, so water lines were run to and from his mother's swimming pool.

Zane remembers when they started to play around with different lengths of headers on his car. "The shorter they were, the better the car ran. I was making a couple of different header styles a week—various lengths, pointing at the tires, pointing up—experimenting with different combinations until we came up with something that worked." After hours of trial and error, the configuration of a short, curved set of individual headers was found to give the increase in power they were looking for. Chet said that their secret finally came out when one of their customers, Frank Cannon, needed a little something extra to help his Chrysler-powered dragster. After the installation of a set of zoomie headers on his car, the rest is history. Featured on the front page of *Drag News* on May 2, 1964, was a picture of Frank Cannon's dragster. The race results at Pomona from April 26 said, "Frank Cannon hits 199 mph at Pomona Drags," and went on to say that out of his six runs, five were over 195 miles per hour, with a 193-mile-per-hour run just off the trailer. He had the only car to run over 190 miles per hour that day and took Top Eliminator. They figured he might have cracked the 200 barrier had it not been a cool day with a strong headwind blowing.

No one could figure out his success, but if they'd looked a little harder (and obviously someone did), they'd have noticed his car was equipped with a different style of header. The pictures in the article show his car with zoomie headers, while all the others were running the standard weed-sweeper style. Suddenly, all across the country, cars were outfitted with zoomie-style headers, and it wasn't long before the 200-mile-per-hour mark was breached. No doubt others may have used something very similar in design in the past, but the Herbert shop was the first to realize the header's performance potential. Where the name "zoomie" originated is anyone's guess.

About today's use of the zoomie-style header, Chet said, "A Top Fuel car gets close to 2,000 pounds of thrust out of the exhaust pipes, shoving the car down. Take those zoomie headers away from those Top Fuel cars, and they'd have difficulty getting into the fives. With straight headers, they'd probably be running in the sixes."

OUTBOARD MOTOR

Always fascinated with innovative mechanical stuff, Chet had seen one item that he'd always wanted to investigate a little further. The opportunity to realize this came in 1971 when the Outboard Racing Federation announced that its world championship races would be held on Lake Havasu, Arizona, the following year. The rulebook stipulated that only one outboard motor was allowed per boat, but with no limit on the engine size.

There are myriad combustion engines with a variety of piston configurations; some are practical and many are pretty radical and just nice to look at. The mechanical device that had intrigued Chet for some time was called the true opposed engine (TOE), which consisted of two pistons, two connecting rods, and two crankshafts utilizing one common cylinder and one spark plug. The cranks are geared together so that each piston reaches top dead center (TDC) at the same time to form a common combustion chamber. The intake and exhaust openings (valves) are located in the cylinder walls, similar to a two-cycle engine. This style of engine had been around for some time, but never used in a production automobile.

Chet's design for a TOE called for a three-cylinder engine block. The crankshafts came from a Kawasaki 750-cc three-cylinder motorcycle, placing one crankshaft at each end of the common block and operated in unison by a set of gears located in the bottom of the engine block. Due to the placement of the pistons, Chet could use the high-pressure induction system of a GMC 4:71 supercharger with Hilborn fuel injection; as one piston moved to close the intake port, the other piston moved to open the exhaust port. The gears that connected the two crankshafts could be adjusted to set the timing, while a pressurized oil system eliminated the need to mix oil with the fuel. The blower was driven off the top of one crankshaft, while a Kawasaki magneto was driven off the opposite crankshaft.

In auto racing, big companies have been known to have a direct influence in changing the rulebook to suit their individual needs. Chet was to find out that this undue influence wasn't necessarily limited to land racing. His outboard motor's dynamic test results got the "Big Two" (Mercury and OMC) concerned enough to register a protest, arguing that the "Herbert Outboard" was actually two engines in one with a common lower unit. Mercury and OMC got their way and the motor was disqualified from entering the race, thus ending Chet's powerboat racing.

THE T-77X

Undaunted by the boating setback, Chet resolved to apply to a race car the long hours of labor spent developing his outboard. Oswego Speedway in Oswego, New York, ran an Unlimited Modified class that suited the capabilities of his engine design. A fellow by the name of Tipke was given the job of designing and building a rear-engine race car for owner Jim Pittilo to accommodate Chet's TOE engine. The combination was given the handle "T-77X."

Using the same basic design as the outboard motor but on a much larger scale, this engine made the boat motor look like a toy.

The race car engine had 8 Kawasaki 750 motorcycle crankshafts, 24 rods and pistons, and a custom-made 12-cylinder engine block. Rather than being supercharged, it used Hilborn injectors to deliver fuel to the high-revving 720 ci that was capable of putting out 1,000 foot-pounds of brutal torque.

In addition to owning the race car, Pittilo was the driver. After making some initial warmup laps at Oswego, he put his foot to it and overqualified the car by breaking the existing track lap record. The powers that be promptly disqualified the car and immediately changed the rulebook regarding engine classification. So much for racing.

Both the outboard motor and the T-77X were unceremoniously retired to the rear confines of Chet's shop where they reside today. Unfortunately, neither engine had the opportunity to really show what it could do, but the T-77X rests against a wall, minus its front wheels, waiting.

GREEN RACE CARS AND SUPERSTITIONS

The Shubert-Herbert cars always stood out with their infamous Shubert Orange paint jobs. Zane was just putting the finishing touches on his latest dragster when he decided on a color change from the standard orange to British Racing Green.

"The first time out running the green car, the clutch blew and cut one side out of the rails," Zane said. "The following week, I blew the front of the engine off, ran over it, and it catapulted me through the air. The next week, the blower blew off, and that kept going on. Finally, Chet says, 'I didn't think you'd have the guts to bring that car out green again.'"

The next week, the newly painted Shubert Orange dragster was once again in the winner's circle.

NITROUS OXIDE

Zane felt that their car was one of the first to run nitrous oxide at a drag strip. It all began at Tony Capanna's in 1964 or 1965, when Zane had their Chevy, equipped with one of Chet's super-long-duration cams (the 400-degree Pulsation 70), on the dynamometer, adjusting the valves. As soon as the engine was fired up, it detonated like crazy and Ron Hammel said to Zane, "I know how to stop that engine from detonating."

"So this guy leaves the dyno room and returns shortly with a pressurized bottle with a valve on top," Zane said. "I had no idea what it contained, outside of some hospital markings on the cylinder."

After fitting a hose on the gas bottle, they installed a 1/8-inch pipe fitting in the Hilborn four-hole injector and connected the hose from the bottle.

Ron told Zane to open the valve on the bottle as he opened the throttle. When the motor was fired up, it detonated like crazy, but as Zane opened the valve, there was instant rpm with no detonation. Then Ron asked Zane if he'd like to run this secret stuff, but only if Zane kept it confidential, although it was not illegal. "In those days, you could run anything that the motor would burn," Zane said.

To conceal what they were up to, a small nitrous-filled fire extinguisher bottle (painted black) was bolted to the belly pan

In 2008, after five-plus decades of grinding camshafts and selling speed equipment, Chet could still be found at his desk taking care of business. *Author photo*

between Zane's legs with a line up to the injector nozzle. To trigger the nitrous, a hydraulic valve was connected to the dragster's throttle linkage.

The use of nitrous produced results that they weren't expecting. "After lining up at the start line, I jumped on the throttle and blew the supercharger," Zane said. This was the first blower Zane ever lost with a fuel-burning car; he had never put more than 20 percent nitro in the tank and usually ran straight alcohol. After replacing the destroyed blower, they gave it another try with the same results. By the third blower explosion, Chet said, "Enough of that stuff," and that was the end of their nitrous experience.

Talking to drag racing reporter-photographer "Digger" Ralph Guldahl about Chet, he mentioned that Herbert once told him in an interview that, "I've never run two races without changing something. The challenge for improvement is why I race. It's no thrill going racing if I don't try something new."

THE MYSTERIOUS PULSATION 400-DEGREE CAMSHAFT

One very knowledgeable and well-respected technical writer contemplated the attributes of the 400-degree Pulsation camshaft in an article he wrote. After analyzing the camshaft, the writer reported that the valve stays open for 40 degrees more than a complete rotation of the crankshaft. The Pulsation 70 grind has a 180-degree overlap, obtained by opening the intake valve 70 degrees before top dead center (TDC) and closing the exhaust 110 degrees after TDC. The intake valve seats itself 150 degrees after before top center (BTC), closing 30 degrees before the piston finishes the compression stroke.

When checking the valve timing of the cam, another authority couldn't believe the degree wheel, but Chet verified that the valves stay open for 400 degrees of crankshaft rotation.

A story told by another specialty manufacturer concerns a time when a very well-known drag racer was using the Pulsation 70 camshaft to set record mile-per-hour runs while being paid to use another cam grinder's decal. That particular cam grinder ended up buying three of Chet's 70 cams to design a similar version of his own.

DRAG NEWS

Although Chet made his mark with roller-tappet camshafts, motorcycles, race cars, and speed records, he also made an imprint on newspaper, with *Drag News*.

Dean Brown first published the newspaper as a bi-weekly in 1954. Chet purchased it two years later and turned it into a weekly paper that became the printed authority for drag racing news across the country. Doris Herbert purchased *Drag News* from her brother in 1959 and managed it up until 1976, when the paper was sold again. Unfortunately, the paper closed its doors the following year.

As a note of interest, Dean Brown went on to open the Fontana Drag Strip in 1960, which was later owned by the world's (unofficially) fastest man, Mickey Thompson.

ADVERTISING

In one of his ads in 1957, Chet presented the "$10,000 Challenge." He was so confident of the superiority of the roller tappet against his competitors' overadvertised flat-tappet camshaft claims that he challenged any of them to a dynamometer test to prove whose cam put out the most horsepower, with $10,000 going to the winning manufacturer. He said that there were no takers.

Herbert Cams never issued a parts catalog in all the years it has been in business. Chet said that he has preferred to deal with his customers personally. By taking this personal approach, he could recommend a camshaft that would accomplish what the customer wanted to do, not what looked good in a catalog.

CHET HERBERT CAMS TODAY

When Chet was confronted with the fact that he was going to be confined to a wheelchair for the rest of his life, he didn't dwell on it but took it all in stride and kept working toward what he wanted out of life. The results of a lifetime spent building a successful manufacturing business, race cars, custom engines, and countless racing victories are more than enough to verify his achievements. What really made Chet stand out from his peers was his belief in the roller tappet. He is credited as the instigator for the use of high-performance roller camshafts in the North American domestic overhead-valve engine.

He also had a strong preference for the Chevrolet V-8 but mentioned that he did grind one Ford flathead V-8 roller camshaft, which is owned by Don Garlits (Garlits was sponsored by Herbert Cams from 1961 to 1962).

Chet passed away on April 23, 2009, but today, Chet Herbert Cams has a large aftermarket automotive parts warehouse to complement its camshaft grinding business. Chet's son Doug began his career at the shop, and he prodded Chet to branch out into the warehousing business. Doug eventually left the family business to open his own very successful parts business out east. Doug also became one of the better-known drivers in AHRA and NHRA Top Fuel drag racing. He was the second driver to ever break the magical 300-mile-per-hour barrier for the quarter-mile.

Both Chet and his sister Doris were inducted into the International Drag Racing Hall of Fame in 1993.

FUEL INJECTION
ENGINEERING
COMPANY

LOS ANGELES
CALIFORNIA

HILBORN
INJECTOR

CHAPTER 9

Hilborn Fuel Injection

STU HILBORN

Author's note: I wish to acknowledge Stuart Hilborn's unpublished autobiography for much of the source material in this chapter, and thank Stuart for graciously sharing that manuscript.

Of all the early speed equipment manufacturers, Stuart Hilborn stands alone with his contributions to the most abstract method of engine modification for performance purposes. What Stuart Hilborn first introduced on the dry lakes of Southern California has become the standard fuel-delivery system in most forms of racing today.

ON THE MOVE

The Hilborn family roots can be traced back to Niagara on the Lake in Ontario, Canada. After graduating from Toronto's McGill University as a pharmacist, Hilborn's father and his new wife set out for Sylvan Lake, a small town near Calgary, Alberta. It was there that his father operated the local drug store and, in due time, Stuart and his two siblings appeared on the scene.

In 1922, the family moved to the state of Washington. After three years in Auburn, Washington, Stuart's father heard that sunny California was the land of opportunity, and the Hilborn family was on the move again.

Making the arduous trip in a four-door Star Touring, the family settled in Pasadena during the Great Depression. Hilborn Sr. found employment as a pharmacist on a part-time basis; luckily, it was enough to get by.

THE CHARTREUSE '40

After graduating from Hamilton High School in 1935, Stuart Hilborn enrolled in Los Angeles City College, where he majored in chemistry. Many years later, he would further his knowledge of chemistry by attending courses at the University of Southern California.

While attending college, he lived with his parents and had to budget carefully; a car was out of the question, but this wasn't a problem in the days of the red car transit system. Los Angeles had a first-rate streetcar service, where riders could travel just about anywhere in town for five cents. But a car did become a necessity upon graduating as a chemist and getting a job beyond the reaches of the red car. After owning a none-too-memorable and unreliable 1932 Auburn, Stuart worked and saved enough to purchase a top-of-the-line 1940 Ford convertible. For the sum of $1,006, he became the proud owner of a flamboyant chartreuse convertible with a black canvas top. The bonus was "the girls loved it," Stuart said. He soon had the flathead hopped up and running with a Winfield cam and dual carburetion.

DRY LAKES

Stuart received his introduction to automobile racing in 1939, when a friend invited him to go up to the dry lakes to watch the speed trials. Once at the lakes, he became fascinated by these backyard hop-up enthusiasts, with their homemade speedsters, and by the speeds at which they were traveling.

Opposite: Stuart Hilborn is suited up in an aviator's helmet, goggles, and bomber jacket, about to climb into his B streamliner to make a run at Harper Dry Lake. The glossy black car really was quite a showpiece for a time when money was tight. *Leslie Long collection*

Inset: The famous logo that has adorned Hilborn-equipped vehicles on asphalt and dirt ovals, quarter-mile strips, dry lakes, salt flats, and even water—anywhere there was a need for high speed. *Author collection*

Bill Warth's Winfield-equipped streamliner is seen at the dry lakes before he sold it to Stuart. The car attained speeds in the 130-mile-per-hour range. *Leslie Long collection*

"Being a chemist, I was completely separated from anything mechanical until I visited the lakes for the first time," Stuart said. It would take several more trips to the dry lakes to convince him to give it a try.

A neighbor, Eddie Miller Sr., would have a great influence on Stuart. Their friendship first developed when Stuart decided to build a car for the dry lakes, and Eddie volunteered to assist him with the project. On a used car lot, Stuart found just what he needed for the lakes, a neglected 1929 Model A roadster, minus the engine.

Miller's mechanical expertise dated back to his involvement with the Duesenberg brothers' Indianapolis racing program. He even drove a Duesenberg 8 to a fourth-place finish at the Speedway in 1921. In Los Angeles, Eddie's mechanical talents were employed by the movie studios for such things as overseeing stationary aircraft engines used for producing wind in movie scenes. Several years after his involvement with Stuart's streamliner, he teamed up with his son Eddie Jr. and built a streamliner for Bonneville. This car had a futuristic, Buck Rogers–type, hand-formed, sheet-steel body, was powered by a full-race flathead Pontiac six-cylinder, and contained many innovations that had the "Miller" trademark stamped on them, such as his own cast-aluminum, chain-drive, quick-change

rearend. This totally unique streamliner made the front cover of *Hot Rod*'s August 1950 issue along with a complete writeup.

With help from Eddie, Stuart purchased a 1934 Ford flathead V-8 to power the roadster. They retained the engine's stock 239-ci displacement but added an aftermarket two-carburetor setup, filled and milled the cast-iron heads, ported and relieved the ports, added a magneto, and installed a one-of-a-kind Miller camshaft to activate the valves. To ensure the engine was well lubricated, two stock oil pumps were modified and welded together.

Miller's hand-ground camshaft is a story in itself. Eddie built a jig out of metal lathe centers to hold the cam while he roughly ground each lobe on his bench grinder. He'd grind for a few minutes, stop and apply machine bluing on the lobe, inspect it with a dial indicator, and continue to grind. This slow, tedious procedure was repeated over and over until the desired profile shape was reached.

"I watched as Miller slowly ground the cam and was truly amazed at his skill and dedication toward the project," Stuart said. "He was a very brilliant and innovative person. Eddie Miller Sr., besides being a very good friend, was my mentor and had the greatest influence on me."

Not satisfied with the performance of the two-carburetor intake, Stuart said Eddie came up with the design for an intake manifold that had four carburetors mounted sideways. Initially, they wanted to use four dual-throat carburetors—one for each corner of the manifold. This would give each cylinder its own carburetor throat. The big dual-throat Stromberg EE carburetors, used on engines such as the V-12 Cadillacs and Duesenbergs, had the proper throat size for the engine, but the cost of buying four of them was prohibitive. They decided to buy one EE Stromberg from the junkyard to use on two particular ports of the engine because of the engine's firing order. The Ford flathead has a firing order of 1-5-4-8-6-3-7-2, with number 1 and 2 cylinders firing after each other. The overlap of the cam keeps both valves slightly open at the same time.

"A poor flow did not exist normally," Stuart said, "but it would exist if one single-throat carburetor was used at that location."

They already had three Stromberg E single-throat

The item that put the carburetor on the back bench when all-out performance was required: the sheet-metal, hand-fabricated fuel injector Stuart built for the flathead V-8 engine in his streamliner. *Author photo*

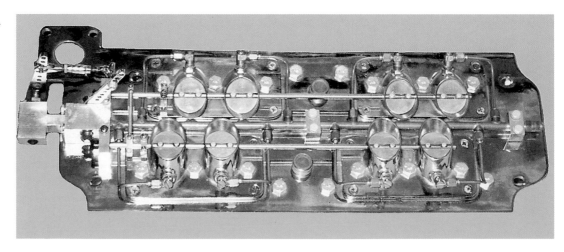

carburetors on hand. By using them in conjunction with the big EE, they ended up with a manifold that gave the same effect as a five-carburetor system.

"It would have been nice if we could've afforded to have four big duals on the intake," Stuart said. "It would have looked nicer and saved a lot of explanations to inquiring people asking about the odd setup."

After working the tuning bugs out of the intake system, it performed very well. The final product was a full-race 239 V-8 flathead putting out nearly 200 horsepower that would prove more than adequate for setting records on the dry lakes.

ROADSTER AND STREAMLINER RECORDS

By joining the Centuries car club, Stuart was able to run in SCTA-sanctioned meets at the dry lakes. With Muroc closed to racing in 1939 and 1940, the meets were held at the Rosamond and Harper dry lakes. It wasn't until 1941 that all the hard work finally paid off and Stuart got his name in the record book. At the September 28 meet, the roadster ran 124 miles per hour on straight methanol, setting a new class record.

The possibility of upping the speed of his record-holding roadster seemed rather limited due to the lack of funds to purchase expensive speed equipment. Stuart knew that it if he wanted to go faster with the equipment he already had, it'd have to be in a car like a streamliner. Bill Worth had his streamliner up for sale, less engine, for $75. Bill had been running a Winfield-equipped Model A in the little car that saw speeds of around the 130 mark. Stuart felt that it would be possible to install the V-8 with some minor modifications to the chassis. The Sunday morning when he and Worth had just finished loading the streamliner onto Stuart's trailer, Bill's wife ran out of the house and yelled, "Pearl Harbor has just been attacked!"

Over the winter months and with help from Miller, the streamliner began to take shape. Alterations to the chassis and body allowed the installation of the '34 V-8. When all the mechanics were done, Stuart applied the finishing touch with a coat of jet-black enamel over the streamliner's body.

That following racing season started well for the new streamliner. On June 14, 1942, it set a new B/Streamliner class record at 137.73 miles per hour. The "B" classification was for nonsupercharged engines between 183 and 250 ci.

SOLUTION TO A PROBLEM

The war was now raging on two sides of the globe. With no end in sight, Stuart enlisted in the air corps in March 1943 and was assigned to the army air corps stationed at Nellis Air Force Base in Las Vegas, Nevada. As an aerial gunnery instructor, he taught recruits how to use the .50-caliber machine gun armaments of the B-17 and B-29 bombers.

With a lot of downtime at the base, Stuart had the opportunity to analyze the various problems he'd been having with carburetion. Running straight methanol at the dry lakes with carburetors that were designed to run on gasoline posed problems. The pot metal of the carburetors would dissolve over time, and the jetting just wasn't large enough to handle the quantity of alcohol that was pumped through them.

"I figured that there had to be a better fuel-delivery system," Stuart said. "If there were some way to inject the fuel rather than running it through a carburetor, it would eliminate all those problems in one big jump."

Upon being discharged from the military, one of the first things Stuart did was to make a prototype injection system out of sheet steel. A surplus aircraft fuel pump provided the pressure to operate the system.

"I knew what was needed for the flow and that the fuel had to be equal in all the cylinders," Stuart said. "The first nozzles were tested using a stop watch and a small scale to determine CCs of fuel per minute [that they would flow]. The original nozzles didn't flow equally, yet they were drilled the same diameter using the same drill bit. After a long and intense study, I figured out that the chamfer of the jet was the culprit. The chamfer at the end of the jet was not as important as the one at the entrance. I discovered that you could chamfer the holes and make the flow rates change, so I chamfered them all the same and ended up with equal-flowing nozzles. This was my biggest obstacle to solve; the rest were minor mechanical problems."

WHY WON'T IT WORK?

Stuart entered the streamliner in a hot rod show that was being held at the Los Angeles Armory and, although he hadn't tried the injection system on an engine at the time, it was on display along with the car. Stuart remembered, "All these technical-type people (some were engineers) looked at my injection and said it'll never work. I asked them, 'Why not?'"

Their response was, "You're flowing the fuel continuously, not timing it; it's got to be timed."

"Again, I asked them why it has to be timed."

Their response: "Everybody times their fuel injection."

Many years later, Stuart read an article published by the Mercedes engineering department that stated that fuel injection did not need to be timed over 2,000 rpm, supporting his reasoning.

INTRODUCING FUEL INJECTION TO THE DRY LAKES

Living in Santa Monica after the war, Stuart joined a local car club called the Low Flyers. Returning to the dry lakes for the 1946 season as a Low Flyer, Stuart raised his old B/Streamliner class record to 139.96 miles per hour running with the four-carburetor system.

As soon as the flowing bugs had been worked out of the injectors, it was time to prove the system with some trial runs. With the help of several friends, the streamliner was trailered up to Rosamond Dry Lake. The motor fired up immediately, and Stuart slowly piloted the car down the lake, increasing the throttle cautiously as he went. After some fine-tuning to the fuel-metering valve and several more runs down the lakebed, the commanding response from the engine confirmed Stuart's belief in his system. No ambulance service was on hand in case of a mishap, so the streamliner wasn't pushed to its limit.

"I did jab the throttle several times, and the quick response was very impressive," Stuart said. "I knew that I had something that had real potential. After taking the streamliner up to what I figured was about 120 miles per hour, there was still plenty of throttle pedal left to go."

When the fuel-injected streamliner ran at its first official dry lakes meet, it caused quite a stir among the other racers. A crowd gathered around the car every time the engine cover was removed, and Stuart was bombarded with questions from the curious and the amazed. Pumping straight methanol through the injectors, he easily took his class win at 136 miles per hour in the maiden running of his fuel-injection system.

ACCIDENT

An incident at Harper Dry Lake during the 1947 racing season almost ended tragically for Stuart. The streamliner hit a rough spot on the lakebed, which spun the rearend around. A tire caught and snapped the wire spokes, collapsing the wheel and causing the car to flip end over end. Crouching as low as possible in the narrow confines of the streamliner's cockpit, Stuart was protected only by goggles, a leather aviator's flying helmet, and a seat belt. He was lucky to survive, but the injuries he did receive were serious enough to have him wrapped up in a body cast for some time. Without a roll bar, his upper back was exposed to the lakebed as the car somersaulted end over end, causing multiple compression fractures to his upper vertebrae.

While Stuart was recuperating, Eddie salvaged what was left of the streamliner. The multiple talents of this genius were once again displayed as he reconstructed the mangled vehicle. The car's body was originally hand-formed from sheet-steel panels, and Stuart recalled, "Miller hammered those body panels back to their original shape. If you'd seen the wreck after the accident, you'd never believe someone could straighten it out, and you'd have never known it [was ever bent] to look at it after he'd finished the job. Miller was a superior body man."

The streamliner appeared on the front cover of *Hot Rod*'s April 1948 issue and was featured as Hot Rod of the Month.

Stuart prepares to climb into his B/Streamliner at El Mirage. *Leslie Long collection*

THE RECORD

After months of recuperating from the almost-fatal accident and realizing just how extremely fortunate he was not to be paralyzed, Stuart decided that in the future he'd leave the driving to someone else. For the 1948 racing season, a fellow member of the Low Flyers car club named Howard Wilson would be riding in the cockpit of the Hilborn streamliner.

During an SCTA meet on July 17, 1948, history was made on the dusty lakebed at El Mirage. Wilson piloted the fuel-injected streamliner down the lake at a record-setting 150.50 miles per hour. It was the first car to break the magical 150-mile-per-hour barrier at any sanctioned meet on the dry lakes. The Hilborn car also set a new B/Streamliner record with a two-way average of 146.47 miles per hour.

That speed record, set by a car using a homemade fuel-injection system, was the catalyst that would change the course of the 31-year-old Hilborn's future.

THE SEEDS OF A BUSINESS

Once he'd proven to all the naysayers that the injection system did actually outperform the carburetor, he was faced with the dilemma of what to do with it. His fellow speed enthusiasts at the dry lakes could see the superiority of this new creation.

The Ford Motor Company even had a writeup about Stuart's new fuel-injection system in its *Ford Times* magazine after his streamliner broke the 150-mile-per-hour barrier.

Dry lakes racing provided him with the initial advertising about this new induction system. With the response he received, Stuart realized that he had a viable, commercial product on his hands.

Stuart had several friends who worked as mechanics on an Offenhauser-powered midget race car. This form of automobile racing was extremely popular with fans throughout the country. Stuart decided to try one of his systems on a midget.

After making arrangements with the car's owner, he made an injector for the Offenhauser engine using the same manufacturing technique (hand-formed sheet metal) as with the original Ford flathead unit. They took the midget out to Carrell Speedway, where Norm Holtkamp was chosen to test drive. He was one of the more skillful midget drivers on the circuit, so they'd be sure to get a valid opinion on the performance of the injector. The very jubilant Holtkamp returned to the pits and couldn't get over the difference in performance of the injectors over carburetors. Stuart was one step closer to opening a business.

THE FINAL PUSH

When the manufacturer of Offenhauser engines (Meyer & Drake) heard about the performance results of Holtkamp's run, it wanted to have a close-up look at this new induction system to see if it would fit into its racing program.

Meyer & Drake had recently installed a dynamometer (one of the first in the L.A. area) and asked Stuart if he would like to try out his injectors on a test engine. For Stuart, it presented a great opportunity to see the potential of his injectors, and he agreed to the proposal. After he and fellow Low Flyer and fuel-injection collaborator Jim Travers installed the injector and related plumbing onto the test engine, George Salih (in charge of the dyno facility) fired up the Offy, let it reach operating temperature at a fast idle, and then gave it several full pulls. Giving a rather mystified look to Dale Drake (it made Stuart concerned), Salih went through the procedure again before shutting it down. Stuart asked them how it performed. Their reply was, "The most horsepower with carburetors was 99 horsepower. With the injectors, it was 110 horsepower."

Meyer & Drake's chief engineer was Leo Goosen, who was one of, if not the, best in the business. Leo had been watching the proceedings of the dyno test and made some suggestions to Stuart regarding the injector system. He advised him to get a pattern made, to cast the injector body in aluminum, and to make some minor changes to the linkage of the prototype. The manufacturers of the Offenhauser said that they'd be interested in the system if Stuart could fill their needs. Stuart replied, "As long as you fellows want them, we'll make them," not knowing that his answer was the beginning of a very long and successful business career.

THE FORMATIVE DAYS

The first production fuel-injection model that came off the Hilborn assembly line was for the four-cylinder Offenhauser 105-ci engine, not for the Ford V-8 flathead as many would be led to believe. The original castings had "Hilborn & Travers" embossed on them, but the partnership dissolved when Jim decided to pursue his racing interests.

Stuart's instincts told him that he had a viable product on his hands, but he still had a full-time job as a chemist at General Paint and was living at home with his family. At first, he operated the business on a part-time basis to see where it was going, but it wasn't long before he left the paint company to concentrate fully on getting the fledgling business off the ground. He said that it was a gamble, but being single at the time, he figured that he could afford to take the risk.

His first shop was in a garage owned by fellow dry lakes racer Willy Dale in Culver City. Things at first were pretty meager—Stuart worked with a gas welder, an electric hand drill, and some assorted hand tools. He did, however, have use of a friend's metal lathe, and over time, when there were sufficient funds, more equipment was purchased. What couldn't be performed in the shop was farmed out to machine shops.

As business expanded and the need for pattern work increased, Stuart took on the creative services of Speedway Pattern in Culver City, owned and operated by Don Nairn.

Little time was left over for dry lakes racing, so the streamliner was sold to Grant Piston Rings after the original prototype fuel injectors were replaced with Miller's four-carburetor intake manifold.

FUEL PUMPS

Stuart originally used a surplus Ranger aircraft fuel pump for the flathead V-8 injection system. It was ideal for this purpose, but the supply was limited. About this same time, Gill Pearson (who worked for the Douglas Aircraft Company) began manufacturing fuel pumps for Meyer & Drake for the 270 Offenhauser. The pump was to replace the hand-operated pressure fuel pumps that were

Stuart pulls up to the starting line at El Mirage.
Leslie Long collection

used with engines that ran carburetors. Pearson manufactured the pump on a part-time basis from his one-man machine shop in Inglewood, and he began manufacturing smaller pumps that were sold to Hilborn for the 105 Offenhauser midget engines. As supply demands increased, Hilborn Fuel Injection began to manufacture its own pumps to control the quality and introduce modifications to the design when needed.

TRAVELING SALESMAN

In order to get the injection systems out to potential customers (midget racers), Stuart teamed up with a top-running midget driver by the name of Ed Haddad. Stuart approached him because he felt that Ed was one of the best all-around drivers on the midget circuit. As a car owner and driver, Ed was only too happy to try out something that might give him an advantage over his competitors, and being pleased with how the injection performed on his car, they struck a deal. For every unit Ed sold as a result of using the injectors on his midget, he would receive a salesman's com-

A copy of the SCTA timing tag showing the run that set the dry lakes on their end—the first vehicle to break through the 150-mile-per-hour barrier there. *Leslie Long collection*

mission. The winning performance of Haddad's midget became his sales tool, and the system worked out beneficially for the two of them. Ed traveled back east to race in the midget circuit, and it didn't take long for the orders to pour in from across the country, as Haddad's fuel-injected 105 Offenhauser-powered midget racked up a long list of victories. Other drivers quickly realized that if they were going to stay competitive, they'd need this latest piece of speed technology.

One thing that Ed mentioned to Stuart after his first trial run with the injectors was the word "nitro."

NITROMETHANE

Stuart was introduced to nitromethane when he worked as a chemist for a lacquer factory. Nitro had been developed by the Commercial Solvents Corporation of Peoria, Illinois, during the war as a substitute for some of the lacquer solvents that were no longer available.

"The first time I ever had an inkling about nitro was when one day a salesman came to the factory selling a lacquer solvent," Stuart said. "This product was available without having to have an OK from the government to buy it. It wasn't until after the war that I'd heard of anyone using it in an engine, and that was in the gas-powered model airplane motors."

The first time he was involved with the use of nitro in a car was when they tested the injectors on Ed Haddad's midget at a local speedway. The injectors were set up to run on methanol and after the original tests were completed, Ed suggested, "How about putting a little nitro in it?"

"Those cars weren't really set up for nitro," Stuart said. "They were running very high compression, which was fine for methanol. We had to limit the nitro to about a ten percent mixture; over that amount usually resulted in a melted piston."

To solve this problem, Stuart knew what the fuel flow should be. By using the theoretical airflow ratios and combustion formulas, he came up with the answer. After making several adjustments to the injectors, the system was capable of running nitro with no problems.

OVERHEAD-VALVE CONVERSION

In 1947 or 1948, Stuart and Jim Travers decided to develop an overhead-valve conversion for the Ford flathead V-8. After studying the Alexander overhead conversion, they felt that there was lots of room for improvement. The problem with the Alexander design was that it left the intake valve in the stock location while incorporating the exhaust valve in the head. This didn't make sense to the boys, and after several lengthy bouts of brainstorming, they came up with a plan. Their design had both exhaust and intake valves in the head casting and was to be available with compression ratios ranging from 8:1 to a high of 14:1.

Jim had found a pattern-maker who worked out of his backyard garage and would make the patterns at a low cost. Using their rough drawings, the pattern-maker produced wooden patterns of equally rough quality. When they decided to cast the heads in iron, the iron foundry wasn't too sure that it could use the poorly made patterns. The iron head castings turned out to be less than perfect and not worth the expense to have them machined. Stuart said that the lack of developmental money killed the project, as neither of them had enough spare cash to complete the job properly.

Around the same time, Jim got a job overseeing midgets for the wealthy oil-magnate Howard Keck. Jim and Frank Coons (another Low Flyer member) would eventually open the doors of Traco Engineering, renowned for building performance engines.

MAHLEN

As business increased, Dale's garage became inadequate, and the operation was moved to another location in Culver City. In no time, this shop also lacked the space Stuart needed, and he found a more suitable facility on Twelfth Street in Santa Monica. Jack Engle, another member of the Low Flyers, would eventually become Stuart's neighbor when he relocated Engle Racing Cams to its new home on that same street.

With the larger shop and plenty of orders to fill, Stuart began buying specialized machinery to make manufacturing an in-house operation, excluding the raw aluminum castings. The only problem was that he hadn't yet learned how to use all of the equipment and was in need of a machinist. Someone knew Stuart needed help and sent Mahlen Lameraux around to his shop. Once Mahlen found out that he could work the hours he wanted, provided that he got the jobs done, he thought that this was a great place to work. He could operate most of the equipment and had no problem machining the injector castings.

"Mahlen was a fellow who could do or fix just about anything," Stuart said. "It was never quite first class when he got done, but it worked."

Mahlen owned an old boat down in Santa Monica bay and liked to fish more than work at a regular job. Lameraux also loved his beer and could do justice to the habit.

"One time, Jim Travers, Mahlen, and I went out for lunch," Stuart said. "It was a pretty hot day, so when the waitress was taking our order, I said, 'Please bring us a pitcher

The wrecked Hilborn streamliner is tied down to a trailer and awaiting a tow back to Los Angeles. The picture shows just how extensive the body damage was; oddly enough, the chrome exhaust pipe escaped damage. Note what remains of the left rear wheel, which was the culprit that caused the accident. One wonders how Stuart ever escaped the horrific disaster with no roll bar to protect him. *Leslie Long collection*

of beer.' Mahlen spoke up, saying, 'And bring me one, too!' Despite Mahlen's beer habit, he never was drunk and stayed with me for several years."

SKEPTICS

The door to the racing event of the year, the Indy 500, was opened to Stuart through Howard Keck, who owned the Superior Oil Company and had a passion for midget racing. Keck had hired the talented team of Jim Travers and Frank Coons to keep his stable of cars competitive, and in 1948 Keck fielded a front-wheel-driven, Deidt-built car in the 500. Stuart was asked to crew, and while at the Speedway he learned about the problems the engine tuners were having with fuel distribution in their bulky twin-carbureted Offenhauser engines. The Keck car, with Jimmy Jackson driving, began the race in fourth place and was doing fine until mechanical problems forced the car out on lap 193, finishing in the 10th spot—very respectable for a first-time effort.

The following year, Stuart was once again asked to crew for the Keck car. This time, he came prepared with a fuel-injection system to fit the Indy Offenhauser 270 engine.

In the weeks prior to the race, pit crews at the Brickyard worked feverishly, searching for a little extra speed on the track. The success of the Keck car in qualifying using Stuart's injectors was noticed by the other teams. Bayliss Levrett, who was having trouble getting his car to qualify, was the first car owner to ask Stuart if he could borrow the injection system. After Stuart installed the unit on his car, Levrett took it out for some hot laps and quickly returned to the pits, complaining to his crew, "We can't run it this way; it's got too much power. I'm over-revving the engine." Several gear changes later, the Levrett car not only brought its speed up to 129 miles per hour to qualify for the 500, but it won the $1,000 purse for the fastest qualifier of the day. Bayliss still didn't have enough faith in the injection system to use it in the 500-mile race. The Levrett car and four other cars all used Stuart's injectors to qualify, and they all switched back to carburetors for the race, as did Keck's team.

The injectors added a 10- to 15-percent increase in horsepower (30 to 35) over the dual Riley side-draft carburetors, with 1- to 2-mile-per-hour increases in lap speeds and increased fuel economy.

Keck had enough faith in the ability of his crew that he never expressed an opinion on the fuel injectors or any other part they installed, as long as the results were positive.

Firestone had developed a new racing tire compound for the 1949 race that was reported to possess very good wear characteristics. This gave the Keck crew the idea of running the entire race without having to make a pit stop for fuel. With his chemistry background, it was Stuart's job to check into the feasibility of fuels that could do the job.

"I didn't like the idea of running gasoline with high percentages of methanol," Stuart said. "You have to use a blending agent to keep them from separating, and sometimes they'd separate anyway. Instead of doing this, I said, 'Let's run a different fuel.' Alcohol fuels are much better for racing; if you go to the higher alcohols, you have a longer carbon chain, and you get more mileage that way."

He decided that instead of running methanol or ethanol, they should move all the way up to butyl alcohol (butanol), because the air/fuel ratio is so much better. The trouble with butyl alcohol is its thick consistency, much like maple syrup.

Stuart knew of two other varieties of butyl alcohol called secondary and tertiary; both are thinner than the original. Tertiary is the better choice of the two, but in cold weather it turns solid. They didn't know how cool the weather would be on race day, so the secondary alcohol was chosen to be on the safe side.

The Keck crew didn't want to arouse any curiosity, "because there aren't any secrets at the track." A barrel of butyl alcohol was ordered directly from Chicago. Jimmy Nairn picked the barrel up at the trucking company's loading dock and removed the identification label from the drum before delivering it to the Keck garage at the Speedway.

Stuart had to guess at the jet size for the carburetors in order to accommodate the amount of fuel that he wanted to run. As soon as they fired up the engine, their neighboring (downwind) pit crew inquired about the strange smell that was coming from the Keck car. Keck's crew explained that it was a fuel additive they were trying out. Out on the track, the car performed very well, considering that the fuel had never before been run in an automotive engine to their knowledge. When Jimmy Jackson returned to the pits, he told the crew, "It's a little lazy, but not bad, and I feel that it can be raced this way." The only adjustment was to lean it down. Jackson started in seventh after qualifying with a speed of 128 miles per hour and finished 500 miles later in sixth place.

The *Keck Special* was the third car to ever run the Indianapolis 500 nonstop. The first was Dave Evans in a Cummins Diesel in 1931, and the second was Cliff Bergere in the *Noc Out Hose Clamp Special* in 1941.

Stuart credits the tires they were running that year as the major reason for their success. No doubt his knowledge in choosing a fuel with an unknown track record and his ability to make it work in the engine were also major factors.

Even though Stuart's injectors got Howard's car into the show again, the fuel system wasn't used in the race. The injector had yet to be a proven article in a long-distance race like the 500, and car owners were still skeptical of the device.

FUEL INJECTION WINS
1952 "500"

TROY RUTTMAN

Sets New Record of 128.922 m.p.h.

Also used by: 2nd, Jim Rathmann—3rd, Sam Hanks

Out of 33 Starters, 26 were equipped with Fuel Injection, and 13 out of the 14 cars finishing.

Also used on car driven by Bill Vukovich, which set Qualifying Record for 10 laps—138.212 m.p.h. & 1 lap—139.427 m.p.h. and led race for 152 laps.

Fuel Injection is for racing only, and is available for the following Engines: All Offys, Ford V8, Ardun Ford, Chevrolet, GMC, Cadillac, & Chrysler

Fuel Injection Engineering Co.
formerly
Hilborn-Travers Engineering Co.
5641 HANNUM AVENUE • CULVER CITY, CALIFORNIA
Phone: EXbrook 7-0164

The turning point for Hilborn Fuel Injection came in 1952 when Troy Ruttman won the Indy 500; out of 33 starters at the Brickyard, 26 ran Hilborn injectors. *Author collection*

DEMISE OF THE CARBURETOR

At the Speedway in 1950, Mauri Rose placed the *Keck Special* third from the front with a qualifying speed of 132 miles per hour with the help of Hilborn injectors. Of the 13 cars that qualified for the race using Stuart's fuel system, 5 of them left the injectors on for the race. Mauri drove the fuel-injected car to a close third-place finish behind Bill Holland and winner John Parsons.

The following year wasn't favorable to the Keck outfit. Again with Mauri in the cockpit, they started the race from fifth place only to end up in fourteenth after a wheel collapsed on lap 126, spinning the car into the infield. Lee Willard, driving the *Belanger Special* on carburetors, won the race, while the next six finishers were all running Hilborn fuel injection. Nineteen fifty-one marked the last time that a carbureted car would win at Indianapolis.

Stuart's injectors were used by 23 of the 33 cars to qualify in 1951. Eighteen cars used the injectors during the actual race.

Of the eight cars running at the end, six were fuel-injected. This result removed any doubt that the fuel injectors could run the full 500 miles without problems. It made the majority of car owners and mechanics realize the benefits of the fuel-injection system over the carburetor. Walt Faulkner drove the *Agajanian-Grant Special* (equipped with fuel injection) to a top qualifying speed of 138 miles per hour for one lap and averaged 136 miles per hour for four laps to break the track record set in 1946 by Ralph Hepburn in the *Novi Governor Special*.

Only six short weeks before the 1952 race, Frank Kurtis produced a rather radical car design for Howard Keck. The Kurtis-Kraft 500A had a low center of gravity with the engine offset and tilted to the right, allowing the driver to sit alongside the driveshaft. It changed the weight distribution between the wheels, improving the handling in the turns and reducing tire wear.

Keck entered the car under the name *Fuel Injection Special*. It was done as a favor to Stuart for his years of valuable technical support, and because Keck now believed in the injectors. Also, Keck wasn't interested in a corporate sponsorship and having to put up with their meddling CEOs.

Howard didn't ask Mauri Rose to drive in 1952 because he wanted a new driver who had more aggression, determination, and hunger to win. He held a meeting with Travers, Coons, and Stuart to get their input. Of the several names that were mentioned, the best ones were already signed up for the 500.

"Then I suggested Bill Vukovich," Stuart said. "I had run an injector test with him, and Jim and Frank had raced against him in the midgets. We all agreed that he was absolutely the most aggressive driver in racing. Keck was sold on the idea. Vuky had never done well at Indianapolis because he had never had a first-class car to drive. We could take care of that." Billy Vukovich was hired for the job, and this choice would pay off for the Keck team.

In 1959 Mickey Thompson drove his Hilborn-equipped four-engine *Challenger* streamliner to a record high speed of 367 miles per hour. *Author collection*

The following year, 1960, Mickey Thompson ran his *Challenger* streamliner to an all-out speed of 406 miles per hour on the Bonneville Salt Flats. All four supercharged Pontiac engines were equipped with Hilborn injectors. *Author collection*

Stuart Hilborn and Herb Porter approached AiResearch with a business proposal in which they would develop an injection system for its turbochargers if they were given the exclusive dealership from AiResearch for the racing applications. *Author photo*

Bill set the second-highest qualifying lap speed of 138 miles per hour, just 1 mile per hour slower than the Novi-powered *Novi Pure Oil Special*. However, due to his late qualifying date, Vukovich had to settle for eighth on the starting grid. Bill led the field for an unparalleled 150 laps, but with only 9 to go and a 22-second lead, the steering gave out and sent the car into the wall, resulting in a 17th-place finish. Fortunately, Vuky received only minor injuries and the car sustained slight damage. Vukovich would drive the *Fuel Injection Special* into the winner's circle at the Speedway for the next two years.

VICTORY AT INDY FOR HILBORN FUEL INJECTION

In the 1953 Indy race, the Keck outfit came back with a vengeance. Vukovich drove the *Fuel Injection Special* to the winner's circle, leading every lap but five. He was the first driver to win from the pole position since 1938. Not only was this win a major boost for Stuart's fledgling business, but also he got married in Detroit several days after the race.

It has been said by many racing automotive authorities that the most important technological development at the Speedway was the Hilborn fuel-injection system. It did away with carburetors, which at times proved troublesome, it provided better fuel economy, and it added approximately 30 horsepower to the 270 Offenhauser engine. Although the injectors didn't have the dynamic range of a racing carburetor such as the Riley,

they were ideal for engines that ran at constant high rpm, such as those at Indianapolis. They were much more efficient than carburetors because of increased volumetric efficiency and reduced fuel consumption.

The 1954 Indianapolis 500 would be the crowing glory to all of Stuart's long, arduous efforts in developing his injection system and getting racers to accept it. This race was first time that every car in the field was equipped with Hilborn fuel injection. It was also the last year for a Howard Keck car to run at the track. Fittingly, Vukovich took the checkered flag one last time.

FUNNY-LOOKING ROCKERS

Before Chevrolet first introduced its revolutionary 265-ci V-8 in 1955, it provided test engines to certain specialty equipment manufacturers to be evaluated for performance purposes. When GM factory rep Mauri Rose showed up on his doorstep with one of these funny-looking V-8s, Stuart wasn't too impressed with what he saw. The first time Stuart removed a valve cover and saw the funny-looking rocker arrangement, he thought the engine wouldn't make it, and he actually second-guessed his decision to make an injection unit for the engine.

After a prototype injector had been installed on the engine and bench run, Stuart began to see the potential of Chevrolet's newest creation. In due time, Hilborn Fuel Injection manufactured more injection systems for this tremendously popular small-block Chevrolet V-8, with its funny-looking rockers, than any other automobile engine.

NOVI

Novi is a legendary name in the history of the Indianapolis Speedway that had the misfortune of never making it to the winner's podium. The Novi engine was a marvelous piece of engineering and powered cars that did everything but win the race. Stuart said that he built an injection system for the Novi to replace the troublesome carburetors, but the engine still had unsolvable problems. Novi mechanics diligently searched for what ailed their engine. The Granatelli brothers discovered the Bosch ignition was mistimed direct from the factory in Germany. When Jean Marcenac originally installed the ignition (not realizing the factory error), he unknowingly set too much advance in the timing. In regard to the strengths and weaknesses of the Novi engine, Stuart felt that the blower was inefficient and that it should have had five main crankshaft bearings rather than three to better support the high-horsepower output of the engine.

TURBOS

The turbocharged Indy Offenhauser that was introduced to the Speedway in 1966 was the direct result of efforts made by Stuart and Herb Porter to salvage the engine before it was completely eliminated from competition at the track.

Bob DeBisschop, an employee at AiResearch (who had served on the A. J. Watson Indy racing team), approached Herb Porter, who was chief mechanic of Roger Wolcott's stable of Chrysler-powered race cars, about the possibilities of installing a turbocharger on an Offenhauser engine. Porter agreed to the

idea and would furnish a race car, provided that Stuart Hilborn supplied the fuel-injection system for the outfit. Stuart and Herb approached AiResearch with a business proposal in which they would develop a turbo program if they were given the exclusive dealership from AiResearch for the racing applications of their turbochargers. AiResearch liked what it saw and signed a contract with Hilborn Fuel Injection to develop an injection system to coordinate with its turbochargers.

Stuart spent a considerable amount of time on the flow stand before getting a proper flow curve. Once they were ready, Herb borrowed a 183 Offy engine from Vince Conze (Conze Machine Shop) to be used as a test mule.

Meanwhile, another force was busy developing a GMC-blown Offenhauser. Dick Jones, who was head of Champion Spark Plug's racing division, had been working on outfitting the Offy with a GMC supercharger. When he heard about what Hilborn's group was up to, he offered them the opportunity to bring their turbocharged engine over to Champion's dynamometer facilities for a comparison study. After the turbo engine was allowed to warm up, a full pull on the dyno produced 575 horsepower, while Jones' blown Offy put out 125 horsepower less, coming in at 450 horsepower. All Dick could say was, "Well, that's the end of the GMC blower."

Herb and Stuart ventured into the turbocharger/injector business, but because there was no one else in it at the time, all the parts they needed had to be designed, tested, and manufactured from scratch. Everything from the stainless-steel wastegate systems to injector designs came about through extensive development work and countless hours in the dynamometer room.

LOGO

The distinctive Hilborn Fuel Injection logo came into existence just before taking the first injector system to the 1949 Indianapolis 500 race. Stuart had made a fuel system especially for the big 270 Indy Offy that was the mainstay at the Speedway.

Jimmy Nairn, a friend of Stuart's, had explained to an acquaintance about the new fuel-injection setup and what Stuart was attempting to do with it. This unnamed contributor, who was a fireman by occupation and part-time artist, came up with a sketch that would become the Hilborn logo. "I loved it," Stuart said of seeing the sketch depicting a hand holding a syringe, the thumb ready to depress the plunger. "In fact, it was so nice that when Chevrolet first came out with their own fuel injection for the public, they copied the darn thing, not exactly, but very similar. I thought that it was good publicity for my own fuel-injection system."

TODAY

Electronic fuel-injection systems have become the norm, feeding gasoline to everything from the daily grocery-getter to race cars.

Now in business for more than half a century, the Hilborn Fuel Injection legend continues on into the new millennium. Today, Stuart continues to spend countless hours in research and development. He is an integral part of the continued success of the Hilborn family-run business, where his daughter Edris runs the office, while his son Duane manages their ultra-modern machine shop.

Reflecting back on all his years in business, Stuart feels his greatest achievement occurred in 1954, the year that the entire Indianapolis 500 field was Hilborn-equipped.

CHAPTER 10

Howards Racing Cams

HOWARD JOHANSEN

Hﾠoward Johansen was far from a normal speed merchant in the sense that he didn't confine himself to producing only camshafts. Like the prolific Lou Senter of Ansen Automotive, Howard delved into a variety of automotive equipment and participated actively in racing, both as a competitor and car owner. During the golden years of drag racing, Howards Cams was a vibrant company that was held in great esteem among his competitors.

GROWING UP ON THE FARM

Born in Polk County, Nebraska, on January 25, 1910, Howard was one of eight children in the Hans and Myrtle Johansen family. Howard began to show signs of being overly resourceful at an early age, beginning about the time when he removed all the casters from their beds. He attached them to wooden race cars he'd made and took the cars outside to play on a pretend race car track. Another time, he disassembled the cream separator. Unfortunately, the folks returned home in time to find the machine scattered about the floor in pieces. Under the threat of cruel and unusual punishment (he thought so), it was put back together in better running condition than before. Howard's interest in automobiles was tweaked the time he wanted to see if the compression could be improved in his dad's Model T by pouring hot lead through the spark plug holes. Howard was quoted as saying, "It worked, but it sure painted the inside of the tailpipe."

THE MOTORCYCLE

By the age of 18, Howard built a homemade motorcycle that he rode throughout the local hills with a fellow bike rider. While out riding one day, both boys had a little competition to see who could ride the farthest without using his hands. Howard was ahead of his friend when his front tire hit a rut, upsetting both him and the bike. He was struck in the head by the other motorcyclist's tire and received a severe head injury.

Howard was hospitalized for an agonizing 30 days with severe facial fractures around one eye. As he was being discharged from the hospital, he was given a Coke bottle–thick pair of glasses and told that he'd be cross-eyed and would have to wear the corrective glasses the rest of his life. As soon as he got home, the glasses were in the trash can. With the same absolute self-determination he showed all his life, Howard performed eye exercises daily for several months until his vision returned to normal. He didn't need glasses again until the ripe old age of 75.

HOWARD'S AUTOMOTIVE REPAIR GARAGE

By 1941, Howard was married and working as an auto mechanic in Shelby, Nebraska. That same year, he received his draft notice and was given the choice to either be inducted into the military or to get a job with some defense-related industry. California, with all its naval yards and aircraft factories, seemed to be an opportune place to seek employment. He loaded up his '32 Ford convertible with a toolbox and his worldly belongings packed in the rumble seat, and with a motorcycle in tow behind, he and his young wife, Liz, headed west.

As the war was coming to a close, Howard was already making plans for the future. He'd noticed

Opposite: Howard Johansen adjusts the Cadillac V-8 in the Bebek brothers' CRA track roadster that held the lap record at Carrell Speedway in 1953. Howard built the engine and the fuel injection system. *Courtesy Don Johansen*

a large stack of 30-inch-square metal sheets in the scrap-metal yard at Vultee Aircraft, where he worked. His supervisor said that they were his if he removed them immediately. Howard planned to use them to construct a building; he and his brother-in-law had already bought a vacant corner lot at 10122 South Main Street in Los Angeles with intentions of opening an automotive repair shop and service station once the war was over.

After getting the building permit for the shop, he began construction by welding a framework out of steel piping and then welding the thin metal sheeting to the skeletal structure. One day, a building inspector stopped in to check over the proceedings. He informed Howard that any welding on the building could only be done by a certified welder. Howard inquired about getting himself certified and was told that he would have to take a certification course. He passed with the highest score ever recorded at the testing center.

The shop quickly evolved into a high-performance manufacturing business, and in short order, he became heavily involved in car racing.

CAM GRINDING

During the war years at Vultee, he began to experiment with camshafts by setting up a homemade jig on a lathe, and he practiced until he had the basic fundamentals worked out. He then converted an old belt-driven lathe into a cam grinder by installing a rocking table and a tool post grinder.

It is not known where Howard came up with the data for his first cam grind, but like the majority of other grinders of that generation, it could have been taken off a Winfield or even a Riley or Bertrand profile. That old cam grinder is now a forgotten piece of history and sits neglected, rusting away behind the Menifee machine shop.

RACE CARS

After the war, the CRA was formed as an affordable racing venue for amateurs, but its focus quickly changed from semi-street roadsters to all-out race cars. The CRA events drew a huge following and offered hands-on experience for any driver who had aspirations of moving up into the big leagues. Numerous equipment manufacturers got involved in the CRA racing circuit, including Al Sharp,

On September 15, 1946, Howard entered his newly completed four-port Riley–powered '23 T roadster at Gardena Speedway's half-mile dirt track, placing second in the semi and winning the ten-lap main. Seen here in car No. 52 and averaging 70 miles per hour, Howard is following eventual semi winner Andy Linden, driving the flathead-powered No. 51 pickup. *Courtesy Don Johansen*

the Spalding brothers, Chet Herbert, Nick Brajevich, Phil Weiand, Barney Navarro, and others.

Howard first got into the local track-racing scene in 1946, when he built and drove his own roadster. On Sunday, September 15, 1946, at Garden Speedway, Howard drove a four-port, Riley-equipped, '23 T roadster to a second-place finish in the semi and won the main feature, which wasn't too bad for the car's first outing. In the 10-lap main, Howard's car averaged 70 miles per hour on the half-mile dirt oval.

Although he did spend some time behind the wheel of the track roadster, Howard knew that his driving career was over after he crashed a somewhat radical midget he'd built. Always on the cutting edge of innovation, the midget was designed sidewinder-style with a Ford V8-60 engine mounted sideways in the car's chassis, using a heavy-duty chain to drive the rear axle (like an oversized go kart). While practicing in a vacant lot, he flipped the unstable midget and quickly realized that he was better at preparing a race car than driving it.

The four-port Riley in the track roadster was eventually replaced by a variety of engines, including an Ardun-equipped Ford, GMC six, flathead V-8, and finally a Cadillac. In 1951, when his GMC-powered roadster driven by Charley Carr set the lap record on Carrell Speedway's half-mile dirt track, one reporter for *Hot Rod* said that Howard's car, "stormed ahead of the field in a startling display of pure, unadulterated power."

He sent the track roadster with driver Pat Flaherty to race in the lucrative Hurricane races in the Chicago area. The Hurricane Racing Association, which was promoted under the guidance of the Grantelli brothers, held races at Chicago's Soldier Field and other tracks in the Chicago area.

One thing Howard could do instinctively was to pick out a driver who had talent. He hired such notable drivers as Andy Linden, Dick and Jim Rathmann, Pat Flaherty, George Amick, and Jack McGrath. All of these drivers would eventually race at the Indianapolis Speedway.

When the Cadillac engine was in the roadster, George Amick held the lap record of 19.90 seconds at Carrell Speedway until the track closed its doors. Amick went on to earn the Rookie of the Year award by finishing second in the 1958 Indianapolis 500.

THE LITTLE INDY 500
In 1948, the officials at CRA came up with the idea of putting on their own Little Indianapolis 500 at Carrell Speedway in Gardena. It would be a 500-lap, 250-mile event held on the half-mile dirt track during the Memorial Day weekend.

Howard entered a roadster driven by Pat Flaherty, who unfortunately ended up in the wall during practice. Dempsey Wilson, whose luck also had run out with a blown engine, had qualified in 17th starting position. It was too late for Howard to repair his car in time for the race, and it was obvious that Dempsey and company weren't about to accomplish too much with a dead engine. It didn't take long for the fellows to combine forces by installing Howard's hot Mercury V-8 in the Dempsey Wilson car, and history was made. Winning the Little 500 opened the door for

Dempsey as a race car driver, and Howard gained notoriety as an engine builder and camshaft grinder.

DRY LAKES RACING
In 1950, Howard joined the Glendale Coupe and Roadster Club, which ran under the Russetta Timing Association banner. Joining the club allowed him to compete at dry lakes meets. He also joined the American Racing Club to compete in SCTA events.

Howard instantly made a name for himself by showing up at a RTA lakes meet with a not-so-pretty, fenderless '35 Ford coupe powered by a mammoth, 510-ci, 360-horsepower gasoline engine. The 1931 Marmon V-16 engine was mounted behind the driver's seat. True to a Howard car, it was not pretty, but it was functional and ran like hell. He was not one to spend a lot of money on decorative frills and chrome parts for race cars, as he built them to do one thing: win races. The '35 Ford set the D/Coupe class record at 150 miles per hour with a one-way run of 160 miles per hour.

While the coupe was being built, an astonished bystander named Don Turner observed the construction. Don was employed at McGurk Engineering and was in the habit of going over to Howard's shop Saturdays after work to see what was happening. On this particular Saturday afternoon, "Whispering" John Meyers was installing pistons in Howard's V-16 Marmon engine. Don asked him what they were going to do with the huge engine, and they told him they were going to run it in a '35 Ford coupe at the lakes. When Don didn't see the car, he asked where it was. Meyers replied that someone had it out on an errand. Don then asked when they were going to race it. John answered, "This weekend." Don couldn't believe that Howard and his crew were going to have the coupe race-ready in time for the lakes meet the following day, so he sat down to watch the action.

When the car finally arrived, they quickly hauled out the stock engine and anything else that wasn't necessary and lifted the car up on a dolly. Howard took a hot wrench (welding torch) to the chassis and body panels to make room for the Marmon engine and tranny mounts. The Ford was finished and ran the next day at the lakes. Don said that if he hadn't seen it for himself he'd never have believed it.

After retiring to the farm, Howard converted a Spartan travel trailer into a motorhome using two Corvair engines with automatic transmissions. He installed windows up front, and Dodge truck steering gear. The engines ran independently of each other with their own set of driving wheels. *Author photo*

This is the result of Howard turning Tony Dedio's '34 Ford sedan into a dry lakes racer powered by a fuel-injected GMC six-cylinder. Ugly but fast is the best way to describe the yellow beast with its hand-painted signage and masking tape around the side windows to assist streamlining. It set the B/Sedan record of 141.17 miles per hour at a Russetta Timing Association dry lake meet in 1951. *Courtesy Don Johansen*

For the last RTA meet of the 1950 racing season, the Marmon was installed in the rear section of a '29 Ford. It set the record for D/Roadster and had the fastest speed of the meet at 156 miles per hour, even with poor surface conditions and a shorter course. Howard had collected enough points to finish 10th overall in the RTA individual point standings for his first racing season at the lakes.

The following year, he was well prepared in the engine department with a highly modified, 292-ci, GMC six-cylinder stuck in a B/Sedan '34 Ford two-door sedan. This sedan was a typical Howard car—fenderless, chopped and channeled, and with a '40 Ford hood for streamlining—not very pretty. Over the 1951 racing season, he removed the GMC and installed it in a modified Crosley sedan that set the record in B/Modified Sedan at 148 miles per hour at the RTA season finals. He also claimed the association's Top-Point Championship. During the same show, he removed the GMC and installed it in Al Barnes' '29 roadster. With Bob Rounthwaite driving, it set the B/Roadster record and posted the second-fastest time of the meet.

Howard took the Crosley to Bonneville that same year to run in two different classes—B/Modified with the GMC six, and D/Modified with the Marmon. He captured both classes with runs of 131 and 156 miles per hour, respectively. The record-setting Crosley's hood was littered with holes to accommodate both engines' exhaust headers.

DEDIO'S '34 SEDAN

Howard was one of those rare types who could make do with whatever was on hand to complete a task and make it work. This ability showed itself plainly when he was in need of a race car for a dry lakes project. One of his employees, Tony Dedio, had casually mentioned once that his old 1934 sedan would make a good race car. When Tony walked to a nearby restaurant for lunch one day, Howard was overheard saying: "Dedio won't mind."

Upon returning to the shop, Tony saw his car lying on its side and Howard busy with a hot wrench. The sedan was gutted, chopped, its fenders removed, its front end was replaced with a modified '40 Ford hood, and a fuel-injected GMC six-cylinder was in place of the flathead. It was far from pretty, but Howard had his race car and no doubt Tony was well reimbursed for the sedan. Howard raced the chopped '34 at El Mirage and set the B/Sedan record with a 141-mile-per-hour effort. Don Johansen said that after the car was finished, Tony stood back for a couple of minutes and finally said, "It really doesn't look too bad, does it?"

TWIN-BOOM STREAMLINER

Bill Burke started the practice of using a single, surplus, aircraft fuel tank for a dry-lakes streamliner body. Howard took it one step further, designing his streamliner around two 150-gallon aircraft fuel tanks arranged in a catamaran fashion. His first twin-tank car was built for the opening of the 1949 Bonneville National Speed Trials.

Don Turner recalled that Howard had first installed cable steering in the twin belly-tank streamliner. When he arrived at Bonneville, the officials ruled against the steering, so he had to make a trip into Wendover to replace the cables with an automotive-type steering mechanism.

The framework of the streamliner consisted of two independent angle-iron frames connected by struts and a live rear axle, while the aircraft fuel tanks had been split lengthwise to form the tops and bottoms of the vehicle. A full-race Mercury V-8 was mounted in one of the tanks, which was connected to a modified '37 Ford rearend that spun a heavy-duty 1-inch chain via a sprocket to the live-axle—go kart style. The opposite tank contained the driver's cockpit, with a large container of water (engine coolant) situated behind the driver's compartment to help offset the weight of the engine. The streamliner turned 167 miles per hour one way with a 147-mile-per-hour average. Dissatisfied with the car's performance, Howard cut the streamliner up when he returned to Los Angeles and started plans for a revised version. The original car did make the front cover of *Hot Rod*'s December 1949 issue, however.

For the 1952 Nationals, Howard introduced a completely new twin-boom streamliner powered by a potent little 296 DeSoto V-8. This vehicle was much more refined than the original, sporting a streamlined, fully enclosed cockpit where Lloyd Scott took care of the driving chores. The 375-horsepower methanol-fueled engine was equipped with custom-built aluminum heads, fuel injection, pistons, and camshaft, all manufactured by Howard. It had a 30-gallon water tank stationed in front of the driver's cockpit, with a 6-volt water pump to circulate coolant to the engine.

Unfortunately, the car didn't achieve its full potential at Bonneville because of a faulty transmission. Howard had used quick-change gears in a two-speed, homemade transmission. After the second run for the streamliner, he changed the gears to increase the car's speed. The replacement gears were installed improperly, and the teeth sheared. As Lloyd Scott attempted to shift into high range, he actually geared down. The car ran a clutchless system and couldn't take the sudden downshift. Lloyd was traveling in excess of 225 miles per hour at the time, and he was very lucky that no damage occurred outside of the transmission case, which could have resulted in a drastic accident. Scott did get inducted into the 200-Mile-Per-Hour Club for his efforts, with an unofficial speed estimated to be approximately 275 miles per hour and a best official speed of 171 miles per hour. The car also experienced handling problems, which Howard traced to an inadequate wheel caster.

The car returned to Bonneville in 1954, this time powered by a 258-ci Dodge Hemi V-8, but it failed to live up to expectations.

GOLETA 1949

The drag racing that began in July 1950 at Orange County Airport is considered to be the opening of the first recognized drag strip in the country to run on a regular schedule, but one drag race predates that opening. In 1949, a local car club held an organized meet on a two-lane service road at an airport just outside Goleta, California. That day's event was punctuated by a grudge match runoff between Tom Cobb and Fran Hernandez.

Unbeknownst to the rest of auto racing's fraternity, Fran was running a secret additive (nitro) in his carbureted V-8 flathead roadster, while Tom drove a blown GMC flathead V-8 in his coupe. After defeating Cobb in the runoff, Fran loaded his car on a trailer and left the meet, leaving no chance for a rematch.

Meanwhile, Howard had also entered a car in the event with Eddie Osipian as the driver. Eddie's alcohol-burning flathead (built by Howard) was installed in a modified Howard track roadster. All unnecessary interior items were removed, the body and engine were moved back toward the rear for better weight transfer, and bald track tires were installed for better traction. It may well have been the first car built strictly for drag racing!

At the end of the day, Eddie was the Top Eliminator of the meet and the winner of the world's first-ever organized drag race. Twenty years later, Eddie teamed up with Danny Porche and Jerry Johansen in the Howards Cams *Rattler* AA/F dragster with Larry Dixon in the driver's seat. Dixon set the low ET and the track record of 6.81 seconds during the 1969 Winternationals at Pomona. The restored *Rattler* now resides in the NHRA Museum in Pomona.

HOWARD 12-PORT

Howard was one of the first to use Harry Warner's 12-port GMC head, recognizing the advantages of its design. Even though he had great success with the Warner head, Howard felt it could be improved upon, as he wasn't totally satisfied with Warner's 90-degree valve layout.

Placing the valves directly over the cylinder limited the sizes of the valves. Howard came up with a design incorporating ideas such as angled valves that provided better breathing and allowed larger valves. His aluminum head weighed 37 pounds (less valves)

Howard's B/Modified Sedan Crosley waits to make a pass at Bonneville. It ran 131.96 with a 245-ci GMC six at Bonneville in 1951. Note the exhaust ports along the side to accommodate either a GMC six or a V-16 Marmon. *Leslie Long collection*

and was designed with a flat combustion chamber similar to that of the 1928 Chevrolet four-cylinder.

Two versions of the Howard 12-port GMC head were offered when it was first introduced in 1952: the standard overhead-valve configuration and a single overhead-camshaft layout. The standard 12-port incorporated bronze valve inserts, had large individual ports, a wedge-shaped combustion chamber, used '51 Oldsmobile rocker arms, and still weighed half of what the stock Chevrolet cast-iron job weighed. On the dyno, a 298-ci GMC engine equipped with Howard's head, fuel injection, pistons, and camshaft put out 303 horsepower on straight gasoline. With the can tipped to 30 percent nitro, the engine produced 351 horsepower at 4,500 rpm.

Once Howard reached his goal with a project, it was usually set aside in favor of another challenge. Several decades later after the Howard head's introduction, Bob Toros of Venolia Piston Company talked Howard into reintroducing the GMC head. Howard looked upon the project of updating the old head as a reason to build a race car for Bonneville that would be powered by one of his 12-port GMCs. The job of manufacturing the head was a collaboration between Bob Toros and Nick Arias of Arias Pistons, with Nick eventually taking over the project to produce a modern, high-tech version of the original Howard 12-port.

DYNAMOMETER

Howard's dynamometer came from a war surplus dealer who had a stock of them and thought that they were some sort of large water pumps. Tony Capanna of Wilcap bought two of these $250 hydraulic brakes and informed Howard of the find.

Howard built his dyno as a noncorrecting dynamometer, meaning that whatever reading it showed on the scale was the true reading. A truck transmission was installed between the engine and the water wheel to step down the rpms for the water turbine.

The transmission and water wheel were joined as one unit so that the torque readout would be more accurate. The complete dyno package was installed on a frame with wheels so it could be moved about as needed.

Howard always put his equipment through extensive dyno testing and field testing under actual racing conditions before selling it to the public. Bob Johansen said that his dad's philosophy on dyno testing an engine was, "It needs to hold the full pull for thirty seconds, and if it doesn't last, we'll find out why it failed and fix it."

CURIOSITY

Howard's curiosity was on display for Joe Panek of Roto-Faze Ignitions one time when he was at Howard's shop on business.

"I watched as Howard was standing on the dyno. He was holding onto a 4:71 GMC blower mounted on a Chevy engine. One arm was wrapped around the blower for support, and the other hand was operating the throttle. He was so engrossed in what he was doing, looking directly down into the fuel-injector body, that he didn't notice his overalls smoldering nor the insulation on the spark plugs melting; he was running the exhaust directly out of the block, no pipes."

According to Ed Iskendarian, in that situation Howard was observing how the curved impellers of the GMC blower had a tendency to push the fuel to the back side of the blower case.

LOGO

The first Howards Cams logo came out in the early 1950s and consisted of a profile of two camshaft lobes with the name "Howards" and an Indy-style race car with No. 7 on the side of it.

The second design is one of the most highly recognizable logos of all the specialty manufacturers. The red ring gear with black and white lettering has graced many of the nation's top race cars and was designed by longtime Howard employee Al Barnes.

HOWARDS RACING CAMS

Ever since he first became totally involved in manufacturing racing equipment and building race cars, the original steel-clad building was sufficient to house the business. But by 1957, the speed equipment end of the business had increased dramatically and a 5,000-square-foot cement-block building was added. The camshaft part of the business increased to the point that six brand-new Norton cam grinders were purchased just to keep up with orders.

When it came to manufacturing new camshaft cores, Howard's camshafts were on the verge of being overbuilt. His steel-billet mushroom camshafts were ground from 4140 chrome-moly bar stock. The majority of other grinding outfits used 8620 alloy billet, which was more than suitable for the job. The 4140 offered longevity and could be reground up to 10 times without sacrificing wear characteristics, whereas 8620 cams were heat-treated to a depth of only .030, prohibiting regrinding. Howard's

Like everyone who went into the cam business before Storm-Vulcan introduced their grinder in 1953, Howard built his own and is shown here performing his magic on a camshaft.
Courtesy Don Johansen

Howard removes the piston grove from the top of a cylinder in an engine block as his wife, Liz, watches attentively. *Courtesy Don Johansen*

heavy-duty cams were cut off of bar stock that came to the shop in 20-foot lengths. The steel-billet flat tappet cams were ground from chrome-moly bars and heat-treated all the way through, not just case hardened on the outside.

HOWARD AND WEIAND COLLABORATE

There were unwritten alliances among several of the early equipment manufacturers when choosing speed parts for cars that they sponsored. Ed Iskenderian and Vic Edelbrock worked well together, as did Howard and Phil Weiand.

One of the more unusual but successful dragsters to hit the quarter-mile in the mid-1950s was the Howard and Weiand–sponsored twin-engine *Bustle Bomb*. It wasn't the car's two engines that made it unusual, but rather the location of the engines. This car was set up with a Cadillac in the rear, the driver in the center, and an Oldsmobile in front. One engine would be used to launch the car, and the other would kick in once under way. Both engines powered the rear wheels.

It set a top speed of 151 miles per hour and fast time of 10.48 seconds at the first NHRA Nationals at Great Bend, Kansas, in 1955. It was also the first car to exceed the 150-mile-per-hour barrier and was probably the second most successful twin-engine

car, next to the Bean Bandits' twin-flathead dragster. Lloyd Scott, Noel Timney, and George Smith shared ownership in the *Bustle Bomb*. George owned the Caddy, while the Olds belonged to Harvey Goldberg, who worked at Howard's shop.

Two other well-known cars that Howard and Phil mutually sponsored were the record-setting *Tucson Speed Sport* roadster and the *Money Olds Special*, which was the first car to go 140 miles per hour on gasoline. The cars were all equipped with Howard and Weiand equipment. Both manufacturers capitalized effectively on the success of these cars by sharing the advertising costs in numerous magazine ads.

MIXMASTER AND THE DESOTO V8

Not content with setting records on land, in 1952, Howard moved into powerboat racing by sponsoring a 266 class hydroplane called *Mixmaster*. Howard prepared 276-ci DeSoto hemi V-8. By developing the engine on the dyno and replacing factory cast-iron parts with aluminum. Performance aluminum heads were cast that weighed only 31 pounds compared to the 56-pound cast-iron factory jobs. The 24-pound factory timing chain cover assembly was replaced with an aluminum 5-pound part. The valves were activated by a billet camshaft with lightweight mushroom lifters. Only the bottom end was left basically stock. Howard even developed a fuel-injection system for the motor.

Over the years, there has been much speculation on how Howard reduced the cubic-inch dimension of the DeSoto. Don Johansen recalls that his father sleeved down one cylinder to come up with 264 inches. Howard knew the only downside of using a smaller piston was a decrease in horsepower from that particular cylinder, as long as that piston weighed the same as the others. Simplicity at its best. Even with one oddball cylinder, the DeSoto pulled 310 horsepower on straight alcohol. The *Mixmaster* set the world record at the 1952 Orange Bowl Regatta in Miami with a two-way average of 122 miles per hour and a high one-way run of 127.

The *Mixmaster* was a threat wherever it competed until disaster struck at Marine Stadium in Long Beach. Bud Meyer was attempting a high-speed run when the rudder broke, destroying the boat and leaving Bud looking for another ride.

HOWARD'S 1955 CHEVY

When Chevrolet first introduced its new line of automobiles for 1955, it had a winner that was outfitted with what has become the best engine ever produced, next to the V-8 flathead. Specialty manufacturers labored long hours to develop speed equipment for this particular engine, and Howards Cams was no different.

Howard bought a '55 Bel Air coupe originally for his wife to drive, but his curiosity as to how the car would perform at the drag strip won out. The Chevy would prove to be an ideal rolling testbed for engine modifications and camshaft designs he had in mind, providing first-hand results under actual racing conditions.

He removed the stock factory 265 V-8, to be reinstalled at a later date. The shop already had acquired several engines from

Howard and eldest son, Jerry, pose with the remnants of a stripped-down track roadster powered by a Howard fuel-injected GMC six with a 12-port Howard head. The track roadster had been converted for the quarter-mile drags. *Bob Toros photo, courtesy Don Johansen*

Howard's aluminum 550-ci V-8 powers Roy Miersch's dragster on fuel to the tune of 189 miles per hour with an 8.20 ET. Note the pressurized oil tank in front of the engine. *Courtesy Don Johansen*

GM to experiment with, and it was with one of these engines that Howard was able to test his ideas. First, the engine was bored and stroked out to 306 ci. He wasn't comfortable with GM's stamped-steel rocker arms, as they hadn't been proven under severe racing conditions at that time, so they were replaced with the more conventional shaft-type. The tops of the heads were machined to fit the rocker arm assembly, which consisted of Ford rocker shafts and Howard magnesium adjustable rockers fitted into special aluminum rocker stands. An experimental flat-tappet camshaft was installed along with an Edelbrock manifold topped off with

three Stromberg 48 carburetors. The flywheel was replaced with a Howard 12-pound aluminum wheel, a La Salle floorshift transmission replaced the Chevy outfit, and the stock rearend was removed in favor of a Ford unit. The factory stock engine had been dyno tested to 135 horsepower. After the modifications, Howard was able to pull 274 horsepower on gasoline.

Howard wasn't a driver, and one of the few cars that he personally competed with in drag racing was this Chevrolet. At Santa Ana, he drove the car to 105 miles per hour, raising the class record by more than 5 miles per hour. He also entered the Chevy in the C/Gas class at the 1955 NHRA Nationals at Great Bend, Kansas, and won the class trophy at 94 miles per hour.

HOWARD'S ALUMINUM V-8

Don Johansen described the lightweight, hemispherical-valve, aluminum V-8 engine that his father designed and built as "reverse engineering." Don said that his dad designed the engine around the largest aftermarket pistons that he could buy at the time, which resulted in a huge (for those days) 550-ci engine. Because he wanted to use hemispherical heads, the first engine of choice was the 392 Chrysler, but the center bore spacing was too close. Instead, Howard started his aluminum engine from a 430-ci Lincoln V-8—the engine's 4.900-inch bore spacing allowed for a stronger cylinder wall and stronger main webs, and the bore could be enlarged.

As the engine was to be used only for drag racing, Howard designed it without any water jackets, resulting in an almost bulletproof block. Decades before carbon fiber, Howard thought to replace the stock metal valve covers (copied from a DeSoto hemi V-8) with replicas made of fiberglass to save weight. The valves were operated by a custom, mushroom-tappet camshaft, and the Hemi heads, which were machined from solid aluminum alloy stock, were fashioned after Chrysler heads. The original version of the engine was built to run without an oil pump and instead utilized a pressurized oil reserve tank with a pressure valve that released oil into the engine while it was running. After several mishaps with burnt rods, Howard finally installed an oil pump in the engine. The oil pan is almost nonexistent because the crankshaft rides well up into the thick webs of the block. The engine was first run on a fuel-injection system designed by Howard that later was replaced with a GMC blower.

The aluminum engine was tried out in Roy Miersch's dragster for trial runs, with a best run of 189 miles per hour in 8.20 seconds on injectors. It was too bad that Howard didn't take the engine to the next level. He left the development of aftermarket aluminum V-8s to the likes of Keith Black and others who followed much later.

Howard did still use aluminum as a replacement metal for much heavier cast iron, marketing Chevrolet V-8 alloy heads that he'd developed originally for his twin-engine dragster. These Chevy aluminum heads were first introduced in 1962. They weighed 42 pounds less than the stock cast-iron units, were equipped with larger ports and valves, had a higher compression ratio, and were sold complete and ready to install.

CHEVROLET STOCK CARS

The performance division of GM gave two new 1957 Model 210 Chevrolets to Howards Racing Cams to be turned into stock cars to compete in the West Coast NASCAR and United States Auto Club (USAC) circuits. Regrettably, by time the cars were delivered to Howard's shop, the racing season was one-third over. The two Chevys ran under the Enoch Chevrolet banner and were driven by Rex White and Marshal Sargent, with Ron Bush (of Bush's Vacuum Brakes in Paramount, California) as their crew chief. Rex would go on to win a NASCAR championship later in his racing career. The two Howard-prepped cars competed throughout California, Oregon, and Washington, placing eighth and tenth in the final point standings in NASCAR's Western Division for the 1957 season.

The Chevys were hauled to the races on trailers towed by pickup trucks, whose braking power couldn't always be depended upon for emergency stops while traveling through the mountainous highways of the Sierra Nevada and the Cascades. Howard designed a trailer-brake setup in which the trailers had their own set of hydraulic brakes to assist in stopping, similar to what's available today on many trailers.

HOWARD'S RODS

Howard was first introduced to aluminum rods through a 392 Chrysler engine, compliments of Iskenderian Racing Cams. In 1958, Isky had made eight sets of aluminum rods out of flat stock on a trial basis. Some of them were sold, and some were loaned out on a free-to-use basis. One racer whose Hemi was equipped with Isky's free-to-use rods sold the race car, with Isky's rods still in the engine. As luck would have it, the new car owner happened to be sponsored by Howards Cams.

The Howards-sponsored car had an engine explosion at the drags, and it was only after tearing the engine down that Howard had a good look at these newfangled rods, and he liked what he saw. He appreciated the attributes an aluminum rod had to offer to a highly modified engine and, after a bit of brainstorming, he was in the forged-aluminum rod business. Howards Cams was the first aftermarket outfit to offer forged rods, with superior strength and manufacturing costs over that of a rod cut from flat stock. The rods were manufactured completely in-house, excluding the raw Alcoa aluminum alloy forgings. These forged rods are still manufactured in the same Howards Cams shop today by Howard's youngest son, Bob Johansen.

THE *WARD-HOWARD CAM SPECIAL*

Howard was most renowned for his unorthodox approach in building race cars, and some cars were so innovative that they caused considerable interest wherever they made an appearance. The one Howard car that stood out over the others was the twin-engine job built in 1957, and even though there were already twin-engine cars in competition, his twin was different.

What made this dragster unique was the side-by-side engine arrangement. It would have been much easier to go with an inline setup. The idea behind having the engines arranged side by side was to have the weight far back to the rear of the car to give the

slicks as much bite as possible. The engine on the driver's right faced forward, and the one on the left was reversed; using this setup nullified any effects of engine torque rotation. The reverse-facing engine had a Howards aluminum flywheel bolted to the front hub of the crankshaft. Its two ring gears meshed with the two ring gears of the adjacent engine to act as one common drive. Howard reported that there was never a problem with the alignment or with overheating of the gears. The front and rear engine mounts were attached to both engines so they worked as one solid unit. The mounts were also adjustable, allowing the use of several different driveshaft lengths so the engine weight could be transferred differently to suit track conditions. In keeping with the uniqueness of the car, a modified rearend similar to a live axle was used, with one large aircraft-type disc brake mounted on the left wheel for stopping power.

The dragster started off powered by two '57 Chevrolet 283 engines bored and stroked out to 339 ci and fed pump gas through three carburetors. The first major event for the dragster was at the 1958 Oklahoma Nationals, where it broke a rear axle during eliminations. After the Nationals meet, Howard realized that the car needed more power, and he began to experiment with chain drives for GMC blowers.

The dragster was upgraded for the 1959 racing season with more powerful engines and a streamlined aluminum front fairing. The Chevy engines were now 318 ci each, equipped with hand-fabricated chain drives turning over 4-71 blowers with four Stromberg 97 carburetors mounted on top of each blower. Together, these engines pumped out 840 horsepower on gasoline.

Glen Ward

WARD-HOWARD CAM SPECIAL
WORLD'S FASTEST – QUICKEST DRAGSTER

"Real Gone Gasser" 177.85 MPH-8.85 Seconds

A promotional ad for the *Ward-Howard Cam Special* twin-engine Chevrolet dragster driven by Glen Ward. At the time Howard didn't want to be identified as the car's owner racing against others using his camshafts. Note the single Hilborn injectors on the blowers. *Courtesy Don Johansen*

Once the blower drives had proven themselves, Howard went into production with cast-aluminum encased chain drives.

The original driver of the dragster was Glen Ward, who piloted the car from 1957 to 1959. The three Johansen brothers accompanied Glen to the big NHRA meet in Detroit. On their way home, they stopped off in Oklahoma for a race meet, and the dragster was totaled at the end of the strip when the brakes failed. The wreckage was returned to Los Angeles and rebuilt, but the accident meant that Glen, although not seriously injured, would not be driving the dragster for some time. Jack Chrisman took over the reins of the car from 1960 to 1961, and Glen returned to drive it for the 1962 season.

When Chrisman took over the controls from Glen Ward, the reconstructed car went on to win Top Eliminator at the 1961 NHRA Winternationals with an 8.99-second ET and 170 miles per hour. This particular version of the *Cam Special* had the frame extended with a sheet of plywood up front to help in streamlining.

THE *HOWARDS TWIN-BEAR*

After Jack Chrisman won the 1961 Winternationals, he and Jerry Johansen—Howard's eldest son—set out to conquer the NHRA World Points Drag Racing Championship. This quest meant they'd have to travel throughout the summer, competing in a variety of drag racing events held across the country. In preparation for the tour, the engines were completely gone over, and the fuel injectors on the blowers were switched over to Scott injectors. The dragster was given a fresh coat of white paint. The fellow who painted the car also did the lettering and drew two cartoon bears, representing Jack and Jerry, on the front—hence, the "Twin-Bear" dragster.

Jerry Johansen, all of 19 years old, was the sole pit-crew member and chief engine mechanic for the entire summer of racing. It didn't take long for the dragster to become known nationally as the *Howards Twin-Bear*. With the combination of Jack's superlative driving technique and Jerry's mechanical wizardry, the dynamic duo won the NHRA Points Championship.

Glen Ward once again took over the driving duties for the following season. At the 1962 NHRA Winternationals, he set Top

Pictured with the *Twin-Bear* dragster after winning NHRA's first World Championship are, from left, driver Jack Chrisman, engine tuner Jerry Johansen, and car builder Howard Johansen. *Courtesy Don Johansen*

Time for the meet at 176 miles per hour and tied for low ET with "Sneaky" Pete Robinson at 8.50 seconds.

Over the five-year lifespan of the *Howards Cams Special/Twin-Bear* dragster, the car held an enormous amount high-speed and low elapsed-time records and won Top Eliminator throughout the country.

Howard's twin-engine design must have looked solid from an engineering viewpoint, as far as Jim Nelson and Dode Martin of Dragmaster fame were concerned. They built the successful *Two-Thing* twin-engine dragster, emulating Howard's engine layout. The *Two-Thing* proved quite successful in competition and, ironically, took Top Eliminator at the 1962 Winternationals.

THE HOWARDS BLOWER DRIVE

The GMC Roots blower really came into its own after the NHRA placed a ban on hot fuels. Without the help of nitro, racers were faced with increasing the cubic inches and/or installing a supercharger. Blowers were either mounted on top of the engine and driven off the crankshaft snout by means of belts or chains, or were mounted on the front using a Potvin-type drive.

The Howards blower drive for the Roots supercharger came about as a consequence of the *Howards Cams Special* twin-engine dragster. When the car was first built, the engines were equipped with carburetors, but after the 1958 Oklahoma Nationals, Howard realized that to be competitive, superchargers were the way only to go. At the time, no one type of blower drive dominated the racing scene. Some used chain drives, some ran V-belts or Gilmer belts, and some ran front-mount drives. The Gilmer belt hadn't proven its supremacy at the time, leaving Howard to choose what would be the most suitable for him.

The chain drive won out in Howard's estimation, and he hand-fabricated two drive systems for the twin-engine dragster. After the chain drives had proven themselves on his car, Howard refined the design and put it on the market. The Howards blower system consisted of a No. 40 double-roll chain drive that was lubricated by engine oil and encased in the heavy-duty cast-aluminum housing. By the time Howard introduced the blower drives, however, it was too late to make an impact on the market. Several other companies introduced Gilmer-belt GMC blower drives that were much lighter and less complicated, spelling an end to the chain and V-belt units.

CHROME WHEELS

The phenomenal growth in aftermarket custom wheels began in the 1960s and did not go unnoticed by Howard. Rather than investing in expensive tooling for sand-cast, molded wheels, Howard felt that the job could be done with a line of pressed-out-steel chrome wheels. He would produce the center, and the rims were purchased from the manufacturer. In the beginning, the wheel centers were cut with a homemade automatic flame cutter and then sent out to be hydraulically pressed into shape; this procedure lasted until the costs of pressure-forming the centers increased to the point that Howard figured the job could be done in-house for less money.

A surplus store outfitted him with the hydraulic-ram cylinders and controls necessary for the job. Bob Johansen remembered his dad going off to the store and returning with nine large hydraulic cylinders and heavy-plate steel, and in no time he had constructed a machine that was capable of forming the wheel centers. Howard also designed and fabricated his own chrome-plating tanks and polishing equipment.

Bob said that his father never worked from blueprints; at best, he would use a rough-drawn sketch, and the rest just came out naturally. He could mentally visualize each step in the project.

One of the more notable customers to run Howard's wheels was the team of Sox and Martin. Ron and Bud campaigned their Howard-cammed A/FX 427 Comet (outfitted with Howard's wheels) to win the Factory Stock Eliminator at NHRA's 1964 Winternationals. The Sox and Martin shop in North Carolina was an eastern rep for Howard's products.

ADJUSTABLE ROLLER TAPPET

After several years of methodically studying the problems associated with fine-tuning a full-blown racing engine, Howard felt he'd solved part of the problem. He conceived a method to advance or retard camshaft timing by up to 15 degrees using an adjustable tappet that allowed for proper valve timing in whatever rpm range an engine tuner was striving to achieve.

One of the advantages of these lifters was that the timing could be adjusted for each individual cylinder. They also allowed the same camshaft to be used in either a blown or normally aspirated engine simply by rotating the tappets for more or less overlap. They were offered with offsets ranging from 5, 10, or 15 degrees and essentially provided the engine tuner with a single, multipurpose economical camshaft.

Bob Johansen said that he and his father spent many hours down at the library searching through the patent records for adjustable tappets and found none. Howard received a patent in 1960 for the innovative adjustable roller tappet that he advertised as having over 45 different duration settings.

CAM WARS

Many times, humor crept into the competing ads for various cam manufacturers, and no one in the business could do it better than Ed Iskenderian, as Howard was to find out.

The ad that really got the friendly advertising rivalry going between Isky and Howard was Howard's ad portraying the 5 Cycle camshaft as something rather humorous. His ad showed five cartoon stick bicycle riders in a line with the fifth cyclist dressed as a clown. The four riders represented the four cycles of an engine, and the guy with the clown outfit represented the "other" cycle, i.e., Isky's much-ballyhooed 5 Cycle camshaft.

This ad provided Isky with more fuel to fan the flames of the Cam Wars. Howard may have been a genius when it came to mechanical things, but he was no match for the wily mind of Ed Iskenderian. Isky simply adopted the clown for his own purposes and used that clown so effectively in many of his ads that one would have thought that the clown worked at Iskenderian Racing Cams.

The gasser-class cars became favorites with the cam grinders to boast their superiority claims. Howard even sponsored Doug Cook in a B/Gas '41 Studebaker sedan and later Cook's '37 Chevy coupe C/Gasser, before Cook teamed up to form the Engle-cammed Stone, Woods, and Cook Willys coupe team. Each cam-grinding outfit had its share of dragsters, gassers, et cetera, to bring to the reader's attention all the attributes of its product.

WINGED EXPRESS

Probably the most highly recognizable car that carried the Howards Racing Cams decal was the notorious *Winged Express* AA/FA of Al "Mousey" Marcellus and "Wild" Willie Borsch. This record-setting Fuel Altered roadster was usually driven by Borsch with only one hand on the steering wheel. Borsch suffered from narcolepsy, and it's said that occasionally, Willie would fall asleep, strapped in the race car while lined up in the staging lines.

At the 1968 Winternationals, Willie ran an unbelievable 7.29 seconds; the ET needed to qualify for Top Fuel Eliminator

A Howard's decal shows the Howard bear riding a Howard steel wheel while holding a cam in one hand and an aluminum rod in the other. *Author photo*

As the Howard twin-Chevy dragster evolved, so did its fuel-delivery system. Howard replaced the bulky eight Stromberg 97s with two four-barrel carbs. *Leslie Long collection*

(AA/FD) was set at 7.28 seconds. Mel Scott of Scott Fuel Injection said that at the following Winternationals, Willie qualified the car for Top Fuel Eliminator, bumping Don Garlits in the process. Unfortunately, the Altered was voted out of Top Fuel by concerned, and possibly intimidated, Top Fuel pilots, who said that a Fuel Altered shouldn't compete against dragsters. The Marcellus and Borsch team was removed from the Top Fuel bracket, and Garlits was reinstated.

Besides the full quarter-mile, smoke-filled, record-setting runs and a driver steering with one hand on the wheel, the Marcellus and Borsch roadster will be remembered for the huge wing sitting above Willie's head. Al Barnes, the shop manager at Howards, was the one who suggested they install a wing above the T roadster to improve the handling during high-speed runs.

LIZ JOHANSEN

The old maxim that "behind every successful man is a woman" holds a lot of water, and Liz Johansen was the woman behind Howard. She was the one who kept the company sailing in a straight line, allowing her husband the freedom from daily business concerns to concentrate on the manufacturing end. Liz not only ran the office and helped out elsewhere in the shop when needed, but had time to raise a family of one daughter and three sons.

Bruce Larmer remembered a time as a teenager visiting the Howard shop to buy parts for his club's drag car. At that time, Bruce was a high school student and a member of the Vulcans car club, as well as the driver for the Vulcan's supercharged Chrysler '32 Vicky, which was featured in *Hot Rod*'s 1961 yearbook.

"When I arrived at Howards, an overhead door was open and an engine was being run on the dyno. I walked over to the doorway and watched as the engine howled away, and then what really impressed me was how Liz, who was also watching the show, picked up a wrench and walked over, without batting an eye, to the racing motor and tightened up several exhaust header bolts that had shaken loose. I was amazed by her casual attitude, as if this was an everyday thing . . . knowing how my own mother would have reacted in a similar situation."

Lou Senter of Ansen Automotive told of the time when the great Mickey Thompson made a friendly $200 wager with Liz Johansen. Mickey lost but didn't have the funds on him to pay up. Every time they would meet, Liz would jokingly ask for the $200, and Mickey would always pull out a $1,000 bill and ask for his change. This scenario went on for several years, until one time Liz calmly reached into her purse and produced eight crisp $100 bills. Among lots of laughter, Mickey paid off the bet.

NOTES FROM TED FRYE

Ted Frye was the traveling sales representative for Iskenderian Racing Cams, and for a hobby, Ted ran a record-setting belly tank at the dry lakes. He said that even though similar specialty manufacturers competed for the same piece of the market, conversation was always friendly among the majority of manufacturers.

One time at the lakes, an announcement came over the PA system saying that Howard Johansen needed to borrow a welding torch.

"The only thing that was available was a cutting torch, and Howard had to weld a small-diameter, solid-steel driveshaft," Frye said. "Nonplused with having to use a cutting torch, I watched as Howard simply laid the snapped shaft on the lakebed and welded the broken pieces with ease."

Howard once mentioned to Ted how he had recently gotten a very large water tank for free. A neighboring farmer had a huge round water tank half buried in the ground and said that it was free to anyone who wanted it, providing they removed it themselves. Howard had a use for the tank and went over to study the situation. While he was sizing up the tank, he noticed a water truck parked at the far end of the field. The truck had brought in a load of water for irrigation purposes, and Howard went over and asked the driver if he could buy some water. After he'd explained to the driver what he wanted the water for, curiosity got the better of the driver, who told Howard he could have the water for free. The driver had to see this plan in operation.

Much to the dismay of the curious onlookers, Howard slowly poured water into holes that he'd dug around the sides of the tank.

He continued pouring until the tank finally loosened itself and began to float upward enough to allow him to pull it out with his tractor.

"It always amazed me the way Howard looked at and overcame adversity," Frye said. "Problems that would have the average person ready to throw in the towel and walk away only seemed to challenge Howard's mechanical prowess."

A RECORD OF INNOVATION

Howard's talents and interests weren't fixed solidly in any one direction. It seemed that whatever field he delved into, he was successful.

In an article, the automotive authority Don Francisco described Howard as the "Master of Ingenuity." Auto historian Mark Dees called Howard the "Quintessential Hot Rodder." Both quotes pretty well sum it up. There were other great speed equipment innovators of that era, but few (including Lou Senter) could measure up to Howard's prolific record of development and experimentation in the hot rodding field. He ventured into untried and unproven areas, and he did it his way.

No doubt there were numerous projects Howard worked on that didn't see the light of day or were simply forgotten about. An early example of one of those projects came from the confines of the garage behind his house, before the Main Street shop was built. Don Turner remembered the day when he showed up at Howard's house just in time to see one of these innovations put to the test. Howard had installed a hydraulic brake system of his own design on the front end of a Harley-Davidson motorcycle. To see if the idea worked or not, Howard offered the bike to one of the guys who was always hanging out at the garage. It was only after the fellow raced off down the street that Howard remembered that he should've warned the rider to be easy with the front brake when stopping.

Apparently, the brake performed perfectly; as the rider came roaring down the street and yanked hard on the front brake lever, the front wheel locked instantly, causing the bike and rider to do a complete flip. Don said that he and the others just stood there with their mouths open, watching in disbelief. A Hollywood stunt driver couldn't have done any better, and fortunately the rider wasn't hurt seriously.

Another commodity that Howard possessed was a seemingly natural ability to observe or find a practical solution to any problem, no matter how complex.

Don Turner related another story about when Howard bought a new German-made milling machine: "Al Barnes was trying to figure out how to place a piece of odd-sized work on the bed of the mill to machine it. Howard looked at it for a bit and said that it was no problem, and proceeded to weld it to the bed of the mill. He told Al to just chisel off the welds on the bed once he was through machining the piece."

Howard's trademark overalls were a carryover from the early days of growing up on the farm in Nebraska. At one reunion he and Liz attended, Howard was dressed in a suit, and numerous people attending the reunion asked about his overalls, saying that

Here's the rare Howard's adjustable roller cam decal that was to advertise a one-shot, cure-all lifter that never caught on with racers. *Author photo*

no one could recognize him without them. The following year, he showed up at the reunion wearing his overalls under a sport jacket, shirt, tie, and a smile.

Like many of his peers in that early specialty-manufacturing period, Howard Johansen lacked a formal education and never sat in on an engineering class at college. This absence of higher learning was the last thing to deter or stand in his way of becoming successful in whatever endeavor he turned his hand to. He'd built a business that was well known in the world of racing and, true to his nature, when the novelty of manufacturing speed equipment wore thin, he didn't hesitate to hand over the reigns to his son and move on to things that held a greater interest for him.

Howard Johansen passed away at the age of 78 on October 25, 1988.

CHAPTER 11

Iskenderian Racing Cams

ED "ISKY" ISKENDERIAN

Edward "Isky" Iskenderian, a.k.a. the Camfather, is the father of the modern-day performance camshaft and is known to performance aficionados the world over.

The Iskenderian family can trace its roots to Armenia, where Ed's father was a blacksmith before immigrating to the United States and settling in California. Edward Iskenderian was born in 1921 in Tulare County near the city of Cutler, and after a failed grape crop due to frost devastated the family financially, the Iskenderians moved to Los Angeles and settled in the Palm Grove and West Adams area, where Edward's father opened a shoe repair business.

Even as a young teenager, Ed showed signs of budding entrepreneurialism, possessing a natural knack for electronics and repairing radios for neighbors as well as selling radios he'd reconditioned. Around that same era, he also first encountered a gow job. Ed said that he was about 12 years old when he began to notice a type of car that was completely different than the run-of-the-mill vehicles that inhabited the roadways. These street rods were mainly Model Ts void of all unnecessary parts and propelled with hopped-up four-cylinders. Ed and his buddies found out they could see more of these cars up at Muroc Dry Lake.

"Once we got there, we realized we should've brought more blankets; it's awfully cold at night," Isky said. "We'd get up there about midnight and have to wait until daybreak to warm up. Some of the guys would be tuning [their cars] up, and some would be foolish enough to go out in the dark and try out their cars, and there were accidents. We sure got a good look at a lot of different cars. We learned a lot from what the fellows had built, and we kind of dreamed up what we were going to do ourselves.

"I remember one time we didn't have a ride up to the dry lakes, but we'd go to Bud Hines' shop on Highland Avenue near Hollywood, because all the racers stopped there on the way to the dry lakes. No one had room until Johnny Junkins came by towing his modified roadster. Junkins said that I could ride in the race car if I wanted to, and in case it came loose on the tow bar, I could steer it.

"Once we got to the dry lakes with the modified, Junkins had one of the best cars up there. He attracted a lot of attention, and it was fun to be with him and the car as everyone came over to look at it."

When Ed first began to play around with cars, a kid could easily pick up an old relic of a Model T that had been sitting in someone's yard for the princely sum of $5 or so.

"If you dragged a Model T home and put it in your backyard in those days, a lot of dads wouldn't allow it. They'd make you get rid of it, but not my dad. My dad was fascinated by the fact that I was fooling around with it. He'd come by and say, 'Edward, how do you know about these things?'"

While attending grammar school, Isky met John Athan, a fellow student who was good at repairing bicycles. Ed's own English-made bike had developed gear problems and was in need of repair. Since that first meeting in 1934, the two have remained the best of friends.

Lou Senter, Nick Brajevich, Bill Brown, and others all attended the same school system. In junior high, "Racer" Bill Brown was a classmate who went on to become a technical writer for *Hot Rod* and later started Racer Brown's Camshaft Engineering Company. Brothers Don and Jimmy Nairn, owners of Speedway Pattern and Nairn Machine Shop, respectively, were classmates and lifelong friends of Ed's, as was the multitalented Bobby Meeks, a driving force behind the Edelbrock dynasty.

Opposite: Ed Iskenderian and his famous Isky roadster. Ed purchased the '24 T-bucket, in substantially less modified form, for the princely sum of $25 from his friend John Athan. That was in 1938, when both were still in high school. *Courtesy Ed Iskenderian*

Above: Isky and longtime friend John Athan, 1938. Isky's prized Maxi F-heads still have their stock configuration of two valve covers per head. *Courtesy Ed Iskenderian*

The Maxi heads required sealing the exhaust ports in the engine block. The engine was already in the roadster, so the car was propped up on two wheels, and the ports on one side were filled with molten lead. Then the procedure was repeated on the other side. Isky and a friend took the opportunity to make this gag photo. *Courtesy Ed Iskenderian*

After grammar school, Ed attended John H. Francis Polytechnic High School in Los Angeles because of its excellent machine shop courses. He finished off his last year (1940) of education at Dorsey High School, located only three blocks from where he lived.

THE ISKENDERIAN ROADSTER

Since the days when the youth of America first began transforming Henry's Model Ts into hopped-up warriors of the road, there were always a few rods that stood out from the rest. To achieve a pedigree, the builder or vehicle had to have attained a reputation of one form or another. A good example of this is the Elvis roadster. Elvis didn't own it, but he drove the car in the movie *Love Me Tender*. As a result, this roadster gained enough notoriety to make it a very desirable and extremely expensive hot rod.

Obviously, the Iskenderian roadster has become highly recognizable because of the person who built it so many years ago and who still owns it today. It's a genuine, untouched hot rod from the early days. Like Athan, Isky wasn't planning on his car someday becoming famous; he just wanted a hot rod to have fun with.

The origins of the Isky roadster go back to 1938, when it was purchased from John Athan. For $25, Ed received a fenderless '24 T-bucket—minus the turtle back—and an Essex rolling chassis. The parts were disassembled and, because his father was using the family garage at the time, Ed rebuilt the frame under the back porch of his parents' apartment building. The T body was stored on the roof of the family garage until the garage became available to complete the project.

At first, just to get the roadster on the street, it was outfitted with a 21-stud V-8 with stock carburetion and exhaust system and a stock T radiator shell. Later on, the radiator shell was replaced with a creation fabricated out of two 1933 Pontiac grilles. For engine gauges, he installed a coveted Auburn dash, and he

engine-turned the stainless-steel firewall to highlight the engine compartment. Eventually, the '32 V-8 was ported and relieved, a Winfield camshaft was installed, and an Edelbrock slingshot dual manifold replaced the stock unit.

The engine's cast-iron heads remained factory original, although he performed some work on the combustion chambers; when the opportunity came along to remedy this, he jumped on it—a set of aftermarket Maxi F-heads. These heads were developed originally to prevent overheating problems on Ford trucks that were pulling under heavy load conditions. This particular F-head design had the exhaust valves located in the heads while retaining the stock intake valves in the block. The Maxi heads that adorn the Iskenderian roadster were purchased from Rex A. Head. Isky said, "When I heard these heads were available for $65, I jumped on it; they made it look like an overhead-valve V-8 engine."

When Isky was installing the Maxi heads on his engine, the exhaust ports in the engine block had to be sealed off, which he accomplished by pouring enough hot lead into the ports to make them flush with the block deck. As the engine was already in the roadster, he propped the car high up on two wheels. This way, Ed could fill the exhaust ports with molten lead and then repeat the procedure by lifting the car up on its other side.

The Maxi heads also came with a hidden cost—several days spent making each custom copper head gasket by hand. Also, after having a student at Santa Monica Tech make up a wood valve cover pattern, Ed had a set of covers cast in aluminum with the name "Iskenderian" handscribed along their length. These full-length custom valve covers replaced the factory jobs that consisted of two small covers per head. Along with the new heads on the engine, Ed fabricated chromed exhaust headers that joined into one larger pipe that ran the full length of the roadster.

In 1940, just after the car had been put on the road, it ran 111 miles per hour up at Muroc. At a Western Timing Association meet at El Mirage in 1942, running with the F-heads and slingshot manifold, Ed managed a very respectable 120 miles per hour in the V-8 Modified class. In those prewar days on the dry lakes, probably one of, if not the, fastest-running roadsters belonged to Vic Edelbrock Sr. Ed said that he'd wait until Vic was about to make a test run. Ed would pull up just off the racecourse beside him, and as soon as Vic took off, Ed would chase after him, keeping to the sidelines, seeing if he could keep up. Vic was a little faster.

When *Hot Rod* first came out in 1948, one of its monthly features was the Hot Rod of the Month, which included the car's picture on the front cover and a writeup about the vehicle's particulars. The Iskenderian roadster made the front cover of the June issue, along with an informative report inside the magazine. At the time of the article, the car had a Navarro dual-carburetor intake manifold. Eventually, it was replaced with an Edelbrock triple manifold, which it has to this day. The last time the roadster was licensed for the road was in 1951.

ROTARY-VALVE ENGINE

Maybe it was because John Athan was one year ahead of Isky at Polytech High, but each friend had to show the other that he was more knowledgeable in technical matters than his buddy, and this contest still exists today!

"John thought he really invented something, and that was a rotary-valve engine," Isky said. "Instead of poppet valves, he figured, 'Why not use a rotary valve?' So he went to the library and found out it had already been done, but he still wanted to make one. We used to think, 'Why not take a Buick straight-eight engine and take the head off and make a head with a big long tube—a rotary valve. No valve springs would be needed.' One day, I got the idea that I thought I could make one for a one-cylinder Briggs & Stratton engine in just a few days. So I made it, but leakage was a problem. It would idle pretty quiet, but soon as you'd open the throttle real quick, it would chirp like a blown head gasket. It would rev way up, and it finally threw a rod."

This rotary-valve experiment was based on a 1-inch-diameter tube that served as both the intake and exhaust manifold. It was welded to a 3/8-inch steel plate on one side of the pipe. The plate acted as the head for the engine. Next, the lawnmower carburetor was attached at one end of the tube via a welded mounting flange. A smaller-diameter but longer tube was inserted into the other end. A portion of the smaller tube stuck out of the end of the larger tube, acting as the exhaust pipe. The small tube also had a sprocket attached to it, which was driven by means of a bicycle chain from a corresponding timing sprocket on the crankshaft. The smaller pipe had two holes drilled through it, corresponding to the two holes in the steel plate. These holes were timed with the piston, acting as intake and exhaust valves, and were sealed from each other by a plug inserted into the tube. The underside of the plate was domed to act as the combustion chamber, and a spark plug hole was drilled and tapped on an angle next to the tube. Lastly, the L-head engine's valves were sealed, as they were no longer needed. Unfortunately, leaky seals caused the engine to throw a rod when it over-revved.

A scene out of 1940 with Isky and John Athan doing some four-wheeling behind Dorsey High School and stopping long enough for John to record their adventure on film. *Courtesy Ed Iskenderian*

Today, that rotary head resides somewhere in the Iskenderian archives. If he'd had a proper bearing seal and a lot of research-and-development time, who knows where Isky could have gone with it.

THE AIR COMPRESSOR

After graduating from school in 1940, Ed and John both got jobs at the Bethlehem Steel Shipyard, where they received a quick lesson in the art of heavy-duty fabrication welding. With the war raging in Europe, one could pick and choose his job if he had the qualifications. Ed and John agreed they'd be better off—and better paid—working in machine shop work, for which they had training. They applied and secured employment with the Martin Tool & Die machine shop in Torrance as machine operators, and whenever the two worked the evening shift, it was part of Ed's job to turn off the massive air compressor at the end of the shift.

It all ended one evening, as their shift was over and the shop was being shut down, John accompanied Isky over to the control panel, and as the two were deep in conversation, Ed absentmindedly shut off the air line, not the power switch. The huge, one-lung compressor kept pumping away, rapidly building up pressure. It blew before Ed had time to realize his mistake. The head was launched off the top of the cylinder, accompanied with a crescendo of escaping compressed air, straight up through the tin roof. The two stood there stunned for what seemed like an eternity, until they heard a loud, dull thud as the displaced compressor bounced off the shop roof and onto the ground. Ed was unceremoniously asked to leave.

Ed had been running a little sideline machine business from a garage behind his parent's apartment house. The back-alley Iskenderian Machine Shop consisted of a couple of metal lathes, a drill press, a band filer, and the usual assortment of hand tools, which was sufficient to do subcontract work for the larger outfits. It became his full-time job after the incident at Martin, and he kept it open until he received his air corps notice.

WORLD WAR II

With the choice of serving his country on land, water, or in the air, Isky decided on the army air corps, figuring that flying an airplane would come naturally as a result of his mechanical ability. He completed the ground school for pilot training at a base in Santa Ana, California, in 1944. But the air training, which was done in Scottsdale, Arizona, slowed down the process of becoming a pilot. It took Isky 13 hours to solo, whereas the average for solo flying was around 8 hours (some things just don't come easily, mechanical skills or not), although while in training at Scottsdale, the husky 21-year-old did break the situp record in the military's physical training program. Regrettably, even his physical strength couldn't help him complete the pilot training. He was transferred over to air transport command, where he served on C-54s commuting from the mainland to bases throughout the South Pacific with priority military personnel and supplies.

The rotary-valve engine experiment Ed undertook at Polytechnic High School. The engine still resides in Ed's archive. *Courtesy Ed Iskenderian*

ISKENDERIAN INTAKE MANIFOLD

Once the war was over and he was discharged from the service, Ed was eager to get his hot rod back on the road. He got to thinking about ways to pull a few extra horses out of his flathead. He decided on more carburetion. He'd seen other rods where the owners had fabricated their own manifolds, and he figured he could do that too.

He had his buddy Don Nairn of Speedway Pattern make up patterns for the cast-aluminum carburetor mounting bases. A flat piece of 1/8-inch-thick stainless plate was cut to the desired shape. For aesthetic appeal, Ed engine-turned the plate using an electric drill, cork, and valve-grinding compound. Four Ford Chandler carburetors were mounted sideways and placed directly over the ports, one carburetor throat per intake port.

Once the manifold was completed and installed on his engine, and with a little adjusting, it looked mean and performed fairly well on the street. While driving out to the dry lakes to a speed meet, Ed decided to see what she'd really do. The roadster could only reach about 96 miles per hour up the Mint Canyon Highway before it peaked, whereas it had seen 120 miles per hour with the Edelbrock slingshot manifold in a prewar event at the lakes. As soon as he arrived at El Mirage, the quad was unceremoniously replaced with the Edelbrock, which he'd taken along just in case. Obviously, one small venturi per cylinder was not enough to produce the results that Isky was searching for.

That dust-covered, four-carburetor Iskenderian manifold hangs as a memento on the wall in one of his storage rooms today—a reminder of those youthful, carefree days.

TRACK RACING

The one and only time Ed ever raced on an oval track, he lost to a three-wheeler. The Davis Automobile Company had Joe Thorn design a compact three-wheel car that was contracted out to race car builder Frank Kurtis to construct. The vehicle consisted of an aluminum body with room for two passengers and utilized a 60-horsepower Hercules four-cylinder engine for motivation.

Robert Petersen of *Hot Rod* needed some publicity shots showing this revolutionary new car in action, and Isky and John Athan were invited to race their roadsters against the three-wheeled vehicle. The race track proved a little too narrow for the roadsters to pass the nimble, three-wheeled wonder.

ISKENDERIAN RACING CAMS

Isky figured that a cam ground specifically for his Maxi heads' valve layout would be a step in the right direction. On the advice of Jimmy Nairn, he went over to Clay Smith's shop in Long Beach. (It could be said that Jim was the instigator in the birth of Iskenderian Racing Cams.) Ed was told that it'd be a good month before the cam would be ready, as Clay's time was already stretched to the limit between his involvement with several race teams and engine building, as well as grinding cams (with a hand-operated grinder). The delay got Ed thinking that if there was such a great demand for performance camshafts, maybe he should get into the business. He could see that there was a heavy demand for speed equipment with the increased popularity of car racing and hot rodding; automobile racing was growing at a tremendous rate.

With his machinist's background and years of hot rodding experience, the idea of starting a specialty manufacturing business, even though he had no knowledge of camshafts or how to grind them, seemed quite plausible. The first step was to pay a visit to Ed Winfield for advice. Winfield was a true mechanical genius when it came to the intricacies of the internal combustion engine. It is well documented that Winfield either took a liking to you, or he didn't. Fortunately for Isky, he was accepted into the confines of Winfield's confidence. Once he could see that this enthusiastic youth was serious about getting into the business, Winfield told Isky that there was a good business in grinding cams, but he himself wasn't interested in cam grinding on a large commercial scale. Winfield spent the time to show Isky how a camshaft grinder operated and allowed him to copy his own homemade camshaft grinder. Winfield would offer guidance in camshaft fundamentals in the years to come.

"When I first started in the business, I felt like I was horning in a little bit on Winfield's business because he'd been nice to me," Ed said. "I bought my first cam from him, and he showed me his machine. I saw how it worked." Note that the original Winfield camshaft grinder that Isky copied so many years ago now resides in the Iskenderian factory as a tribute to his mentor.

Once he decided to go ahead, Ed found affordable shop space in a corrugated tin building at the rear of the Mercury Tool & Die machine shop at 5977 Washington Boulevard in Culver City. John Athan and Warren Lipper were co-owners of Mercury and rented out a portion of the unused building to Ed for $25 a month. The tin building, with a dirt floor and no heating system, had been hastily erected during the war to house large stamping presses.

Ed picked up a used cylindrical grinder at an auction sale for $600 and, with the use of the Mercury machine shop, he fabricated a rocking table and cam follower to turn it into a camshaft grinder. This particular machine is reputed to have done over $1 million worth of grinding and is still in constant use today.

In the beginning of this cam-grinding venture behind the Mercury machine shop, Ed used his home address on 4807 West Adams in Los Angeles for any advertisements. A business-college student was hired on a part-time basis to take dictation and correspondence while Ed worked the camshaft grinder.

INTO PRODUCTION

Once he had his camshaft grinder, Ed needed to have a performance cam to offer to the public. The first creditable Isky flathead profile was based on a 0.320-inch-lift camshaft; the base circle was ground down, giving an additional .312 inch in lift and producing a considerably higher lift than a stock job.

For a trial run, the cam was installed in John Athan's roadster. According to John, "The engine really wound out and could light the tires in second gear with no difficulty. I went down Culver Boulevard, and when I put it into high gear, the clutch slipped even with my reinforced clutch; it'd never done that before. I was going about seventy-five to eighty and put in into high, and it slipped and I had to let up so it'd grab. I told Ed it was unbelievable. Ed knew

that he was on the right track; all you needed was lift, because all the flathead had was a tappet spring and a lightweight valve. You didn't have a rocker and a bunch of stuff. Everyone, including Winfield, had been conservative with their lifts."

Being the new kid in the cam business didn't help when Isky first opened for business. Without a proven track record to back up the performance of his cams, most of the local speed shops wouldn't carry his product. Ansen Automotive and Karl Orr's Speed Shop were the exceptions. The local boys who either raced the dry lakes or oval tracks were running Winfield, Harman & Collins, Weber, or several of the lesser grinders who had already established a name for themselves. Ed depended on kids who were just getting into the sport and didn't know one cam grinder from the other. Unfortunately, these inexperienced kids were not about to set any speed records at the lakes or on the race track.

"I had a hard time at first getting the masters right," Isky said. "I started grinding these flathead cams and had no sales, of course. I finally did make a few cams that looked a little funny and looked a little more radical than any of the others that were on the market, and I went around to the speed shops to see if they would buy them.

"I was a little ashamed of these cams because they had no clearance ramps. When these new fellows who bought my cams came down the street, you could hear [them] coming a block away with tappet noise."

What jump-started his business, along with the majority of the other parts manufacturers, was the introduction of *Hot Rod* in 1948. All it took was a 2-inch ad in the magazine's second edition to bring in customers. Ed received a call from a NASCAR team (E&E Racing) from out east. The fellow placed an order for two new 1007 track-grind camshafts at $20 apiece and, as he was in a hurry for the cams, he wanted them sent by airmail.

The early Iskenderian track cams had a fast action with no clearance ramps, but as long as drivers weren't concerned with lifter noise, they worked fine. These cams had a broader torque curve with good midrange power.

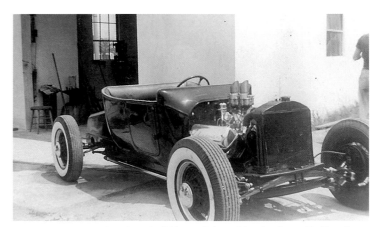

Isky's roadster is fresh out of the paint and body shop. Notice it still didn't have a grille shell or the Edelbrock slingshot manifold. *Courtesy Ed Iskenderian*

Here's a closer look at the Isky roadster's most famous feature: the custom-cast aluminum valve covers inscribed with Ed's last name. *Courtesy Ed Iskenderian*

"The short timing and fast action produced a noisy slapper cam," Isky said. "Fortunately, the simplicity of the Ford flathead V-8 valvetrain allowed one to get away with a not-so-gentle cam on the race track." These track cams gave the NASCAR boys passing power where it was needed to win races. Those orders from out east were instrumental in assisting Iskenderian Racing Cams through the make-it-or-break-it stage in the early days of business.

Needing to increase sales, Ed turned to mail order and set up a series of dealerships across the country. Anyone who wrote in for information about cams was offered an Iskenderian dealership. When there were enough to make up a list, he advertised them as Iskenderian dealers situated throughout the country. No doubt the Los Angeles speed shops did Isky a favor by not selling his camshafts—it forced him to look elsewhere for customers, introducing him to the power of advertising.

When Isky first opened shop, he set a goal of selling at least five camshafts a day, which equated to a profitable $100. He reached that goal within the first year.

Ed's primary business values were prompt service and good value for the buck. Shortly after opening the business, he had stocked up on preground camshafts so there would be no delay in delivery. Walk-in customers could simply exchange their used cam for one already preground. This policy also meant there was no delay in keeping up with mail-order deliveries. Isky also offered new cam cores for those who wanted to spend the extra money.

At first, like the few cam grinders of that era, he concentrated on grinding the popular Ford/Mercury V-8 and the Model A and B camshafts, which were the bread and butter for the cam shops. One day, Kenny Harman of Harman & Collins stopped in and offered to grind any non-Ford camshafts on a subcontract basis.

"One time, I sent them [H&C] a V-12 Cadillac cam that came in," Isky said. "After sending the cam back to the customer, he paid me a visit and said, 'This thing doesn't run worth a damn.'

H&C mistakenly put a flat-tappet profile on hydraulic cam. That's when I made my first hydraulic [cam]."

Later on, when the partnership of Kenny Harman and Cliff Collins dissolved, Isky found that he was the largest racing cam grinder in the country. Collins retained the H&C name, while Harman opened KH Cams, but neither business ever equaled the success of the original company.

Besides selling camshafts, Isky realized there was a good market for performance valve springs. He sold the heavy-duty Lincoln Zephyr spring as an Iskenderian performance valve spring. The Zephyr valve spring was more than adequate to meet the engine requirements of those early days, but as cam profiles became more radical, it became necessary to provide stiffer springs to control the valve action. Soon, spring manufacturers were called upon to come up with suitable heavy-duty valve springs to meet Iskenderian's demands for the performance camshafts.

EXPANSION

During his first year in business, Ed suffered greatly from bronchitis. The illness would impair his breathing to the point that he had to leave the cold, damp shop behind Mercury Tool & Die and go home to recuperate.

After spending a year learning the camshaft trade in the drafty tin building, it was time for a better—and warmer—shop. He relocated to a shop on Western Avenue and hired his first full-time employee, Norris Baronian. Frank St. Amant also worked in the office on a part-time basis and would later become the office manager. This shop soon proved unsuitable, and in 1950, Iskendarian moved to 5000 West Jefferson Boulevard, just across the street from Vic Edelbrock's shop. This location proved quite favorable for both parties, as Vic was constantly running dyno tests on engine-manifold combinations. Invariably, Isky would get the job of supplying a cam with whatever profile was required. It was a good, mutually beneficial, working relationship.

Hop Up magazine did a monthly series called "Meet the Advertiser" to introduce its advertisers to the readers. In the April 1952 issue, a two-page spread on Iskenderian Cams showed a picture of Ed sitting at a drafting table with a slide ruler in hand. It was a short story, but it did mention that the 30-year-old father with two sons had no intension of doing anything else but grinding camshafts.

As the business grew, so did the need for larger facilities. First, Isky built a shop on a vacant lot he'd bought on Slauson Avenue in Culver City. Later, expansion made a move to Inglewood Avenue in 1957 necessary, but the Slauson shop was retained. Now, Iskenderian Racing Cams was operating from two locations to fill the huge volume of orders. Ed would manage both operations during the day, while Norris Baronian oversaw the night shift at Inglewood. (Norris would eventually leave and open Norris Cams.)

Operating the business from two different locations presented its share of problems until the opportunity came along to purchase a mammoth complex that originally had been built for aircraft maintenance. In 1965, Iskenderian moved into its present location in Gardena that consists of a four-building complex totaling

50,000 square feet situated on property a city block long. After that, all the manufacturing was done under one roof, while the Inglewood and Slauson facilities were turned into warehouses.

T-SHIRT ADVERTISING

Isky may not have been the originator, but he certainly was among the first to turn T-shirts into a medium for corporate advertising.

Isky was confronted with this business opportunity as a result of sponsoring a couple of fellows who were going to attend the 1950 Bonneville National Speed Trials. He donated $100 toward the traveling expenses of Norm Lean and Doug Harrison, who were towing their Isky-cammed flathead C class '32 roadster to the salt flats. To show their appreciation for the financial assistance, the two grateful racers stopped at a silkscreen shop before leaving Los Angeles for Bonneville and had the Iskenderian Racing Cams logo screened on their T-shirts. The two young hot rodders ran a strong 132 miles per hour on the flats. It was not enough to capture a class win, but they did capture the attention of others at the meet with their screened Isky T-shirts.

The effect of this small act of appreciation by Norm and Doug toward their sponsor would have far-reaching consequences, introducing the T-shirt as an advertising medium for specialty manufacturers. Being an intuitive businessman, Ed could see the potential advertising value using this medium. The cost of a T-shirt in relation to its advertising value was phenomenal. He seized the moment, and it wasn't long before the Iskenderian logo was seen coast to coast, anywhere racing enthusiasts gathered.

VALVE TIMING FOR MAXIMUM OUTPUT

Probably the most useful booklet put out by any aftermarket specialty manufacturer for the amateur or professional engine tuner was titled *Valve Timing for Maximum Output* and contained a wealth of practical information regarding performance engines.

The idea to publish such an informative booklet came about after Ed had read an engineering book on the topic of timing for maximum output. He felt that by offering a booklet that explained the how's and why's, the camshaft buyer would have a working knowledge of exactly how the valvetrain functions and how to go about setting it up properly. It has grown in size from when it was first offered in 1948.

ANTIBOOTLEG SEAL

The novel idea of using an antibootleg seal was a consequence of the shop receiving numerous complaints from owners about their poorly ground Iskenderian camshafts. Upon examining these cams, Ed realized that his cams were being copied, and not well. The inferior imitations were costing Ed both sales and the reputation of his company.

Knowing that any machine shop that had a camshaft grinder with a copying device could produce substandard copies of any cam it wanted, and with a set of punches could put whatever name it wanted to on it, Ed figured that there had to be a way to overcome these forgeries. He recalled seeing how the railroad companies would place seals on the locked cars to ensure that their boxcars

This photo was taken in the alley behind the Iskenderians' apartment building in 1942. From left are Bob Gilcrest, Fred Brail, and Doug Fenn. Note the single taillight in the center of the turtle trunk and part of a sign on the garage behind them. This was Isky's machine shop prior to going into the army air corps. *Courtesy Ed Iskenderian*

weren't tampered with. With this in mind, he came up with the antibootleg seal, which was introduced in 1954 and proved to be a great advertising and marketing tool. The customer was guaranteed that if a camshaft had the Iskenderian seal attached to it, it was the genuine article.

HARD-FACE OVERLAY

When General Motors first introduced the overhead Oldsmobile and Cadillac V-8 engines, their cast-iron camshafts were not really suitable for regrinding, as the soft iron cores couldn't hold up to the punishment of a racing engine. The innovative Chet Herbert had the market sewn up with his steel-billet roller camshafts until the introduction of the hard-facing process.

The idea to hard-face a cam was derived from the flathead V-8 days. Ed remembered that after installing a reground camshaft, the end of the valve stems had to be built up by welding on a wear-proof material in order to get the desired valve lash, as adjustable tappets were not available at the time.

To combat the premature wearing of a reground cam, Ed came out with a system he called "hard-facing" in 1950. It involved building up the cam lobes with an alloy and then grinding to the desired profile. Initially, this alloy was ballyhooed as a top-secret product, but in reality it was called Wall-Colmony No. 4 and was a tungsten-carbide chrome-nickel alloy. To keep this product a secret from the competition, Isky would purchase the stuff through a welding supply house in 100-pound lots under an assumed company name and would have a courier pick it up.

At first, the alloy was welded directly onto the cam lobe and then ground, but this procedure proved difficult at times when grinding the desired shape on the lobe. Ed then came up with a system of first grinding the desired profile, grinding a 3/8-inch-wide groove into the toe of the lobe, and then filling it up with weld material. The grinding was then completed to a bulletproof finish.

This hard-facing process is still in use today by engine builders that need a camshaft to survive the severe punishment of long-distance racing (e.g., NASCAR) and where the rulebook disallows the use of a roller cam.

CONTINGENCY MONEY

At one time, the only thing a driver won at the drag strip was a trophy, possibly cash or a treasury bond, a kiss from the trophy queen if he was lucky, and bragging rights. Those were the days before companies got on the bandwagon, realizing that offering contingency money, points, and so on to racers who put their company decals on their race cars was good for business.

"We started the contingency program for drag racing by giving $500 for Top Eliminator by accident," Isky said. "I was surprised when I learned in the 1950s that the Champion man was right there at Indianapolis, and when you pulled into victory lane as the winner, you not only collected your winning purse, but if your Offy was equipped with Champion spark plugs, you got money from the Champion Spark Plug Company.

"Well, we advertised in *Drag News*. Even though we didn't win, we got a lot of publicity out of it. The NHRA Nationals were coming up at Indianapolis, so we put up $500 for Top Eliminator, and we won. Well, Norris (Baronian) was my factory rep out there at the Nationals, and he came back with a little message from the other 27 different classes saying, 'How about something for us?'

So the next year, we put up $100 for the class winners, and the next year [1963], we had 27 class winners and we paid $500 to Top Eliminator. We had it all to ourselves for a while; at this time, NHRA didn't have a contingency program."

ADVERTISING

An Iskenderian ad from the 1964 era pretty well sums up the life and times of Iskenderian Racing Cams and its owner: "The Penalty of Leadership is that the little guys are always gunning for the big guy." If Ed had never ventured into the camshaft business, he would have made a wonderfully successful advertising executive. He seems to have an inherent knowledge of how to market a product that appeals to the customer.

Even though a manufacturer may have a quality product that is used by the majority of winning cars, no one will know unless it's brought to their attention, usually in the form of advertising. By the late 1950s, various specialty companies began to advertise specific cars that were winning races by using their products. Some of these sponsored cars competed in the same classes, and it soon became a challenge for the advertiser to come up with an innovative ad to catch the reader's attention.

In 1958, Howards Cams ran an ad in an attempt to inject some humor about Isky's unbelievable 5 Cycle camshaft, which backfired on the competitor with an ironic twist. A Howards ad depicted a series of five cartoon bicycle riders with the fifth cartoon rider dressed in a clown's outfit. Each cyclist represented the four cycles of an engine, and the fifth, as far as Howards was concerned, was a clown. Ever ready to seize the moment and not to let an opportunity slip by, in the same magazine, the Iskenderian ad depicted a caricature of a clown driving a brand-new Chevrolet pickup truck with the box of the truck filled with trophies and a bicycle. A Chevrolet pickup had actually been presented to the winner of the NHRA's Top Eliminator at the 1958 National Championship meet at Oklahoma City. It just happened to be the Iskenderian-sponsored Cyr and Hopper dragster powered by a 5 Cycle–activated Chrysler.

Prepared to serve his country and save the world, a young Ed Iskenderian is seen decked out in his army air corps uniform. *Courtesy Ed Iskenderian*

Home on military leave in 1942, Isky brought along Fred Brail for home-cooked meals and a ride in a genuine California hot rod. Note the Edelbrock slingshot manifold. *Courtesy Ed Iskenderian*

To take full advantage of the success of the 5 Cycle and the hilarious clown escapade, Iskenderian Racing Cams even issued a 5 Cycle decal depicting a clown riding a bicycle and holding onto a large trophy.

In a brilliant move, Isky employed the services of perhaps the greatest drag racing cartoonist ever, the renowned Pete Millar. The liberties that can be taken in the form of a cartoon were more than exemplified in Pete's "Isky 'toons." Some bordered on defamation, but all contained loads of humor. Enough of these strip cartoons were produced that eventually Pete published two volumes solely on Iskenderian Racing Cams. The cartoons poked fun at some of Ed's cam grinding competitors as well as certain engine builders and drag racers. Millar placed Ed's face on the Statue of Liberty, and he created a depiction of Isky as the "Camfather." One strip was a takeoff of the Charles Atlas beach scene ad, where a skinny (well-known drag racer) guy with his lady friend were intimidated by an overgrown bully (another racer). Ed is shown at the bottom of the strip as a muscle-bound promoter from Iskenderian Racing Cams offering to "make a new man out of you in only 5.97 seconds." That was the magical elapsed time set by T.V. Tommy Ivo, who was the first drag racer to break the six-second barrier and an Iskenderian customer. Oddly enough, the skinny little guy in the cartoon ad looked sort of like Tommy.

The sky was the limit when it came to Ed's imagination for advertising. In one ad, there was a picture of Albert Einstein and a quote: "Einstein Discovered the 4th Dimension. Ed Iskenderian . . . the 5th Cycle." How can anyone compete with that?! Another ad pictured Ed looking at a camshaft with Antonio Stradivarius admiring one of his violins. It was excellent advertising for the Camfather.

SEMA

In 1963, Ed Iskenderian was appointed president of the newly formed Speed Equipment Manufacturers Association with Roy Ritcher, Bob Hedman, Bill Garner, Dean Moon, Al Segal, Vic Edelbrock Jr., John Barlett, and Phil Weiand as directors of the board. In its first year of operation, the association had close to 40 members.

The word "Speed" in the acronym "SEMA" was eventually changed to "Specialty" to appease certain bureaucrats who associated speed with the carnage of accidents caused by reckless teenage hot rodders on the public roads.

In 1985, Ed was inducted into the SEMA Hall of Fame.

DYNAMOMETER

The Iskenderian shop was one of the first camshaft grinders to acquire a dyno to test its camshafts. Its first dynamometer was a beam-balance style purchased from Vic Edelbrock for $1,500, but it was resold to Iskenderian dealer Ted Kessler in Buffalo, New York.

"We went up to San Francisco to the Hall-Scott Engine Company (it had been involved in engine manufacture during World War II), which was auctioning off equipment," Isky said. "We bought two Taylor dynamometers for $600 apiece. We set one up and started to test every day. Luckily, we had Joe Milliard running it, and then we got 'Bones' Balogh, who was a godsend because he ran Chevys at the drags." Bones was with Isky from 1959 to 1966 and then moved over to Venolia Piston Company.

When Robert "Bones" Balogh was asked how he got his nickname, he replied that when he was in high school he was a skinny kid; someone attached the name to him, and it has stuck ever since. As well as being a very proficient dyno man, Bones has had a successful drag racing career that has extended from 1958 to the present date.

FORCED-INDUCTION DRIVES

After the NHRA imposed its ban on exotic racing fuels (nitro) in 1957, engine builders had to look elsewhere for the horsepower needed to win races—to blowers and big cubic inches. Race cars had been using superchargers of some description since long before the war, but it was the GMC Roots blower that racers and specialty manufacturers were turning their attention toward. This particular blower was plentiful, economical, and a means of acquiring large amounts of horsepower without having to resort to hot fuel mixes. By 1958, Chuck Potvin had fully developed his front-mount blower drive, which was marketed through the Moon Company. Numerous other companies offered top-mounted GMC blower drives as an alternative. And although he had no prior plans to enter that particular line of speed equipment manufacturing, Isky found himself in a situation that seemed to push him toward it.

"I used to follow the government surplus bulletins," Isky said, "and I noticed there were 1,500 brand-new (GMC) blowers sitting up in Tooele, Utah, near Salt Lake City. They had been sitting there ten years or more, and the government was putting them out on bid. I went to Vic Edelbrock [Sr.], and I said, 'You know the Chevrolet V-8s getting popular and this [6:71] blower is a little too big, but if we can reduce the gear ratio between it and the crankshaft, we can run them slow. We can move the blower forward a little bit so there's room for the distributor in the back. If you

In 1942 while on leave from the army air corps, Isky borrowed his brother Luther's Triumph motorcycle to pay his friend John Athan a visit at the Mercury Tool & Die shop. *Courtesy Ed Iskenderian*

Louis Senter's Ansen Automotive was one of the few Los Angeles speed shops to take Ed and his fledgling business under its wing. Karl Orr was another early supporter. *Courtesy Ed Iskenderian*

make the blower manifold, I'll make the Gilmer belt pulleys for it, and I think we can sell them.'

"Chuck Potvin got an idea that he should loosen up the blower by turning the OD [outside dimension] down about .005 of an inch. His idea was that if it backfired it wouldn't bend the rotors. So, we used to send our blowers to Potvin to have them machined down. Of course, it recycled a lot of air and it wasn't long before the guys said that they wanted them tighter.

"One day, a junkman sold us a heavy blower off a diesel engine. We noticed it had plastic sealing strips on the tips of the rotors. I said, 'That's what we ought to do. We ought to put a Teflon strip in there and really tighten up the blower, and if it touches the case it'll be just Teflon.' Pretty soon, we were installing Teflon in the blowers."

Jimmy Nairn of Nairn Machine developed a method of machining a dovetail groove along the outer edge of each rotor. Then a strip of Teflon with a dovetail profile was installed in the groove, which assisted in closing up the internal clearances, making a more productive blower.

The Iskenderian blower drive was designed so the top and bottom pulleys were interchangeable, giving the unit the ability to over- or underdrive the blower. Isky made blower kits for Chevy, Chrysler, Oldsmobile, and Pontiac. You could buy the whole kit complete with a Gilmer belt.

At a time when drag racers were beginning to trade in their multiple-carburetor setups for superchargers to stay competitive, it was Isky who outfitted "Big Daddy" Don Garlits with his first GMC blower. As a point worth mentioning, Iskenderian Racing Cams was also Big Daddy Garlits' first sponsor. In 1959, Garlits, being the top dog out east, was challenged to come west and compete in three meets for some serious West Coast–style

racing. At the time, Don was running eight Stromberg 97s on top of a Crower U-Fab intake manifold, an Isky cam, and some goodly doses of nitro in his dragster. A few of the West Coast boys, including Art Chrisman, were already running GMC blowers on their fuel-burning rigs. The first of the three meets was the Smokers car club–sponsored United States Fuel & Gas Championship race held at Famoso Raceway, about 20 miles from Bakersfield (not NHRA sanctioned), where Don managed a 172-mile-per-hour run before throwing a rod. Chrisman won the meet with his blown Chrysler. After the race, Isky had Garlits and Setto Postoian (another eastern racer) return with him to the shop, where he outfitted both of their cars with GMC blowers. Don kept the carburetor outfit on top of his blower and went on to win the next two meets at the Kingdom strip in Lodi, California, and at Chandler, Arizona.

Even after Garlits and Postoian had the Jimmy blowers installed on their respective cars, they each retained their eight carburetors. This setup made visibility rather difficult for the driver, but there was also an interesting feature with these carburetor setups. At Bonneville, Isky had noticed an odd number of fuel lines going to a group of Stromberg 97s situated on top of a blown engine in a belly tank belonging to Tom Beatty. It seems that Tom had gone to the guru himself, Ed Winfield, to inquire about how to eliminate fuel shortages to the engine when running multiple carburetors on fuel.

"When you convert the 97 carburetors to alcohol, you use twice as much fuel," Isky said. "You have to bore out the needle and seat, and it's unknown whether you're passing enough through the needle and seat to keep the float full. So Winfield had worked with Beatty and told him how to run part of the fuel into the bottom of the bowl with a certain-sized jet. You figure that

75 percent is going into the bottom of the bowl without a needle and seat, and the needle and seat with the float will make up the rest. This way, you are sure to have plenty of fuel in the bowl. As soon as you leave the line under power, you turn on the line to fill the bottom of the bowls, and you shut it off at the end of the run, otherwise you'll flood over." Beatty ran this setup on his GMC-blown 303 V-8 Oldsmobile-powered D/Lakester at the 1958 Bonneville Nationals, where he ran a very fast 232 miles per hour in an open-wheeled belly tank.

They used Winfield's setup on the Garlits and Postoian engines with 16 individual fuel lines feeding the eight Strombergs perched on the blowers.

"Boy, it was a lot of plumbing," Ed said, "and was dangerous too."

CAMSHAFTS

Over the years, Isky has come up with some memorable names for his various camshaft grinds. Names like Superlegerra, 404 Constant Acceleration, Polydyne, and 5 Cycle are all familiar to speed enthusiasts worldwide. His first camshafts were similar to everyone else's in those times (excluding Winfield), as the industry was getting a handle on the intricacies of cam design. It was a challenge to come up with a winner, which Isky did with the 1007 track cam that proved very successful with the NASCAR crowd, and with the mushroom track grind that really set the wheels in motion. But any Ford V-8 aficionado worth his salt knows that the fabulous 404 was the hot ticket in the realm of flathead power.

Ed Winfield assisted Isky in those early days, and in turn Isky lent assistance to Frank McGurk. In 1953, Isky and Frank collaborated on a camshaft design for the Chevrolet six-cylinder. The outcome of this union was that McGurk opened his own cam-grinding business, and Isky had what he called the Iskenderian Dual-Pattern camshaft to add to his catalog.

"(Frank) was a friend of mine, and he specialized in six-cylinder Chevrolet camshafts and wasn't a threat to my own cam business," Isky explained. Not too many of us would invite more competition to the dinner table.

When the Chrysler Corporation unleashed its Hemi-head V-8 to the motoring public, its ability to breathe deep wasn't overlooked by the racing fraternity. The combination of the Hemi and GMC blower proved to be successful and became a common sight at the drags. A California drag racer by the name of Ernie Hashim, who ran a speed shop in Bakersfield, helped Iskendarian Cams establish its reputation as a leader in Hemi performance. His front-mounted, GMC-blown Hemi had set the quarter-mile speed record prior to Cook & Bedwell with a run of 153.11 miles per hour.

The friendship between Ernie and Ed began well before drag racing ever came onto the scene. It started before the war, when Ed was driving his roadster on his way to visit some relatives and stopped into Hashim's service station for gas. Ernie was impressed with the hot rod, and he held Isky up long enough to take some pictures of the car. In the postwar era, Ernie opened a speed shop and got involved in drag racing, and he was one of the first to get his hands on the newly introduced Chrysler Hemi V-8. A local

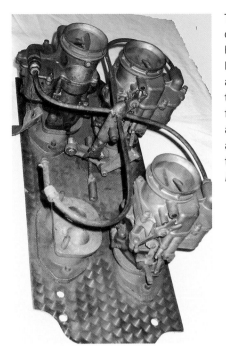

The Iskenderian four-carburetor manifold built by Isky in the late 1940s. Notice the engine-turned aluminum mounting base, the thoughtfully designed fuel block and gas lines, and the linkage bell crank attached to the base of the fuel block. *Courtesy Ed Iskenderian*

Chrysler dealer had to replace a new engine in a customer's car and gave the slightly damaged one to Ernie. Because of his chance meeting with Ed years earlier, he decided to go with an Isky cam in the dragster he was building.

The Infamous 404

Lady Luck was shining on Ed the day a customer walked into the shop to inquire about having an Offenhauser midget engine's camshaft repaired. Some of the lobes had been damaged, and once the repairs had been completed, Ed made a copy of the cam. He liked the looks of the cam's profile (No. 4 Offy grind) and figured it would be interesting to try out in a flathead. The master cam was set aside for the time being, but when the day came that he had a request for an extra-wild flathead cam, Ed remembered the Offy profile.

"These guys [S&S Speed Shop up in Fresno] phoned up, and they wanted something radical," Ed said. "I said, 'If you guys really want to do something radical, I'll grind you one.' It went like a bomb. It had good low end and top end too."

To overcome the inverse flank of the Offenhauser cam lobe, he came up with the idea of taking the contour off a 1923 radius tappet designed by the renowned engine builder, Harry Miller.

"Fred Offenhauser went to Ed Winfield for help to update the Miller racing engine after purchasing manufacturing rights at the bankruptcy auction," Isky said. "Winfield said he could improve on Miller's radius cam and came up with the type-four Offy radius cam."

Many years later when Ed Winfield had retired to Las Vegas, Isky would occasionally pay him a social visit. Usually, the conversation would get around to the merits of camshaft design, and Isky related the story about how he copied the Offy No. 4 cam profile onto a flathead camshaft. Winfield revealed that it was one of his cams.

He couldn't make them fast enough for Offenhauser. Winfield told Isky, "I made a master so they could do their own."

The 404 cam was originally ground on 1932 Ford V-8 camshafts due to the wearing characteristics of the steel cam, but as the supply of '32 cams ran out, the 404 was successfully ground on cast-iron cams. As for performance, the low spring pressure, short timing, and high lift gave it a fantastic midrange power, working exceptionally well in an engine that had a very light valvetrain like the flathead Ford V-8.

It became known as the "Constant Acceleration" cam and was probably responsible for more flatheads winning races than any other cam grind. It would be a tossup between the 404 and Potvin's 425 Eliminator as to which had the better top end, while the 404 had the midrange—both could claim to be the number-one flathead camshaft.

Most likely one of the more notorious drag cars to run a 404 was Californian "Jazzy" Jim Nelson. His modified Fiat Topolino coupe ran a fully modified nitro-burning flathead that was a force. At NHRA's first National Meet at Great Bend in Kansas in September 1955, the coupe ran an incredible 10.90 ET, which was the second lowest for the meet, and set the A/Competition Coupe class record at 132.93 miles per hour. Nelson and that Fiat put a lot of so-called dragsters on the trailer, making him one of the best salesmen for the 404 flathead cam.

The 5 Cycle Camshaft

The term "five-cycle" originated with the Italians as part of the technical language used to describe the overlap period in a Formula One racing engine. Drag racing chassis builder Scotty Fenn visited Isky one day and talked about this Italian five-cycle cam affair, and he suggested that Ed should grind a five-cycle camshaft. The idea was intriguing, and Isky could see the advertising potential behind such a claim. He filed the idea away in his mind for the possibility of exploiting it at a later date.

The shop that Ed built on Slauson Boulevard in Culver City in the early 1950s. John Athan now owns the shop; for years it was filled from the floor to ceiling with used cams and grinding wheels. *Courtesy Ed Iskenderian*

That chance came when a couple of drag racers from San Diego named Emory Cook and Cliff Bedwell had Bruce Crower build a Chrysler Hemi for their dragster. Crower suggested that they should contact Iskenderian Cams for advice on selecting a camshaft, as he used Isky cams for his own engines. Sensing that the Cook and Bedwell car would make an ideal testbed for a new, radical cam he'd been developing, Ed sponsored the car.

Crower assembled the 354-ci engine using his company's six-carburetor U-Fab intake manifold and his dual-disc clutch assembly, and with the Iskenderian cam, the car was debuted as the *Isky-U-Fab Special*. Needless to say that when the dragster set a new speed record of 166.97 miles per hour (Lions Drag Strip in 1957)—11 miles per hour over the existing record—Isky announced the new "5 Cycle Hyperbolic Crossflow 7000" camshaft to the world.

The crossflow incorporated in the cam timing had a longer duration than normally used at the time. This extra-long overlap period helped scavenge the combustion chamber and worked as a cooling cycle to effectively combat detonation. When all was said and done, the Cook and Bedwell machine was advertised as being the World's Fastest Dragster at 169.32 miles per hour in 8.89 seconds.

"I saw the significance in five cycles," Isky said. "It's a lot better than four cycles. [To say that] I'm going to put an extra cycle in the engine, that's quite a publicity stunt." Leon Cook, Iskenderian Cams' advertising man, took full advantage of the speed record set by this revolutionary new five-cycle cam, much to the chagrin of his competitors, as seen in their own advertising disputing the fifth-cycle theory. Up to that point in time, all who'd ever given combustion engines even the slightest thought knew there were two types: two- and four-cycle. When Iskenderian Racing Cams introduced a five-cycle camshaft, eyebrows were raised.

550 Superleggera

"This is the camshaft that placed Iskenderian Racing Cams at least five years ahead of my competitors," Isky said. "At the time, there seemed to be a limit on how long a cam you could put in an engine. One day, we decided to lengthen the duration about 20 to 30 degrees [retaining the same lift], and we called them the 7,000- and 8,000-rpm camshafts.

"We plotted [the horsepower curve] out, and we noticed three dips in the power curve. I said, 'Maybe our dyno is kind of old and maybe it's not that accurate,' so we didn't pay much attention to those dips, though I had read where harmonics in the valvetrain can repeat like this. We decided to make a soft-action cam with high lift [550 inch] and an unheard-of long duration—we were getting 1.3 horsepower per cubic inch with a 283.

"When the first 283 came out, we bought a new Corvette short block for about $400. It was an all-stock 283 with the best stock heads Chevrolet had at that time [no porting or valve work], which were double-hump. We had either an Edelbrock or McGurk long manifold with eight 97 carburetors on it. It was a top-end, high-performance engine, so we decided to make this radical cam. I thought it was just an experiment and didn't know if it'd run in our engine. To our amazement, all of a sudden it jumped 75 horsepower just from that cam alone, and the carburetors didn't have to be adjusted or anything; the venturis automatically compensated for the extra airflow and gave more fuel. Peak power was about 7,000 to 7,500 rpm and even had good power at 8,000. We kind of held back on that cam for a little bit, and we came out with 505A, 505B, 505C, and so on—hot, but milder cams.

"Top engine builder Dave Zeuschel came by one day and said that he wanted me to make him a 'superleggera' cam, and I said, 'That really sounds good, but what does that name mean?' Well, in Italian it means 'super light and fast,' so we used that name right away.

"I told McGurk about [the camshaft]. 'Oh, bullshit,' he said. 'But Frank,' I said, 'this is high lift.' Frank told Isky that a Chevy V-8 was all done at 5,000 rpm and that a Chevy wouldn't produce power at 7,000 or 8,000.

"He didn't realize that you need a very soft-action valvetrain," Isky said. "It was like Winfield's style. With Winfield's cams, you didn't need heavy valve springs; he always had a soft action."

Mickey Thompson was another nonbeliever about the horsepower claims coming out of the Iskenderian shop.

"Mickey Thompson phoned up and said that the 505 was a lot of bull and that our dyno was worn out," Isky said. "I said, 'If you don't believe it, how about if we put our motor on your dyno.'"

Bones went over to Thompson's state-of-the-art dyno facility and allowed Mickey to run the engine personally. The first run was up to 5,500 rpm. Bones told him to take up it to 6,500, which he did. Again, Bones told him to take it up higher, but Mickey said that he didn't want to be responsible for blowing up the engine. So Bones took over the controls and got the engine up to 7,000 and did another run at 7,500 rpm. Mickey couldn't believe it and stated that the so-called stock Corvette V 8 (excluding carburetion and camshaft) was all tricked up inside, but the pan was pulled to reveal all stock GM parts.

One of the earlier cars to run the 505 with a great deal of success was a Potvin-style GMC supercharged Oldsmobile dragster owned by Dick Guyetto. To make the most of the clown

controversy, the Iskenderian-sponsored car was known as the *Isky 505 Clown* dragster.

With further development on the dyno and using a 555 Superleggera in a near-stock Corvette 327, they got 462 horsepower at 7,500 rpm on pump gas—an amazing 1.41 horsepower per cubic inch. Later on, they reached 1.74 horsepower per cubic inch from a carbureted Chevy on pump gas—572 horsepower!

NASCAR Cams

Isky's relationship with Vic Edelbrock Sr. went back to the early 1950s, when the two first began to collaborate on engine testing. When Vic needed camshafts for a performance package that he was putting together for a Detroit auto manufacturer, he knocked on Isky's door. Vic had a contract with Mercury's performance division to come up with a NASCAR-legal performance kit for its stock cars. The deal was for 500 kits, which included intake manifolds, camshafts, chilled iron lifters, and dual valve springs. This homologated the performance parts so that they would be considered original factory equipment and thus legal for NASCAR racing. At that time, the factory was having problems with premature camshaft wear under extreme racing conditions.

"The only way [to fix this] was to hard-face the cams and use special chilled iron lifters," Isky said. "It was the only solution I knew, unless we went to a roller cam, but you couldn't put a roller cam in the Y-block because of the tappet bore design." The Iskenderian Y-block hard-faced camshaft was the only one on the market that would hold up under the severe racing conditions of the NASCAR speedways.

Although Isky's cam, dual springs, and lifters were thoroughly tested, along with the Edelbrock equipment, on Vic's dyno prior to shipping the stuff off to Mercury, there was a fly in the ointment—ignorance. At the races, the Mercury cars began to experience problems with valvetrain breakage. When they ran on the rough surfaces of the speedways, it caused the rear tires to break free and spin, over-revving the engines to the point that the valvetrains malfunctioned. Fortunately for all concerned, Californian Gus Davis was working for Holman & Moody in Charlotte, North Carolina, building Grand National engines for Ford. After disassembling and repairing numerous Mercury engines, he realized the problem was inadequate spring tension. He solved it by installing a Pontiac inner valve spring. He got Mercury to list the Pontiac inner spring in its parts catalog. Later, when Gus mentioned to Isky what he'd done to rectify the problem, Isky told him that his kits originally contained two valve springs, but that Mercury's factory rep had said that the inner springs weren't necessary, so the kits were never shipped with them.

Besides supplying camshaft kits for Mercury, in 1957, Isky supplied approximately 100 racing cams to Pontiac's racing division for its stock car program.

Polydyne Cam

The Polydyne camshaft profiles were very successful for Iskenderian. Their performance in racing engines won acclaim in many different fields of racing. The "Poly" name was taken from the mathematical polydyne formula, and Ed liked the system and used it in his advertising. He introduced this grind series as the Iskenderian Polydyne Profile, accompanied by a cartoon drawing of a parrot sitting on a camshaft.

The crew at Isky's knew that they had a winner with the Polydyne Profile after testing a 327 Chevrolet on the dyno. The modifications were kept to a minimum in order to test an engine that the average performance enthusiast could affordably duplicate, with stock heads, high-compression pistons (retaining the stock bore and stroke), an Edelbrock six-carburetor Ram Log manifold supporting Stromberg 97s, and a flat-tappet Polydyne profile camshaft. This combination produced an astounding 437 horsepower at 7,500 rpm on straight gasoline.

PATENTED ROLLER TAPPET

The use of roller tappets in an automotive engine can be traced back to the infancy of engine design, but the flat tappet won out early on because it was more economical to mass-produce. A variety of U.S. auto manufacturers did incorporate the roller tappet in their engines, but not the mainstream companies. Chet Herbert first introduced the roller as an alternative performance upgrade in the domestic postwar automobile engine. The difficulty Chet, and others who followed him into the roller tappet business, encountered was how to prevent the roller body from rotating once it was placed in the lifter bore. Proper alignment was needed for it to follow the contour of the camshaft lobe.

Isky could see the writing on the wall for roller camshafts; there were a lot of benefits to using a roller. In 1958, Iskenderian Racing Cams introduced its patented self-guiding roller tappet. Ed was the fourth person in the United States to ever have been granted a patent on a roller tappet.

The Isky tappet bodies were lengthened to bring them above their bosses and had an interlocking guide blade attached to each lifter that, when set in alongside the other lifters, prevented tappet rotation—simple and effective. These patented self-locking keys eliminated the need to machine or modify the engine block. One benefit of the longer tappet body was that shorter pushrods had to be used, making the pushrods less prone to flex at high rpm. Isky also introduced the Ultra-Rev kit to complement the roller cam, preventing lifter bounce at high engine speeds.

PATENTED HYDRAULIC LIFTERS

Hydraulic tappets proved problematic under racing conditions until the anti-pumpup tappet was invented. Isky put a patent on his performance hydraulic lifter after proving it could perform under the toughest of racing conditions.

Circa 2006, Ed examines the intake manifold he manufactured for his roadster after World War II. Topped with four Ford Chandler carbs, the manifold didn't perform up to snuff on the way to El Mirage, where it was unceremoniously replaced with Ed's trusty Edelbrock slingshot. *Author photo*

His anti-pumpup lifter contained a specially designed valve that was inserted into the tappet, with a second hole in the lower side of the tappet to act as a relief port. This mechanism opened up this second port as the lifter was beginning to pump up from high revs. The port bled off excess, trapped oil in the lifter, thus preventing the valves from being held off their seats, which would cause a drop in compression and horsepower.

ALUMINUM RODS

The use of aluminum rods in automotive engines was chiefly reserved for racing engines. In the postwar era, there was a phenomenal growth in the number of aftermarket manufacturers offering everything the engine builder could use—except aluminum rods. Iskenderian Racing Cams was the first company to offer this type of alloy rod.

The idea came by chance from Iskenderian customer Burt Looney of Oklahoma, who drag raced a prewar Oldsmobile coupe powered by a supercharged V-8 Oldsmobile. It seems that Burt stopped into Isky's shop while on his way to a race meet at Bakersfield, and over the course of his conversation, Burt mentioned that he made his own aluminum rods out of flat stock. He showed Ed several spare rods that he'd brought with him. Isky was impressed with the rods and, seeing a marketable angle, asked Burt if he would mind if he took a drawing off one of the rods.

Isky had Mark Cravens of Cravens Tool in Van Nuys, California, manufacture eight sets of aluminum rods for the popular Chrysler 392 Hemi. "We sold four sets and loaned out four sets for people to try," recounted Isky. One of the race cars that received the free rods on a trial basis was sold—complete with Isky's rods still in the engine. This particular drag car was then sponsored by another leading camshaft company.

"One day out at Riverside, they threw a rod on the drag strip," Isky said, "and they foolishly enough announced over the PA, 'Will anyone who found that rod on the drag strip please return it to _____Cams? We want it back to see what happened to this engine.' Well, we thought that was really funny. We knew it was one of our rods in that engine that'd never been paid for."

In 1958, Isky Cams advertised aluminum rods for the Chrysler Hemi V-8 and is credited as the first performance manufacturer to offer aluminum rods for a postwar American V-8 engine. Its original rods were machined from flat stock, but the high production costs of the labor-intensive manufacture, and increases in horsepower, caused Isky to switch over to much stronger aluminum forgings. As the popularity of the rods caught on with the racing fraternity, Isky also came out with aluminum rods for the Chevrolet V-8.

HIYA, PAL!

These words have been heard by performance devotees since the earliest days of Iskenderian Racing Cams. Isky explained that his trademark salutation came to him out of necessity, due to the large number of customers that came into his place of business. Over time, it became nearly impossible to remember the names of repeat customers who occasionally came into the shop. Ed has always been a very gregarious individual, and not being able to put a name to a face when it walked into his shop didn't sit well with him— that's when he came up with the phrase. Obviously it worked; when you first meet this gentleman, he makes you feel that you've been good friends for a long time. It's genuine.

"Authority is taken, not given." This quote from Isky could best be described as a personal mantra that he adopted at the beginning of his illustrious career in the automotive field. Iskenderian Racing Cams rose to the top of the performance camshaft business at lightning speed, regardless of the cam grinders that were already in existence when he began. He constantly pushed forward in product development and didn't spare the dollar when it came to advertising. Early on, Isky took the stance that his company was the leader in the cam-grinding section of the specialty market and acted accordingly—and the unparalleled growth of his business proved him correct.

A rule that he learned early on in business was "you're only as successful as your customers," and he was always willing to lend assistance to some up-and-coming racer who looked like he knew what he was doing. In a lot of cases, it panned out for both of them. There have been many who might not have achieved the racing success they had if not for the generosity of Ed Iskenderian.

In his autobiography *Challenger*, Mickey Thompson credited Isky with supplying the money to have six engines built (two were

Circa 2006, Ed poses with the cam-grinder he built, which has turned out an estimated $1 million worth of camshafts. *Author photo*

spares). The hard-pressed Thompson was struggling to build a streamliner when Ed donated $1,200 to Mickey so that he could pay Frits Voigt to build the Pontiac engines for the *Challenger* streamliner. He also contributed complete camshaft packages and other speed equipment toward the four-engine streamliner. Isky's generosity paid off in the form of valuable advertising ink after Thompson put the streamliner over the magical 400-mile-per-hour mark on the salt flats at Bonneville.

Ed was on the great Smokey Yunick's short list of personal heroes. Smokey was quoted as saying, "Iskenderian was the Henry Ford of the business—he got the price down and marketed to the masses." Smokey didn't put up with any B.S. or hand out compliments unless they were warranted.

Today, sons Richard, Ron, and Tim run Iskenderian Racing Cams with their father not very far off in the background. Isky is at the shop daily to take care of personal correspondence and even grind the occasional specialty camshaft for an old client or an obsolete cam profile that the company no longer carries in its catalog.

Iskenderian Racing Cams may not hold the top-dog position that it once had. But regardless of how time treats the other speed merchants, a name that will always surface on automotive enthusiasts' minds when the subject of performance equipment comes up in conversation is Iskenderian—the greatest name in the field of racing camshafts.

CHAPTER 12

McGurk Engineering

FRANK MCGURK

After the mighty flathead V-8 knocked its little cousin, the Model A four, off its pedestal, the majority of any specialty manufacturer's sales was for equipment designed to hop up the side-valve V-8. Although the Chevrolet and GMC six-cylinders made a showing in racing circles, these engines never had a following like the flathead.

Fortunately for those who wanted something else under the hood other than that flathead, there were outfits such as McGurk, Nicson, Horning, and the Spalding brothers who specialized in speed parts for the six-cylinder crowd.

Exactly why Frank McGurk chose the underrated Chevy-GMC six rather than the popular flathead is anyone's guess, but his unrelenting dedication in developing specialty equipment for this engine earned him the moniker "Mr. Chevrolet" among his peers. The now-defunct *Speed Age* magazine, in one of its 1953 issues, described Frank McGurk as "the foremost Chevrolet engine expert in the country."

BEGINNING

Frank was born and spent his childhood growing up in the small town of Brea, in Orange County, California. The McGurk family eventually moved into Los Angeles and it was while attending high school that Frank first began to hone his driving skills on the dirt track at Jeffries Ranch in the San Fernando Valley.

Jim Jeffries, an old-time bare-knuckles prizefighter, had an interest in automobile racing. He had a half-mile dirt oval built to hold informal races, providing a good introduction to the world of racing for many aspiring drivers until it ceased operations around 1940.

It didn't take long for Frank to realize that with a bit of luck and a fast car, he could make some good money at racing—winning, for example, a $300 purse for the feature at Oakland's 5/8-mile dirt oval. The fast cars and money had enough appeal that even under the threat of being disowned by his family, Frank quit school, as it was interfering with his driving career, and he went racing full-time. Although his formal education ended in 1934, years later he would pick up metallurgy and mechanical studies on his own.

The first race car that he drove was Ralph Schenk's four-cylinder, Chevy-powered sprint car. Frank raced the sprint from 1933 to 1935 and was listed in the B-driver class when he moved up to the old Legion Ascot Speedway.

While racing at Ascot, he acquired the nickname "Wildman," owing to his foot-to-the-floor driving style. As his driving skills steadily matured, he began to be a threat for the checkered flag, enough so that when Ascot closed in 1936, Vince Conze hired him as his driver. Conze competed in the AAA Eastern circuit, and there Frank's reputation for driving landed him a seat in the 1936 Indy 500.

While campaigning Conze's sprint car out east, Frank racked up a considerable number of wins. One of his favorite tracks was a paved oval in Thompson, Connecticut. This track held several races annually in which the promoter would put up $250 for the fastest lap timed during the main feature. While out on the track doing practice laps, Frank would figure out how fast he had to go in order to collect the prize money. With a stopwatch in one hand and the steering wheel in the other, he pushed

Opposite: One thing about coming in first, besides the trophy and money, is a kiss from a pretty trophy girl, and it seems that Frank McGurk received more than his share. *Dave Ward collection*

the car just enough to stay under the existing record. During the main feature, he'd break the previously set lap record, but only marginally, making sure that the car still had enough speed in it to win the next $250 promotional race. This system didn't work for him every time, but it worked often enough to make him keep coming back to the track.

Vince Conze's cars were in a state of constant experimentation, and Frank was the driver that could make the most of these changes. Vince ran his 220 Offy sprint with a semi-elliptical spring setup while others were running leaf springs over the axles. He and Frank were the first team to use different-sized diameters, with the larger on the outside, for tire stagger.

In an article he wrote, 1949 Indianapolis 500 winner Bill Holland said that the first time he remembered anyone running 100 percent methanol in a modified stock engine it was Frank McGurk. It occurred around 1940 when Frank was running a dual overhead camshaft (DOHC) Cragar on a Model B block that held the one-lap track record at Thompson, Connecticut.

In 1946, Frank joined the Western Racing Association and raced Conze's car, and he maintained two of the hottest midgets on the West Coast that were driven by Danny Oakes and Duke Nolan. He won the "big car" Championship in 1947 and was leading the point standings in 1948 when the WRA was changed to AAA. Frank even tried his hand at several of the popular California Roadster Association events held at Carrell Speedway during the 1948 season.

INDIANAPOLIS 500

When Frank competed at the 1936 Indianapolis 500, drivers at Indy were still accompanied by a riding mechanic—a job that no doubt required more intestinal fortitude than what the driver may have had. For the 500-mile marathon, Karl Hattel sat next to Frank in the *Abels Auto Ford*. Frank had qualified the Cragar-powered race car in 22nd spot at 113 miles per hour, only to drop out on lap 51 with crankshaft problems and finish in 26th place.

The Brickyard was to be jinxed for Frank. For the 1937 race,

In 1936 Frank and riding mechanic Karl Hattel drove the Cragar-powered four-cylinder *Abels Auto Ford* to twenty-sixth place at Indy after dropping out with crankshaft problems. *Dave Ward collection*

Frank was in the driver's seat of the *Belanger Special*, with Albert Opalko as his riding mechanic. Misfortune befell the duo during time trials, when the Miller crankshaft broke, locking up the car's wheels. Sadly, the ensuing crash killed Opalko and hospitalized McGurk for more than two months. This year was the last the Speedway's rulebook called for a riding mechanic to be in the race car.

The next time Frank attempted to drive at Indianapolis was in 1946, in the first race held since 1941, when the Speedway shut down for the war. Again, Lady Luck had forsaken his efforts, as he couldn't get the car up to speed to make the show. Frank returned to the Speedway numerous times as chief mechanic for the J. C. Agajanian racing team.

FRANK MCGURK CHEVROLET SERVICE

Up to the beginning of World War II, Frank made his living by driving race cars. As America entered the war, the helmet and gloves were put away, and he joined the service. He was transferred to North American Aircraft's engine division. From there, he was shipped out east to work for the Packard Motor Company, which manufactured the Rolls-Royce and Merlin aircraft engines. He was in good company at Packard, working alongside Indy 500–winner Mauri Rose.

Once the hostilities were over, Frank returned to Los Angeles, and Bill Krech of Inglewood Tire & Auto on Redondo Boulevard in Inglewood leased a two-bay shop in part of his building for Frank's automotive repair business: the Frank McGurk Chevrolet Service. Obviously, he focused mainly on Chevrolet repairs, but he still raced cars and pulled wrenches on customers' midgets. He could see that there was more money to be made in the performance end of the business, and he wasn't overly keen on just doing general auto repairs.

MCGURK ENGINEERING

By 1951, the business had outgrown Krech's shop and relocated to South La Brea in Inglewood. Now that he was manufacturing speed equipment, the shop's name was changed to McGurk Engineering. It took all of a year for that shop to become obsolete, and Frank relocated to 440 South Market Street in Inglewood. The need for better premises arose again by 1955, and this time it was off to 13226 Haldale Avenue in Gardena.

When Don Turner first went to work at McGurk's, he was given the job of porting and relieving Chevy cylinder heads, as well as filling the combustion chambers with cast weld and then grinding them out to raise the compression ratio. He recalls that when filling the combustion chambers, a lot of them cracked during welding. To rectify this problem, they had small cast inserts made and welded them into the chambers, although it still didn't solve the cracking problem.

When filling the combustion chambers became too labor-intensive, Frank had Don fabricate a piston with a deflector cast on top to fill the chamber. Don remembered putting plasticine on top of a piston and pushing it up into the head to get the desired shape. After shaving a little off for clearance, he sent it off to the pattern maker.

The item that got the ball rolling for McGurk Engineering was Frank's design for a dual intake manifold, advertised as "Balanced Power" for Chevrolets. In designing his dual intake manifold, Frank relied on his years of racing and tuning competition engines, and he remembered how Offenhauser made its carburetor manifolds with flat ends. In order to supply each port equally, Frank installed a baffle plate in the main passage of the manifold that controlled the distribution of fuel and velocity from the two carbs to the three intake ports. In no time, McGurk Engineering was offering two-, three-, and five-carburetor intake manifolds, Venolia racing pistons, Iskenderian cams, reworked cylinder heads, and custom-built engines. Frank advertised that he was the sole distributor for Wayne Horning GMC and Chevy equipment, and when that outfit broke up, he purchased its complete line of Chevrolet manifolds and piston molds.

To help six-cylinder enthusiasts understand the complexities of the engine, in 1950 Frank published the *McGurk Chevrolet Speed Manual*, a booklet on how to get the most from the Chevy. This little instruction manual was not only helpful in engine modification; it was a great promotional tool for his equipment and a good moneymaker itself. He then published another book that was more in-depth and included the Jimmy engine and titled it *Reworking the Chevrolet & GMC Engines*.

Chevrolet V-8s

When GM launched the 265 V-8 in 1955, McGurk Engineering didn't miss a beat and came out with camshafts, pistons, and a three-carburetor intake manifold for it. Frank published another moneymaker entitled *Reworking the Chevrolet V-8*.

Ed Iskendarian remembered McGurk phoning him to discuss the new Chevrolet. McGurk had tried to get an engine but was only able to get some parts. "The rocker arm doesn't have a rocker shaft," McGurk told Isky. "It looks like a little rowboat that rides on a stud and half-ball." Isky replied, "Hold everything; I'm coming right over. There it was—a ball-stud rocker hanging on a stud, which saved General Motors quite a bit of money on the rocker arm assembly."

In 1958, McGurk introduced the Trophy Winner six-carburetor intake manifold. He advertised that this manifold could be converted into a dual carb setup for street use simply by blocking off all four end-carburetor mounts and running only on the two center carburetors. Six carbs would look mean as hell on a street rod, yet you could get the dependability of a two-carb system without anyone knowing it. Don Turner recalled taking raw manifold castings for this manifold over to the Conze Machine Shop for finishing until Frank bought his own milling machine that was big enough to do the six-carb intake.

Although some might compare Chevrolet's 348 V-8 to a boat anchor, Frank's company was one that took the time to develop this engine. One of the aftermarket items it had to make for this particular engine was a cast-iron, wedge-shaped boring plate. The plate was needed if the cylinders were to be bored out because the surface of the cylinder block, unusually, was not at a 90-degree angle to the cylinder walls. The plate assured that the boring bar could be aligned parallel to the cylinder walls. McGurk even offered a stroker kit for the 348 V-8; another kit was offered for the more popular 283 that stroked it out to 306 ci.

Dave Ward recalled that McGurk sold buckets of Chevy six and V-8 head-bolt washers. These flat little donuts came into existence when heads were torqued down a little tighter than normal, and eventually the head bolt would chew into the casting, resulting in loss of tension on the head bolt. McGurk used a die made up to stamp out head-bolt washers that were retailed in packaged sets and sold to outlets such as Honest Charley's by the pound.

Dual-Master Camshafts

Frank moved into the performance camshaft business not by design, but as a result of carrying out a variety of engine modifications for

Action at Carrell Speedway in 1947 has Frank driving the 220 Offy sprint car of Vince Conze past Arvol Brunmier, who is going over the wall. Arvol escaped serious injury. *Rod Larmer collection*

Frank campaigned Vince Conze's *Inglewood Tire Service Special* big car on March 18, 1948, at Carrell Speedway. Here he stops long enough to receive a trophy. He was leading in the Western Racing Association points up until it changed over to American Automobile Association circuit. *Rod Larmer collection*

Frank lines up Vince Conze's 220 Offy No. 1 sprint car, sponsored by Bill Krech's Inglewood Tire, against Kenny Palmer's *Agajanian Special* No. 4 car. Compare the large front brake drum on Frank's car to that of his opponent's car. *Rod Larmer collection*

a magazine article. In 1953, *Hot Rod* collaborated with him on a story about his daily-driven '51 Chevy pickup. Each engine modification was tested out on Frank's 300-horsepower Clayton chassis dyno to show the horsepower outcome, with the camshaft testing left to the last segment. Testing the camshafts involved comparing the factory stock cam to nine three-quarter cams obtained from a variety of unnamed cam grinders. Over the course of the assessments, each camshaft was run in the engine, and several actually showed a power loss at low rpm, where a three-quarter grind was supposed to perform better. Being dissatisfied with the camshaft testing results, Frank felt that he could do a lot better. With the assistance of Ed Iskenderian's wealth of camshaft know-how and grinding facilities, the two designed a three-quarter grind.

As a consequence, Frank decided to get into the camshaft business. As with others entering into this specialty trade, it was made a lot easier by the Storm-Vulcan Company, which in 1953 introduced an affordable camshaft grinder for the engine-rebuilding trade. This particular unit came with a copying attachment that simplified the production of a cam master.

Frank called his new camshaft design the Dual-Master grind, as both the intake and exhaust lobes had different openings, closings, and valve lifts. The dual-pattern cam reportedly had a wider operating range, obtained by using the different valve timings, and offered better low-end torque and overall performance.

The one problem he encountered when grinding '54 and later Chevrolet camshafts was that they were cast iron and could only be used as a three-quarter grind—until he heard about hard-facing. This procedure, popularized by Isky, involved applying material to the lobes that would stand up to the rigors of a full-race cam. The job of hard-facing cams was handed over to Don Turner, who figured out the process through trial and error. Once he had the

process well in hand, he would take camshafts home with him and do the hard-facing in his garage in the evenings to earn extra money.

Isky was the gentleman who set the automotive gurus on their butts when he came out with his legendary 5 Cycle camshaft—that fifth cycle had them guessing. Others were quick to follow, such as Howard Johansen, with his unbelievable eight-cycle grind. Not to be outdone with all this ballyhoo, Frank introduced the 6 Cycle 100X camshaft for the Chevrolet V-8. It was promoted as having all the normal four cycles plus the romantic fifth cycle to produce a revolutionary sixth cycle. Frank must have figured that if they could get away with their unsubstantiated claims, why not join the fray?

Roller Tappets

Since the days when Chet Herbert first popularized the roller tappet, the methods of keeping those tappets from rotating in their bosses was as varied as the number of camshaft grinders. Everyone was trying to figure out the best method of keeping the roller tracking in alignment with the cam lobe.

One method that McGurk found successful was a roller lifter that had a guide strut protruding off the lower portion of the tappet body, which rode along the side of the camshaft lobe, keeping the tappet tracking correctly in the tappet boss. A drawback to this particular design was that the camshaft lobe had to be ground to accommodate the leg extension, limiting the width of the roller by this leg. This design also caused drag on the side of the lobe from contact with the leg.

Another design used a spring wire-loop retainer to hold two adjacent roller tappets in place, preventing any rotation in the tappet boss. This system seemed to have had enough good qualities to put it into production, but McGurk received calls from irate

Frank is in the pole position, driving Vince Conze's 220 Offy sprint car with the staggered front tires. It almost appears that Conze's car is running three tire sizes. *Rod Larmer collection*

racers whose engines suffered major internal problems because of defective wire retainers breaking under stress. Frank acted quickly, and in an attempt to salvage the remainder of his stock, he had them Magnafluxed. A surprising 50 percent of the wires were rejected after being tested, which was enough of a concern to Frank that he considered there might be a flaw in the spring retainer design.

The only way to solve the dilemma was to run a batch of the Magnafluxed retainers in a test engine on the dynamometer and see what happened. Dave Ward said that no matter how hard they revved the engine, allowing the valves to float by using weak valve springs, the only thing that broke was the occasional test engine—the spring-wire retainers held the rollers in place.

Frank still didn't trust the retainers and was nagged by the question of what was he going to do with the thousands of steel roller-tappet bodies.

After studying the situation for some time, he came up with a solution that would save the tappet bodies: using an aluminum, pressed-in extension inserted into the top of the hollow tappet body. They milled a flat spot on the aluminum extension and riveted a guide spool to it that supported a stamped-steel guide wrench. This guide wrench, in turn, attached itself to its neighboring tappet, preventing rotation—simple yet very effective. The reason Dave said that Frank extended the lifter was to use a shorter pushrod; the shorter the pushrod, the stiffer it becomes. Frank did not like the long GM pushrod. McGurk and Iskenderian were the only two cam grinders to use long roller-tappet bodies at that time.

At the 1966 SEMA show, which was held at the Disneyland Hotel in Anaheim, McGurk Engineering displayed an engine equipped with the new roller lifters. Many of the onlookers who viewed the tappet design made the comment that the aluminum-pressed insert would come out of the steel lifter body under hard usage. Frank responded that aluminum out-expands steel. "The hotter these things get, the tighter the aluminum insert will get in the steel tappet," he said.

Dave can remember only one failure ever occurring with this tappet design. A sprint car racer from Texas ran out of water in a 500-lap race and completely fried his motor.

Dynamometer

In addition to his 300-horsepower chassis dynamometer, Frank wanted an engine dynamometer. He located a hydraulic brake that once belonged to the great engine builder Harry Miller, and he redesigned it to be completely portable and self-contained to allow engine testing to be done wherever it was most convenient at the time.

He installed the brake onto a square-tube frame set on casters. It incorporated a heavy-duty truck radiator to cool the test engine, a muffler system, and a fuel tank assembly. Don Turner said that he was in charge of welding up the framework and recalled that when they first built the dyno, it had a tendency to tip backward if there wasn't an engine mounted on the frame. To rectify the problem, he installed heavy weights on the front end of the framework to counterbalance the water brake. The portable rig could easily handle the horsepower made by the six-cylinders, but after 1955, it began to prove inadequate for the more powerful V-8 engines.

The replacement dynamometer was a much larger Clayton model that had to be permanently installed in one location. Don said that he was again assigned to build all the controls for the unit and plumb the engine exhaust pipes into stacks that went straight up through the roof. After numerous complaints from neighbors, truck mufflers were added to help quell the racket.

McGurk Engineering rented out its facilities to anyone who wanted to test the performance of his or her engine. Turner called to mind one customer who brought in a Chevrolet six-cylinder and a newly ground Ed Winfield camshaft to be installed in the engine and tested on the dyno. Don had to phone Winfield for instructions as to how the camshaft was to be timed and what valve spring pressures to use with the cam. Winfield replied, "Use the stock Chevy valve springs, and don't turn the engine over 5,400 rpm. It'll make all kinds of power from about 1,800 rpm up."

Winfield was correct and everyone, including Frank, was quite impressed with how much horsepower the engine actually did make. Winfield told the guy not to leave his engine and camshaft at McGurk's overnight; Ed knew Frank would make a copy of the cam.

Shop Courtesy Car

In the days when he was still doing general auto repairs, Frank would offer a courtesy vehicle if a customer's car was going to be laid up for some time. It was a little white 1936 Chevrolet business coupe in pristine condition. After leaving the auto repair business, he gave the coupe to Don Turner, who converted it into a drag car.

The lethargic straight six was removed in favor of a GMC 302 truck engine that was bored out to 322 ci with three one-barrel carburetors and McGurk's camshaft, valve train, and pistons. At first, they ran into bottom-end problems with the engine. The rod bearings were OK, but the main bearings were giving them difficulties.

Frank took the engine over to the Spalding brothers—also Chevrolet specialists—and tried out the GMC on their dyno facilities (before he got his first dyno). With a strobe light they were able to see that once the engine was running over 7,000 rpm, the crankshaft would try to straighten itself out and do the main bearings in. From then on, the engine was kept below seven grand at the strip and there were no more crankshaft problems. The best top speed Don ever got out of the coupe was a respectable 117 miles per hour on gas. Frank even gave the quarter-mile a try, winning the fendered-coupe class at Santa Ana in November 1950, and winning again in the heavy-coupe class at Santa Ana in February 1952. As their interest in drag racing petered out, the 322 Jimmy was sold and the stock engine was reinstalled in the coupe. Don used it for several more years as his daily transportation vehicle.

Another hot Chevy coupe came out of the McGurk shop in the early 1950s. Frank's foreman, Sam Matsuda, ran a 1939 coupe

After installing a modified Oldsmobile V-8, three McGurk employees admire Frank's Kurtis 500 sports car. From left are shop foreman Sam Matsuda, Guy Allen, and Don Turner (behind the steering wheel). *Don Turner collection*

with a modified Chevy six that ran 130 at the dry lakes and was clocked at 105 on the strip. This car used Hilborn fuel injection when racing and a three-carburetor setup on the street. It was featured in *Hot Rod*'s October 1952 issue.

KURTIS 500S

The shop that produced the fabulous Kurtis-Kraft Indy roadsters, midgets, and sprint cars came out with the 500S sports car. Based on the Indy-style chassis, it was at home on the track or street. Like his race cars, Frank Kurtis sold the 500S as a rolling chassis, leaving the drivetrain up to the buyer's discretion. In 1953, McGurk bought one of these sports cars and had his crew install a Cadillac V-8 with a lightly modified Hydro-matic transmission that came out his pickup. Don Turner fabricated a floor-mounted shifter for the car out of some scrap material that worked perfectly. Don always felt that his shifter should have been put into production.

The Caddy was bored out to 354 inches and outfitted with McGurk 8:1 compression pistons, an experimental camshaft with solid lifters, a Weiand dual-quad intake manifold equipped with adapters to take on four Stromberg 97 carburetors, a Vertex magneto, and a Belond exhaust system. The package put out approximately 325 horsepower at 5,000 rpm. A '40 Ford rear axle with a Halibrand quick-change center section was installed under the rear of the car.

Even with the Hydro-matic, the car performed well on the racecourse, as Frank scored a second-place finish in a five-lap race against Bill Stroppe's strong-running, Mercury flathead-powered Kurtis 500 during the first-ever Santa Barbara Road Race.

Frank also set a new sports-car record of 106 miles per hour with the Kurtis at the Santa Ana drags.

1955 CHEVROLET

When Frank's father retired, he went to work for Frank as his parts deliveryman. When Chevrolet unleashed its fabulous V-8 to the American public in 1955, Frank bought a two-door sedan equipped with the V-8 as the shop delivery vehicle. The car was also used as a mobile testbed to try out various speed parts that they were developing. His father had problems with the McGurk aluminum flywheel that was installed in the car. Frank's flywheels were finally subcontracted out to Tony Capanna's Wilcap shop, and the problems got under control. The Chevy's 265 engine was upped to 292 inches, turning it into a strong runner, but when the engine was again enlarged to 306 with a quarter-inch stroker, it didn't show any significant gains in performance.

In 1956, Frank took the Chevy with the hopped-up 306 V-8 to the L.A. Drag Strip and set the record for the postwar street car class at 102 miles per hour with a 14-second ET. His claim to fame with the car was when he beat fellow speed parts manufacturer Howard Johansen in his '55 Chevy at the strip.

CHEVY II

In an effort to gain an advantage over their peers, it was customary for Detroit automakers to supply specific specialty manufacturers with their latest engines to play with. McGurk Engineering was on the list when Mauri Rose (three-time Indy winner, by then a factory rep for GM) delivered a Chevy II four-cylinder engine six months prior to its release to the public. By the time GM was prepared to unveil the Chevy II, McGurk had already pulled 230 brutal horsepower out of the little four-cylinder, which had been designed for economy driving.

In order to get the jump on the competition, Frank bought approximately 700 unfinished steel-billet roller camshafts from the Walker Machine Company for the Chevrolet four- and six-cylinder engines. McGurk Engineering now had a monopoly on steel-billet cam blanks, as Walker Machine was the sole manufacturer of the billets. Other cam grinders were obligated to buy billet blanks from McGurk until more were available from Walker.

MCGURK-CUMMINGS SUMP PUMP

For years, aircraft engines had incorporated dry-sump oiling systems, enabling the aircraft to fly inverted. The usage of the system in auto racing had made Frank a dry-sump advocate. It was around 1958 or 1959 when Frank and Mark Cummings first formed a partnership in the dry-sump business.

Dave Ward said that it all began with an Arizona sprint car owner named Al Kitts. Kitts had machined a drive out of a piece of cast iron, with a Hilborn fuel-injection pump mounted on one side and an oil pump on the other side. He attached the unit to an aluminum front timing-chain cover. Al was racing at a meet in California where Frank and Mark happened to be, and while walking through the pits the two noticed Al's homemade sump drive. Frank questioned Al as to why he didn't make the crossdrive out of aluminum, which would have been a lot lighter. Al replied that he didn't know how to construct a wooden pattern to make a casting for the drive.

As luck would have it, Mark was the pattern shop foreman for Alcoa Aluminum and, like Frank, had done a fair bit of circle racing. Both fellows could see a potential business venture in marketing the drive. With Kitts' permission, know-how, and assistance, the three drew up plans for a front-mounted accessory crossdrive that operated a water pump, oil pump, and fuel-injection pump and was designed for the Chevy four, six, and V-8 engines. The finished product consisted of a cast timing cover that

had the water pump driven off the crankshaft and the oil and fuel pumps driven off the camshaft. The unit contained dual oil pumps, one for the engine oiling and the other for crankcase scavenging.

The McGurk-Cummings dry sump system was manufactured by Mark and marketed through McGurk Engineering. According to Dave Ward, they sold the drives faster than Mark could make them and there was always a backorder for the units. Besides the front-mount accessory drive for the circle-track racers, they later came out with a VW version once the Bug engine became all the rage in off-road vehicles.

With the demise of McGurk Engineering, Dave and Mark worked together selling the units from Dave's home for about three years until Mark passed away, and regrettably, the McGurk-Cummings crossdrive slipped into obscurity.

UNDER NEW OWNERSHIP

In October 1968, McGurk Engineering was sold to Iskenderian Racing Cams. Emphysema compelled Frank to get out and enjoy what time he had left. Frank once told Isky that he'd originally taken up smoking to make him appear older than he really was when he first began his racing career.

Once the sale was finalized, Frank and his wife, Madeline, moved away from the smog of Los Angeles to the more tranquil surroundings of Escondido, California. Frank's company was relocated to Isky's shop, where Dave Ward—McGurk Engineering's longest-serving and now sole employee—ran the business as a separate identity under the Iskenderian roof.

McGurk Engineering took up an area of about 30 by 30 feet, enough room for Dave to operate the two Storm-Vulcan cam grinders, a straightening bench, and a hydraulic press and to place some storage cabinets. He ran the business at Isky's for 11 years, doing all the cam grinding, assembling roller tappets, correspondence, and so on, basically operating a business within a business. In 1979, McGurk Engineering came to a final close when Dave retired.

Although McGurk Engineering is no more, Frank's roller-tappet design and some of his racing camshaft grinds (Dave designed many of the later McGurk grinds) were merged into the Iskenderian parts catalog.

The McGurk roller lifter was one of the main products that Iskenderian Racing Cams wanted when they purchased McGurk Engineering after Frank decided to retire. *Dave Ward collection*

CHAPTER 13

Navarro Racing Equipment

BARNEY NAVARRO

Like several other speed merchants of his day, Barney Navarro had a passion for one engine only: the infallible Ford flathead V-8. Barney concentrated all his efforts solely on that engine. Unfortunately, when Ford put aside its flathead V-8, merchants like Barney got out of the speed parts business. The demise of the flathead wasn't the end of his involvement with auto racing by any means, but never again did he venture into the world of manufacturing speed equipment.

THE EARLY YEARS

The seeds of mechanical curiosity were planted early, beginning at the age of three when Barney received a live-steam model engine from his father. The simplistic design of this mechanical marvel and other such toys left an imprint on the young lad's mind that would shape his future. Barney felt he was fortunate that his father had the foresight to encourage his son's natural curiosity of the world around him and to assist in developing his mental and motor skills with mechanical toys. This close father-son bonding left Barney with an acute memory of his early days and of the enthrallment he held for his mechanical toys and their intriguing designs.

Barney's early grasp on mechanics became more apparent when he and some neighborhood friends built wooden push carts to race down LaLoma Road, which was a fairly steep piece of paved asphalt. As he was speeding down the makeshift racecourse, and actually passing cars at times, he realized a wide wheel stance and a lower center of gravity provided much better handling.

In 1929, the family took the train to New York City, where they lived for nine months. For the return trip home, Barney's father bought a used Willys Knight that was in need of an engine rebuild before he could set out on a long journey.

"My dad rented space in a shop, and at the age of ten, I became a gofer, as I assisted in the engine overhaul," Barney said. "In the same shop, another fellow was attempting to rebuild a Wills Sainte Claire with an overhead-cam engine. I learned a whole new vocabulary resulting from his cussing as a result of lack of proper tools to do the job, and no doubt knowledge to do the work.

"It was helping my dad work on the Willys Knight sleeve engine and later on helping him do a valve job on one of those 'miserable' Chevrolets, that my interest in mechanical devices intrigued me. It wasn't until I had studied physics that I really began to understand the fundamental principles involved."

He figured that the most unusual engine he'd ever encountered was his dad's Willys Knight sleeve-valve creation. What was different about this type of engine was that the carburetor and exhaust were on opposite sides of the block and it used cylinder sleeves with two slots moving up and down rather than poppet valves.

"I felt that it'd have been interesting to have tried a blower on it," Barney said. "With the intake on one side and the exhaust on the other side, [it was] like a four-valve Hemi except using slots for valves."

Opposite: Barney Navarro's roadster gets a push-off down the dusty El Mirage lake bed. Notice his head is well above the roll bar. *Courtesy Barney Navarro*

Navarro employee Bob Trummel's roadster is parked next to Navarro's shop on Verdugo Road in Glendale in 1948. The car is sporting Barney's 3:71 GMC blower and four-carb induction system. It set its class record at the dry lakes. *Courtesy Barney Navarro*

HIGH SCHOOL

The trials of scholastic learning never held any obstacles for Barney as he completed his academic courses at Eagle Rock High School while enrolled in evening machine-shop courses at Glendale High. During high school, he and a friend, who was quite knowledgeable in electronics, designed electric guitar amplifiers that they sold to a very limited market.

At the shop course in Glendale, Barney was given an opportunity to put what he was learning to use. The Weaver brothers, Bernard and Bob, had built a midget to race at the Gilmore track and asked Barney if he could help them with their problem—they had a Locomobile straight-eight automobile engine but only needed half of it, as the rulebook limited their class to 135 ci. The engine was a one-piece block with two separate overhead-valve heads, each servicing four cylinders. After cutting the engine in half, Barney recalled that the Weavers' Locomobile-powered midget may not have been the fastest car at Gilmore, but it worked.

Upon graduating in 1937, Barney worked a variety of jobs until 1941 when he landed a position as a machinist at Heidrich Tool & Die.

HOT RODS

Barney's first recollection of gow jobs went back to the 1920s, when he saw stripped-down, fenderless Model Ts.

"These early rods had Z'd frames, most used Franklin front axles, and some were so low that they couldn't pass over the traffic buttons that separated the road lanes; they really impressed me with their cornering and acceleration abilities."

When he turned 16 in 1935, Barney bought his first car, a $50 '29 Hudson two-door sedan powered by a six-cylinder F-head engine (like a Riley two-port, but with only one intake port). He wanted a bit more pep, so at night school he machined the stock carburetor manifold, which was cast into the block, allowing him to install dual carburetors. He knew that George Riley of Riley Carburetors & Camshafts had ground racing cams for Essex engines and that the Essex was nothing but a Hudson with four cylinders. There had been a number of Essex-powered midgets that ran at Old Legion Ascott and were pretty quick. Barney was looking at his Hudson as an Essex-and-a-half, but with much more power. He gave the stock roller cam to Riley with instructions to regrind it with a flat-tappet performance profile, because he had little faith in roller lifters and their excessive spring tension.

In 1940, he joined the Glendale Stokers car club, which competed under the SCTA banner. It was a relatively new car club and held its meetings in Paul Swanson's body shop on Colorado Boulevard in Glendale. Some other members in the Stokers club of that era were Tom Beatty, George Hill (who drove the *City of Burbank* streamliner and was involved in the movie industry), and the talented Doane Spencer, whose fabulous '32 highboy roadster set the mark for other hot rod builders.

Barney eventually acquired a '39 Ford two-door sedan. The stock cast-iron heads were milled 1/16th of an inch and re-domed approximately .030 inch, so he still had the piston coming up close to the head (for good squish). The valve cavities were fly cut to give them room in the head, and a Weiand high-rise dual carburetor intake was installed; it was the first intake manifold that Phil Weiand ever produced and was used as payment to Barney for machining 10 raw manifold castings. Barney met Phil through some of the Stokers club members.

On November 14, 1941, Barney removed the engine from the '39 Ford, installed it in a modified dry lakes roadster, and flat towed the race car up to Muroc Dry Lake for the last event to be held on the lake before the military took it over. Because of the extremely large crowds and long line to race, he only got one run of 107 miles per hour in for the day. While waiting in line to run, a photographer from *Hop Up* magazine captured Barney standing beside his roadster with his foot up on the tire.

During the early dry lakes meets, there were times when cars that competed in the same mile-per-hour bracket would be grouped together and run simultaneously. Like a cavalry charge, there would be as many as 10 cars running abreast down the course. It wasn't too bad for the front-running car(s), but those left behind had to contend with thick clouds of blinding dust and could only hope that they were headed in a straight line and wouldn't run into someone or vice versa.

"It was the one time in my life that I was really scared," Barney said. "All you could see was dust, and [you could only] hear other cars around you. You had to drive by instinct." It was a means of allowing a large number of cars to compete, but the need for safer running conditions came about after a string of serious and sometimes fatal accidents.

POSTWAR

Once United States declared war, Barney was drafted, trained as a navigator by the air corps, and eventually stationed in Fort Worth, Texas, for the remainder of the war. During this time, curiosity about the runner design of Ford's stock intake manifold got the better of him. He removed his car's intake and made rough drawings, using modeling clay to duplicate the passages. After studying the firing order and runner layout of the stock manifold, he understood why the stock runners went where they did. This research would later be the basis of the Navarro 180-degree dual-intake manifold, which followed the same induction sequence as Ford. Borrowing from the Ford design was Barney's secret to an intake that outperformed many other aftermarket manifolds. He felt that, with all the resources the engineers at Ford had at their disposal and the money that went into research and development on the flathead V-8, the fundamental design of Ford's runner passages had to be correct.

After being discharged, he worked at Lockheed for a short period before returning to Heidrich. Barney's plan was to eventually open his own speed equipment business.

FLATHEAD V-8

When it came to making a choice of engines, Ford's flathead V-8 appealed to Barney for a variety of reasons. His appreciation for this particular engine was first tweaked when he was a passenger in a friend's new 1935 Ford, doing 72 miles per hour in second gear. Barney figured that any engine that could take that kind of abuse had something going for it. It was then that he began to read up on the technical specifications of the engine. He liked what he saw, despite the fact that it had a tendency to burn oil, siamese-centered exhaust ports, and no water passage on the back ends of the block around the exhaust passage, causing the block to get hot.

"The exhaust is the greatest flaw in the flathead Ford," Barney said. "Ford's first V-8 [experimental] had the exhaust coming out the ends of the block, and if they'd done that, plus separated the center ones, you could make that damn flathead outperform a lot of overheads. I remembered watching the heavily laden Ford trucks going over the Ridge Route [heading north out of L.A.] at about five miles per hour. You could see the back of the engine block was red hot because the side panels were removed to aid cooling.

"Not everyone knows, but the cars that were sent out here west of the Rockies had bigger radiators. When you got cars that came from the east, you had a big problem."

NAVARRO RACING EQUIPMENT

As Barney planned to make his intake a reality, he had his girlfriend at the time—who happened to be an artist—draw a dual-intake manifold design from the rough drawings he'd made while stationed in Texas. With the drawing and the clay runners that he'd made, he paid a visit to Hermann Husbey's pattern shop on Fletcher Drive in Glendale.

Victor Caliva, owner of the Aircraft Foundry Company and a friend of Barney's, did the castings for his manifolds. Later on when Barney contemplated casting some high-compression cylinder heads but was shy on capital, Victor financed the heads and paid for the patterns. The gross cost of a raw head casting at the time was $10. One day, Barney got a shock when he stopped in at the foundry and found a stack of cylinder head castings taller

Two Navarro dual-intake manifolds. The one on the left features the exhaust-heated "dog bone" exhaust heater adapter to assist in cold-weather driving. The unit on the right has the adapter replaced with an exhaust-riser plate bolted to the manifold for summer driving. *Courtesy Barney Navarro*

than himself. He calculated that there was close to $7,000 worth of rough castings piled up in the stack. Victor let him take the financed castings back to his shop and pay for them as they were sold. Had it not been for Victor's generosity, Barney's business would never have grown the way it did. Barney rented facilities at Heidrich over the weekends to machine manifolds and heads.

Navarro Manifolds

When the original Navarro dual-carburetor manifold appeared in 1947 it wasn't equipped with a heat riser, so there was a bolt-on cast-aluminum attachment that was sold as an extra. This cold-weather dog-bone–shaped device came about after he experienced carb freeze-up during a 1945 winter road trip from Texas to California. The Weiand manifold wasn't equipped with a heat riser.

The first Navarro manifolds were designed with a center plate between the two carburetors that could be removed in favor of the dog-bone heat riser for cold weather use. This riser consisted of an intricate casting that allowed hot engine gases to circulate around the bases of the two carburetors. It was manufactured from 1947 to about 1952. Because of the demand by collectors of flathead equipment and nostalgia buffs, Barney later put these risers back into production.

In its infancy, Navarro Racing Equipment operated out of Barney's home garage. With the first batch of manifolds machined and ready for sale, Barney loaded up the trunk of his '42 Ford and drove around to the speed shops in L.A. The first sale was to Roy Richter of Bell Auto Parts, and then it was over to the Clay Smith and Danny Jones shop. Finally, he dropped into Karl Orr's Speed Shop, where he sold the remaining intakes. Regarding Clay Smith and Danny Jones, Barney said, "I went into their shop the first day I went out selling stuff, and I unloaded a good portion of my trunk at their place. They believed in my product."

Within a year, business had grown to the point that he needed a machine shop, and Barney moved to one that was zoned commercial on 718 Verdugo Road and Windsor in Glendale. Noisy visitors to the shop prompted the city council to force him to relocate, which he did, to 5142 San Fernando Road.

To attract attention to his latest shop, he painted over the front window with silver paint, excluding an opening large enough to display a Navarro-equipped V-8 flathead engine. Kenny St. Oegger dubbed it the "Peek-A-Boo Speed Shop." In the beginning, it wasn't unusual to find Barney hustling between two or three machines at the same time. When he could afford it, he hired fellow Stokers club member Tom Beatty to work in the shop. Beatty would eventually make quite a name for himself on the dry lakes and at Bonneville.

The Navarro three-carburetor manifold came out in 1948, but when some manufacturers introduced a four-carb intake, Barney drew the line. He never had much faith in the four-carburetor manifold and did enough research to prove that his triple intake was more efficient than a four.

"You have a firing order that you have to conform to, and you can't do it properly with four," Barney said. "Actually, the three will work better than the two. What you can do is remove the acceleration check valves in the two end carburetors and only keep the check valve in the center carburetor, because you only need acceleration pump fuel to get it off the line."

Despite his faith in the three-carb setup, Barney came out with a flathead four-barrel manifold, thinking that it would be an instant success. He designed it to be used with the new $45 Lincoln carburetor—the same carb used on the Lincolns that won the Carrera Panamericana. The Navarro four-barrel intake was also the only one that allowed trouble-free installation of the newly designed McCulloch supercharger, which could be purchased through Navarro as a complete kit that included the supercharger (4 pounds boost), manifold, and Lincoln carburetor for $340. Unfortunately, sales were poor; Barney didn't consider that the majority of hot rodders preferred the eye-appeal of three or four carburetors sitting on top of their engine, not one big, squatty, ugly carburetor, even though one carb would be a lot less complicated to tune. Also, the four-barrel manifold was introduced at a time when the overhead-valve engines were moving in.

Though he only made flathead intakes, Barney was very well versed on how manifolds function and the theories behind the workings of such; he chuckled about the time he was over at Mickey Thompson's shop and Mickey was testing a manifold that had a small glass window installed at each end of the manifold body. He showed Barney with amazement how the gas condensed on the inside of the manifold into little puddles on the bottom of the plenum chamber, but Barney had known about this for years.

Navarro Cylinder Heads

A year after introducing the dual-intake manifold, Barney came out with a high-compression cylinder head. He said that that many of the other head manufacturers were more concerned with temperatures and high compression ratios, and were not too concerned about the breathing aspect of the head.

The crow-foot chamber that he used gives a deep entry into the cylinder (clear across the cylinder), giving maximum compression; it's not a straight cut, but a moon-shaped cut. Sir Harry Ricardo originated this design. Ed Winfield used it on one of his first Model A heads, but shortly after he'd released the head, Chrysler bought the patent rights from Sir Harry and sent a letter to Winfield requesting that he cease using that chamber design. Ed complied but found himself in a bind, so when he re-designed his head, he told everybody that the straight-across cut didn't make any difference in performance. "But it did make a difference," Barney said. "You get the maximum compression and airflow by using that type of chamber [crow-foot]."

By the time Barney incorporated this design into his heads, the original patent had already expired. Also, the Navarro heads conformed with the stock piston configuration. "To get the turbulence you need, you want the piston to go as close to the head without hitting," Barney said. "This squishes the fuel charge into the spark plug area at an extremely high rate. As a result of this fuel mixture turbulence, you don't need much spark advance. That's the secret to making a flathead work."

When the Navarro cylinder head was first introduced, the flow characteristics were better than any other specialty head on the market, including the stock Ford head. To prove his point, in 1948, Barney had an independent engineering firm (the Pichel brothers) run airflow and horsepower tests.

"They reported that my equipment out-flowed and was better than what already existed on the market," Barney said. To give proof of the power that his equipment made, Barney would often challenge others to a chassis dyno test, and he always came out on top.

The only time there was ever a Navarro 21-stud cylinder head was the time Barney converted a set of early aluminum 21-stud heads that belonged to Tom Beatty. "We filled the stock heads and ground out a Ricardo chamber in them," Barney said. "Using a stencil, we sandblasted my name on them. For years, people were wondering about the 21-stud heads that I manufactured." Beatty ran 136 miles per hour at the lakes with those Navarro 21-stud heads.

Barney's oxygen setup at the 1950 Bonneville meet—before he fried the pistons. Using a mix of alcohol and oxygen he ran 136.77 at the dry lakes with this configuration compared to 102 miles per hour without it. *Leslie Long collection, Courtesy Barney Navarro*

Superchargers

Barney had read about supercharging in a British publication called *Speed and How to Obtain It*, along with several other articles about the Roots-type blower. They described how to almost double the horsepower of an engine using one of these units, and Barney felt that this was one way to get large amounts of raw horsepower economically, provided you knew what you were doing.

No one up to that time had installed a GMC blower on top of a flathead V-8, so it was to be a learning curve. The project made him one of the forerunners in supercharging the postwar North American production automobile engine. Kong Jackson of Kong Ignitions sold Barney his first blower, a 3-71 GMC, for the price of $60. The blower came from a GM diesel engine that powered a World War II landing craft.

Using some wood and plaster, Barney created a pattern for a blower manifold that would accept the 3-71. In the days before the cogged Gilmer belt was available, it was a choice of using a chain or V-belt drive; Barney chose the latter. The V-belts on a multi-spooled pulley system would slip, peel off, or disintegrate because of rapid overheating. Heat was the biggest problem for the blower drive, and it was especially apparent on the race track. Finally, Barney licked the problem by making air-cooled drive pulleys. He drilled into the face of the pulley and then at right angles into the base of the V. The perforated pulley acted as a centrifugal fan, drawing air in to cool the V-belts—simple, yet very effective.

To prove that his blower system worked, Barney took a stock 239-ci Ford V-8 and added 8:81 cylinder heads, a Winfield camshaft, Spalding ignition, and the 3-71 blower adorned with four Stromberg 48 carburetors mounted sideways. Dyno tests showed the blown engine produced 237 horsepower at 5,400 rpm on straight alcohol. The same engine, normally aspirated, pumped out 170 horsepower.

Bob Trammel, one of Barney's employees, owned a 268-ci flathead-powered T roadster, and it was the first vehicle to try out the Navarro blower drive. Trammel was about to drive the roadster back home to Montana and figured he could sell it for big dollars if there was a timing tag from the dry lakes attached to the dashboard. After installing the blower, Barney drove Trammel's roadster to a 143-mile-per-hour run at El Mirage. This roadster even appeared in one of the early issues of *Hop Up*.

THE *RUST BUCKET*

After the success with the blower on Trammel's engine, the next car to try it was Tom Beatty's roadster, appropriately called the *Rust Bucket*. At the lakes and at Bonneville, Beatty's car either broke a speed record or just plain broke. Barney mentioned that Tom took delight in having his cars look awful and go fast. One magazine article about Beatty's car quotes a tech inspector at a lakes meet, saying it (*Rust Bucket*) was the safest car at the meet, but that was debatable. Beatty's roadster had only several bolts and numerous locking pliers holding the body to the frame. The instruments were taped and wired to the steering column, a couple of leather straps held the engine hood in place, and a paint job of red primer

finished off the car. It was powered by a '32 V-8, and with Barney's blower setup, the roadster was clocked close to 150 miles per hour on the dry lakes.

Being a racer at heart and having gained a good insight into the blower business at Barney's, Beatty eventually opened his own shop specializing in blower installation kits.

NAVARRO–BEATTY TANK

Once Stuart Hilborn's streamliner breached the magical 150 mark at El Mirage, Barney looked for something that'd do maybe 200.

"I told Beatty that we needed a belly tank, and since Tom lived next to my shop, it would be real convenient to build the car," Barney said. "Tom had a covered carport where he could do the welding and assembly work. Unfortunately, Beatty would only go so far on welding the chassis and wanted to get rid of my plan to use 3/4-inch OD chrome-moly aircraft tubing and just use a couple of Model T rails in its place. I told him, 'Beatty, you've got only one life to give to this damn foolishness, let's make it safe.' " Under duress, or so it seemed to Barney, Tom continued to build the chassis according to Barney's plans. Tom did all the assembly and welding except for the independent swing axle.

The unique swing axle assembly that had removable floating axles was designed and built by Barney. "I believed that half of the cars that were turning turtle on the lakes were doing so because they had open driveshafts," Barney said. "Say you have an 800-horsepower engine that produces 800 pounds of torque, and you're going down that course. The driveshaft is trying to tip that car to the tune of 800-foot-pounds, 1 foot away from the pinion. Say your axle's 3 feet long. You divide that 800 by 3, which gives 266 pounds of torque trying to tip the car. That's what gets a lot of fellows in trouble who have sprung suspension cars and lots of horsepower. You can counterbalance this by preloading all four springs on the car."

When Barney came out with the flathead V-8 four-barrel manifold, he offered as an option a package deal containing the manifold, a Paxton supercharger, and a new Lincoln carburetor. *Courtesy Barney Navarro*

To give credibility to this theory, in the early 1960s, Barney tried it out on a Plymouth belonging to Ed Dempsey of Concrete Coring Company that had a 427 wedge with a 13:1 compression ratio. After installing dual turbochargers and lowering the compression, the engine output 800 horsepower. "The car ran straight as an arrow after I had preloaded the suspension to counteract any effects of engine torque," Barney said.

The 1,500-pound Navarro–Beatty belly tank's 295-ci '48 Mercury engine was equipped with a converted 4-71 GMC blower that put out 10 psi via a Navarro-engineered blower drive consisting of four 1/2-inch V-belts with four Stromberg 48s flowing straight alcohol. The unique rear suspension design and the powerful supercharged engine allowed Tom to set an all-time high top speed for lakesters at 188.28 and set a D/L class record at 185.80 miles per hour during the 1951 Bonneville Nationals. It was the tank's first appearance on the salt flats.

The 1952 Bonneville Nationals held a surprise for many who believed that an open-wheeled belly tank couldn't top the 200-mile-per-hour mark. Beatty ran 203 and set the two-way record at 197.17 miles per hour. Again, the rear swing axle was believed to have contributed to the high speed by improving the car's traction. During the week-long meet, Tom destroyed two engines, five pistons, and three cylinder heads. It was reported that his lakester could be heard for the full length of the six-mile racecourse.

Barney got what he'd set out to do: press coverage of a record-setting car running Navarro equipment. The Navarro–Beatty belly tank was featured as the Hot Rod of the Month in *Hot Rod*'s October 1952 issue.

NAVARRO ROADSTER

Barney felt it was time he had his own car to help promote Navarro Racing Equipment and with the assistance of Tom Beatty put together a dry lakes 1927 T roadster in a four-day marathon of intense labor. It would be the perfect car to test his newly built 176-ci, de-stroked, GMC-blown 245-horsepower flathead V-8.

The engine for this project was a 1941–1942 replacement block that had a Mercury water jacket and Ford cylinder cores. The engine was de-stroked, and Barney had the crankshaft metal sprayed and then cut down from 3 3/4 inches to 3 inches, resulting in 176 ci, small enough to put the roadster in the class he wanted to run. The metal-sprayed crankshaft called it quits after one season of hard usage.

The second crankshaft was a takeoff of a borrowed 180-degree casting pattern from Charlie Brayden of Norden Machine Works. Barney made some pieces to put on the throws to get rid of that extra 3/4 inch of stroke and then had a casting done, resulting in a cast-manganese-molybdenum-steel 180-degree crank with a 3-inch stroke. To counteract the negative effects of the siamesed exhaust ports, Barney chose a 180-degree crankshaft to eliminate the crossover exhaust problem, but the 180 had its own inherent problems. It could not be balanced properly and would vibrate, which he experienced at Bonneville.

"Speeding down the lake, I watched the tachometer needle break off at the indicating end, and then the tail broke off due to

The Navarro "four-day" roadster at El Mirage in October 1948. The roadster took four arduous days of intensive labor to get ready for the meet. It was powered by a 3:71 GMC blower with four side-mounted Stromberg 97s sitting on a 176-ci V8-60 turned over by a 180-degree crankshaft. What made this car unique at the time was the installation of a GMC blower on top of a flathead V-8. Barney was breaking new ground. *Courtesy Barney Navarro*

A close-up of Barney's V-belt-driven 3:71 GMC blower installation with four Stromberg 97s mounted sideways due to lack of space. Note he used four belts to drive the supercharger, with a fifth to drive the water pump. *Courtesy Barney Navarro*

the vibration coming out of the engine," Barney said. "The engine was bolted directly on the car's frame with no rubber mounts." That engine with the 180-degree crankshaft and its 3-inch stroke could spin the engine at 8,000 rpm (Barney's Rambler 6 also had a 3-inch stroke). With the short stroke, the 180 crank, and the high revs of the engine, Barney claimed you could run it that way all day long.

Ed Winfield ground a special steel-billet camshaft for the altered firing order of the 180 crankshaft. Barney mentioned that because of the cam's fast action and the high rpm, some of the valve stems dented the lifters just as the engine was putting out 218 horsepower on the dynamometer.

"Winfield made a billet cam for my 176 V-8 because I knew that the reground Ford cores would bend as a result of having the lobes and shank ground to get a high lift," Barney said. "With only three cam bearings, the reground camshafts had a tendency to bend under all the valve spring pressure. I used mushroom lifters with the camshaft—I am not a fan of a roller tappet. A flat or mushroom lifter gives a quicker lift with less spring tension and no side thrust." Barney machined his own mushroom lifters and had them hard chromed. The GMC blower was putting out 16 pounds of boost with only a slight machining of the blower housing to allow the rotors to spin at a higher rpm than they were originally intended to run.

The roadster's frame consisted of a couple of 1937 Willys frame rails with crossmembers made from Ford driveshaft tubes, and the engine was mounted 18 inches back in the chassis. An in-out box connected the engine up to a quick-change rearend. The engine hood, nose piece, engine side covers, and cast-aluminum grille shell were all built by Art Ingles. (Art worked for Kurtis race cars and is also credited for being the originator of the go kart.) Barney put the finishing touch on the roadster with a deep red, almost maroon, paint job and prepared to run it in A/Modified (the smallest engine-displacement class).

The 3:71 GMC breathed enough life into the engine that it eventually put out 270 horsepower at 6,500 rpm, pushing the roadster to a record run of 136.77 during the SCTA's first 1948 meet of the season at El Mirage. Later he moved the record up to 146.86 miles per hour—on 176 ci! During the opening of the Bonneville National Speed Trials in 1949, Barney's roadster was timed at 147 miles per hour, and later on at an SCTA meet in July 1950, he was moved up to B class with the addition of the GMC blower. At the SCTA Fall Finals meet that same year, he was experimenting with an 88-ci flathead V-8 that ran 92 miles per hour.

Barney built his roadster as a dual-purpose vehicle, competing in both the dry lakes events and in the popular CRA events. Driving on the wide-open flats of the dry lakes was one thing, but tearing around a dirt track inches from competitors was another, and Barney knew he wasn't qualified for that type of racing. He went through several drivers to find one who could handle the car and its incredibly responsive engine. He recalled that the car upset several drivers because of the high rpm. A normally aspirated track roadster with a flathead engine of around 300 ci would run in the neighborhood of 5,000 rpm. When they drove the Navarro roadster, with its tiny blown engine screaming upward to 8,000 rpm, they were tricked into thinking that they were traveling much faster than they actually were. One driver who impressed Barney was Walt James, who put the roadster in the trophy dash right alongside Troy Ruttman, an Indy 500 winner. Walt had never driven the car before and just climbed in, did half a hot lap, and then signaled that he was going to do his qualifying lap. Walt James was one of the West Coast's top roadster drivers and one of the founding members and president of the CRA.

Unfortunately, the roadster never made a dent in the oval-track scene, which can be partly blamed on the problems Barney encountered with V-belt drive. If the Gilmer belt had been available at the time, things may have turned out differently.

Barney felt that he could have gotten over 150 miles per hour at the lakes if he'd given it a little more side clearance at the connecting rods.

"I have never seen a race car engine come apart because it was too loose," Barney said. "I've seen a lot come apart because they were too tight. Beatty's rust-bucket engine made lots of noise and held together."

The Navarro roadster was the only supercharged vehicle to run with the same engine at both the dry lakes and in oval-track competition. He also mentioned that he ran in the smallest displacement class because the whole idea was an experiment to see how much power he could get out of a small engine, and the skill needed to achieve this goal would be good for advertising. Sadly, his ideas ran contrary to a world that thinks that biggest is best.

Today, the Navarro roadster has been fully restored by its present-day owner and is on display at the NHRA Museum in Pomona, California. Unfortunately, the original engine is owned by another car enthusiast.

O/STREAMLINER CLASS

The shapes and sizes of vehicles running at the annual week-long speed event held on the salt flats of Bonneville, Utah, is as diverse as the list is long. The sanctioning body tries its best to offer a class to accommodate pretty well every car or motorcycle that arrives at the meet. In 1950, Barney made the pilgrimage to run a 176-ci V-8 in two different classes. In the A/Modified Roadster class, he'd outfitted his engine with an experimental dual-carburetor oxygen-injection system, and in the B/Modified Roadster class, the engine would be running the GMC blower.

It was still early in the week when, during a high-speed run, he felt the car begin to slow down and surmised that he'd just burnt a couple of rods. Upon pulling the pan and surveying the damage, he concluded that the engine was toast. But Barney had always been an astute thinker and, after considering the damage,

A contemplative Barney stands next to his roadster at El Mirage after pulling the head off the V8-60 to discover several broken pistons. Note the rear tires are off the ground to assist in turning over the engine. Tom Beatty and his wife are in the background with Tom's *Rust Bucket* roadster. *Courtesy Barney Navarro*

he decided to convert what was left of the V-8 into a four-cylinder. That'd leave him with 88 ci, enough to run in the O/Streamliner class that was open and in which no speed record had been set.

Once the engine was dismantled and the damaged rods and pistons were removed from the crankshaft, Barney used a hack saw to cut the four destroyed rods off at the rod caps so they could be reinstalled on the crank to hold the bearings in place. A piece of string and a stick were used to simulate a beam balance to verify that the cut-off rod ends would be kept within a tolerable weight of each other. The unused exhaust ports were covered over with pieces cut from a beer can, and all unused intake passages were also blocked off. To qualify for the streamliner class, Barney taped cardboard over the rear section of the body panels. As a gag, he even added a cardboard tailfin on the trunk lid like some of big streamliners used to stabilize the cars at high speeds.

No one objected to a cardboard streamliner; in fact, it stirred up a lot of good humor among his fellow racers. When the cardboard wonder was taped up and ready to go, it was given a trial run to be sure that it would hold together at high speed. With the roadster-streamliner creation fastened down on the trailer, Barney gave it a successful 90-mile-per-hour test ride down the highway behind his car.

The push car had to stay behind the cardboard streamliner for a considerable length of time to get it up to speed, as it was running an in-out box and, with the small engine, it needed lots of help to get it up and moving. After establishing a new O class record of 78.67 miles per hour (two-way average) at Bonneville, Barney left the engine in the car to see how much more he could get out of it. Keeping with his wry sense of humor, the unused cylinder head was replaced with a piece of clear Plexiglas that made more than one curious spectator take a second look!

Barney explained that the rods seized at Bonneville due to the original design of the 180-degree crankshaft. "Brayden designed his crankshaft with a diagonal bar, which dates back to the Model T. It wants to straighten out at speed, which bends the crank, putting the bearings in a bind and seizing the rod bearings."

OXYGEN

With a good handle on chemistry, Barney had experimented with a variety of fuel compounds in search of optimum horsepower. This search for an alternative fuel led him to oxygen, which has the ability to produce enormous amounts of horsepower.

"Nitro is just a foot in the door," Barney said. "I could build an engine with no intake valve; just squirt a liquid oxygen mix [oxygen and alcohol] directly into the combustion chamber."

His little 176-ci flathead V-8 ran 102 miles per hour on dual carburetors at the dry lakes; with the same setup, but with oxygen injection, the roadster ran 137 miles per hour. During the fall meet at the lakes in 1950, his B/Modified Roadster ran 146.81 miles per hour with the oxygen-carburetor setup.

His use of oxygen was kept a secret, even when *Hop Up* magazine wrote a feature story on Barney in its August 1951 issue. The reporter followed Barney step by step throughout the article, beginning by taking pictures of him building and installing the flathead into the roadster, traveling up to El Mirage Dry Lake, and actually running the car. He even photographed the dual carburetors with the oxygen injectors, and still no one picked up on what Barney was doing.

Alas, Barney ran into an alcohol and oxygen mixture that proved too combustible. Two round stacks over the carburetors had one line connected to an alcohol tank and another line attached to the pressurized oxygen bottle that was mounted inside the car. Each carburetor had a regulator that controlled the amount of oxygen being injected into the top of the carburetor as the carburetor linkage pushed the butterflies wide open. During one particular run on the lakebed, the engine backfired, igniting the oxygen and alcohol injectors, and one carburetor disappeared like magic, leaving only the throttle body base. The intense heat of the backfire instantly vaporized the pot-metal carburetor body, coating the interior of the engine and exhaust pipes with pot metal.

"If you ran more than 30 percent oxygen," Barney said, "the charge in the combustion chamber would ignite too easily, from any extreme hot spot, causing the charge to backfire through the carburetor."

The navy had discovered the same thing, unbeknownst to Barney, during the same period. Its program was called "High Altitude Power Augmentation" and experimented with feeding extra oxygen into aircraft engines at high altitudes to gain more power in efforts to replace the turbocharger. The navy found that 30 percent oxygen was about the highest ratio it could run safely. Normally, the atmosphere contains about 21 percent oxygen.

Barney felt that he could have gotten more horsepower and speed out of the engine if he'd experimented with water mixed with alcohol because the rapid combustibility would have been cut down. A 50/50 water and alcohol mix was used to cool the charge being injected into the engine of the P-38 aircraft, which had an emergency setting that gave almost 70 inches of boost. Used for any great length of time, that kind of boost would destroy the engine. Yet it was nothing for the Unlimited Hydro class powerboats, which used aircraft engines, to be running as high as 125 inches of boost and consuming as much water and alcohol as gasoline.

Ollie Morris of Santa Ana also played around with the volatile stuff. For several years, Ollie just about owned the Orange County drag strip with his *Smok'n White Owl* flathead-powered dragster, and, like Barney, he kept his use of oxygen a secret. A small bottle of oxygen was installed inside his race car, and he only used it if he was about to lose a race. Like Barney, he also experienced the occasional mishap.

TRICKY COMPETITOR

The first car that A. J. Watson ever took to compete in the Indianapolis 500 was a Maserati chassis powered by a Navarro-built V-8 Ford—a bored and stroked flathead equipped with Navarro heads and a triple intake manifold.

By the time the ill-equipped Watson team reached Chicago, it realized that there wasn't enough money to continue on to Indianapolis. Out of desperation, the team took on the sponsorship of a large, well-known auto parts warehouse distributor in Chicago. The only condition that the new benefactor demanded of the Watson team was replacing the Navarro parts with their own brand. Unfortunately for the Watson team, this outfit's inferior equipment couldn't supply the same performance. No matter how Dick Rathmann pushed the Maserati, he just couldn't get it up to speed to qualify for the 1948 race.

The following year, Barney built another engine for Watson's car to compete at Indy, and this time he was prepared, as Watson was still running under the Chicago outfit's sponsorship. Barney had come up with a strong deterrent to prevent anyone from removing his cylinder heads and intake manifold from the engine. He bored through the head and into the large, round, center water hole in the engine block, bored into the siamesed exhaust passage, and, after threading the opening, installed an exhaust pipe into the hole. The cost of making custom cylinder heads to accommodate this new exhaust port would prevent anyone from tampering with the Navarro heads. Despite the looks of it, Barney said that this center exhaust outlet didn't affect the engine's performance one way or the other.

When A. J. arrived at his sponsor's shop in Chicago, he refused to remove the Navarro triple intake in favor of his sponsor's dual. Not to be outdone, the sponsor had the Navarro name removed from the cast-aluminum cylinder heads and intake manifold with a die grinder.

Before A. J. Watson made a name for himself as one of the foremost race car builders of his day, he raced track roadsters as well as his Indy Maserati. A. J. competed in West Coast CRA events and traveled back east to run in the lucrative Hurricane Racing Association circuit that was based in Chicago. Watson had to run under an assumed name when competing in the HRA events, as competing in both racing venues was regarded as a conflict of interest by both sanctioning bodies. In order to sneak in under the wire, Watson registered his roadster with CRA as

The infamous Tom Beatty *Rust Bucket* roadster with Barney's 3:71 blower protruding from the engine hood. The car looked like hell but was very quick. *Courtesy Barney Navarro*

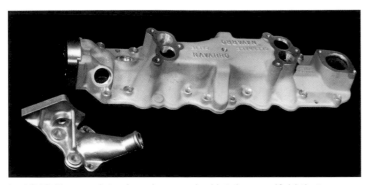

In 1949 Navarro introduced a new dual-intake manifold that incorporated an exhaust riser, thus eliminating the costly dog-bone exhaust heater adapter. *Courtesy Barney Navarro*

a Navarro Racing Equipment entry, which provided Barney with good advertising every time Rathmann raced the car.

WRITING

Barney originally got into technical writing to counteract the biased reporting he found in some automotive magazines. These magazines showed favoritism to certain manufacturers—those with either large advertising budgets or with political pull. This bias hurt outfits whose equipment was omitted. Barney confronted Rolland "Rolly" Mack, who was the advertising rep for Petersen Publishing, about this seemingly unfair practice. Rolly knew about Barney's wealth of technical know-how and suggested that if he wanted change, he should write some articles himself. Rolly said, "Publicity is the main thing, even if it's negative publicity."

The in-depth technical material came from Barney's schooling in chemistry and physics. He combined sound mechanical knowledge with a natural insight into the fundamental rules that governed these subjects.

Barney wrote scores of tech articles for a variety of automotive magazines. One article from 1952 concerned Ford's Fordomatic automatic transmission, and Barney used his own '51 Ford two-door sedan as the test subject. This car was his personal daily driver, as well as a tow car for his roadster and powerboat. He had massaged the engine to make sure the car had enough grunt to pull a loaded trailer over some of the steep passes encountered on the way to the dry lakes.

The flathead was bored out to 284 inches, and new pistons, a Vertex magneto, a Winfield camshaft, a dual intake, and 7:75.1 heads were installed. It could go from 0 to 60 miles per hour in 11.5 seconds while its stock counterpart made the same acceleration in 17.82 seconds. Barney found that Ford's automatic could take the added abuse of extra horsepower and haul a load on lengthy trips throughout California's hot desert climate.

When *Hop Up* magazine performed a road test on Ray Crawford's 1953 Lincoln entry in the '52 Pan Am race, it requested Barney's '51 Ford be part of the article as well. The *Hop Up* crew took the Lincoln on a 300-mile roadtrip out into the desert and back with Barney's Ford accompanying them. The article mentioned that the 205-horsepower Lincoln was no match for Barney's 170-horsepower Ford in acceleration, but it could outhandle the Ford with its heavy-duty, prepped suspension.

BOAT RACING

Sometimes things occur quite by chance, such as how Barney got involved in powerboat racing. It was in the early 1950s when Kenny St. Oegger came into the shop to inquire about what could be done to improve the set of Navarro cylinder heads he'd bought. After a lengthy conversation with Ken, boat racing had piqued Barney's curiosity. Initially, he started off by helping out in St. Oegger's pit, but over time he found himself riding in the cockpit as a co-pilot, or riding mechanic, in an erratic-behaving 70-mile-per-hour crackerbox-class speedboat. This style of powerboat places the driver and co-driver to the very rear of the flat-bottomed hull with a direct-drive inboard engine positioned directly in front of them, providing an unpredictable ride at the best of times.

When Ken purchased a three-point, Hallett-built, hydroplane hull, he sold the engine out of the crackerbox and let Barney run the boat with his own engine under the name "Navarro & St. Oegger." When Barney had reached the point that he was totally disenchanted with the car racing scene, he sold the roadster, complete with the GMC blower setup, and concentrated solely on powerboat racing.

266 CLASS

When Ken acquired the Hallett boat, he departed from the usual choice of engines and installed a 12-port Wayne Horning Chevrolet six built by Harry Warner's employees Nick Arias and Bob Toros. The engine was mounted in the boat on a 7-degree incline to assist in streamlining and to lower the center of gravity; it allowed Ken to run the exhaust along the bottom with a Hilborn injection system on the upper side. The low angle of the engine gave the boat great handling.

The industrialist and powerboat enthusiast Henry Kaiser eventually bought Ken's boat and about a year later called Ken to ask if he could repair it. He and Barney went to Kaiser's mansion on Lake Tahoe. The two worked on the boat's engine for hours, and it was close to midnight when they finally found the problem and test fired the engine.

"You could imagine what those six open stacks sounded like rebounding around the quiet shores of Lake Tahoe at midnight," Barney said.

The next morning, Kaiser's right-hand man, "Handy" Hancock, came out to see them. Barney figured they were in for it, but Hancock was smiling and told them they did the right thing by starting up the boat.

"He said Mrs. Kaiser told him that the old man was just laying there in bed, staring up at the ceiling, until he heard the engine start up; he smiled, turned on his side, and went to sleep," Barney said.

Kaiser's pier, where the two worked on the powerboat that night, was later used as a location in the first *Godfather* movie.

Barney prepares to make a run at a 1950 El Mirage meet. Note the blister on the engine hood to cover the four Stromberg 97s on the GMC blower. *Courtesy Barney Navarro*

Barney comes off a high-speed run during a 1950 El Mirage meet. He's wearing aviator's goggles and a protective face mask but has no roll bar. *Courtesy Barney Navarro*

7-LITER

Being a dedicated and well-heeled speedboat enthusiast, Kaiser owned more than one boat. His other craft was called *Restless 32-H* and was also docked at Tahoe the day Ken and Barney were there. It was powered by a twin McCulloch–blown early 426 Chrysler Hemi. It happened that there was a race being held locally and Ken talked Kaiser into letting Barney drive the boat. Afterward, Barney and Henry discussed what the boat needed and struck a deal where Barney would take the boat back to his San Fernando Road shop in Glendale for some upgrades.

Borrowing a set of Hemi-head patterns from Clark and Tebow of C&T Automotive that were originally designed by Al Sharp, Barney did some alterations to suit his needs and had a set of aluminum heads cast. Sodium Dodge truck valves were used for the exhaust, the McCulloch blowers were replaced with a Hilborn fuel-injection system, and an aircraft starter motor was fitted to the back end of the crankshaft, as the engine sat reversed in the hull and the prop shaft ran directly off the crank snout. A heavy-duty 24-volt aircraft battery was installed and could be relocated to balance the boat, and with 50 percent nitro and 50 percent alcohol in the tank, Barney could easily hit 135 miles per hour down the straightaway.

In 1956, Barney won his first 7-liter race, competing against the talented boat designer Richard Hallett. Barney covered the 2.5-mile course with an average of 83.88 miles per hour to win the race and set the Five-Mile Competition world record.

Barney developed a rather unique air-cooled, double-walled, exhaust header system consisting of outer sleeves surrounding each individual exhaust pipe, with about a quarter inch of clearance around the inside pipe. The outer pipes started several inches from the header flange on the block and extended past the inner pipes so the high-velocity exhaust gases leaving the smaller pipes would create a vacuum between the two, drawing cooling air into the base of the larger diameter pipes. These headers proved to be lightweight, very effective, and relatively inexpensive.

All good things come to an end, and when Barney saw Ken almost get killed in a race, he knew it was time to hang up the gloves. It happened while he and Ken were racing in Hawaii, and Ken flipped his craft, with almost fatal results. The seriousness of the accident made Barney realize that it could be him next, and that was enough to make him quit racing.

LOGO

Logos, especially when they were put out in decal form, proved to be a highly successful form of advertising for specialty equipment companies. By 1950, Barney knew that he needed something that would grab the eye, and a friend whose father was an art director for Warner Studios designed the Navarro Racing Equipment logo. Barney had told her that it would have to stand out, as the majority of racing cars were either red or yellow. She came up with the flame design, which would show up on just about any background color.

AIRESEARCH

Barney did a fair amount of consulting work for the AiResearch Industrial Division of the Garrett Corporation from 1957 to 1972. One of his more notable projects was designing and manufacturing turbocharger test stands, which essentially ran the turbine portion of the turbocharger using natural gas and air for combustion provided by the turbo's centrifugal compressor. These Navarro-made test stands are still in use today. The turbines were run night and day to evaluate their longevity, as AiResearch wanted to show the Detroit auto manufacturers the benefits of turbocharging for their underpowered economy vehicles. Barney said that the main barrier to the turbochargers' adoption was that the automakers were still relying on carburetors for fuel delivery and did not have injection systems that would have worked better.

NAVARRO TWIN-TURBINE TURBOCHARGER

The most innovative feature that Barney brought to the world of turbocharging was his twin-turbine system. "The conventional turbocharger's operational efficiency range is limited to a maximum effectiveness of approximately 25 percent of the engine's rpm range," Barney said.

In order to broaden the operational range, two turbines are employed in the Navarro concept. Each turbine is mounted on a common shaft and possesses an isolated housing. Initially, one turbine receives the total exhaust gas output from the engine, and a diverter valve blocks the flow to the second turbine. The diverter valve is kept in the single-turbine mode until the exhaust pressure to operate the turbine becomes excessive. Then it is shifted to dual-turbine operation, thereby extending the engine's range of efficient turbocharged operation. An additional advantage of the twin-turbine concept is that it allows total isolation of twin exhaust systems for an engine.

Barney also developed and patented a turbo diverter valve that was used primarily on his race car.

CORVAIR

Barney designed a custom turbo for his 1961 Corvair Monza's flat six-cylinder with an automatic transmission that resulted in speeds up to 94 miles per hour in quarter-mile runs at Lions Drag Strip. In the engine compartment, he mounted a CO_2 tank with a 200-pound regulator that had a line running over to one side of the twin-turbine turbocharger. As the gas pedal was pushed to the floor from a dead stop, the CO_2 from the supply tank spun the turbine to give an instant 45 inches of boost from a standing start. The other side of the turbo would kick in when the engine rpm was high enough to provide sufficient exhaust pressure, and the whole operation was controlled by electrical switches and solenoids. Barney wrote an in-depth report on turbocharging the Corvair for the January 1962 issue of *Hot Rod*.

BONNEVILLE

In 1964, Barney built a twin-turbo setup for Ed Dempsey's large 800-horsepower wedge Plymouth to take to Bonneville. They were aiming for the 225-mile-per-hour mark and successfully made a trial shakedown run. One of the turbos failed during their second run, but the car still managed a very decent 195 miles per hour. Unfortunately for the racing team, the weather conditions changed, preventing any further testing.

"We figured out later that one of the turbos failed because it was blowing through the carburetion," Barney said. "The air was very moist and was cooled to the point where ice pellets the size of a poppy seed would bounce around inside and come back on the compressor wheel. These minute particles of ice would make the leading edge of an inducer look just like a hack saw blade."

Before the turbo had packed it in, the team drove the Plymouth back and forth to the salt flats from Wendover every day rather than spending the time to load and unload it off the trailer. (Wendover is a small town located a stone's throw west of the Bonneville racecourse.) At the end of the day, they'd get out on the highway and, once up to well over 100 miles per hour, they'd cut the engine and coast into town to their motel. In the morning, when they fired up the Plymouth with its open exhausts, they weren't there long enough for anyone to complain or catch their license plate number.

FORMULA ONE

It was through an acquaintance named George Ilinsky that Barney was introduced to Count Volpi of Italian racing fame who was visiting from his home country. The count hired Barney to install the Navarro twin-turbine system on his MV Agusta motorcycle. Once the installation was completed, the bike was dyno tested at the Landy Brothers' shop. Back in Italy, the count took the turbocharged bike to the Agusta factory, but the manufacturer showed little interest in the setup, so Volpi took the bike to the Ferrari factory, where it was put through a dynamometer run. The results were impressive enough that when the count showed the figures to his friend Carlo Chitti, who was in charge of Alfa Romeo's racing program, Chitti contacted Barney about coming to Italy.

In March 1981, Barney was hired to spend a week as a consultant at the Alfa Romeo factory in Milano, Italy. Alfa was having difficulty with its 91-ci, 600-horsepower Grand Prix V-8 racing engine. It performed very well at high rpm, but on a road course, it experienced so much turbo lag that it killed the engine's performance. Alfa felt Barney's twin-turbo system might be the answer to the dilemma.

This view of Tom Beatty's belly tank at the 1951 Bonneville Nationals shows the detailed frame of chrome-moly aircraft tubing, the water tank in front of the engine, a well-protected cockpit, and a copy of Barney's blower setup. It set the D/Lakester record of 185.80 miles per hour. *Leslie Long collection, courtesy Barney Navarro*

Barney is in the driver's seat of Henry Kaiser's *Restless 32-H* hydroplane during a race at Lake Mead in 1956. Once Barney had reworked the boat and Chrysler engine, it became very competitive, collecting several records and numerous wins. *Courtesy Barney Navarro*

After making some suggestions on his first visit, he went back the following month to see how the engineers were progressing with his program. Regrettably, they hadn't followed up on Barney's suggestion to couple the turbos in close; instead, they had them rigged up to long exhaust pipes. He also wanted them to switch the heads around so the exhaust ports would be on top and the intakes on the outside of the block. By having the exhausts in the center, they could get the right firing order set up, and with short exhaust pipes they wouldn't lose a lot of heat.

"Unfortunately, no one could speak English until the last day when the count showed up to interpret for us," Barney said. "We started to remove pieces of equipment to see where the problem lay. As soon as the two long pipes to the diverter valve were removed, the engine turned 13,000 instantly. I did everything I could to break up the resonance; the long overlap was allowing exhaust to come back into the intake."

Due to commitments back in the United States, Barney couldn't stay to complete the work on the engine; besides, Alfa wanted a quick fix, not the way Barney knew it should be done. At the time he was involved with Alfa, Mario Andretti was the factory driver.

700-HORSEPOWER RAMBLER 6

Barney's philosophy toward mechanical performance was based in the principles of physics. "A lot of people don't understand the physics of what they're doing," Barney said. "That's the problem. If they understood the physics, they'd attack the problem from a different angle instead of just buying parts that somebody else uses."

Before he began the Rambler 6 project, he gave thorough consideration to all the available engines on the market at the time.

AiResearch's Navarro-engineered and constructed turbocharger test stands were in use for many years. *Courtesy Barney Navarro*

He came to the conclusion that the American Motors Corporation (AMC) Rambler 6 was the strongest engine and the best equipped to take the punishment of a 3.5-hour race such as the Indy 500. The Rambler had 1/2-inch head bolts, 1/2-inch main bolts, a port for every valve, eight counterweights on the crankshaft, seven main bearings, a short stroke, and good crankshaft pin and main bearing diameters.

"The crankshaft had what you call 3/4-inch overlap," Barney said. The only drawback with the engine was the lack of head bolts, so he used a spring seal instead.

The turbocharged Rambler was rigged up so that the gas pedal controlled the wastegate. "We set the wastegate at 70 inches of boost," Barney explained. "The harder you pushed on the throttle, the less the wastegate threw away and the higher the boost would be. You could push real hard and get 95 inches of boost at 47.5 pounds of pressure. It was a way of keeping the driver out of trouble," recounted Barney.

AMC manufactured three special cast-iron heads for Barney that contained several extra studs to prevent the head gaskets from blowing. The rulebook at the time stated that the heads had to come off the factory assembly line, so AMC had Barney's custom heads come off the line ahead of the standard stock production heads, following the rulebook to the letter!

"I made special seal rings in conjunction with a modified head gasket," Barney said of the AMC head. "We machined the area surrounding the cylinder bore away and used a 3/32-inch-thick circle-seal spring with a round heel, so when you rocked it, it didn't dig into the block. Every time the engine fires, the head rises and lowers very minutely. You need something that'll give and take the movement between the head and engine block."

Upon completion, the engine was test run over at the Champion Spark Plug dynamometer facility under the capable hands of Dick Jones. Further work was performed on Tony Capanna's Wilcap dyno. The Rambler put out 640 pounds of torque at 4,500 rpm and 700 horsepower at around 6,500 to 7,000 rpm. Barney said that the engine could handle 105 inches of boost with no damage to the engine.

Regrettably, Barney hadn't the time or the means to fully develop projects such as the Rambler 6 and the oxygen-injector system. For a period of five years, Navarro Racing Equipment received $18,000 from AMC to perform work on the Rambler 6; this sum only partially covered the actual costs incurred in developing the turbocharged version of the engine.

When AMC sponsored land-speed record-holder Craig Breedlove to drive a streamliner at Bonneville, it commissioned Navarro to build a turbocharged six-cylinder as one of the engines that was to be used in the record attempts. The ultra stream-lined car was designed to run several AMC engines with hopes of setting several different records, but for various reasons the project never arrived at Bonneville. Breedlove converted the car into a drag strip show car called the *Screaming Yellow Zonker* and toured the country, while Barney's engine was shuffled off into a dusty corner.

Barney with his six-cylinder Rambler–powered race car in a Gasoline Alley garage. Notice the wing mounted on the rear of the car, plus the wood handsaw in Barney's right hand. When asked in 2003 what he was attempting to do with the saw, said he couldn't remember. *Courtesy Barney Navarro*

At their garage in Gasoline Alley, Barney and a crewmember check over the turbocharged Rambler six-cylinder in the Navarro race car. Note the portable electric engine starter by the right rear tire. *Courtesy Barney Navarro*

INDIANAPOLIS 500

The first time Barney traveled to the Speedway was in 1951, and with the exception of a few years, he attended every Memorial Day Classic until 1971. He was there either reporting for a magazine, attempting to get his own car in the show, or assisting a race team in the pits with its race car.

Over the years, the Speedway has attracted just about every type of car–engine combination imaginable, so when Barney showed up with a race car powered by a Rambler engine, the automotive critics took it all in stride. The Navarro Indy car was a Watson car that was a copy of a Rolla Vollstedt car, which in turn was a copy of an original Jack Brabham design. Grover Pope and Norm Hall had bought A. J. Watson's copy of the Brabham from a car owner in Indianapolis. Watson's copy had come in second in the 1964 Indy with Rodger Ward behind the wheel. Many years later, Rodger bought the car from Barney to restore it back to its 1964 spec.

The Rambler-powered car made its début at the Brickyard in 1967 with Norm Hall in the driver's seat. Hall had had his right leg amputated just below the knee after a previous racing accident, and his amputated leg proved to be a major hindrance when driving the turbocharged car, as he needed to move his foot quickly to back off the throttle as soon as the turbo kicked in. Not being totally comfortable with the situation, Norm stepped aside for Les Scott, who ran the AMC Evaluation Teardown Department and raced midgets on the side.

Scott was running about three miles per hour shy of making the show before he ran into turbocharger difficulties. The Rambler was equipped with Weber 58-millimeter side-draft carburetors that were reworked for alcohol and the turbos. Problems developed as the weather turned cool and damp; moisture would freeze as it ran through the carburetors, forming minute ice pellets

that destroyed the vanes of the turbine. To overcome this problem, Barney later came up with what he called the "barn door," which worked with a fuel-injection system. It measured the airflow entering the engine, similar to mechanisms that were used later on fuel-injected passenger cars.

After the failed attempt, Barney bought out his partner's shares in the car, feeling that he would be better on his own. The following year at Indy, Scott again couldn't get the car up to speed even though the Webers had been replaced with the innovative barn-door air-metering valve with port injection. In 1969, Barney was again back at the Speedway with Jerry Titus in the driver's seat. Regrettably, Titus crashed the car while running practice laps.

"I told him to be careful [and that] as soon as the boost started coming in to back off because he couldn't think as fast as that turbo could spin," Barney said. "It spun up, broke the tires loose, and put him right into the wall."

The following year was the last attempt for the aged and outdated race car. Rookie driver Jigger Sirois couldn't get the car to run right because of a faulty enrichment valve, which wasn't discovered until much later. The Rambler had more power, but the car just didn't handle properly, and the drivers of that era really did not understand the subtle technique needed to drive a turbocharged car. When the *Navarro Engineering Special* was running right, it had loads of speed in the straightaway, but it just couldn't make the turns. Compared to the newer breed of well-handling Indy cars, the tired Watson chassis was antiquated. It could not utilize the excessive amounts of horsepower put out by the Rambler engine.

One rather novel feature of the race car was that it had a transmitter that relayed manifold and exhaust pressures and exhaust temperatures to the pit, and as the pressure went up, the transmitter beeped faster, much to the curiosity of the other pit crews. Barney came up with the idea to let him know how the car was performing on the track without having to totally rely on the feedback and memory of the driver. This idea of car-to-pit telemetry is widely used in racing today, most prominently in Formula One.

HI-DOME HEADS

Over the years, there's been a great deal of controversy over just where the piston should be once it reaches top dead center in the flathead V-8. Some theorists suggest it should be flush with the block, some want the piston to travel up into the head (pop-up style), and then there's Barney's version: "Heads are more important than a dual-intake manifold. The heads will increase the torque, and that's what people notice."

The Navarro Hi-Dome cylinder heads were flow tested and achieved a reported 30-percent increase in airflow due to the flat area over the exhaust valve and the high area over the intake valve. The spark plug is located above the exhaust valve, and there is an undercut radius behind the intake. This particular head has a chamber that is designed to raise compression and still allow a high rate of flow.

"The Hi-Dome head uses the same shape as the early Chrysler Hemi pistons to promote turbulence, and they do not 'pop up' into the head," Barney said. "The design places the center of the piston dome up into the head chamber that has a matching shape." The engine builder must use a custom dome piston, such as one from Arias Pistons, to receive total benefit of the head.

HENRY'S ENGINE

About Ford Motor Company's most distinguished engine Barney said, "The flathead V-8 is the symbol of what made the hot rod business evolve and the sport itself. It would never have happened if it hadn't been for the millions of flatheads produced by Ford."

Navarro Racing Equipment remained faithful to the flathead engine, never deviating from its original product line. Other outfits, such as Offenhauser, Edelbrock, and Weiand, which also cut their teeth manufacturing flathead stuff, changed direction to accommodate the overhead-valve engine.

"About 1951, the majority of people who bought flathead equipment were at least thirty-five years of age and had a brand-new Ford or Mercury," Barney said.

He was deeply disappointed with the Ford Motor Company because it never fully developed the flathead to the maximum, and he wished that, "they'd improved the siamese port, the uncooled back section of the block next to the exhaust outlet, and the center main bearing."

Navarro Racing Equipment manufactured speed equipment for these fabulous V-8s from 1947 to 1957, when the engines phased out due to the lack of demand, only to resume manufacturing years later as the nostalgia boom hit.

BARNEY NAVARRO'S LEGACY

"You don't violate the laws of nature; you can't, they're inviolate," Barney said. "If you understand the basic physics, you have

Barney and Jim Miller pose with Chrysler's turbine job that Barney test drove and wrote up in a tech report for a car magazine.
Courtesy Barney Navarro

the problem beat. Now it's a matter of ingenuity and figuring out the limitations of what the rulebooks allow you, working within those parameters."

Aside from their close friendship, Barney was very impressed with Ed Winfield because he was one of the very few people who understood the theory behind the mechanics that made something work. During one of many great conversations with Barney, I asked him: "If you could do it over again, what would you have done differently?" He responded, "I think I'd have been less honest. Ed Winfield once told someone that I will never be a millionaire. I'm too honest!"

Over the years of manufacturing and experimental work, Barney recorded six patents, including a diverter valve, a twin-turbine turbocharger, a concrete wall saw, and a method of cutting radial gears. Unfortunately for Barney, none of his patents ever made him fabulously wealthy; obviously, Ed Winfield was correct!

Throughout his racing career, Barney tried his hand at everything, from the dusty lakebeds of Southern California, the expansive salt flats of Bonneville, and the dirt and paved oval tracks to international road racing, the prestigious Indy 500, and powerboat racing. While active in racing, he served on the board of the SCTA and was a member in both the CRA and the Southern California Power Boat Association.

Navarro Engineering also accomplished its fair share of developmental projects, from perfecting heart-lung machines, turbocharging systems, and testing equipment to research and development work. Alas, time waits for no one, and on August 20, 2007, at the age of 88, Barney Navarro passed away—on his birthday.

CHAPTER 14

Offenhauser

FRED OFFENHAUSER

Almost certainly one of the greatest names in the history of auto racing is Offenhauser. The original Fred Offenhauser was a toolmaker who began working for the Harry A. Miller Manufacturing Company of Los Angeles in 1913. The following year, Fred was put in charge of the developing an inline six-cylinder aircraft engine, which was touted as the first original "Miller" engine. It wasn't long before Fred was considered a master machinist, and with the master drafting skills of Leo Goosen, the two became indispensable in the development of Miller's racing engines. When Harry's company went bankrupt in 1933, Fred bought the rights for several of the Miller engines and retained Leo as the chief design engineer for his new company. The Miller name was dropped in favor of Offenhauser.

In 1946, three-time Indy winner Louis Meyer and his former riding mechanic and crew chief Dale Drake bought the Offenhauser Engine Company, which they renamed Meyer & Drake.

BEGINNING

The Fred Offenhauser we're concerned with was born October 4, 1917, and grew up on his parents' ranch in Perris, California, about 90 miles east of L.A. Shortly after graduating from high school in 1935, his family moved to 1712 Mansfield Avenue in west Los Angeles, just two blocks away from Uncle Fred's engine plant (the original Fred Offenhauser). Fred was hired as a machinist in his uncle's shop, and later on, his younger brother Carl would also join the firm as a machinist. As time went on, Fred developed aspirations of one day taking over the company. But after being drafted into the navy, Fred served out the duration of World War II stationed at Moffat Field in Los Angeles, while the Offenhauser Company put aside its engine business to take on aircraft work for the military.

Once the hostilities were over, the Offenhauser Company resumed engine building, and Fred and Carl went back work for their uncle, but not for long. When his uncle sold the business to Louis Meyer and Dale Drake in 1946, Fred knew that his dream of owning his uncle's business was over for good.

OFFENHAUSER EQUIPMENT CORPORATION

Fred had been chumming around with another Offenhauser employee named Fran Hernandez, who started working for Offenhauser after being discharged from the navy in 1945. Although Fred wasn't personally involved in hot rodding, Fran was, and he was no doubt influential in the pair going into the speed equipment business. Fred left the Offenhauser Engine Company and, with Fran Hernandez as his partner, rented a shop at 8948 National Boulevard in Los Angeles. The shop opened under the "Offenhauser Equipment Corporation" name to capitalize on the name's notoriety.

Using the Offenhauser name opened up a lawsuit with Meyer and Drake over the legal rights to it. The courts finally settled the affair, realizing that there was no deliberate intent by either party to use the Offenhauser name in a deceptive or stolen manner. Each had a legitimate right to the name, and each party had to remain within its own boundaries of specialty manufacturing so as not to compete with one another commercially.

Opposite: Offenhauser's four original employees stand before the machine shop at 8936 National Boulevard. From left are Al Ward, Bob Hughes, Fred Offenhauser, and Fran Hernandez. *Courtesy Fred Offenhauser Jr.*

An inside shot of the original Offenhauser machine shop on National Boulevard finds Bob Hughes checking valve lift on a flathead while Al Ward mikes a piston. Note the stack of V-8 heads on the left. *Courtesy Fred Offenhauser Jr.*

When Fred first opened the doors for business, the shop offered general machine work to supplement its income until there were sufficient sales in the speed equipment line. The machine shop was busy enough that two more machinists, named Bob Hughes and Al Ward, were hired.

After being discharged from the marine air corps in 1947, Hughes had the privilege of being the second employee hired after Al Ward. Bob recalled that he was taken on as a drill-press operator at 85 cents an hour, drilling out heads, intakes, and generator brackets, after Fred taught him how to properly sharpen bits for the drill press and lathe. He spent three or four days learning how to do it just right, as Fred was adamant about having everything done with precision. Fred also insisted that every Saturday morning Bob and the other shop workers come in and clean the machine shop until it was spotless. Over time, Bob was taught how to shrink-fit the ring gear on aluminum flywheels, machine heads and intakes, and perform the tedious job of machining the degree marks on the ignition-adapter plates. Hughes also remembered how, in 1948, a young fellow named Bob Petersen came around to the shop to solicit ads for his new magazine. Although Fred ran only three ads in that first year of *Hot Rod*, the response was overwhelming.

In late 1948 or early 1949, Fred and Fran Hernandez went their separate ways. Fran went over to Edelbrock and eventually on to the Ford Motor Company.

NITRO CARBURETORS

Once the mysteries of nitromethane had become common knowledge to the average racer, there still was the problem of how to convert a carburetor to run on the stuff. The carburetors of choice at the time were the Stromberg 81 and 97 series. Bob had noticed this particular problem after paying a visit to a dry lakes meet, where he saw the difficulties some fellows were experiencing with carburetion.

After dissecting a Stromberg and studying the inner workings, he deduced that the carburetor needed larger dump tubes. He tried out his theory by machining and installing some larger tubes and adjustable jets in a number of carburetors that he then gave

The interior of the Offenhauser shop on National Boulevard. Notice how clean the shop is and the stack of manifolds on the table. From left are Al Ward, Bob Hughes, Fred, and Fran Hernandez. *Courtesy Fred Offenhauser Jr.*

to several racers at the lakes. The results were so good that Bob and Fred began to scour the local scrap yards, buying up all the 81 and 97 carburetors they could find. The carburetors would be disassembled and sand blasted clean, the pot metal was anodized black, and larger dump tubes and adjustable jets were installed. The nitro-friendly carburetors proved to be a hot item, as the shop sold all it could produce.

Fred takes measurements off Chevrolet's new 265-ci V-8 for the Offenhauser three-carburetor manifold pattern. *Courtesy Fred Offenhauser Jr.*

FROM NATIONAL TO ALHAMBRA

The original shop on National Boulevard soon became inadequate for the quickly growing company, and in 1950 it found larger accommodations at 5054 Alhambra Avenue in Los Angeles. Within five years, the company moved up the street to 5156 Alhambra and eventually relocated to its present-day address at 5300 Alhambra. Obviously, Fred liked the area.

OFFENHAUSER EQUIPMENT

Bob said that his machining skills matured to the point that Ted Halibrand asked him if he'd come and do some part-time machine work for him. Ted was a frequent visitor at the Offenhauser shop, as the shop was hired to machine the Halibrand quick-change center sections. Fran had built all the jig fixtures and tooling to hold and machine the center sections.

In 1951, the Korean War erupted, and Bob was recalled back into active military duty to fly Corsairs. He left his wife, seven-month-old daughter, and three-year-old son to fly combat missions in Korea. He hadn't flown since being discharged in 1947. Once his military tour was over, Bob returned to Offenhauser, where Tom Heininger was by then the general manager and Carl Offenhauser was overseeing the machine shop. Another employee, named Jimmy Ayles, also worked in the machine shop when he wasn't behind a drafting board. Bob said that he became the acting sales manager while Fred was out on roadtrips.

Not content to manufacture a line of products for one engine, Fred expanded into areas outside the flathead V-8. By 1953, the Offenhauser catalog listed cylinder heads and manifolds for the V8-85 and V8-60, Chevy 6 intakes and valve covers, Cadillac and Ford OHV 6 equipment, as well as non-Offenhauser stuff. Fred turned Offenhauser into a speed parts warehouse as well as a manufacturer. He traveled throughout the country several months a year, visiting his established dealers and setting up new accounts. Fred could offer speed shops a complete package deal that included Offenhauser products, as well as those from Hedman, Clay Smith, Schiefer, Weber, Hurst, Stewart-Warner, Jahns, Gotha, Hellings, Harman & Collins, Winfield, and so on. When he wasn't out on the road, sales manager Joe Shea would be out pounding the pavement throughout the midwestern, eastern, and southern states with his Offenhauser Power Equipment station wagon. This practice continued until the large discount warehouse distributors started up, as these outfits could sell parts cheaper than Fred could buy them.

CHRYSLER MANIFOLDS

One of the more profitable contracts Offenhauser had in 1953 was with the Chrysler Corporation. This contract was to supply Chrysler with a performance package for its Hemi V-8, consisting of a dual-carburetor manifold and a Belond exhaust system with mufflers. Bob Hughes recalled that he had to make sure the Chrysler orders were shipped on time, and Tom Heininger took care of all the invoicing on the deal. Bob said that he remembered seeing one check from Chrysler for $26,000—a huge pile of cash in those days.

As a side note, Bob and Tom had talked about going into business for themselves, as they could see there were plenty of opportunities in the hot rodding business. About four months after Bob rejoined Offenhauser, he and Tom had a chance to open a business with a silent partner: Harry Weber. Harry was instrumental in assisting them with their business, which became the very successful Webco Corporation.

DUAL-PURPOSE MANIFOLD

Offenhauser introduced what it called a "Dual-Purpose" intake manifold for the new 1954 Ford Y-block—the engine that finally pushed the tired old flathead into obscurity. This particular intake was sold in a package form with easy-to-install parts consisting of gaskets, installation instructions, a throttle linkage and preformed steel fuel lines. "Dual-purpose," meant that this manifold could be set up to function with either two or three carburetors. The buyer could run either configuration while retaining a balanced fuel distribution to the engine by using the cast aluminum carb base-plate to block off the center intake for two carburetor operation. Fred even offered a free article titled "Triple-Threat Power Story," that described the manifold's ability to run two carbs for street use and three for racing, giving the owner two manifolds in one. Bill Drake and Jim Ayles were the Offenhauser technicians behind the development of this manifold.

FRED AND OLLIE

A common denominator in the success of many young companies is the input of intelligent, business-savvy individuals who take an active part in the direction of the company. In all probability, Fred's most fortunate business move was to acquire the services of George "Ollie Morris" in 1954. Fred was never personally into the hot rod scene or racing, and even though he was a judicious businessman, a talented machinist, and he understood the attributes of an engine, with Fran Hernandez gone, the company needed input from the racer's viewpoint.

The influence Ollie Morris had upon Offenhauser's future was monumental. Ollie was a grassroots racer who was weaned on do-it-yourself race car building and engine modifications. He brought a history of successful drag racing and engine building to Offenhauser, he understood volatile racing fuels, and he was a deep methodical thinker when it came to understanding the laws of nature pertaining to the automobile engine. He was also a skilled machinist with a very inquisitive mind.

SPONSORSHIP

In the early 1950s, Ollie was running his own automotive repair and machine shop business in Santa Ana, California. Besides auto repairs, he converted carburetors over to nitro fuel—a service that was popular with racers—and he eventually tied up with Dean Moon to distribute them for him. His racing skills and successes at the drag strip attracted Offenhauser.

"The car gained a bit of notoriety, and that's when Fred Offenhauser got interested," Ollie said. "He'd been semi-sponsoring another car, and it seemed like every time the other guy and I ran off, he'd lose, and there's one thing Fred hated, and that was losing. He approached me one day at the races and gave me his card and asked if I'd meet him at his office on Monday."

Fred wanted to sponsor the *Smok'n White Owl* dragster, and the men came to an agreement in which Offenhauser would be the sole sponsor of the car. Fred offered cylinder heads and intake manifolds and would take care of the engine machining costs. In return, Ollie would modify and develop the equipment, allowing Fred to use these enhancements in production Offenhauser heads and manifolds.

Ollie Morris is busy setting the rocker of a Chevy six as Carl Offenhauser looks on. They're about to test an Offy dual-carburetor manifold. *Courtesy Fred Offenhauser Jr.*

THE FIRST CHEVROLET V-8 DRAGSTER

Prior to the release of its revolutionary 265-ci V-8, Chevrolet had passed out samples of the engine to various aftermarket manufacturers for development purposes. Offenhauser received three engines to develop and, if possible, to test under actual racing conditions. Fred offered to replace Ollie's flathead motor with one of the Chevys so a newly designed three-carburetor manifold could be evaluated at Bonneville. As the engine wasn't ready in time for the salt flats, the team decided to take the *Offenhauser Special* to the 1955 NHRA Nationals at Great Bend, Kansas, instead.

Both Fred and Ollie worked on modifying the Chevrolet, and without any guidelines to follow, the two went with what they thought would suit the engine. The engine was overbored 3/16 inch and stroked to 3 1/4 inches for a 316-ci engine; the overbore would create problems later. The stock rods appeared to be strong enough and were retained, the stock valve springs were replaced by Chrysler springs, and JE Pistons supplied special cast pistons. Both Fred and Ollie's opinions were similar to that of Stuart Hilborn when they first saw those funny-looking stamped-steel rocker arms that were individually bolted to the heads. Not having total confidence in this factory rocker system, it was replaced with a Thomas magnesium rocker-arm kit. Chuck Potvin ground an experimental flat-tappet camshaft for the Chevy, as Ollie was a longtime user of Potvin equipment.

The Chevrolet fit right into the *Smok'n White Owl*—now painted black with "Offenhauser" painted across the body—as if it was built for it. This car became the first dragster to ever run a Chevrolet V-8 engine. By the time everything was bolted down, the team only had time to test run and tune the engine once at the Santa Ana drag strip prior to going to the Kansas meet.

At Great Bend, after soundly beating Mickey Thompson during time trials, Mickey dug into the rulebook and lodged a protest against the Offenhauser car for its absence of rear shock absorbers. The rules stated that cars had to be outfitted with shock absorbers on each wheel, so the car was disqualified. To get around this little setback, a local Offenhauser dealer's shop welded two nonfunctioning shocks onto the rearend; the rules didn't state that they had to be working!

Upon being reinstated, but with further complaints from Thompson, Fred let his well-known temper get the better of him. He pulled the car out of competition and left for California, never knowing how the car would have done in the runoffs. Ollie said that they had a very good chance at winning, considering the ETs he was turning, and the car was one of the few that didn't have any problems with the rough surface of the concrete strip. On the upside, Ollie did make a run of 141.28 miles per hour, becoming the fastest Chevrolet-powered car in the country and winning a Chevrolet V-8 engine from GM for setting the fastest time at the meet with a Chevy engine.

One thing the pair did learn from running a goodly dose of nitro at Great Bend was that it weakened the thin cylinder walls. It caused a power loss and almost destroyed the engine. After the meet, they had to sleeve the cylinders.

"The block was tissue-paper thin in comparison to the V-8 flathead," Ollie said. "We had bored that Chevy V-8 block out to what I thought was a conservative 0.040 over."

Great Bend was a learning experience for Fred and Ollie in modifying a Chevrolet V-8. Afterward, Fred explained all that they had done to the engine to any racer who requested the information.

"What made me fall in love with the Chevy to begin with was you could twist its tail," Ollie said. "It just didn't seem to have any limit, and if you got the valve spring tension right, that thing just didn't have any sense, it'd just keep on going. The flathead would get up to a certain point, and if it didn't fall apart, it was just like it had a governor; that's all it was going to do."

Ollie continued to work for Fred on a part-time basis as a design consultant while maintaining his automotive tune-up and specialty machine shop in Santa Ana. Once the two became involved with other projects at the Offenhauser factory, Fred asked Ollie not to race anymore because he wanted a living engineer, and he convinced Ollie to sell his race car. The gentlemen pooled their individual strengths to come up with some exceptionally interesting and innovative intake manifolds.

DYNAMOMETERS

To promote horsepower and performance-enhancing paraphernalia is great as long as the equipment does what it is advertised to do, and about the only true method of finding out exactly how the stuff performs is try it out on a dynamometer. In keeping with the times, Offenhauser installed a 300-horsepower Clayton chassis dyno in the early 1950s to test various engine components prior to production, and when the need arose, Fred would rent Stu Hilborn's dyno facility in Santa Monica.

"If you're going to do anything with manifolds, you've got to have a dyno," Ollie said. "You can't sit there and theorize and hit 100percent. It isn't going to work."

The time came when the chassis dyno proved to be insufficient for what was needed, and Fred began to search for a replacement.

"Fred found this guy who had a Clayton truck engine dyno," Ollie said. "It was a low-rpm, high-torque [dyno] and could stand up to 1,000 horsepower, but it was a monster."

The truck engine dyno had an operational ceiling of around 3,000 rpm. To overcome the problem, Ollie and Fred installed a 2:1 gearbox affixed to the 4-foot-diameter absorption unit and recalibrated it to read the exact horsepower, taking in the friction loss caused by the gearbox. Once the gearbox had been installed, the dyno was capable of runs into the 8,000-rpm range with no problem. The usual range was limited to around 5,000–6,000 rpm and only reached into the higher-rpm range when running all-out racing engines.

To meet the demands of manifold development, Ollie turned the dyno into a progressive unit, with a complete array of instruments to test more than just horsepower and torque. He purchased all sorts of sensitive aircraft instruments from surplus stores, as the aircraft companies were by then changing over to electronic instruments. Aircraft vacuum gauges were installed to measure manifold pressures and exhaust emission outputs, and a 12-channel strip chart gave an exact readout during engine performance tests. This chart was also connected to the chassis dyno to record test results from either dyno as needed.

Ollie rigged up this sophisticated test equipment to allow printed readouts from each engine cylinder under any kind of

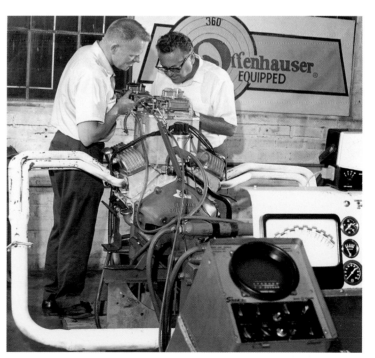

Fred, right, and Ollie Morris check a new D-port runner design placed in Ollie's magic box manifold. The tests proved successful and the runners were incorporated into the Offenhauser Tunnel Ram manifold. *Courtesy Fred Offenhauser Jr.*

Ollie Morris, left, with Carl Offenhauser at the workbench in the dyno room. The "magic box" manifold on the test engine supports dual four-barrel carbs. *Courtesy Fred Offenhauser Jr.*

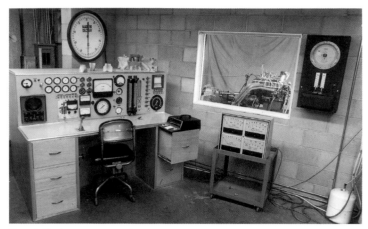

The Offenhauser dyno facility just after the installation of the shatter-proof window and cement-block wall. The test engine blew up the following day and part of the crankshaft bounced off the window. Ollie added the large number of dials and gauges to assist in manifold testing. *Ollie Morris collection, courtesy Fred Offenhauser Jr.*

load or rpm, and it could also record individual manifold and exhaust pressures. He also had the ability to enrich or lean out a carburetor while running the engine on the dyno, without having to shut the engine down or manually change carb jets. Ollie designed a system in which he could pressurize the carb float bowl and simulate up to three jet-size changes. Manifolds such as the Dual Port, the Cam-a-Go, the Super Sonic, and others were developed and refined using this equipment.

FLYING PISTONS

With any form of severe engine testing there's always a story or two about some mishap that took place. Ollie recalled being in the dynamometer room one time while they were running a small-block Chevy that was used especially for high-rpm testing. Ollie used to stand next to the test engines, but after the dynamometer room was renovated, the control panel was separated from the water brake by a cement wall with a large safety glass window to observe the operating engine.

"This particular engine exploded at near 9,000 rpm, and all I remember was a yellow flash and something smashed against the side of the glass," Ollie said. "It was the rear section of the block with the flywheel attached that hit the glass. Had I been there, I'd have been dead. There was only a tiny little nick in the glass where it hit. This happened about two weeks after we installed the safety glass window. One of the pistons and a piece of the rod was lying out in the middle of the street. From the engine to the street was over 100 to 150 feet. It just blew it right out the open door and driveway."

This particular engine was the only one they ever lost due to an explosion and was an all-out racing engine built by Ollie, who installed his own-design, four-bolt main caps long before GM came out with them in its engines.

CLEAN, MEAN, AND LEGAL

When it comes to a patent, it seems that a base patent has no expiration, unlike the normal everyday patent. "They are the absolute first concept; that's the reason why they're almost impossible to get," said Ollie Morris, who holds a base patent for the Dual Port 360 manifold.

Ollie thought, "Why does the manifold port have to be the same size all the way through? Why not make a primary port and a secondary port? The more I thought about it, the more I convinced myself, so I built a manifold in my own shop using a base manifold, fiberglass, epoxy, and this and that. It once backfired on me and blew the manifold all over the dyno shop.

"After numerous dynamometer tests with a prototype Dual Port manifold, and with the facts and figures tallied up, the results proved that we had something exclusive on our hands," Ollie said. "This manifold was a concept patentable item rather than an idea patentable item, and a base patent was taken out on the manifold.

"You take the manifold and divide it in half; the low rpm runs off the primary section. The cubic feet of air per minute that the engine requires is pushed through a smaller hole, which builds up velocity and therefore overcomes the reversion wave. You can take an engine that won't hardly run [because it] has such a robust cam in it, put a Dual Port manifold on it, and it'll run nice as hell."

The Dual Port manifold was not intended to be an all-out racing manifold, but a street performance and emissions manifold. It was ideal for smaller displacement engines that lacked bottom-end performance.

CALIFORNIA HIGHWAY PATROL

To prove the attributes of the Dual Port, Fred contacted the California Highway Patrol (CHP) and the Automobile Club and offered to equip several of their vehicles with the manifold for road tests under actual highway conditions with unbiased supervision.

The CHP delivered three new Chrysler 440-ci Interceptor cruisers to be equipped with the manifolds. They were tested for 100,000 miles, alternating between factory stock and Dual Port intakes. Ollie was in charge of changing the units, and none of the vehicles' drivers knew which manifold was on the car as to not influence their reports. The manifolds more than met the emissions standards, even with the stock emission equipment not installed, but the Chrysler Corporation wasn't very happy with the results and complained to the CHP for installing nonapproved equipment on the engines. But because Offenhauser didn't sell the manifolds and CHP didn't purchase them but only was trying them out, Chrysler's accusations didn't legally hold water.

The Dual Port manifold passed with flying colors, but, Ollie said, "the manifold ended there as far as being a possibility for a factory replacement manifold to meet the emissions standards was concerned."

The two-manifolds-in-one Dual Port was born after approximately four years of extensive developmental work. "To me, an engine is not a piece of mechanical machinery," Ollie said. "It has a personality. Yes, it's a piece of machinery, but this machinery through a billion variables develops its own personality, and if you learn to speak that engine's language, then you can learn to coexist with it. If you're truly trying to build a race engine for performance, and if you don't do what pleases that engine, I'll guarantee you that engine isn't going to run right. The happier the engine, the better it'll run.

"On the dynamometer, I'd read the dials; dials are facts and figures. Again, the basic concept of engineering is to learn to coexist with the laws of physics. You do not violate the laws of physics or nature," Ollie said. Ollie and Barney Navarro's thoughts on engineering come out of the same book.

Dynamometer tests showed the manifold lowered exhaust emissions as a result of better fuel management, and for a high-performance street manifold it was untouchable in its performance. The Dual Port 360 was first introduced to the public at the 1971 SEMA show, where the Offenhauser booth had a flow bench to show how the manifold operated. Fred and Ollie used a clear plastic model with Styrofoam balls, a blower system, and a butterfly plate to represent a carburetor.

"You could actually see the primary and secondary [runners] flowing at two different rates of speed simultaneously," Ollie recalled.

RV PACKAGE

"I tried to convince Fred that we could produce a performance package for RVs that would normalize an engine for the RV owner," Ollie recalls, "allowing him to have a lot more bottom-end torque, which is what an RV needs and where they really hurt is at high altitude."

"The package called for a turbocharger with a control mechanism that fit on top of any Dual Port manifold," Ollie said. "It was a diaphragm velocity control system that kept the primary and the secondary in the manifold separated so all the airflow at low engine rpm was going through the primary. With the turbocharger, you've boosted it even to a higher air speed, and when the valve got to a certain pressure ratio point [terminal velocity ratio of the primaries, maximum volume], then the secondaries would begin to open up automatically. By then, the airflow was nearly supersonic—gave it one hell of a ram effect! It worked much better at low engine rpm with the turbo, and when the secondaries would come in, you'd get the increase in volume that the engine required, so you would again gain performance."

CAM-A-GO

The Cam-A-Go concept was derived from having to constantly adjust the camshaft timing while performing engine dynamometer tests. Ollie Morris invented it in the late 1960s while he was running engine tests at the Offenhauser plant.

"The Cam-A-Go came about as a method of filling a need," Ollie said. "While testing various types of manifolds, it was necessary to have an engine with compatible performance to suit that particular manifold. To save costs and time, I came up with the idea of just altering the camshaft timing by mechanical means for testing our equipment. It started out as an in-house tool."

At SEMA in 1972, Fred (left) and Ollie Morris accept an award from the Hot Rod Industry News for their dedicated effort in automotive research with their dual-port manifold. *Courtesy Ollie Morris*

The Cam-A-Go consisted of a mechanical device that varied the timing between the engine's camshaft and the crankshaft. It could advance or retard the timing up to 10 degrees versus stock timing, and it replaced the stock timing chain, chain cover, and both gears. The package included a cast-aluminum cover containing three gears.

The Cam-A-Go was advertised as a multiple-use tool to help a car owner meet his needs at any particular time. "If he needs more top end he retards it, or more bottom end he advances the cam timing," Ollie said. He stated that the Cam-A-Go had adjustable stops for advance or retard, and, "I made elaborate models that had a variable rheostat that you could dial in anything you wanted," Ollie said. "You could shift the cam at 10,000 rpm, up or down, no problem."

Fred said that he'd take care of the financing for all the pattern work, gears, and so on, and in return Offenhauser kept the exclusive distribution sales rights. It provided Ollie the opportunity to get his idea into production, which he knew he couldn't do on his own.

"We made three models of it," Ollie said. "The Cam-A-Go Automatic, the Mechanical, and the Standard model. The deluxe unit had the adjustable cable to the driver's compartment, where he could change the cam timing by advancing or retarding the timing."

All the machining for the Cam-A-Go was done in-house at Ollie's shop, where five employees worked full-time, as the product was very popular. But the business needed substantial cash input to meet the demand for new models to accommodate a larger variety of engines.

Unfortunately, it was about this time that the big aftermarket warehouses began offering similar products with prices that Fred couldn't match. Offenhauser was not in the position to compete with these large merchandizing giants and dropped its accessory business in the early 1970s. This business change put an end to all products that were not manufactured directly by Offenhauser, including the Cam-A-Go. Ollie couldn't afford to keep the Cam-A-Go business afloat on his own.

As a side note, Ollie did sponsor the twin-blown Chrysler-powered *Freight Train* dragster with his Cam-A-Go and had very good success with the product up until the business folded.

SCHALLER QUARTER-SPEED CAMSHAFT

H. G. Bus Schaller was somewhat of an inventive fellow. He was a motorcycle aficionado who began racing bikes on the dry lakes back in the 1940s and always made a good showing wherever he raced. After many years of grinding motorcycle cams, Bus came up with a double-lobe camshaft design around 1957 that performed with some degree of success in a Harley-Davidson motorcycle. His camshaft received a base patent in 1959 and was written up in many automotive magazines that noted how well it performed and the benefits of this particular design. Even though it was very innovative, no cam company offered to take it over.

Bus, Fred, and Ollie worked out a deal in which they would form a company to go into the camshaft business as three equal partners. Fred would finance the project, Morris would do the engineering layout work, and Schaller would do the manufacturing.

In a standard automotive engine, the camshaft runs at half the crankshaft speed, and the ignition and oil pump run off the cam. The problem of modifying the ignition and oil pump systems for the quarter-speed cam was left up to Ollie to overcome. After considerable work, he developed and engineered a foolproof kit that would readily adapt to most of the popular engines. This type of camshaft needed a special cam gear drive, distributor, gear housing, and roller tappets.

The first installation kit was designed for the small-block Chevrolet, as it was the popular engine of choice. Dynamometer tests used Chevrolet's popular 425 camshaft on a Corvette fuel-injected engine.

"We could take a 425 cam, put it in a standard stock 327 Chevy engine, and it would peak out at about 5,000," Ollie said. "The valves would start to float. We could put the double-lobe cam in it [same grind as the 425, but with roller lifters] and run it to 8,000 rpm with no valve float. We were running valves on the seat at 85 pounds, where normally to get that rpm you had to run 135 to 145 pounds on the seat.

"The main theory behind the quarter-speed camshaft's advantage is two-fold. First is the impact ratio between the cam and the tappet. At 8,000 rpm, the tappet only saw a 2,000 rpm impact ratio. Second is that you didn't have to run a high spring pressure."

While Fred and Ollie were working on getting a camshaft kit ready for production, Schaller struck out on his own and began selling shares in his own double-lobe camshaft business, breaking their business agreement. After a bit of litigation, Fred and Ollie pulled out of the venture and Schaller went his way.

In 1961, Bus and his son, Jim, formed Schaller Cams in Turlock, California. But before the business could really be developed into something, Bus passed away, thus ending any future for the quarter-speed camshaft.

About the most notable person to use Schaller's cam was Mickey Thompson, who used it in his Chevrolet-powered *Harvey Special* entry that Al Miller drove to a ninth-place finish at Indy in 1963.

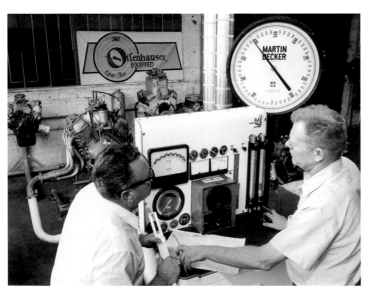

Fred, with the slide ruler, and Ollie Morris run the dyno. The readout on the scale indicates 390 foot pounds of torque at 4,500 rpm from the 427-ci Chev. *Courtesy Fred Offenhauser Jr.*

Carl Offenhauser, left, holds a four-barrel manifold while pattern maker Ron Soll takes measurements. Those are patterns on the tabletop. *Courtesy Fred Offenhauser Jr.*

OFFENHAUSER MAGIC BOX

The "magic box" manifold, as Ollie called it, was used to test various shapes of potential manifold runners.

"It was just a big, aluminum, rectangular box," Ollie said. "Everybody would just laugh about it when they saw it. Inside, it was set up in such a way that I could take the top off it and take the runner sections and change them when we were developing the ram manifold. I would change the configuration of the runners, put them back inside the box, and test the results without having to go to the expense of building a new manifold.

"When you design a manifold for an engine of any given configuration, the receiver area of that manifold is extremely critical, and it's key to the manifold. The runners are important, but it's how the air exits the carburetor and enters the manifold and starts its process of distribution that is the key to the manifold's success."

DIAL-A-FLOW

The Dial-A-Flow intake was a new concept in manifold design with a unique plenum chamber. It could be dialed in with one of three special flow-control inserts for street, street-strip, or strip. Each insert altered the flow, volume, and velocity of the air/fuel mixture. These inserts eliminated the expense of having to replace a manifold for a different application.

"I thought, why not make a manifold that, with an insert, all you had to do was change the insert and you can change the manifold's personality?" Ollie said. "It was aimed at the guy who wanted to modify his manifold without having to replace the total unit; it was an inexpensive method of modifying that part of the engine."

TRACTION MASTERS

In the late 1950s, Ollie took out a patent on traction bars that he'd designed and went into partnership with Fred and Els Lohn of EELCO to manufacture them through the Ollie Morris Equipment Corporation. Each partner contributed to the venture. Ollie's part was to design and manufacture traction bars for various vehicles. EELCO would make some of the parts using its screw machines, and both Offenhauser and EELCO would warehouse and distribute the bars to their respective customers.

After having a very successful year in business, trouble started when a competitor copied the design, infringing on the patent rights. Legal action was taken, and things went downhill after that. Rising legal costs finally killed the business completely.

DESIGN, MANUFACTURING, MARKETING

The Offenhauser line of speed equipment was equal to any in the business because of Fred's dedication to perfection in design, manufacturing, and marketing. The majority of early speed equipment manufacturers evolved into the business as a direct result of personal involvement with hot rods, race cars, and so on. Fred Offenhauser was one of the few who weren't personally involved in any of the above, but he did appreciate performance cars, always drove the latest Detroit muscle car, and was forever trading one

in for another. His son, Fred Jr., remembered his dad jokingly telling him that, "as soon as the cigarette butts get up to the top of the ashtray, I turn it in on a new one." To keep abreast of how his products performed outside of the company's testing facility, Fred would always try out the latest equipment on his own cars to make sure that all the linkages and related parts functioned properly before they were released into the marketplace.

Manufacturing a product is one thing, but it still has to be marketed. There was a fair amount of competition for the flathead V-8 cylinder head and intake manifold market in that postwar era, so making the public aware of your product was essential. Outside of magazine advertising, trade shows were an important venue for the manufacturer to show his wares to prospective buyers and speed shop owners.

Fred traveled to the American Automobile Manufacturers Association (AAMA) show in Chicago, the Pacific Automotive Show in Los Angeles, and similar shows during the winter months to display Offenhauser's latest products and set up new accounts. He even came out with a little promotional item entitled "Offenhauser Powerful News," which was a monthly sales and information newsletter mailed out to Offy dealers across the country.

As time went by, so did a lot of the smaller specialty manufacturers, who for a variety of reasons either failed to keep up with the competition or turned their attention toward other avenues of business. Eventually, the big three emerged in the intake manifold business: Offenhauser, Edelbrock, and Weiand. An astute businessman ran each of these three manufacturers, and it was only after an unfortunate turn of events that one began to fall back. Fred suffered a heart attack that would have a lasting effect on him. He appeared to lose all drive for the business and ceased to advertise his company's products at a time when the Dual Port manifold made up 90 percent of the company's sales volume. The

Fred kneels next to his new Studebaker and talks to the salesman in front of the auto dealership. Fred had a penchant for new cars. *Courtesy Fred Offenhauser Jr.*

In 1955 when Chevrolet released their fabulous 265-ci V-8, Ollie Morris was the first in the country to run one in a dragster. Installing Offenhauser finned valve covers, Ollie is getting the car ready for the first NHRA Nationals at Great Bend, Kansas. *Ollie Morris collection, courtesy Fred Offenhauser Jr.*

Offenhauser manifold lineup was second to none, but without aggressive advertising, sales slipped. Around this time, Ollie Morris left to pursue other business interests, ending any further manifold development. The final straw was when the dynamometer facility was closed down. After 25 years of service with the company, Fred's brother Carl left in 1978 to open up his own shop.

Fred Offenhauser passed away in 1992 at the age of 75, leaving his two sons, Tay (Fred Jr.) and Jim, to continue the family business. Today, customers can still order just about any of the products that Offenhauser ever manufactured. With nostalgia buffs demanding flathead stuff, the company is as busy as ever.

GEORGE "OLLIE" MORRIS

Although the Offenhauser Equipment Corporation story is primarily about Fred Offenhauser and his company, Ollie Morris and his *Smok'n White Owl* dragster played an integral part in directing the company toward the success that it enjoyed. It took the combined efforts of these two players, each possessing different skills, that when melded together made for a winning team.

George "Ollie" Morris began his racing career in the seat of a track roadster just after World War II. He worked the afternoon shift at the Edison Company, which allowed him time to work on his cars and to also have a part-time job in a body shop.

"When I got out of the navy after the war, I tried as best as I could to get an education," Ollie said. "I couldn't work, support a family, go to college, and play with a car. I didn't have the money to go to college, so I took night courses and emphasized courses like math, physics, and so on, that I considered the necessary courses to get the basics of engineering. Money was tight, so any engine modifications were done with whatever was at hand. My track engine was basically a well-tuned stocker."

When the Santa Ana drag strip opened in 1950, it presented a whole new venue of racing. For Ollie, that meant no more countless hours spent repairing damaged body and frame parts after a busy night of dirt-track racing. At Santa Ana, he raced a roadster with varying degrees of success until he teamed up with Harold Dawson and set a record with their B/Roadster in 1952 at a speed of 128 miles per hour.

"The roadster had the firewall removed to save weight and then the engine blew, covering me in hot oil," Ollie said. "Everything came back in my face; that's when I figured, 'Bullshit, I don't need this.' I felt that it'd be a lot safer if the engine were situated behind me. That's when I came up with the famous *White Owl* dragster."

In 1953, with the help of Bruce Terry, he built a radical rear-engined dragster on the ground in his backyard. The chassis was designed while sitting on a wooden box with the '29 frame rails (salvaged from his roadster) alongside the box to give him the width of the frame. The rails were then turned upside down and Z'd in the rear to get the chassis as low as possible. The body was hand-formed and welded out of aluminum, with the rearend open to give easy access to the quick-change gears. Ollie had built an adjustable swing-arm rearend (for better traction), made from Ford driveshaft housings. Unfortunately, the axles kept twisting, and he didn't have the money to have Cook's Machine Works turn out custom heavy-duty axles, so a solid rearend was reinstalled. The short-wheelbase design of the car proved to be very stable in racing, but if Ollie wasn't concentrating, it could be a bear to handle.

To come up with a shape for the body, he did a little testing to find one with the least wind resistance. "Not having access to a wind-tunnel facility, I used a bathtub full of water—crude but effective," Ollie said. "After making various scale models of what was thought would best suit my needs, I'd push the models through the water with a stick and observe the water turbulence around the body. Adjustments were made where necessary with modeling putty to come up with a final shape that proved to be successful on the track."

In order to buy a quick-change rearend for the car, Ollie returned more than 50 trophies to the Santa Ana drag strip, as C. J. Hart had a policy of buying back trophies from the racers for $5 each. He traded in trophies another time in order to buy a Harman & Collins magneto.

"Some people had never seen a rear-engined race car at the drags, and with the body panels in place, they didn't realize that at first glance the engine was in the rear of the car," Ollie said. "The back of the car looked like a Kurtis midget. I even had people comment, 'Why did you put the big tires on the front?' expecting the engine to be in the front of the car. We even put a grille in the back end to fool people and go along with the gag.

"In those days, brand name didn't mean anything to me. I had a chance to buy a used set of Edelbrock heads. The price was right; I paid for them, as new ones were $40. I proceeded to fill and grind the combustion chamber. When it was said and done, Edelbrock would never have recognized them. At the time, I was doing part-time work for Wyse Welding and learned to Heliarc through Wyse."

The No. 606 on the dragster originated from Ollie's days of circle-track roadster racing. It was assigned to him the first time he entered a race, and because he won his first heat race, he decided that it was a lucky number.

"When I worked for the Edison Company in Whittier, California, there was a chrome-plating place next door to us," Ollie said. "They used heavy copper wire as hooks in the chrome tanks. It was hard for them to get hold of copper wire that of large diameter in short lengths. In our scrap, we would have short pieces of heavy copper wire, so I traded them chrome work for the copper wire. Piece by piece, I got the car chromed."

"I got the nickname 'The Mad Chemist of Baker Street.' I lived at 2214 South Baker Street in Santa Ana," reflected Ollie. "I used several different fuel mixes that I would concoct. My main or race-mix fuel was a combination of 97 percent nitro with a little methane, ethyl ether, and hydrazine added, and then enough benzene in it to give it a benzene odor to try to hide the other stuff."

Because of the potent smell coming from his engine, he received another moniker—"Stinky"—and had a Disney skunk cartoon character painted on his crash helmet.

Originally, the car was painted white and, because of its cylindrical body shape, it received the nickname the *Smok'n White Owl* after the White Owl brand of cigars. Harvey Malcolmson of Harvey's Auto Glass sponsored the car and picked up the fuel tab that amounted to about $10 weekly. *Hot Rod* featured Ollie's dragster on the front cover of its November 1954 issue with a fully detailed writeup on the car.

Santa Ana held its fourth-anniversary meet on July 27, 1954, which Ollie won at 140.08 miles per hour, setting the record in D/Roadster class. In the days before the word "dragster" was used to designate certain classes, the cars were known as "roadsters." The *Smok'n White Owl* would run over 145 miles per hour later that season and was entered as a B/Lakester in the 1954 Bonneville Nationals.

Regardless of the success Ollie had with the novel design, few copied the engine configuration. It would be many more years before "Big Daddy" Don Garlits changed over to the rear-engined style, and that only came about after Garlits was involved in a serious accident with his front-engined dragster. Today, Ollie resides in Escondido, California, where he and his grandson are in the process of reproducing that infamous *Smok'n White Owl* car.

The working relationship between Ollie and Fred benefited both parties. Fred Offenhauser was the merchandiser and manufacturer, while Ollie Morris was the designer, holding patents on the Dial-A-Flow, the Super Sonic, the Port-A-Sonic, the Ram manifold, the Dual Port manifold, and the Cam-A-Go. He also mentioned that he's held numerous other patents not directly related to automobile engines—not too bad for a self-taught engineer.

RACING SECRETS BY OLLIE

"I learned real early that these guys who started their engines on nitro usually blew them up right at the line," Ollie said. "I figured out why—the nitro was so rapid-burning at slow engine rpm that

One of the top contenders at drag strips throughout Southern California in the early 1950s was Ollie Morris' Ford flathead–powered Harvey's Auto Glass–sponsored dragster. Shown under new sponsorship, the *Offenhauser Equipment Special* continued its winning ways. That's Thumper, the cartoon rabbit, on Ollie's helmet. *Ollie Morris photo, courtesy Fred Offenhauser Jr.*

you'd fire with the piston coming up and that'd just blow it up. At the end of a race, I'd take the spark plugs out and tow the car back to the pits in gear to purge the cylinders. I'd drain the carburetors and fill the Strombergs [(97s had a little side port] using a hypodermic needle with straight alcohol. Then there was enough alcohol in the carbs to get the engine safely started, and my pit crew could tell by the odor when the nitro started flowing. Until then, I'd back up from the stage line. I wouldn't let myself get staged, and when one of the guys would nod, then I'd roll up. C. J. would always wonder what was the matter, but I never blew an engine up on starting. By then, the engine had come up to temperature, and when I stood on it, the nitro was right there.

"Another speed secret I had that no one ever knew about was I was burning oxygen in the engine. In the front of the car, I had a cylinder that was a bailout [high-altitude aircraft] cylinder with a line running back to the engine. In the bases of the carburetors there were little tubes. I had a switch valve, and with it I could turn the oxygen on, and I only used it in instances of desperation, if it was near the end of the race and the guy was coming up on me. It was highly unpredictable; I might blow an engine.

"The first time I got a set of ForgeTrue pistons from Fred, I gave them back later and jokingly said, 'These are no [blank blank] good.' The dome was actually inside-out. The dome was actually blown down onto the wrist pin by using the oxygen system on them. The pistons did a beautiful job—the engine all of a sudden went flat on top end and didn't burn anything out. Any other piston would have been destroyed along with the engine. Anytime the car was ever shown open, the [oxygen equipment would be removed] because I never wanted anyone to know what I was doing."

CHAPTER 15

Potvin Racing Cams

CHUCK POTVIN

Chuck Potvin, like several of his peers, evolved into a speed merchant after being initiated into the world of high performance on the dusty dry lakes of Southern California. He started off just like thousands of other speed-hungry kids of that era, enjoying the thrill of unrestricted wide open lakebeds as their personal race tracks. What set him apart from other enthusiasts was his ability to build modified ignitions that really worked. In today's world, Chuck Potvin is best remembered for producing legendary camshafts for the Ford flathead V-8.

FROM RABBIT HUNTING TO CAR RACING

Chuck and a school chum named Doug Hartelt were first introduced to the sport of racing in 1937 while on a rabbit-hunting expedition at El Mirage Dry Lake. The two teenagers had driven up for a weekend of camping and hunting, but their shooting attracted attention from some SCTA members who were holding a race meet in the same vicinity. As compensation for being asked to stop shooting, Chuck and Doug were offered the opportunity to take their '32 roadster through the speed traps. This little episode sparked an interest in racing that would one day lead Chuck to open a successful speed equipment business and for Doug to become a notable driver and engine builder.

While attending Anaheim High School from 1935 to 1939, Chuck, Doug, Dick Kraft, Kenny Lindley, and the Palm brothers had a car club called the "Plutocrats," which was disbanded after graduation in 1940 in favor of the Hollywood Lancers (later known as just the Lancers). This club allowed them to run their cars at SCTA-sanctioned meets, as the SCTA rulebook specified that each car club had to have a minimum number of members in order to participate. Once in the Lancers club, Potvin, Kraft, and Hartelt became common fixtures at the lakes meets, competing with their similar souped-up, V-8-powered '32 roadsters.

Chuck had a natural gift for mechanics, and while still in his late teens, he successfully modified his own ignition. The ignition performed so well that others wanted one. Soon, he had a small part-time business converting Zephyr ignitions in his parents' garage on West Broadway in Anaheim. His business was short-lived, as he enlisted to serve in World War II, but after tests revealed his high technical skills, he was assigned to work on aircraft carburetion in the engine department of the Douglas Aircraft Company.

POTVIN ENGINEERING/POTVIN AUTOMOTIVE

After the war, Chuck resumed his ignition business behind his parents' home under the name of Potvin Engineering. With the huge postwar surge in auto racing, business was brisk for the young entrepreneur who, in addition to the already profitable ignition business, took on a distributorship of Evans Speed Equipment for Orange County. After several years, he finally outgrew the residentially zoned shop in his parents' backyard, and in 1948, he bought a corner lot on North Los Angeles Street and East Wilhelmina in Anaheim. There, he erected a block building that was a little larger than a two-car

Opposite: Photographed in front of Potvin Automotive in 1948, this is Doug Hartelt's flathead V-8–powered '25 T that set the B/Roadster class record at the lakes with a speed of 135 miles per hour. By the size of the trophy on display, the car was a winner. Note that decked-out flathead on the stand behind the roadster. *Leslie Long collection*

Inset: The famous dinosaur was incorporated into the Potvin logo to represent the idea that his camshaft grinds were proven out on the dynamometer (i.e., "dyno") prior to their marketing to the hot rodding public. *Author collection*

A young Bill Jenks is parked in front of his high school in his cherry '32 high-boy roadster. In 1946 the 16-year-old drove the car 102 miles per hour at the lakes. *Leslie Long collection*

garage. By mid-summer that year, Potvin Automotive was advertising in *Hot Rod* that it was handling aluminum flywheels and Cromwell leather racing helmets in addition to the dual ignitions and Evans equipment.

Wanting to get into the ever-growing speed equipment market, Potvin could see that the performance camshaft field held good possibilities. In his teenage years, he'd run Pierre Bertrand cams and always had good luck with those grinds. In the postwar era, Clay Smith had taken over the deceased Bertrand's business and was running it under the name of Smith & Jones. Chuck had met Clay at Bertrand's shop in the prewar days and was well acquainted with the two fellows.

Ron Roseberry of R&L Chassis in Anaheim remembered that Chuck once told him how he got into designing camshafts. "The credit goes back to Chuck's old high school shop teacher, Claude Booth," Ron said. "Claude was instrumental in helping him with the mathematical equations necessary for fundamental camshaft lobe design and the technical aspects of camshaft grinding."

Chuck built his first cam grinder the same way everyone else did before commercial units were available. Using the base of a Storm-Vulcan crankshaft grinder, he made up a rocking table and had Conze Machine Shop manufacture the intricate index plates. The rocking table allowed the camshaft to follow the shape of a master cam and make contact with the grinding wheel. By 1949, business had reached the point that there was no time for racing, so the cars of Doug Hartelt, Bill Jenks, Ollie Morris, and Otto Ryssman would be used to test the latest cam designs. Chuck advertised very little in the early 1950s and included the statement, "no correspondence please," in his advertisements.

THE DINOSAUR AND THE DYNAMOMETER
From his days working in Douglas Aircraft's engine department, Chuck knew that the only way to actually know the full potential

of any engine modification was to try it out on a dynamometer. A surplus store supplied an English Heenan & Froude water brake, which Chuck redesigned to suit his needs. The dyno was capable of pulls to 600 horsepower and could sustain speeds up to 10,000 rpm. Chuck added a flywheel and starter motor as permanent fixtures to the structure, making it more convenient when testing an engine, and he equipped exhaust pipes with heavy-duty mufflers to keep peace with the neighbors.

Chuck incorporated the picture of a dinosaur into his logo to represent that "every Potvin cam design is dynamometer tested and proven for the utmost in performance before being put into production," according to longtime friend Leslie Long. Les first met Chuck and Doug through mutual friends at the dry lakes in 1947, and while attending junior college in 1948, he would stop in to the shop after class. Years later, Les and Bill Hays were both involved in Stinger Ignitions.

Les Long related the following anecdote about when Chuck first got the dyno. In the early 1950s, Harold "Shorty" Post was proprietor of the Post Body Shop in Orange, California, and Chuck had the dynamometer set up in Shorty's body shop prior to installing it in his own shop. One Sunday night, they fired up a six-cylinder GMC engine. Les, Doug, Shorty, the town's two police officers, and several onlookers watched Potvin get the engine ready to fire up on the dyno. Just before the test was to start, the two officers excused themselves, as they didn't want to be within earshot of the racket that was about to take place. Even though the dyno was inside the shop, the unmuffled exhaust system shot directly outside through a hole in the wall. Leslie said, "In those days, the police didn't have radios in their patrol cars, and in an emergency, the station house would turn on a flashing light at the plaza, and the patrolling officer would call in from a call box. The two policemen said, 'Wait before you start this up until we go somewhere out of town.'"

THE SHOP
A fair amount of work was accomplished in the Potvin shop, considering the size of it. It contained two camshaft grinders, a master cam generator, a dynamometer, and several metal lathes. At the height of the company's business, an addition was added to the front of the building to accommodate shipping and office space. Even after all the years those two grinders and Chuck's homemade master cam generator were used, they're still in operation today in the skillful hands of Bill Jenks at Mooneyes.

Chuck originally designed all the flathead cams and most of the overhead flat-tappet cams, as he was never partial to the roller-tappet camshaft. Once Chuck had taught Bill how to design camshafts, Bill came up with some of his own designs. When Dean Moon bought out Potvin, Bill designed the roller-tappet camshafts that were sold under the Moon brand. British Leyland hired Potvin Automotive to design and grind a series of performance camshafts for several of its cars. Bill said he designed and Potvin ground hundreds of cams for Triumph TR3 and Spitfire sports cars. The name "R. W. Kastner" was stamped on the end of the camshafts, and they were sold in Leyland's English parts catalog. Potvin also ground performance camshafts for Pontiac's racing division, with a GMC parts number stamped on them. Bill designed these camshaft profiles and ground them on camshaft blanks sent from the Pontiac factory.

Like a lot of other manufacturers, when he first had a look at Chevrolet's new V-8 in 1955, Chuck was skeptical of the valvetrain and commented to Ollie Morris, "Those pistons don't move up and down; they just sit in one spot and vibrate." The engine had a very short stroke compared to most of the existing engines of that era. Ollie ran a Potvin cam in his Chevy V-8 dragster when he entered the NHRA's first National Meet at Great Bend, Kansas.

NITROGLYCERINE—THE REAL STUFF

Otto Ryssman lived on an orange farm, and in those days, farmers were allowed to purchase dynamite for land-clearing purposes. This was a time when racers were concocting anything and everything in search of a more potent fuel. Occasionally, Chuck would have Otto buy a half-dozen cases of dynamite for the purpose of extracting the nitroglycerine. He would somehow safely heat the dynamite to extract the nitroglycerine and then combine it with alcohol. By trial and error—obviously not too many errors—he came up with a formula for some hot racing fuel. As nitromethane became more readily available, it put an end to this hazardous practice.

Leslie Long recalls that in the early 1990s, the local news media reported that several cases of old discarded dynamite were discovered in an old lady's garage in Anaheim. It was the same garage that Potvin rented for storage many years earlier.

THE 425 ELIMINATOR

Initially, Chuck used a modified version of a Bertrand camshaft as a basis for his grind until he got a handle on the art of camshaft design. It was a time when the Ford V-8 ruled supreme, and in keeping with the majority of his fellow grinders, Chuck put out a variety of flathead grinds. Like Iskenderian with his renowned 404, the camshaft grind that made the name Potvin synonymous with power was the fabulous 425 Eliminator. It rivaled the Isky 404 for supremacy, and the two camshafts created many a debate over which was best. Even today, this debate will occasionally crop up in the conversations of old-time racers.

"The 425 had more upper-rpm, while Isky's 404 had more midrange torque," Bill Jenks said. "The 404 wouldn't buzz as tight as the 425. One of the most successful drag race cams ever ground for a flathead Ford was the 425. Isky's 404 was an excellent cam; there were a lot of winners with both cams."

It appears that regardless of the strengths and weaknesses of each camshaft, in the end they came out about equal in performance. A 1954 Potvin ad stated that 65 percent of all the times turned in at drag strips in Southern California above 130 miles per hour were by Potvin cam–equipped cars. Bill also mentioned that the super-race Potvin 3/8 grind (derived from the .375-inch lift) came in a close second to the 425 Eliminator in performance.

Isky said of the 425, "Potvin decided that he had to go high lift with the stock tappet. We were always afraid to overrev the stock tappet, but the spring pressures were light, and he did a pretty

A pair of Chuck's SCTA timing tags from El Mirage, 1946. *Leslie Long collection*

good job with the Potvin Eliminator. He ran a high lift on a stock tappet and got away with it too."

Ollie Morris was the first to run the Eliminator in a race car. After installing the 425 in his rear-engined dragster, his car became the nemesis to many on the drag strips of Southern California. The best he ever ran with the Potvin-assisted flathead was 144.33 miles per hour.

"The 425 had an extremely abrupt lobe, and across the top it had a little kicker radius," Ollie said. "That cam can only be ground on a '32 steel-billet cam because of the base-circle height." Today's 425s have to be ground on a special steel-billet cam.

Another well-known record-setting vehicle to enjoy the merits of the 425 camshaft was the '42 Merc V-8-powered dragster of Art Chrisman. This legendary classic now resides in the NHRA Museum, but in 1953 it was the first car to break the 140-mile-per-hour barrier. On February 8, 1953, during a meet at Orange County Airport, the car ran 140.08 miles per hour and set a new track acceleration record of 9.04 seconds.

George "Ollie" Morris grew up several blocks from Bill Jenks and the two attended junior high together. Both were good friends with Chuck Potvin. "I knew Chuck when he first started out in a garage behind his mum's house in Anaheim doing ignitions," Ollie recalled. "Chuck would get some of the wildest ideas about cams and he'd come over to the house two or three o'clock in the morning and bang on the door with a cam in his hand. He'd be just wild-eyed. He hadn't any sleep for three days. He would get an idea and just plow through. Well he had this cam and he called it a 300. I looked at it and said, 'Chuck, you've got to be kidding.' The lobe was almost square and flat across the top. Chuck said, 'No, it'll really work on the top end.' He wanted me to enter it in the race Sunday. I said, 'Chuck, this is Saturday night. I am not going to go out to that garage and tear the engine apart to put a cam in it for tomorrow.'

"I ran it the next week. The thing that surprised me was that I had to tow the car to nearly 40 miles per hour to light up, and when it did start, the stand-off on the carburetors was phenomenal. Boy, did it come on at the top end, but can you run a flathead at 8,000 [rpm]? It started coming in real strong at about 6,500. This 300 camshaft or 'bread loaf' got its name because it had horrific duration. It was a dog off the line, but once you got to the higher rpm ranges, then the cam started to work pretty good. You had to use a mushroom lifter with it."

FIRST AND LAST EMPLOYEE

Bill Jenks' hot rodding days began back in 1946, when he turned 16 and could legally drive his '32 highboy roadster. That November, after joining the Lancers car club, he went to his first dry lakes meet and posted a 102-mile-per-hour run. Not only was he a first-timer; he was the youngest driver at the meet.

An accident caused by brake failure would be the catalyst that set the course for Bill's future. He was driving a '37 Olds coupe, saving the roadster for lake racing. Living in the vicinity of Potvin's shop, Bill would occasionally hang out there. One day in 1949, he pulled into Potvin's lot and applied the brakes, but the car kept rolling. The Olds smashed into a cement block wall, pushing the wall into Chuck's desk, and moving the desk and Chuck back several feet. Fortunately, the only things besides the wall that received damage were the desk, the front end of the Olds, and Bill's ego. After surveying the damage and knowing that this very

Three dry lakes roadsters are on display in front of Potvin Automotive in 1948. From left are Doug Hartelt with his roadster, Jim Starr and Bob Comstock with their roadster, and the Palm brothers' roadster. *Leslie Long collection*

apologetic teenager hadn't the funds to cover the repairs, Chuck offered Jenks the opportunity to work off the expenses, telling him, "It will be safer for all to hire you and get you off the streets."

Bill became the first full-time employee (and the longest-serving) in the Potvin shop. There were five full-time employees in the busiest years. Once Chuck taught Bill how to convert Stromberg 97 carburetors to alcohol and rebuild dual ignitions, he had time to concentrate on grinding cams and doing development work on the dynamometer.

The Korean War commenced in June 1950, and Bill was called up the following month for active duty overseas. Two years later, with his military stint completed, he stopped in to Potvin's shop for a visit, and Chuck asked, "Ready to go back to work?" Bill hadn't intended on retuning to his old job but figured it'd do until something better came along. By then, Chuck had enough confidence in Bill's mechanical abilities to teach him how to operate the cam grinder.

Before the Korean War, Bill raced his roadster at the lakes, field-testing Chuck's latest camshaft grinds until the engine finally blew and the car was parked in the garage for another day. After returning to work at Potvin's, he got married and, in due time, became a dad. The roadster was dragged out, dusted off, and sold—a story that has a familiar ring for a lot of hot rodders.

Bill remained with the shop until it was sold to Dean Moon, and he continued on working under the Moon name until it in turn was sold to Mooneyes USA. As of today—over half a century later—Bill is still grinding cams (his own designs and Chuck's) on the original Potvin grinders. Bill Jenks is the sole remaining employee of the once renowned "Potvin Cams," all because of an old car with faulty brakes.

DOUG HARTELT: UNSUNG RACER

With every success story, there are many individuals behind the scenes who contribute to that success, but the light never seems to find them. Such is the case with Doug Hartelt. Doug's passion for racing was forged back in 1937, when he and Chuck were rabbit hunting up at El Mirage. He became a standard fixture at lakes meets and was involved in the earliest days of drag racing. Doug's cars always ran either at the top of his class or in close proximity to it. He took the B/Roadster class at a 1947 meet with a two-way record run of 129 miles per hour and a one-way run at 135 miles per hour. Doug's '25 T was even faster than some of the C class cars. Because money was a scarce commodity in those early days, in place of racing pistons, Doug sawed off the skirts of the stock pistons and left his Mercury V-8 block unported. Once Chuck got into the camshaft business, Doug's cars became a mobile testbed for Potvin cams.

When he wasn't straightening out body panels or painting cars at Harold Post's body shop, Doug and his T roadster could be found at the dry lakes, Bonneville, or the drag strip. Doug ran his '34 chopped, fenderless coupe in RTA and SCTA meets. In 1954, the car ran 173 miles per hour at the dry lakes and 122 miles per hour at the Santa Ana drags with a Hilborn-injected 364 Chrysler on methanol.

THE *POST STREAMLINER*

Doug Hartelt was employed at Shorty Post's body shop, where the *Post Streamliner* was born. The car was designed and built by both fellows in the body shop and was noticeably different than other streamliners of the day. The driver's seat was offset to the left like a normal car, and the engine rode in the middle. A large water tank for engine coolant sat on the right side of the car to balance things out. A sturdy tubular frame was covered by a hand-formed, streamlined, aluminum body and was designed to handle a flathead V-8 or a Chrysler Hemi.

The streamliner was introduced at the dry lakes in 1952, powered by a full-race, Potvin-built Mercury V-8, and later that year it went to Bonneville powered by Hartelt's Chrysler. Stuart Hilborn had given Chuck a fuel-injection system to try out on the salt flats. The team encountered problems with the injectors until discovering that the fuel hoses were interfering with several of the intake ports. The car ran great after adding short velocity stacks to the injector bodies, capturing the C/Streamliner class with a 217.65-mile-per-hour average.

The following year, Chuck and Doug took over the *Post Streamliner*, leaving Shorty's name on the car, and competed on the dry lakes with Otto Ryssman in the driver's seat. In a July RTA meet at El Mirage, Ryssman drove the streamliner to a blistering 203-mile-per-hour record run, being the first to break the 200 mile-per-hour barrier at an RTA-sanctioned meet. It was the fastest time ever recorded at any dry lakes meet held in California up to that date. Later on at Bonneville, the streamliner ran a sleeved-down 303-ci Hemi in the C class.

For the 1954 Bonneville meet, Sandy Belond sponsored the Potvin-Hartelt streamliner and repainted it as the *Belond Equa-Flow Exhaust Special*. Ryssman was to compete in the B, C, and D/Streamliner classes with two Chryslers and a sleeved-down 257-ci DeSoto V-8. Ollie Morris was also a part of the team and entered his rear-engined dragster as a lakester, competing in the B, C, and D classes, and he was to share the three engines with Ryssman.

After making several runs down the racecourse, the fellows wanted to try a higher gear ratio than they had with them, so they decided to use larger diameter Firestone Bonneville tires. To accommodate the larger tires, the inner wheelwells of the streamliner had to be hammered out. Unfortunately, this would prove to be the downfall of the car. A strong crosswind began to blow just as the streamliner got up to the starting line, and all runs were put on hold until the wind died down. As soon as the wind subsided, Otto was given the OK to proceed, but the winds picked up again when he was well on his way down the course. The sidewind was strong enough to push the body over enough to make contact with a tire. The streamliner had been clocked at 224 miles per hour and was decelerating when the right rear tire blew, sending the car into an uncontrollable spin. It then rolled a reported 15 to 20 times over about 300 yards before coming to a stop. Though the aluminum body was destroyed, Otto was saved from serious injuries by the integrity of a well-constructed frame. He was lucky to have survived the horrific ordeal with only minor

cuts and bruises, and he received the trophy for the fastest D/Streamliner. Otto had more 200-mile-per-hour runs than anyone else at the time.

"Chuck was running the *Post Streamliner* with the big engine, and I was running the B engine, which was a DeSoto, and that first day we qualified for open-wheeled lakester," Ollie Morris said. "I went in early because I would rather run in the morning when the wind was less [problematic], and Ryssman wanted to run that afternoon for the record run because he figured that he had a better chance. That's when he blew the tire and flipped it. Chuck came in from the salt bed and said, 'No more. You're not going to run the car. Put it on the trailer. I'm going home.' It was his engine, so that was the end of that."

FRONT-MOUNTED BLOWER DRIVE

In 1952, Hartelt began running his radically chopped '34 Ford coupe and replaced the well-worn flathead with a '51 Chrysler V-8. He purchased the 331-ci Hemi from a local Chrysler dealer that was replacing problem engines that were under warranty and selling the broken engines to local racers for $50 each. Over the next several years, the engine was enlarged to 364 ci. With Hilborn injection, it put out 370 horsepower on methanol. Stuart Hilborn had given Doug an injection unit to test out on the Chrysler. The coupe was a constant competitor at the lakes in both RTA and SCTA events, with runs in the 170-plus range. At Santa Ana, Doug was getting speeds in the low 120s.

The use of superchargers at the dry lakes was nothing new, but when Doug saw a GMC blower sitting in front of a flathead V-8 in Tom Cobb's coupe during a meet, it aroused his curiosity. Cobb originally mounted the blower on top of a flathead and then relocated the unit to the front of the engine. Doug liked the idea, because having the blower sticking up above the engine hood created wind resistance and interfered with the driver's line of

Doug Hartelt grew up with Chuck and was a staunch supporter of Potvin equipment. Moving up from a dry lakes roadster, Doug successfully campaigned this modified '34 Ford coupe with a V-8 flathead and later a blown Chrysler Hemi at the strip, the lakes, and Bonneville. *Leslie Long collection*

vision. Front blower drives were nothing new in the automotive world, but for a backyard hot rodder, finding a way to adapt a blower to the front end of a Chrysler V-8 and having it perform well posed numerous problems.

Doug designed and fabricated the front drive for a 6-71 GMC blower and used a Crower prefab intake manifold to provide runners for the blower. He adapted Hilborn's fuel-injection unit to the intake side of the blower. After preliminary testing, he told Hilborn that there wasn't enough fuel getting to the engine, and Stuart didn't believe it. Doug then installed eight injector jets to feed fuel directly into the intake manifold runners in conjunction with the existing injectors on the blower. By adding a second fuel pump, the engine's fuel problems were licked.

Hartelt's successful blower-drive design proved itself at the drag strip in Calvin Rice's car. On its maiden run at Santa Ana, it registered a speed of 133.33 miles per hour and got up to 142.56 miles per hour later in the season. Fine-tuning began to show results when, in February 1956, Calvin tied Ed Losinski's strip record at 149.68 miles per hour. Doug is credited as the first to install a GMC blower on the front end of a Chrysler Hemi, and the Potvin blower drive no doubt owes its birth to the inventive mind of Doug Hartelt.

POTVIN BLOWER DRIVE

The NHRA brought its fuel ban into effect after the 1956 Nationals, and racers began to look elsewhere to replace the liquid horsepower. At a time when the majority of engines were normally aspirated with multiple carbs or fuel injection, many began to explore the GMC blower. The success Doug had with his blower drive made Chuck realize that there was a market for a setup of this style that provided a positive locked drive, better visibility, and a lower center of gravity.

The original design was sold as a do-it-yourself kit that had to be welded together. The customer had to send his GMC blower

in to Potvin Automotive, where it could be inspected for any defects and fitted with an oil line for the drive gears. An engine adapter housing was then installed on the blower to ensure the customer's blower and the kit were compatible and there would be no problems in assembly. It was then returned to the customer for completion.

The first blower-drive kits comprised two drive sprockets with a chain, flame-cut parts for a log-type intake manifold, hoses, clamps, a pop-off valve with springs, and the cast engine adapter housing. As sales increased, the intake manifold was changed to cast aluminum with a common plenum chamber that fed all eight intake ports and resulted in an increase of almost 30 horsepower. Chuck recommended the use of three Stromberg NAR-6B updraft aircraft carburetors with the larger 6-71 (two for the 4-71) blower when running gasoline, and if using fuel, the carbs had to be anodized. These surplus aircraft updraft carburetors could be purchased from Potvin or through Moon for $30 apiece. Updrafts were favored because they prevented fuel leakage into the blower that might occur when the engine wasn't running. According to Bill Jenks, "The carbs worked very well—bitch'n."

Not wanting to be involved in merchandising, Chuck allowed Dean Moon to become the exclusive distributor for the Potvin blower drive, which retailed for $220 in 1958. The following year, an overdrive adapter was available that allowed the engine tuner to achieve a variety of blower speeds for various racing conditions. It was optimistically advertised that it'd take about seven minutes to install a blower kit on an engine. All the buyer had to do was slide the assembly onto the front of the engine and bolt it into place, and then bolt the connecting tubing that joined the blower to the intake manifold. About 14 bolts and 16 hose clamps needed to be tightened. Probably the most notable and recognizable race cars to use the Potvin blower system were Dean Moon's *Mooneyes* dragster and Dragmaster's *Two-Thing* twin-engine dragster; both were record holders.

Chuck rebuilt GMC blowers for racers for $50—the same labor rate GM charged. The only difference was that he set them up to racing specifications. A $30 charge could set one up to fit

Ollie Morris' infamous Harvey's Auto Glass–sponsored rear-engine dragster at Santa Ana, where it approached the 140-miles-per-hour mark. The nitro-burning flathead was a winning testimonial for the Potvin 425 Eliminator camshaft. *Ollie Morris photo*

In 1959 Chuck chose the name Drag-N-Fly for his go kart–manufacturing business. As the advertisement states, the ready-to-run $169 kart came complete with a Clinton A-490 engine. *Author collection*

a Potvin drive. Chuck's workmanship was good enough that Mickey Thompson had him build the blowers for his four-engine, land-speed record-setting *Challenger* streamliner.

DRAG-N-FLY

A fellow by the name of Art Ingles, who worked for Kurtis-Kraft, is credited with starting go karting when he built a small motorized kart to have some fun. By 1959, the popularity of karting was in full swing, and it caught Chuck's attention. The idea appealed to him enough that he had another building put up adjacent to the cam shop to manufacture go karts under the name "Drag-N-Fly." The kart came ready to run with a Clinton A-490 engine and retailed for $196 in 1960. Chuck even went so far as to produce a cast-aluminum Potvin exhaust megaphone for the little engine.

Bill Jenks tried his hand at racing these little speed demons, and finishing in second place in a major race was a personal best in his short kart racing career. Bill said that many of the kart manufacturers sponsored factory teams that traveled in converted buses to various races, such as the 100-milers held in California and Mexico.

By 1962, Chuck was getting out of the manufacturing business altogether and sold the Drag-N-Fly kart manufacturing business to Ray Tourse in Riverside, California.

TIME TO SELL

Ed Iskenderian was always very sociable with the other manufacturers and would occasionally drop into their shops for a visit. On one such visit, Potvin told Isky, "I'm not going to grind any more Chevy cams, because I can't compete against the price of a Duntov cam." At that time, a cast-iron blank core was around $12, yet you could buy a hot-performing Duntov cam for $19. It was said that most of the leading road racing Corvettes on the West Coast circuit were running factory Duntov cams over aftermarket cams. Les Ritchey, the owner of Performance Associates in Covina, California, who was a well-respected engine tuner and drag racer, said, "Chevrolet was putting some cam grinders out of business due to the factory Duntov camshafts."

After spending the better part of his life involved in the speed equipment business, Chuck finally had enough, and in 1961 confided in his longtime friend, Leslie Long: "There's no future in cam grinding. Edelbrock is the largest company, and they've got five employees. There's no future in racing, so I'm quitting." The following year, Potvin Automotive was sold to Dean Moon.

Dean kept the camshaft grinding and machine shop end of Chuck's business in Anaheim until 1967, when new accommodations were built next to Moon's shop in Santa Fe Springs. Fred Larsen, who retired from the navy in 1962, started working for Moon in Anaheim with Bill and moved with them to the new location. Bill and Fred ran the machine shop facilities at Moon's for over 40 years together, doing camshaft grinding, gas-tank and hubcap fabrication, and whatever else it took to keep the doors open.

AFTER POTVIN AUTOMOTIVE

After leaving Potvin Automotive and the kart business behind him, Chuck went to work in the dynamometer facility of the Atlantic-Richfield Testing Center in Anaheim. It's not known how long he stayed at the job, but it wasn't more than a year or so. Leslie Long reported that Chuck did some freelance writing for an automotive magazine under a *nom de plume* of "Nivtop"—Potvin spelled backward.

Chuck Potvin passed away in 1975. Fortunately, the revival of the Ford flathead V-8 by nostalgia buffs has created a demand for the legendary 425 Eliminator camshaft and has kept the name "Potvin" from drifting into obscurity.

No doubt one of the best-known racers to use Chuck's front-mount supercharger setup was Dean Moon. He liked it so much that he eventually purchased the rights to it along with the Potvin camshaft business. This is a highly polished Potvin blower drive attached to the Chevy V-8 that powered the record setting Mooneyes dragster. *Author photo*

The very amicable Bill Jenks began his career at Potvin in 1949 and has continued to design and grind cams and weld aluminum fuel tanks at the Moon facilities, making him one hell of a longtime employee. *Author photo*

CHAPTER 16

Scott Fuel Injection

MEL SCOTT

Even though Milford "Monk" "Mel" Melvin Scott Jr. wasn't among the early speed equipment manufacturers, his 97 fuel injector was as unique as its inventor, and the mark he left in the short time that he was in business is well worth documenting.

FROM MODEL AIRPLANES TO THE DRY LAKES

Intrigued by anything mechanical, especially if it had an engine, Mel got involved with gas-powered model airplanes when he was very young. By the age of 14, he'd installed a Servicycle engine on his bicycle. In 1948, Mel and his brother, Bob, built a midget racer powered by an overgrown 80-ci Indian Chief motorcycle engine. On weekends, they'd sneak in and race around the running track at University High in west Los Angeles, where Mel won two varsity letters in gymnastics.

After the midget experience, Mel graduated to Whizzer motorbikes. In no time, he had modified the little 2.5-horsepower engine to produce a whole lot more power. The dependable L-head four-stroke design was transformed using Mel's own F-head design that incorporated an overhead intake valve.

Mel got involved in amateur flat track racing, competing with a 21-ci BSA. While racing some friends on a dried-up riverbed, the throttle stuck wide open on the alky-burning JAP bike he was riding. The resulting crash left him with a broken nose that needed plastic surgery to repair. He figured he got off lucky, considering the severity of the incident.

After the bike episode, Mel felt that four wheels might be a bit safer. He built a modified fenderless 1927 Ford T pickup with the box shortened to about 3 feet in length. His choice of engine was what made the street rod different: a hopped-up 1935 four-cylinder Willys engine. Mel fabricated the dual-carburetor manifold and the exhaust manifolds from old bedposts, as well as the two carburetor air breather stacks. The twin exhaust pipes ran the full length of the truck. Trying to locate a starter for the engine proved to be a bit difficult, but that didn't prevent him from driving the hot rod until he found one; in the meantime, he had to park the car nose-down on a sloping street to allow for a rolling start.

Without the finances to join a car club, Mel would borrow Ted Lapadakis' membership card to run under the Almega club at the dry lakes. The best run Mel ever got out of the little 135-ci Willys at the lakes was 104 miles per hour. The pickup was totally void of any safety features—no seat belts, no roll bar, or crash helmet, just a solitary oil pressure gauge and surplus air force goggles to help the driver see through the dust on the lakebed. Occasionally, accidents did occur at the lakes; Mel recalled the time he was finishing a run and turned around just in time to see the Spalding brothers' *Wayne Horning Special* streamliner come tumbling through the speed traps.

EARLY EMPLOYMENT

After graduating from University High in 1949, Mel got a job with the Transco Products Company, which manufactured aircraft components in Culver City. Though he started off sweeping floors, within 12 years he'd worked his way up through positions as an assembler, machinist, toolmaker, model maker, electrical and mechanical technician, and finally headed the environmental laboratory as a test engineer.

Opposite: A proud 16-year-old Mel Scott with his just-completed '27 T pickup powered by a modified 135-ci four-cylinder Willys engine. Note the dual straight pipes and the high-mounted steering wheel. *Courtesy Mel Scott*

Before he graduated to four wheels, Mel was involved with the two-wheelers. Here he is running his 21-ci BSA flat-tracker at a dirt track . . . obviously safety equipment was not a concern. *Courtesy Mel Scott*

To further his education while working full-time, Mel enrolled in UCLA extension courses. He also took a correspondence course through the Canadian Institute of Science and Technology, from which he received his degree in automotive engineering. During the same period, he received tutoring from the many engineers at Transco. Eventually, the long hours of hard work and studying paid off, as Transco made him an associate engineer.

FUEL INJECTION

Mel built his first fuel-injection system in the late 1940s for a stock, six-cylinder-powered, 1940 four-door Chevrolet. He couldn't afford speed equipment to hop up the engine, but he felt that he could at least improve on the fuel-delivery system. After reading up on fuel injection, he set out to make his own system.

He fabricated the injector out of a piece of exhaust tubing. A modified valve cock became the barrel valve that would meter the fuel. Mel used an electric fuel pump to pressurize the system. To kept things simple, the fuel pump had a separate shutoff switch that had to be manually turned off when the engine wasn't running.

The separate shutoff setup wasn't the most foolproof design; one day, Mel was running late for work and absentmindedly forgot to shut the pump off after parking the car. Upon returning to the car after work, he quickly realized what had happened when he recognized the strong smell of gasoline. Taking a chance, he carefully drove the car over to his father's nearby service station and drained the fuel-contaminated oil out of a very clean and, luckily, undamaged motor.

From December 1950 to November 1956, Mel served in the army active reserve in California. He was assigned to the 763rd Ordnance Maintenance Battalion of the 63rd Infantry Division, in charge of supervising the maintenance of tanks, trucks, and diesel/gasoline engines. When he was called in for active reserve duty at Camp Roberts, he took along the homemade fuel injector with the idea of perfecting it in his off hours. At the base, he had access to a Jeep and, seeing as how the injector fit right onto the vehicle's engine, Mel continued his research complements of Uncle Sam. When he was honorably discharged on November 29, 1956, he'd attained the rank of sergeant first class.

THE POOR MAN'S FUEL INJECTOR

The idea to make a commercial fuel-injection system happened while Mel was racing his pickup at the dry lakes and he first saw Stu Hilborn's injection setup. With the knowledge he acquired from experimenting with the Chevy injector, Mel felt that he could do something similar to Hilborn's system, but on a simpler and less expensive scale.

After studying the situation for some time, he realized that the good old Stromberg 97 carburetor was plentiful and already widely used by the racing crowd. Mel designed a very simplistic system in which the injector body bolted onto the base of a 97 carburetor, ending up with what he liked to call the "poor man's fuel injector."

To keep the startup costs in line, Mel made his own wood patterns and machined them at Transco after working hours. The first attempt at making the 97 fuel injector was in 1957. Mel tried it out on a friend's V8-60-powered midget race car, which won the trophy dash the first time out. This particular injector had a sliding needle valve and constant fuel flow with no variation of pressure, as a hand-pumped pressurized tank supplied the fuel. Because the midgets were always humming at high speeds, the idle wasn't too important for this type of injector. The unit operated on a constant pressure between 2 to 7 psi, and a fuel pump could be used if a fuel-pressure regulator was installed between the injector and gas tank.

Rod & Custom published an article about Mel's new fuel-injection system that was being used on the midget. The results of dynamometer tests performed with the injector were published in the January 1958 issue and produced huge interest. After receiving a flood of inquiries, Mel decided to put the injector into production. *Rod & Custom* published a followup article on the injector in its September 1958 issue and reported that with slight design changes and further fine-tuning, the injectors showed an increase of 35 horsepower over a stock four-throat carburetor on the dyno facilities at Performance Associates in Covina, California. The tests were performed on a '57 Ford engine equipped with a three-carburetor Edelbrock manifold with two Scott injectors and one carburetor.

The only problem with the original design was the constant-flow injector. "You had to know how to drive them," Mel said. "You had to keep the engine rpm up when you left the line, as they were strictly for racing. An ideal setup that could be used on the street was to run two fuel-injection units and one carburetor with progressive linkage on a three-carburetor intake manifold. This setup was good once you put your foot in the throttle and the fuel-injection units cut in." Used in conjunction with carburetors on a multiple-carburetor manifold, these injectors could easily be used on street rods.

SCOTT ENGINEERING

At the age of 27, Mel found himself holding down a full-time job at Transco and running a fuel-injection business in his spare time. Ads for Scott Engineering began to appear in *Rod & Custom*, offering the 97 fuel injectors for the low price of $24.95. The enormous response to the ads was more than Mel ever anticipated. He was so overwhelmed with orders that he brought Ron Hess into the fledgling business as a partner. Ron was a finishing carpenter by trade, and he undertook the making of the wood patterns for the injectors and ran the business end of the shop, while Mel looked after the product development in design and research. In the beginning of their venture, they had permission from Transco to machine the injector castings in Transco's machine shop after working hours, but the quantity of orders made it necessary to rent a shop.

With the success of the 97 injector established, Mel turned his talents to the GMC supercharger, the ultimate piece of speed equipment to complement any engine with loads of horsepower. Like his injector-carburetor design, the GMC injector was simple and uncomplicated. It consisted of two aluminum tubes approximately 3 inches in diameter welded to a cast base plate. Aluminum butterflies were mounted to a throttle shaft from a stock carburetor, and a fuel metering housing machined out of brass regulated the fuel flow. In keeping with the idea of making the injector simple and user friendly, Stromberg 97 carburetor jets were used because they were readily available, inexpensive, and accurately manufactured. These jets were used in all of Mel's injectors so the racer wouldn't have to buy a load of expensive specialty nozzles, just over-the-counter, economical, and easy-to-change Stromberg carburetor jets.

The unique feature of this Scott design was having the fuel injected above the butterfly, eliminating the need for aerated nozzles. Mel felt that the fuel was vaporized better when it passed with high velocity around the butterfly during idle, and when the throttle was opened, the fuel was deflected off the butterfly for better distribution into the air stream.

As business grew, the variety of Scott injectors increased to include several different universal-style single-throat injectors, injectors for the popular Chevy II four-cylinder racing engines used in midgets, and four blower injectors designed for the three GMC supercharger sizes. The universal single-throat injectors were designed to mount on just about any type of carburetor manifold (provided the bolt holes lined up), were numbered 400, 500, and 900, and were designed for foreign and domestic engines. Advertising claimed that they idled as well as, if not better than, carburetors, outperformed the majority of carburetors, and could be used with gasoline, alcohol, or nitromethane. All Scott injectors had the fuel nozzles located above the butterfly to keep the nozzles from being subjected to high vacuum at idle and preventing an over-rich condition inside the manifold. All his injectors, excluding the 97 model, used a Scott centrifugal fuel pump that produced a pressure curve that increased with the rise in rpm, resulting in a fairly even air/fuel mixture ratio.

Probably the most highly recognized induction system that Mel ever designed, aside from the original 97 carburetor unit, was the low-profile Scott Superslot Fuel-Injection System for the 6-71 GMC blower. In the days when dragsters were run with the engine up front, a large GMC blower with an injector and air scoop perched on top impeded the driver's visibility at the best of times. Mel felt that if he lowered the height of the injector, it could have only beneficial results. The increased visibility offered by this design, combined with its highly identifiable, low, wedge-shaped, air scoop, soon

A fabulous picture of Mel and a passenger in Mel's '27 T pickup following the patrol car off the lake bed at Rosamond. What makes this image really interesting is Stuart Hilborn's streamliner making a high-speed run in the background. *Courtesy Mel Scott*

became a favorite among the drivers of front-engined dragsters.

This oblong GMC blower injector was only 1 3/4 inches high and was sold in a kit form that included the slot injector, pump, shutoff valve, air scoop, fuel lines, and a jet blank that could be drilled out for the proper size with the help of a chart. The Superslot had two nozzles placed above the butterfly and was designed for maximum fuel distribution. One nozzle was located in the center of the casting, which passed 75 percent of the fuel, and the other was near the front of the casting. Mel found this design worked best in combination with the curved GMC Roots blower impellers' tendency to force the fuel to the rear of the supercharger housing. This simple and user-friendly fuel-injection system was easily adapted to either gasoline or racing fuels by simply changing the jets.

In late 1964, the Mickey Thompson Equipment Company made a business arrangement with Scott Engineering that made it the sole distributor of the Scott Superslot Fuel-Injection System. This deal ran through to 1967. Thompson would purchase a minimum of 240 units per year at $135 each and marketed these units as the M/T Scott Superslot Fuel Injection.

KARTS

Scott Engineering was the only specialty company to manufacture fuel injection for karts when the karting craze hit Southern California. Mel developed an injector that operated on a gravity-feed system and performed very well—well enough that the Go Kart Company bought the rights to the injector. Scott Engineering continued to manufacture the units under the Go Kart name and sold them as fast as they could be produced.

The last injection system produced by Scott Engineering before it closed its doors in 1966 was a direct-port unit using the Corvette fuel-injection manifold. Mel utilized the base of the factory Corvette fuel-injection manifold, as the injector was designed to bolt directly onto the Chevy manifold.

CENTRIFUGAL PUMP

The fuel pump was a key component of Mel's injector setups. A paper by Robert H. Goddard regarding research into fuel pumps that were to be used in liquid-propellant rockets was enough to sell Mel on the idea of a centrifugal pump. Goddard concluded in his research that the centrifugal pump was superior because of its high volume and dependability.

"With this type of a pump, you don't have to bypass anything," Mel said. "You don't have to run a bypass line; you run it right up to the injector, and when you shut it off, [the fuel] just recirculates in the pump. It is not like a positive pump where you need a bypass line. This is a desired feature, as there is always a head of fuel available when the throttle is popped open with no drop in pressure.

"This pump will go from about eight to sixty pounds pressure as the rpms go up. As the rpms go up, the pressure goes up." This style of pump has a much wider pressure range than the positive-type pump and can pump twice the volume of fuel.

A discarded vacuum cleaner provided Mel with the basis for his first prototype fuel pump, as there were no commercial centrifugal pumps readily available that would suit his purposes. His decision to manufacture a pump came about after taking a vacuum cleaner apart to study its rotary impeller. By machining the vacuum's large impeller (which was designed to pump air) down to a suitable diameter to push fuel, Mel had his impeller problem solved. The pump housing was machined from aluminum stock. The homemade pump proved to be very satisfactory after testing, and with several minor changes to the design, Hess made wood patterns for the various fuel-pump parts and put them into production.

The Scott fuel injection gave better midrange power on the drag strip because the pump provided fuel pressure that was more in tune with the engine's demands versus a positive-type pump.

Two early Scott injectors on an Eddie Meyer manifold powering a Ford V8-60 midget racer. This particular application for his homemade injector was what started Scott Fuel Injection. *Courtesy Mel Scott*

WINNERS

Howard Johansen, owner of Howards Cams, gave Scott Engineering a large boost as a speed equipment manufacturer. Johansen was well known as an innovator and was on the cutting edge with many of his projects, such as a twin-blown Chevy V-8-powered dragster. What made this particular car radically different was the innovative way Howard set up the drive between the two engines, and he won a lot of races with it.

In the 1950s, Howard had designed and fabricated his own fuel-injection system for a DeSoto V-8 engine. He'd used a centrifugal pump with the injectors but had trouble when he bypassed the fuel; the fuel got so hot in the tank that it would throw the metering off, resulting in a poorly running engine. Not wanting to go through those earlier injection problems with his new car, Howard called Scott Engineering. Mel sent several injection units over to Howard's shop and then waited for a phone call from him, but it didn't come. A short while later, Mel was reading *Drag News* and saw a picture of Howard's twin-engine dragster winning Top Eliminator at Long Beach Drag Strip. It was obvious that Howard had known how the injectors worked the minute he saw them. The Howards Cams dragster went on to take the first NHRA World Championship meet in 1961 equipped with Scott injectors on its GMC blowers.

The low-profile Scott injector dominated the major drag racing events in 1963, with Roy Davis winning the NHRA World Championship, and the Hirata and Hobbs AA/G dragster driven by Bob Vodnik taking Top Eliminator at the '63 NHRA National Championship at Indianapolis. There, the Scott injector was used on four of the eight Top Eliminator qualifiers. The Hirata and Hobbs team repeated its win again in 1965. Dick Vest won the World Series Championship with Speed & Sport taking runner-up, and Sandoval and Madden won the United Drag Racers Association (UDRA) Top Eliminator—all equipped with the Scott. Frank Pedregon, one of the more colorful drag racers of the 1960s, used Scott injectors in his notorious fuel-burning AA/FC. Frank received the nickname the "Flamin' Mexican" from the way his Fiat-bodied dragster would always catch on fire. Bits of rubber thrown off by the slicks would collect in the wheelwells of the metal Fiat Topolino body and be ignited by the nitro flames coming from the zoomie-style exhaust headers.

Mel told of the time when the Sandoval and Madden dragster ran 196 miles per hour in the quarter-mile at San Fernando (no one had run that fast at the time), equipped with a Scott Superslot injector on the blower. After the run, the announcer said that the race officials didn't get a time on the car, as nobody had run that fast before, so it must have been an error in the timing system. The Sandoval and Madden car did another run at 195 miles per hour to back it up. Their car also took Top Eliminator that day.

During *Hot Rod*'s Sixth Annual Top Fuel Championship races held at the Riverside drag strip in 1968—several years after Scott Engineering had closed its doors—Larry Dixon was piloting the Howards Cams *Rattler* dragster. As it approached the starting line to make a qualifying run, the announcer belched out, "Here comes that Howards Cams car to the line, running those antiquated Scott injectors." The *Rattler* went on to win the meet, defeating many top-name racers and later was featured on the front cover of *Hot Rod*'s August 1969 issue. In December 1968 at Irwindale Dragway, the *Rattler* dragster became the world's fastest AA/F dragster with a 236.84-mile-per-hour run.

Probably the most memorable and spectacular race car ever to use a Scott injector was the infamous *Winged Express* roadster of Marcellus and Borsch. With this 200-mile-per-hour fuel-burning AA/FA blown-Hemi roadster in the capable hands of "Wild" Willie Borsch (notorious for his one-handed driving skills), it produced speeds that embarrassed many Top Fuel dragsters. "Mousey" Marcellus said that at the 1968 Winternationals they ran a 7.29 ET using a brand-new Scott slot injector they'd bought from Mickey Thompson for $50. Apparently, Mickey was overstocked with the units and couldn't sell them because the venturi area was too small for the new, larger engines, but after that 7.29-second run, Thompson sold every injector he had for $200.

There is also a story about the time Willie qualified for the 32-car Top Fuel field after bumping "Big Daddy" Don Garlits out of the lineup. As the story goes, a meeting of concerned dragster pilots, who no doubt were a little worried that they might lose out to the ultra-quick Fuel Altered, held a vote not to allow Willie to run in the show.

SCOTT RESEARCH AND DEVELOPMENT

Even though Scott Engineering had been closed for many years, Mel still kept an active interest in the research and development of induction systems and pumps. Over the years, he has custom-designed and manufactured fuel pumps for a variety of racing teams and companies. One of the more notable jobs was designing and building a custom fuel-delivery system for Butch Blair's Top Fuel sand dragster in 1987. This sand dragster set an all-time record of 147

miles per hour with an ET of 2.26 seconds for the 100-yard run. The following year, Blair ran the former Joe Amato dragster on the asphalt quarter-mile, winning Top Eliminator at the last Bakersfield Fuel & Gas Championship at the old Famoso Drag Strip, and finishing third at the NHRA World Finals that same year. Mel designed the custom high-speed centrifugal pump that turned 16,000 rpm (flow tested to 60 gpm at 200 psi) and was used in conjunction with an Enderle hat and a modified Enderle barrel valve. This particular setup on Blair's engine would produce brilliant exhaust flames that none of the other cars were getting, and no one could figure it out.

"The centrifugal pump always has a head of fuel, whereas a positive pump has as much as the pump is going to produce, and it's bypassing all the rest of the fuel," Mel explained. "When you shut the bypass, there are milliseconds involved in all this operation, and they've never been able to have a tremendous load of fuel when they first leave the line. That's when you want it, because the engine is pulling down—it wants to be loaded up. Blair would get these exhaust flames, and no one else would, but now they're all getting them because they got all these down nozzles."

The Scott Injector Pump was a high-speed, high-volume, turbine fuel-injector pump that operated up to 18,000 rpm with a fuel flow up to 70 gpm at 200 psi. It could be tailored for a variety of fuels and used on unblown, blown, and turbocharged engines. An article in *Super Stock* magazine reported that when Gene Snow installed a Scott pump in his car at the 1986 International Hot Rod Association (IHRA) Winternationals, it delivered so much more fuel than any conventional pump that the motor simply couldn't handle the fuel load. At the time, Bill Standridge of Bakersfield was running the Scott Injector Pump business.

Another idea Mel developed was a takeoff on his old Stromberg 97 injector, only this new fuel injector was applicable to the Holley

Scott injectors and fuel pumps were designed for a lot of applications, like this unit to fit onto a four-barrel manifold. *Courtesy Mel Scott*

In the 1960s one of Southern California's Top Fuel dragsters was the Sandoval & Madden front-engine job seen here setting top time at the San Fernando Raceway meet with a 196-mile-per-hour run using the Scott slot injector unit. *Courtesy Mel Scott*

One of the cars that made a name for itself in the Gasser classes was Al Hirshfield's early Willys coupe equipped with a Scott injector system on the GMC-blown Hemi. *Courtesy Mel Scott*

four-barrel carburetor base. It was designed so that at the drag strip, all a racer had to do was to remove the upper portion of the Holley carburetor and attach his injector to the base using the existing linkage. After the racing was finished for the day, he could just reverse the installation procedure. Again, Mel had come up with a simplified and inexpensive injector unit. Not wanting to tie himself up in a production business, he sold the induction system to Ron's Racing Products of Tucson, Arizona.

Always up for a challenge, in the mid-1980s Mel got a request for a simple injector unit for a six-cylinder Chevy-powered dragster. Using exhaust tubing as an intake manifold and one of his fuel-injection bodies, Mel came up with a very economical but high-performing induction system.

MOTO SKEETER

One of Mel's nonautomotive ideas during the mid-1960s was a rather odd-shaped little mini-bike called the Moto Skeeter. It was advertised as being "low cost and dependable transportation" and could be purchased either without an engine at $179 or with one at $249. The bike's 4-horsepower engine, in conjunction with the fluid transmission, was more than adequate to provide trouble-free riding.

The scooter was quite simplistic in design, as the sturdy frame consisted of extra-large-diameter exhaust tubing, lights, fenders, large, comfortable handlebars, and a two-person padded seat. A washing machine torque converter acted as a fluid transmission (replacing the usual centrifugal-type clutch), and the bike had a disc brake on the rear sprocket.

Mel and Ron Hess began to manufacture their Moto Products mini-bike at Ron's father's shop in Van Nuys, until financial woes set in and they couldn't afford to have the bike certified for road use. They found a buyer for the mini-bike, but unfortunately the deal didn't pan out. The Go Kart Company was just about to add the Moto Skeeter mini-bike to its lineup when

it went out of business—before Mel and Ron received any money from the sale.

AFTER SCOTT ENGINEERING

Mel treated his business more as a hobby; while it was in operation, he continued to work full-time at Transco. His partner, Ron Hess, also worked at Scott Engineering on a part-time basis, continuing to work as a finishing carpenter full-time. After Scott Engineering closed in 1966, Ron went on to open up his own cabinetry business.

Mel put everything in storage after a deal to sell Scott Engineering fell through. Mel said that he and Lou Baney were going to form a partnership in the fuel-injection business, but he's very happy he didn't, saying that he would have missed out on the great adventure-filled life that he and his wife, Elle, have shared together.

All the wood patterns for the company's fuel-injection systems were left at Frank Medeiro's aluminum foundry in Culver City for storage.

"Regardless of how poorly made my patterns were [before Ron Hess was on the scene], Frank wouldn't say anything, and if need be he would repair the mistakes so he could cast the parts for me," Mel said. While Mel and his wife, Elle, were away in Southeast Asia, the aluminum foundry was sold, and the new owners disposed of all the Scott Engineering patterns.

TRAVELING AND PATENTS

Strange as it may be, sometimes even something as minor as a stray piece of wind-blown paper can have an effect that will change a life for years to come. This oddity occurred quite by accident to the Scotts. Mel said that he and Elle were sitting on the beach when a piece of newspaper blew up around their feet. Upon glancing at it, they noticed an ad that read: "American President Liner to the Philippines, $1,000 roundtrip." The trip included stopoffs at numerous islands along the way. With Elle's parents living in the Philippines, they felt that it would be a great way to go for an extended visit.

After a stay in the Philippines, they moved on to Hong Kong, where Mel worked as a mechanical engineer at the Taikoo shipyard, supervising the construction of military landing ships and the rebuilding of diesel engines, generators, cranes, windlasses, and so on.

From March 1967 to May 1970, Mel was employed by the U.S. Army, Air Force, and the Marines, stationed in Vietnam as a field engineer. He was in charge of maintaining and supervising the installation of motion picture equipment in military movie theaters. Duty station was at Okinawa with temporary duty in Taiwan, the Philippines, Japan, and Korea. While they were in Vietnam, Elle worked as a handwriting analyst for the U.S. Military Police.

After returning to the United States in 1970, Mel went to work for the Von Brimer Scientific Laboratories in Las Vegas, Nevada, as a design engineer until 1972. At this facility, he was involved in the research and development of exhaust afterburner systems that reduced the pollutant emissions from automobiles.

From 1972 to 1984, Mel acted as a consulting engineer for the hardware division of STP Corporation in Santa Monica and for Olson Engineering in Huntington Beach. He was granted six United States patents, one Mexican patent, and one Italian patent, all relating to air computers and exhaust gas recirculation (EGR) valves. He licensed his patented EGR valve to STP, which in turn was sold to the Russians for their Lada cars. These cars had to meet certain emissions standards before being allowed into Canada and Sweden. In 1970, all automobiles had to be retrofitted with an EGR valve or similar device to reduce exhaust pollutants. At the 1974 Indianapolis 500 race, 17 out of the 33 race cars were equipped with Mel's patented EGR valve on their Offenhauser engines, and three of those cars finished in the top 10.

Always ready to broaden his horizons, in the late 1980s, Mel freelanced as an investigator of automotive mechanical failures to determine the legitimacy of those failures. During this same timeframe, he and Elle completed the advanced course at the Rouse School of Special Detective Training and in 1989 became private investigators. In 1992, Mel and Elle traveled to Vietnam for a client whose relative was declared missing in action during the war. Their client wanted to know if the stories about American soldiers being still held in prisoner-of-war camps were valid. After an intensive search with no restrictions and total freedom to travel wherever they wanted and to speak to whomever they wanted to, their conclusion was that there were no POWs remaining in Vietnam. However, they did uncover various scams perpetrated by unscrupulous people trying to attain money for false information regarding so-called U.S. POWs still held in Vietnam. They returned to Vietnam again in 1995, and the U.S. Embassy in Vietnam confirmed their findings.

RETIREMENT

Being retired allows Mel the freedom to research and develop what he enjoys the most: anything mechanical that burns nitro or rocket fuel. In his much younger days, he flew gas-powered model airplanes and built model pulse- and ram-jet engines. Today, he has rekindled his fascination with these engines. One of his latest projects was designing and making a turbojet engine out of a KKK turbocharger.

Mel's present-day workshop contains everything from a homebuilt rotary engine, a homemade turbine engine with an afterburner made from a jet aircraft starter motor, a nitro-burning lawnmower engine equipped with an F-head (reminiscent of the Whizzer head he designed and built 50 years earlier), a performance muffler of his own design, a subcompact Suzuki automobile that will get a humongous pulse-jet engine mounted to its roof to run at the Carlsbad Drag Strip, several old Honda motorbikes converted to run on nitro (Mel has a real thing for nitro), and numerous wooden patterns for fuel injectors and pumps hanging from the rafters. Though he stopped commercially manufacturing fuel injectors and pumps in 1992, he will occasionally make one for a friend if pressed.

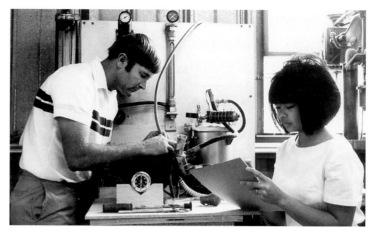

Mel and his wife Elle at work in their Santa Monica shop in the 1960s, flow-testing a fuel injector. *Courtesy Mel Scott*

NITROMETHANE

Mel has always had a fascination and respect for the raw power that nitromethane can produce, and he holds thoughts on today's Top Fuel cars and their dangers.

"They have to cut the fuel flow back to at least 37 gallons a minute or you're going to have an adiabatic compression," Mel said. "If this happens with liquid nitromethane, you're going to have an explosion. It's a time bomb, a class 'A' explosion. A prime example of this is the terrible explosion when Doug Herbert's engine blew apart at Pomona in 1999. I'd already written a letter to NHRA about this exact situation shortly before Herbert's explosion.

"NHRA have done something better than restricting it to thirty-seven gallons a minute—they cut the fuel to ninety percent. When you add ten percent alcohol into nitro, it takes that sensitivity and drops it way down. As an example of how volatile nitro is, if you put nitro in a beer can and drop it from a building, it'll just splat onto the ground. However, if you put nitro into a steel cylinder and drop it off that same building, you'll have adiabatic compression. It's got nowhere to go; it'll just explode. The Hirata and Hobbs engine explosion is a good example of what can happen. They were firing up their unblown fuel car running one hundred percent nitro, and the engine had an adiabatic compression explosion, which totally destroyed the engine and seriously injured Kenny Hirata."

IN RETROSPECT

Mel says that the main reason his injection business didn't achieve greater status was directly related to the lack of marketing knowledge. But he still wouldn't have traded all the experiences that he and Elle have had for a successful manufacturing business.

During all that's already been mentioned, the Scotts have lived in 7 different countries, visited 85 countries, and managed to visit every communist country except Albania.

When asked what he felt was his greatest achievement throughout his much-varied career, he looked at his wife, Elle, and said, "She is!"

CHAPTER 17

Sharp Speed Equipment

AL SHARP

As one of the pioneers in the specialty equipment business that emerged after World War II, Al Sharp was a successful speed merchant as well as an astute businessman with a prolific number of nonautomotive manufacturing concerns.

THE BEGINNING

The Sharp family moved from Ohio to Southern California and settled down in south Los Angeles near 118th and Broadway Boulevard when Al was one year old. He graduated from George Washington High in 1938. During his high school years, he was introduced to the world of hot rods, becoming a member of the Idlers car club and occasionally racing at the dry lakes with a '32 roadster.

Growing up in an age when speed equipment was almost nonexistent, particularly for cash-strapped teenagers, Al and his club members had to rely on their own ingenuity to squeeze a little extra out of their engines. At the time, Al was running a Meyer dual-carburetor intake on his flathead and figured that if two carbs were better than one, four of them could perform miracles. Keeping it as simple as possible, he cut out a piece of flat plate aluminum and welded on four mounting flanges to accept four Amal carburetors that sat directly over the intake ports. He recalled that the homemade intake looked pretty hot when it was mounted on the engine, and it worked with varying degrees of success, but he eventually went back to the more dependable dual intake.

There was upkeep in running a hot rod, and in order to pay the expenses, he got a part-time job after school at Lumley's Auto Wreckers on Main Street in Los Angeles. It was rigorous work tearing cars apart at the wrecking yard, but he became very well acquainted with automobile construction. He didn't mind getting greasy working on his own car, but the thought of a career at Lumley's was enough to set his sights on becoming a technical engineer. Finances prevented him from enrolling in an engineering course upon graduation, so he had to get out and make a living. Al realized that if he were a skilled tradesman, it'd mean a bigger paycheck, so he applied for a job as an apprentice pattern-maker in the local foundry. Al became a self-taught engineer by studying everything he could find about engineering and design.

THE SOUTH PACIFIC

When United States went to war in 1941, Al was working at the naval yards in Long Beach as a pattern-maker, which deferred him from military service. But as the war progressed, Uncle Sam came calling, and Al was shipped to the South Pacific to serve as a pattern-maker for the navy.

While stationed in the Pacific, he forged a reputation for himself with the repair of a large bronze propeller from a cruiser that had arrived at the repair shop with a bent blade, caused by hitting a coral reef. Al's chief warrant officer began to heat the end of the blade to straighten it when Al chipped in, telling him that the prop was already very malleable and that heating it would cause it to fracture and probably drop off. His superior reprimanded him for his lack of knowledge—imagine a kid telling an old salt with 20 years of naval experience what to do! The chief carried on and pounded

Opposite: At the strip with the infamous 554 coupe. Cigar chomping Al Sharp is working on the engine with unknown man in the middle and Gene Mooneyham on the left. Courtesy Al Sharp

The speed parts that began a successful manufacturing career for Al Sharp. In the foreground is a Sharp dual manifold; in the rear is the first commercially successful triple, introduced in 1948. *Courtesy Al Sharp*

the heated blade with a sledgehammer and knocked it right off. Embarrassed, and a little more than peeved, he looked up at Sharp and said, "I suppose you can fix it?"

Al replied, "Just drag it over to the foundry, and I'll show you."

When Al first landed at his posting, he noticed that they had an Ajax electric furnace that no one had been able to figure out how to operate. Al was lucky enough to get it going.

"First, I made a plaster cast from one of the remaining good blades, attached it to the broken one, and then embedded the lot in a sand flask," Al said. "After removing the plaster cast and cutting two large sprues [one on top and one in the bottom] in the sand mold, I melted down about six hundred pounds of bronze, which raised more than a few eyebrows. I then made a large number of pigs [containers to catch the overflow molten metal] and started to pour the melted bronze into the top sprue. As the hot molten metal filled the cavity, it passed through the bottom sprue into a pig. The liquid hot metal slowly began to melt the broken edge of the blade and melded together with the new casting. After filling about forty pigs, the bottom sprue was shut off, and the casting was left to slowly solidify overnight."

The following day, everyone, including the commanding admiral of the island, showed up to see the results of the new kid's work. The blade was removed from the sand mold, and the risers were cut off, ground, and buffed.

"I took a twenty-pound sledgehammer and placed another piece of bronze on the tip of the newly cast blade, and asked the chief to hit it," Al said. "Swinging as hard as he could, all that came out of the chief's mouth were several words of profanity. I'd

seen this type of repair done on a much smaller scale and figured that molten metal is all the same, regardless of the size." From then on, until the end of the hostilities, Al could do no wrong.

Upon being discharged from the service at the end of the war, Al made a rash decision and went directly into his own business. From a financial standpoint, it was a risky venture, having a total of $1,176, and $1,000 of that was borrowed from a friend. But it was enough to purchase the woodworking machinery needed to make foundry patterns.

SP PATTERN SERVICE

Before Al really got going, Gordon Pilkington joined him as a partner. They called their new business SP Pattern Service.

"Gordy was a much better pattern-maker than I ever was, but I had the ideas and would scribe on a piece of paper, and Gordy could do what I wanted," Al said. "It worked beautifully."

Besides the commercial pattern side of the business, Al produced speed equipment patterns for himself and others. Over the next several years, as the performance market grew like a runaway weed, SP Pattern made patterns for numerous manufacturers, including Ford V-8 head and intake patterns for Grancor Speed Equipment of Chicago (the Granatelli brothers), Chevrolet manifold patterns for McGurk Engineering, GMC intake patterns for Howards Cams, patterns for Braje, Jeep patterns for Vic Hickey, a Ford flathead six-cylinder head pattern for Lyle Knudsen, and more.

One customer from that era was Tony Capanna of Wilcap. Tony had Al design a special gearbox pattern for his dynamometer. The box had to have the ability to withstand the abuse of high rpm and heavy torque loads from high-performance engines. The

The controversial runner layout of the Sharp flathead V-8 four-carburetor manifold. Al's competitors said it was too much carburetion for the engine. *Courtesy Al Sharp*

two remained friends over the years and, oddly enough, it was Tony's son who later brought the line of Sharp speed equipment back into production for the nostalgia market.

By the mid-1950s Al had branched out into other business ventures, and SP Pattern was sold to Lyle Knudsen. Many years later, Al and Lyle formed a partnership to construct several large commercial buildings.

MANIFOLDS

In postwar America, it seemed that every conceivable manner of automobile racing took off like never before, creating a demand for speed equipment that the small number of existing specialty manufacturers couldn't keep up with. Al had some ideas about what would make a decent intake manifold, so Sharp Speed Equipment was created as a secondary business to the pattern shop.

His first offering was a Ford V-8 two-carburetor intake. In 1948, he introduced the first commercially successful triple-carburetor flathead manifold, and again in 1952, he was ahead of the competition by bringing out a four-carburetor manifold.

"I didn't care for the stock Ford port passages, so I developed my own high-velocity direct runners with as few bends as possible," Al said. "The three-carburetor intake is very efficient and will flow over a wide range. At low speeds, you don't need the same volume as in the top end, but the fuel mixture must flow freely, so when the throttle is pushed to the floor, there are no flat spots in acceleration."

By 1953, Sharp Speed Equipment was manufacturing intakes and heads for the flathead six-cylinder Plymouth and Dodges, intakes for the Chevy six, and a now-rare four-barrel intake for the flathead V-8.

HEADS

As soon as the manifold business was up and running Al looked into producing high-compression heads. He had heard that the Nairn brothers (Don of Speedway Pattern, and Jimmy of Nairn Machine Shop) had a set of Ford V-8 cylinder-head patterns. John Athan of Mercury Tool & Die had made the patterns, which he originally designed to be cast in iron. The Nairn boys had several sets cast with "Nairn" on the heads in anticipation of marketing them, but that's as far as they ventured.

Thinking that he could save himself the work of having to carve out his own head patterns, Al borrowed the patterns from Don and Jim, changed the name to "Sharp," and cast a set of heads in aluminum. The heads were to be installed in a track roadster, as he wanted to try his hand at racing.

Al quickly found that the heads caused the engine to overheat. He did not know that Athan designed the patterns to be cast in iron, so the wall thickness surrounding the combustion chamber area wasn't as crucial as it was with aluminum. Under racing conditions, the heads didn't have the internal water capacity to cool properly. Al completely redesigned the interior water passages and modified the combustion-chamber shape, and after several tries came up with a head that incorporated flow ribs inside the water cavity.

"My heads were relieved toward the exhaust valve, using the theory that if you scavenge the cylinder and get the spent gases out, it won't pollute the incoming charge," Al said.

Besides the conventional-type heads for the Mercury and Ford V-8s, Sharp Equipment also produced heads to accommodate pop-up pistons.

TRACK ROADSTERS

In order to gain the maximum exposure for his equipment, Al looked at the racing venues around Los Angeles and settled on the California Racing Association. The CRA track roadster shows drew an enormous spectator following and would be ideal venues to show off the Sharp performance line. After driving his own car in several races, Al concluded that driving wasn't his forte and put Red Amick in the driver's seat. Later, he sponsored Del Baxter's track roadster with Troy Ruttman as the driver, and in 1947, Baxter's car took the CRA Championship at Carrell Speedway.

His involvement with track roadsters gave Al the idea to design and manufacture a three-carburetor manifold. It caught a lot of flack from his competitors until they saw the outstanding results on the track, whereupon they too began manufacturing triple-carb intakes.

After two short years in business, Sharp Speed Equipment offered a long list of equipment, including dual and triple manifolds, generator brackets, safety hubs, foot pedals, Chevy-six manifolds, Plymouth-six heads and manifolds, as well as camshafts from Tom Spalding Cams. With the introduction of *Hot Rod* in 1948, and after placing a fairly large ad in the first issue, business increased dramatically.

SAFETY HUBS

Sometimes it takes a truly unfortunate accident to put safety features into practice, and such was the case with the spectator fatality that occurred at Carrell Speedway. During a race, a rear wheel came off Del Baxter's car and bounced up into the stands, killing a little girl. Regrettably, at the time, there wasn't a safety device available that would keep a loose wheel from leaving the vehicle if an axle broke. The accident deeply bothered Al, and he took it upon himself to find a solution to prevent any further such mishaps. He came up with a design for the safety hub—an

uncomplicated device designed to keep the wheel attached to the axle housing. It was made for Ford rearends but could be adapted to other brands. This item was an instant success and became a mandatory item in track racing. Sharp began to sell thousands of these units throughout the country.

At the first *Hot Rod* show at the Los Angeles Armory (1948), the Sharp Equipment display booth offered a raffle prize for a set of safety hubs. The young fellow who won them didn't exactly know what they were for. In a quirk of fate, that same kid—Gene Mooneyham—came to work for Sharp Engineering several years later and stayed for 14 years. Gene Mooneyham started out at the bottom at Sharp's and eventually became the shop foreman and a longtime friend of Al's. (Nick Arias of Arias Pistons was another early Sharp employee. He'd just been discharged from the military in the early 1950s and landed a job at Sharp. Nick recalled that it was there that he learned

Al puts the finishing touches on a Sharp-equipped V-8 flathead.
Courtesy Al Sharp

FOOT PEDALS

The Sharp cast-aluminum foot pedal came about because Troy Ruttman was having a problem with his foot slipping off the gas pedal of Del Baxter's track roadster while racing. After spending a little time thinking about the dilemma, Al took an outline pattern off of Ruttman's shoe, and from this rough outline he made a cast-aluminum foot pedal. Gordy Pilkington meticulously hand-carved the nonskid, diamond-shaped, tread design into a wood pattern for the pedal. At the track, Ruttman received a good amount of ribbing from other racers when they saw this large aluminum gas pedal in the roadster, but it wasn't long before the merits overcame the jokes, and the pedal became a very popular item. Ultimately, hundreds were shipped across the country to speed shops. Again, it didn't take long for other manufacturers to bring out their version of the Sharp pedal.

D&S INTAKE MANIFOLD

The nondescript D&S flathead V-8 two-carburetor intake manifold still shows up on occasion at automotive flea markets, and its lineage can be partially traced back to Sharp Speed Equipment. The D&S intake manifold was sold through the Clark Headers shop and other outlets as an inexpensive hop-up item. Al had picked up the patterns for this oddball intake at an auction and never knew the parentage of the manufacturer, or if it had ever been put into production. The manifold design didn't meet his standards, and he wouldn't sell the manifold under the Sharp name. Instead, he entered into a sideline business with Clark Headers, which said it could sell lots of manifolds as long as the price was right. It wasn't the best manifold on the market, but it filled the gap for budget-minded hot rod enthusiasts.

DRAG RACING, ROSES, AND NITRO

In the early days of drag racing, the adventurous, including Al Sharp and Art Chrisman, tried out different fuel formulas in attempts to gain the upper hand on the strip. These two speed enthusiasts were running nitro in a dragster before the fuel became well known. Nitromethane has a very distinctive smell, and they tried everything imaginable to disguise the odor, even some perfume donated by Al's wife. When word got out about the perfume, Tom Medley drew up a cartoon for the September 1952 issue of *Hot Rod* showing roses coming out of an engine's exhaust pipes.

In 1953, Art was the first to break the 140-mile-per-hour mark during a drag meet at Santa Ana. His 304-ci '42 Merc-powered fuel dragster with Sharp heads and a four-carb manifold ran a record-setting 140.08 miles per hour and set a 9.04-second track acceleration record. Al sponsored Art's coupe at the 1953 Bonneville Nationals. Chrisman set the B and C/Competi-

The 554 1934 Ford shows a full-blown Chrysler with Al's cast-aluminum blower scoop and Sharp heads. Al is on the left. *Courtesy Al Sharp*

The old saying "Necessity is the mother of invention" prompted Al to come up with this portable engine stand after stubbing his toe in the dark. *Courtesy Al Sharp*

tion Coupe class records at 160.17 and 163.63 miles per hour. Al recalled that it was his idea to attach modified wringer washing-machine lids to the car's wheels for better streamlining.

THE INFAMOUS 544

Like a lot of hot rodders, Gene Mooneyham was involved in dry lakes competition and ran a 1934 Ford sedan with his friend Carl Johnson. The car was raced as a sedan from 1951 to 1953. Then they decided it'd go faster if they weren't pushing so much air with that large body and replaced it with a $5 1934 coupe body. The flathead was eventually replaced by a blown Hemi, and Al got into the action in 1959 by taking over Carl's interest in the coupe.

They installed an Enderle barn door–style fuel injector atop the GMC blower, and during a run, fuel was drawn out of the

injector by the slipstream and deposited on the car's windshield. To overcome the problem, Al designed a cast-aluminum air scoop that extended above the engine hood and fit onto the injector body. When Kent Enderle saw this neat setup, it gave him the idea to put the injector butterflies in a scoop rather than down in the injector body. Sharp Speed Equipment did up the patterns for Enderle's new-style injector scoop, which eventually became the trend for the fuel-injection industry.

Many times a new idea is discovered by accident, such as the time when Al and Gene were building up two identical Chrysler engines for the coupe and uncovered a horsepower secret quite by accident. One day, they stopped for lunch while in the middle of honing out one of the engine blocks. After lunch, Al went back to finish the job, but he had forgotten which cylinder he had ended on, so he measured each cylinder and, to his surprise, the cylinders that had already been honed were found to be out-of-round in several spots.

Retracing what he'd done before lunch, he concluded that the block had been sitting out in the sun and heated up enough to distort the cylinder walls minutely. To rectify the problem and get all the cylinders the same, the block was heated with a torch and the cylinders were honed.

The other engine had already been assembled, so this process was only performed on the one engine. Later at Bakersfield, the pair ran the engine that hadn't been hot honed and then, out of curiosity, decided to run the second engine in the car. Running the same heavy load of nitro, the coupe picked up significant miles per hour on the top end. After that, every engine they built was hot honed.

The best the Mooneyham and Sharp coupe recorded was 186 miles per hour at 8.96 seconds with Larry Faust in the driver's seat. On occasion, Gene would drive the car, until he had a near-fatal disaster when the brakes failed. Many years later, the restored Mooneyham & Sharp 544 coupe found a home in the Don Garlits Museum in Florida.

M&S HEADS

When Al bought into the 544 coupe, he also began developmental work on aluminum heads for the race car's Chrysler engine. He felt that he could design a lightweight head that could easily outperform the cast-iron heads, and by 1963, the coupe was outfitted with a set of "M&S" (Mooneyham and Sharp) heads. He designed them with larger water passages and proper routing to eliminate hot spots, and grooves for O-rings, but for economic reasons, the heads used stock Chrysler valvetrain components. A special feature that Al implemented was what he called the "cartridge fire." To eliminate preignition from a hot spark plug, he isolated the electrode of the plug in a small cavity above the combustion chamber. Each head weighed in at 35 pounds, which was about half of a cast-iron head, and retailed for $995 a set.

Approximately 10 sets of these aluminum heads were manufactured and sold to other engine builders, but without a sufficient return on investment to keep the venture going, and with other projects in the works, Al sold the head patterns to Bruce Crower

The completed and ill-fated Ilin fiberglass sports car that looked like a cross between a T-Bird and a Lotus Elite. *Courtesy Al Sharp*

of Crower Cams. A set was installed on the Hippo and Alexander fuel-burning 300-ci Chrysler dragster, which turned a very respectable 199.10 miles per hour.

Sharp also manufactured cast-aluminum valve covers for the Chrysler Hemi. When Al retired from the speed equipment business, he sold the patterns to Dean Moon. Al said that if you look on the inside of a Moon Hemi valve cover today, you'll see the initials "M&S" in the casting.

TEFLON SEALS

When Al and Gene heard that Jack Chrisman and Harry Duncan's dragster was up for sale, they thought it was too good a deal to pass up. The dragster had originally been built to carry a small Dodge V-8, but to make it really competitive, Al and Gene installed a big blown Chrysler between the rails. Jack Chrisman was in charge of driving the dragster, but with the added power, the car's short 96-inch wheelbase proved almost uncontrollable. The handling problems ended after 24 inches were added to the wheelbase.

Once they'd a chance to run the car for a while, Al noticed that the engine seemed to be starving for fuel at the top end of the strip, even though they were using the largest pump that was available. He figured that he could design a pump that would do the job and bought the largest impeller he could find. With the new pump in

place, the dragster picked up almost 6 miles per hour.

Besides a new fuel pump, they felt the dragster needed an updated fuel shutoff valve, and Al would design it. Al's error of using Teflon washers between the two plates in the shutoff valve wasn't noticed until making some runs at the strip. The washers lost their shape after being used several times, causing a leakage problem that could have proved disastrous for both car and driver. It was then that Al remembered Teflon doesn't retain a memory unless it is under compression. He was so irritated with himself and with the leakage problems that he reinstalled the original shutoff valve rather than finding a replacement material for the washers.

HAIRY OLDS

During the 1960s, exhibition drag cars evolved and filled the spectator stands wherever they appeared, performing wheel-standing feats, smoking rubber for the full quarter-mile—anything to put on a good show. Manufacturers were quick to see the advertising potential, and George Hurst was one of the first to jump on the bandwagon and sponsor several outstanding exhibition cars carrying the Hurst logo. In 1966, Sharp got involved with the Hurst *Hairy Oldsmobile* project, a highly recognizable Toronado that could smoke all four tires the full length of the strip and that was an instant hit with racing fans. It was a fairly easy stunt for the Toronado to perform, with its two 1,050-horsepower blown 425 V-8s powering all four wheels. Sharp designed and manufactured blower manifolds, front engine covers, and custom valve covers for the two Toronado engines.

WORLD'S FASTEST MAN

Craig Breedlove became a household name when the young hot rodder from Southern California set the land speed record with a jet engine–powered car on the Bonneville Salt Flats. In 1967, Craig and Al formed a partnership called the Spirit Equipment Company with the intention of cashing in on Breedlove's popularity. Al would take care of the designing and manufacturing, while Craig would carry the marketing and public relations end of their business. One of their main products was a new blower manifold design that they planned to patent as a diverter manifold. At the time, other manufacturers' blower manifolds had a flat plenum base, which led to fuel puddling on the floor, whereas the Spirit manifold made any surplus fuel drain toward the valves. Gene Mooneyham now manufactures this blower manifold.

Another product was aluminum heads for the Ford flathead V-8 with the name "SPIRIT" cast on them—a rare find today. The partners also manufactured cast-aluminum timing chain covers and valve covers for the Chrysler Hemi. Unfortunately, the business never really caught on and was shelved.

Al and Craig worked together on several other projects, including the notorious *Screaming Yellow Zonker* rocket-propelled exhibition drag car, which was later sponsored by English Leather. The *Zonker* was originally built as part of AMC's efforts to set a number of class records at Bonneville using several different AMC engines. One was a turbocharged six built by Barney Navarro.

RACING

Before making the transition to the quarter-mile, the '34 coupe competed at El Mirage, where Al first got a chance to get behind the steering wheel. He'd just gotten the car up to speed at the top end of the course, when one of the tires hit a small rut. Before he could get off the accelerator, the engine overrevved and blew its insides out. From then on, as far as he was concerned, someone else could drive the temperamental coupe.

After Al purchased a new 1957 Jaguar convertible, he was

rather curious to see what it had for power, and he entered it in a race at the Riverside International Raceway. Vapor-lock difficulties he experienced on the track were enough to turn him off the Jaguar, and a short time later he happened to drive by a used car dealer and noticed a Mercedes coupe sitting on the lot. This Mercedes would have retailed around $9,700 new in 1955 and had a $6,000 tag on it. With only 150 miles on the Jaguar's odometer, a trade-in was made, and Al happily drove away in the Mercedes. This particular model was the famous gullwing coupe that had rare aluminum body panels and a 183-ci, OHC, straight six-cylinder gasoline engine.

Al recalled the day he set a class record at El Mirage in the Mercedes, which came with a lesson on valve clearances. His buddy Jack Heiht was a Mercedes mechanic and had worked on the engine and set the valves the night before an RTA meet and trailered it up to El Mirage the following day. When the Mercedes was started and allowed to warm up, the valves rattled like crazy. They discovered that they had 0.029 inch clearance. Thinking back on what they had done to the engine, they realized the valves had been set when the engine was cold. When the engine warmed up to operating temperature, the camshaft towers expanded and threw out the settings. After adjusting the valves, Al piloted the Mercedes down the lakebed for a 136.57-mile-per-hour record run. The best he'd ever gotten out of the car on previous runs was 128 miles per hour. Heiht backed up the record run when he drove the Mercedes to a 136.44-mile-per-hour run. The only trophy Al ever kept and valued was the one he received when he drove that Mercedes to the B/Sports Car class record.

DIVERSIFICATION

Sharp was a diversified company that was involved in everything from mold pattern production and speed equipment manufacturing to aircraft and missile work. For the aircraft industry, it manufactured fiberglass radomes (long, stream-lined nosepieces containing radar equipment for jet fighters used by the French and Israeli governments). The company also designed and built an integral weaving machine that created a fiberglass honeycomb material. When the company was at its peak, Sharp had 30 employees working in either the pattern shop or the foundry.

LOGO

Several Sharp logos were used over the years, but the one that Al favored most was created by Ed "Big Daddy" Roth. Ed Iskenderian may have popularized the T-shirt as an advertising medium, but Roth's genius helped turn it into a canvas of airbrushed crazy cartoon monsters and wild cars. Roth's Sharp logo, with the legend "Best on the Block," depicted a guillotine and a hapless victim.

ILIN SPORTS CAR

Raymond Development Industries of Huntington Park, California, contracted Sharp in 1961 to construct an operating prototype sports car called the "Ilin." The deal called for two fiberglass luxury four-door sedans to be built, along with all the tooling needed to put the car

Of the many Sharp decal logos, this one, designed by the legendary Ed "Big Daddy" Roth, was Al's favorite. *Courtesy Al Sharp*

into production. An Israeli automobile company had commissioned the project with had plans to manufacture the car in Israel.

The Ilin body was designed by Howard "Dutch" Darin of Kaiser fame, who specified that it be built around a Studebaker Golden Hawk V-8 drivetrain. It was to be fitted to a modified Studebaker 120-inch wheelbase frame and weigh approximately 2,600 pounds with a four-door hardtop fiberglass body, chrome-plated fiberglass bumpers and grille, and a genuine burled-walnut dashboard. A clay model of the car vaguely resembled a cross between a Ford Thunderbird and a Lotus Elise.

Although the project was a mammoth undertaking, it didn't deter Al. Ed Pelot was the multitalented shop superintendent on the project and the driving force that kept things running smoothly. He ironed out any wrinkles that came up during the car's construction. To begin, a plaster cast of the clay model was made and then expanded on a loft to allow them to make full-size wooden mockup templates. The mockup was designed to separate, allowing the fenders, doors, hood, deck lid, and roof sections to be removed in order to make the individual fiberglass molds.

Darin had been very explicit that there were to be absolutely no changes in the car's design in any form because a change would destroy the car's aesthetic value. Al said that those demands had to be overlooked when it came to the windshield. To get a custom window, a buck was taken off the mockup and sent out east to an automobile window manufacturer for an estimate. Upon receiving the enormously overinflated cost for the custom window and after picking themselves off the floor from laughing so hard Al figured there had to be a better and much cheaper way to get the windshield. Al's experience at Lumley's Auto Wreckers finally paid off: visiting the local wrecking yard, he found a Ford windshield that would be a perfect fit, except for about 3/4 inch difference on the layback and about 1/2 inch on the tilt back. The front of the mockup was quickly recontoured to accept the windshield, and the "Ford" insignia was sandblasted off the glass with "Ilin" engraved in its place. When Dutch came to view the car's progress, Al asked what he thought of the windshield. Dutch said, "It is beautiful; how much did it cost?"

Al said, "Fifteen thousand dollars."

Darin just about fainted until Al confessed, "Dutch, I hate to tell you this, but that's a Ford windshield."

Dutch said, "Tell me what you changed."

Al replied, "You tell me what I changed."

"Well, I can't see the difference."

"That's what I thought," Al answered.

Sharp essentially did everything on the project but the upholstery and painting. These two items were subcontracted out to Gaylord Upholstery in South Gate and John Camarano of Jerry's Auto Body in Bell.

The Ilin project required about 1 1/2 years to complete with 15 full-time pattern-makers and a cost of $185,000. From the very beginning of the project, Al had mentioned to the owners that they should have schematic prints for the car and that his draftsman could create the blueprints as the car was being built. The investors said that the prints could be done more cheaply in Israel.

This decision proved to be a very costly mistake on the owners' part. The two cars and related material were packed up and shipped off to Israel, where they were not allowed into the Israeli port of entry because there were no official papers, written documentation, or prints as to the manufacture of the cars. The complete package was returned to the United States, and it ended up in Detroit. What happened after that is anyone's guess.

Al Sharp passed away on September 16, 2004, marking the end of another legendary speed merchant whose name might have disappeared had it not been for the resurgence of interest in the good old days of hot rodding and flathead V-8 speed equipment.

In this 2003 photo, Al holds what he felt was one of his more memorable speed parts: the commercially successful four-carb manifold that he introduced in 1952. *Author photo*

CHAPTER 18

Spalding Racing Cams & Ignitions

BILL AND TOM SPALDING

This story is about two brothers, both merchants of speed equipment and both successful in their chosen fields. The Spalding legacy began on an orange ranch situated between Azusa and Glendora, California, in the early 1900s. The younger of four Spalding sons, William (Bill) Andrew II was born on January 17, 1917, and his sibling, Thomas (Tom) Powell, was born on January 25, 1920.

The boys grew up on the 22-acre orange farm and were well acquainted with the daily routine of milking cows, caring for chickens, turkeys, and hogs, weeding the family vegetable garden, and horseback riding. Besides caring for the livestock, there was always work in the orange orchards, pruning, picking, and lighting smudge pots when the temperature dipped near the freezing mark.

Bill Spalding recalled that the best part of those early days was being allowed to drive the farm machinery. "We all worked on the orange ranch and learned how to drive everything when we were kids. We got our driver's licenses early in those days."

1923 CHEVROLET TOURING

In 1930, their father presented his two youngest sons with a well-used '23 Chevrolet Touring that he'd purchased for $5. This gift set the course for their future. With 22 acres to practice on, it didn't take long for the boys to learn the fundamentals of operating a car. More than once, they removed the engine's cylinder head to clean any carbon deposits that may have built up from cruising the back 40, but they mainly did it out of curiosity, to see what made an engine tick. Bill said their father was always helpful in answering the multitude of questions they asked him about the mechanical pieces of machinery on the ranch, something that helped develop their understanding of mechanics.

After driving around the ranch for some time, the Chevy was finally licensed for the road. It was then that they looked for ways to improve the performance of the old Touring. To improve the looks of the car, they replaced the stock solid-steel wheels with wire jobs off the family's '29 Ford Touring, after coming up with their own design for a wheel adapter.

1928 FORD TOURING

"When Tom and I were still in our early teenage years, Dad bought us a '28 Ford Touring car," Bill said. "We tore that thing down and made a hot rod out of it. I remember in 1932 this guy drove in our laneway with a brand-new Ford pickup V-8, and he challenged us to a race. So we went out to Gladstone Avenue, and I beat him the first fifty yards, and then he went on by us like a bomb. That's how we got started."

In 1934, Tom, Bill, and some friends first attended one of the impromptu race meets held up at Muroc Dry Lake. As fortune would have it, their cousin Arthur Powell, who also lived on an orange farm, was a good friend of the famous racing engine builder Harry Miller. Miller gave a Miller-Schofield head to Arthur, who in turn gave it to Tom and Bill.

Opposite: Bill and Tom Spalding's Unlimited Modified roadster. It's outfitted with Riley OHV heads on a 1935 flathead V-8, a Mercedes blower atop a homemade manifold, and two Stromberg 48s. Note the nicely fabricated exhaust flowing into large-diameter collector pipes. *Courtesy Bill Spalding*

"The first thing that was hot on [the '28 Touring] when we drove up to the dry lakes was that overhead-valve head," Bill said. "The intake valves were about two inches in diameter, and it was a cam driving the intake only; the exhaust valves were in the stock position.

"At first, we just went up to Muroc to see what was going on. John Blackwood drove his stock '31 roadster up there too, and it was a good thing because our Miller-Schofield froze up the cam, so he towed us home with a rope."

Bill recalled later on that after they'd assembled the engine and were pouring the oil in, they noticed a small speck of dirt in the oil. They all felt that it was too small to interfere with the operation of the engine. He said they should have been more careful, because after disassembling the seized cam bearing, they discovered that minute object had caused the oil blockage.

By the time the Ford was ready to be replaced, it'd gone through a metamorphosis of engine modifications. They tried just about every performance head that was available at the time—Winfield, Acme, Miller-Schofield (Cragar), two-port and four-port Riley, McDowell, Dryer OHV, and possibly others. Bill said that he couldn't remember the number of heads they went through on that car.

1929 ROADSTER
In 1936, the Touring was set aside for a 1929 Ford roadster rolling chassis, from which they removed the fenders and running boards, and installed a flathead V-8.

"We went to L.A. and bought a 1935 Ford V-8 engine from a junkyard for $35 and installed it in our '29 roadster," Bill said.

"Tom milled the stock aluminum heads about one-eighth of an inch on an angle to obtain more compression, but he retained enough clearance for the valves."

They both had a hand in porting and relieving the engine intake passages, while Bill fabricated a two-carburetor intake manifold topped off with a pair of Stromberg 48s and a homemade exhaust system. Kenny Harman, who was working for George Riley at the time, ground the engine's camshaft.

"We used to go down to George's shop all the time and became good friends," Bill said.

Once everything was bolted in place, the car was taken up to Muroc for the speed trials, where they reached a disappointing 96 miles per hour before encountering ignition problems. The tachometer they'd installed showed the ignition cutting out at 4,750 rpm.

SPALDING MANUFACTURING COMPANY
After returning home, Tom, Bill, and John Blackwood disassembled the distributor and studied the problem. They concluded that if there was a second coil and a condenser, it might resolve the situation. These theories were tested on the Ford 40-B distributor in their shop class at high school.

"We moved one of the stock points," Bill said. "The stock Ford distributor had two sets of points pivots. We separated that, and put two coils and two condensers in that stock Ford ignition. By moving that point just so many degrees, it made it come out just right. Four of the cylinders functioned from one set of points, and the other set serviced the other four cylinders. Immediately, we got over six thousand rpm just as soon as we fired it up.

"We started the ignition business out of our shop at home, and Tom stayed in that business his entire life."

After the distributor proved successful, Tom and Bill paired off and opened their own part-time business, while John Blackwood started an ignition business. The brothers ran the Spalding Manufacturing Company from the shop on the orange ranch and charged a $25 exchange fee for a modified distributor. An ad run in a 1938 SCTA newsletter announced that the Spalding Manufacturing Company's modified had set the V-8 record at Harper Dry Lake with a Spalding ignition and listed their shop's address at 417 South Ben Lomond Avenue in Azusa, California.

Bill and Tom's father with the 1910 Harley-Davidson that he crashed at Pismo Beach en route to San Francisco in 1911. *Courtesy Bill Spalding*

A copy of Bill Spalding's SCTA timing tag for the B/Streamliner that set a record speed of 128.75 miles per hour on October 29, 1939. *Courtesy Bill Spalding*

DRY LAKES MODIFIED

Even though they had the ignition problem licked, Bill and Tom figured they'd reached the roadster's limit, so they put together a car built solely for racing, with an all-out racing engine and a much-modified chassis with a cut-down and narrowed body. Apparently, the boys were given a set of rare Riley overhead-valve heads for a 21-stud flathead V-8 by a race boat owner who couldn't get the setup to work properly. What really set their modified apart from the other dry lakes competitors, besides the Riley OHV heads, was that it had a Mercedes Roots blower forcing air into the engine. Bill purchased the blower from a foreign-car repair shop in Los Angeles for $100 and made an intake manifold to adapt the blower to the Riley heads. Kenny Harman came up with a suitable camshaft grind for the engine.

This setup proved to be very successful, with a two-way record at Harper Dry Lake of 120.5 miles per hour on October 2, 1938. Bill said that it reached an unofficial 145-miles-per-hour reading on one early-morning run when the conditions were perfect at the lakes. On August 24, 1941, they pushed the car up to 128.93 and later to 132 miles per hour in the Unlimited class V-8 Modified. Although they ran a modified body, because of the blower and Riley conversion, they were placed in the Unlimited class.

With the Spalding Manufacturing Company bankrolling their racing exploits, the brothers decided to go all out and build a streamliner for the dry lakes.

THE *CARPET SWEEPER*

This particular car was a stop-and-stare vehicle whenever it appeared at a dry lakes meet. The brothers made the leap from their record-setting modified to a record-setting full-bodied streamliner after seeing Jack Harvey's car. Harvey's prewar streamliner was one of the first—if not the first—full-bodied cars to run at the lakes. The design of this mammoth, flat-sided, airfoil-shaped vehicle, nicknamed the "Coca-Cola Stand" (no doubt in reference to the material that made up the car's metal body), was the Spalding brothers' inspiration. At the young age of 18 and without fully comprehending the complexities of airflow, resistance, lift, and so on, Bill used a piece of chalk to sketch out a design for a streamliner on the cement floor of their shop.

The basis for the streamliner was an Essex automobile frame surrounded by a steel skeletal framework and covered with thin sheets of steel to form the body; aluminum sheeting was too expensive. The corners of the body were rounded where the flat sides joined the flat deck, the nose sloped downward to a narrow rectangular opening across the width of the car to feed air into the engine and radiator, and the front wheels were left open to allow for turning. A small vertical vent on each side of the car allowed air to exit from the engine compartment, and the long tail section was similar to the nose as it slanted toward the ground. A side view of the streamliner resembled a cross-section of an aircraft wing—lots of lift. The driver was outfitted with the standard pair of old aviator's goggles, a leather flying helmet, and a safety belt. The twin-carbureted 1935 V-8 engine from their '29 roadster was used to propel the liner.

The *Carpet Sweeper* streamliner attracted a huge audience whenever it was at the dry lakes. It ran a Kenny Harman camshaft, the Spalding's converted ignition, and a homemade dual carburetor intake on a '35 21-stud V-8. Here, Tom, Bill, and an assistant push the streamliner to the starting line with the hood off the engine compartment. The car was officially timed at 128.75 miles per hour with runs in the 130 range. If it had gone much faster, the airfoil design would have proven disastrous for the driver. *Courtesy Bill Spalding*

With only the framework and engine completed, the vehicle performed high-speed runs up and down Gladstone Avenue, and by the tachometer, it was doing 80 miles per hour in low gear and approximately 120 in second. The brothers didn't confine racing to the dry lakes; before the streamliner was outfitted with its metallic skin, the car was involved in a little drag racing. They took on all comers at the drag strip, defeating everything from hot rod roadsters to motorcycles.

"I nicknamed the streamliner the *Grey Ghost* due to the gray paint job," Bill said. "It sounded kind of romantic, but as far as everyone else was concerned, it was branded the Spalding brothers' *Carpet Sweeper*, obviously due to the car's sloping, narrow, oblong front end."

The best two-way run average for the record-setting B/Streamliner was 128.75 miles per hour. Bill recalled that unofficially the car did get up into the 130s. The brothers took turns driving at the lakes, and for the short time the streamliner was running, its record was never bettered by a competitor. It's been reported that Tom and Bill were among the first to run alcohol in a Ford V-8 flathead at the dry lakes.

Bill mentioned that they'd discussed removing the bolted-on tail section of the streamliner in an attempt for higher speeds, but unfortunately they never got around to doing it. Had the tail section been removed, the car's top end speed may have been much higher.

"We probably would have gone ten miles faster; the car handled rather squirrelly because it was trying to lift the back section."

The brothers' involvement with their race cars only lasted until they'd achieved their goals, and as for the streamliner, plans had already been drawn up for something new. The *Grey Ghost* was unceremoniously dismantled for parts needed for the next project, and the remains were put aside and sat neglected for several years until the war. While her sons were serving in the military, Mrs. Spalding put the piles of sheet metal and steel framework out for the scrap-metal collectors to assist in the war effort.

POSTWAR

Once the war was over, Tom and Bill picked up where they'd left off with Spalding Ignition. There was an endless demand for speed equipment, and a hot ignition system was an integral part of any racing engine. Even though there was stiff competition from outfits such as Kong, Potvin, and the like, rebuilding and converting stock ignitions and repairing magnetos were the makings of a business.

Unfortunately, the business didn't expand fast enough to support both brothers, and when Bill was offered a job with the Harman & Collins camshaft company, he gave his part of the ignition business to his brother. Less than a year later, Bill left Harman & Collins to open his own camshaft-grinding business, and later on the two brothers united their businesses under one roof and changed the name to Spalding Custom Cams & Ignitions.

In 1953, Tom decided to invest in an automotive parts manufacturing opportunity in Mexico, leaving Bill to run both businesses. The venture in Mexico proved to be a washout, and Tom returned to Los Angeles the following year to take over the reins of the ignition business, about the same time Bill was offered a job with Ford. The camshaft-grinding division of the Spalding business was eventually sold off, and Tom moved the shop to 1617 South Myrtle Avenue in Monrovia, operating under the name of Spalding Products. Later on, he would move again to 454 East Duarte Road in Monrovia.

Tom realized that modifying stock ignition systems wasn't adequate to meet engine builders' demands for high-revving racing engines. In 1955, he came out with a totally new dual breaker-coil performance ignition system called the Flamethrower, which was guaranteed to work up to 10,000 rpm. He spent a considerable amount of time field-testing the system with promising results

and proved that the Flamethrower could meet the demands and perform under almost any racing situation. To show the effectiveness of his new ignition system, Tom installed the Flamethrower on a stock Studebaker V-8 and gained 12 horsepower with no other modifications to the engine.

Besides automotive ignitions and magnetos, Tom got caught up in the karting craze that took Southern California by storm in the late 1950s. He built a custom dynamometer to test out kart clutches and ignitions of his own design, receiving a patent for a centrifugal-type clutch in 1962. An article written by John Christy for the February 1961 issue of *Hot Rod* covered Tom as he ran dyno tests on a variety of kart engines. His dyno worked so well that, for $5, he offered complete plans on how to build a precision self-contained kart dynamometer mounted on a portable stand. The plans were sold through Kart-Tek, a subsidiary of Spalding Products.

A year later, he made the front cover of *Hot Rod*'s June issue with an English Anzani racing outboard motor–powered kart that he'd built to compete in the Super C class. The unique thing about the kart, besides the Anzani motor, was a gearbox designed by Tom that mounted to the engine's crankshaft to reverse the output rotation of the chain. It ran a double row of chains to handle the alcohol-burning, water-cooled, rotary-valve, 36-horsepower miniature monster, which was equipped with oversize disc brakes. How it fared on the track is not known, but surely it must have been an attention-getter.

When Ford introduced its DOHC Indy V-8 to the Speedway in 1963, the once-formidable Offenhauser was unceremoniously sent to the rear of the pack. To compensate for the horsepower discrepancies of the Offy, which hadn't seen any major modifications since its conception, numerous tests were performed with turbochargers and blowers with varying degrees of success. One dynamometer test indicated approximately 700 horsepower at around 6,000 rpm when the mag failed. Being constantly plagued with magneto failures, Dale Drake called on Tom to see what he had in the way of an electronic ignition system. After installing one of Tom's electronic outfits on the test engine, it perked up to 8,000 rpm without a miss and made more horsepower to boot. The Spalding electronic ignition was one of the driving forces that

The successful Hartman CRA track roadster as seen at Carrell Speedway and equipped with a Wayne-built 220-horsepower 12-port Chevrolet six-cylinder using a Spalding ignition and racing camshaft. From left are Wayne Horning, unknown, Bill Spalding, Harry Warner, Johnny Hartman, and Al Janick. *Dan Warner collection*

A 1950 Spalding advertisement by Tom used the CRA track roadster. *Courtesy Bill Spalding*

helped put the Offenhauser back into contention until its final run at the Speedway in 1980.

Tom received a patent in 1972 for his very innovative Spalding BDI ignition system. This capacitor discharge–type system consisted of a BDI trigger that provided the signal for the electronic power pack to fire. This trigger device consisted of an infrared light source, a rotating shutter, and a photo light detector. The BDI system was accurate and stable up to 15,000 rpm because of its solid-state electronics, and dyno tests showed a horsepower increase of up to 10 percent over other racing ignitions and magnetos. Spalding BDI ignitions were manufactured for domestic and foreign cars, all forms of race cars, and even motorcycles.

The success of the BDI ignition caught the attention of auto-parts maker Echlin, which was in the process of procuring profitable speed equipment manufacturers for its list of holdings. Tom decided that Echlin's offer was too good to refuse and turned over the keys to his business later in 1972. The Spalding Products name was dropped in favor of Accel, and for the next two years, Tom remained with his former company as head of research and development.

After a long and very successful career in speed equipment manufacturing that began in the 1930s, and after enjoying almost 30 years of retirement, Tom passed away on September 26, 2001, at the age of 81.

SPALDING CUSTOM CAMS

In the early speed equipment days, the only way to get your hands on a camshaft grinder was to make your own, as commercial units were prohibitively expense. So Bill purchased a used Landis cylindrical grinder for $3,500 and installed a camshaft grinding attachment of his own design. He made his own cam masters, and his first design was for the Chevrolet six, rather than for the popular Ford flathead V-8 that the majority of the cam-grinding shops of that era began with (excluding Chet Herbert and his Chevy roller-tappet camshafts). Spalding Custom Cams opened for business in Glendale, California, in 1947.

Bill recalled his first customer was Nick Brajevich, who had a Wayne 12-port head–equipped, Chevy six–powered CRA track roadster. The cam for this car had to be ground from a billet, as the Wayne head placed the exhaust ports on one side of the engine and the intake on the other, changing the stock valve layout. Nick's roadster hadn't accomplished much on the track, but in the first race after installing the Spalding 280 camshaft, the roadster set fast time in qualifying, took the eight-lap dash, and went on to win the main.

Before leaving to go work for Ford, Bill turned over the cam side of the business to his his nephew, Volvey Ayers Spalding II, to whom he taught the intricacies of camshaft grinding on the Landis grinder, as well as a smaller grinder used for motorcycle camshafts. Like his uncle, Volvey stayed with the cam business until something better came along. Less than a year after taking over the business, he sold Spalding Custom Cams to the Palmini Engineering Company of South San Gabriel, California. (Once Bill's business was no longer associated with his own, Tom renamed the ignition business Spalding Products.)

Bill said that about the most unique engine he ever ground camshafts for was a DOHC converted Studebaker V-8 engine designed by a good friend, Willis Utzman. Bill ground the engine's original four billet cams, which were later replaced with some ground by Ed Winfield. The engine also ran a Spalding ignition system. This engine was built to power an Indy car owned by J. C. Agajanian. During shakedown runs for the 1953 Indianapolis 500, the car broke the 200-mile-per-hour barrier, but that's as far as it got. At the time, it was the only engine besides the Novi to break the 200 mark at the Speedway. The only fault of the engine was that when Utzman turned the engine's crankshaft on a lathe and the bed wasn't long enough to handle the full length of the crankshaft, so he made an adapter to fit onto the crank's snout. This adapter turned out to be the demise of this fabulous 32-valve engine. When a member of the pit crew attempted to start the engine with a portable handheld starter, the added snout piece twisted, causing internal problems that ended any further running of the engine. Why it was never remedied and tried again is anyone's guess, but fortune saved the engine from extinction, and it is now on display in "Speedy" Bill Smith's fabulous museum in Lincoln, Nebraska.

THE SPALDING TRACK ROADSTER

The California Racing Association became a major player as it quickly grew from its humble beginnings of stripped-down street roadsters to well-disciplined, race-bred track roadsters. As the popularity of roadster racing grew, numerous speed equipment manufacturers either sponsored a car or directly fielded their own, as it was a great way to try out new products and also was effective advertising. Bill and Tom felt that a roadster would prove beneficial to their businesses, but it had to be a first-class project. As the saying goes, "No one remembers who came in second place."

Once plans were drawn up, it took only three weeks of concentrated work to come up with one of the most beautiful track roadsters that ever participated on a dirt track. The two brothers took a $5 1925 Model T body and transformed it into a thing of beauty; everything was done to perfection. Because of the class

The immaculate Spalding CRA '25 T track roadster looks its best. The boys didn't neglect a thing when they built this beauty. What wasn't painted bright orange was chromed. *Eric Rickman photo*

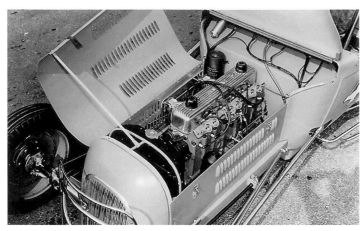

The Spalding track roadster's Wayne 12-port-equipped and Hilborn-injected 248-ci Chevy six. Naturally, the engine ran a Spalding ignition and camshaft. *Eric Rickman photo*

rules, the frame had to be that of an auto manufacturer—no prefab jobs. Tom wanted to use a Willys auto frame, but he couldn't find one that didn't have its share of stress cracks, holes, and general wear. To circumnavigate this little obstacle, he welded up an exact copy of a Willys frame. The frame passed tech inspection with no question of its authenticity. They put the same torsion bar and arm setup used on Kurtis midgets on the front end—easy enough, seeing that Bill's shop was located next to Johnny Hartman's shop, which manufactured torsion bar suspensions for Frank Kurtis. Hartman was already running the same style of front end on his own Chevy six–powered roadster that proved to be a record-setter both at the dry lakes and on the track.

A Pat Warren open-tube, quick-change rearend was installed to save weight. It was one of the first open-tube units ever manufactured and the first open-tube quick-change ever used on a track roadster. The aluminum radiator shell was hand-formed by the talented Art Ingles. Art worked for Frank Kurtis, manufacturing race car bodies. He also made the nosepiece for Barney Navarro's track roadster and is credited as the innovator of the kart.

Wayne Horning built up the 1949 248-ci Chevrolet six outfitted with a Wayne 12-port head, cast exhaust, and a three-carburetor manifold. The rest of the engine ran 14:1 compression, an in-out box, and a Spalding camshaft and ignition. Later, the three-carb intake was changed over to six carburetors, and in 1950, it received the first fuel-injection system that Stuart Hilborn manufactured for a Chevrolet. The body and frame were given a brilliant orange paint job, while everything else was either chrome or cadmium plated. Tom even had made his own cadmium-plating outfit and plated many of the car's smaller parts that weren't chromed. He wrote an article for the October 1950 issue of *Hot Rod* with the instructions on how to make a cadmium-plating setup.

The first time out for the roadster was on the mile dirt oval in Phoenix, Arizona, in 1950. Even though the track was in poor condition, Roy Prosser pushed the Spalding roadster to set fast time for the meet as well as a new lap record. Prosser went on to

take the eight-lap event, and in the main, he almost lapped the entire field. But, because of the rough track surface, the gas tank straps broke, forcing the car out of the race. Of the 30 roadsters that began that main event, only six cars crossed the finish line.

For its next five races, it set fast time, won both the eight-lap events and the mains in all five races, and all at different tracks. One of the main advantages the Spalding roadster had was its horsepower-to-weight ratio—more than 300 horsepower on alcohol to a lightweight 1,375 pounds—while the majority of track roadsters were running the heavier flathead V-8s with less horsepower and torque.

The car was finished in time to participate in the 1949 Bonneville National Speed Trials, taking its class in B/Modified Roadster. The following year, the roadster placed second with a run of 144.69 miles per hour. Once the bugs were worked out, the roadster ran a very fast 146 miles per hour in B class at an SCTA El Mirage lake meet.

The Spalding roadster had several drivers, with Roy Prosser as the main driver. Future Indy racer and camshaft grinder Dempsey Wilson was one of the drivers to race the car, and he had the reputation of crashing the roadster whenever someone spun out in front of him.

As the 1950 racing season came to a close, Tom and Bill decided to sell the car, as there wasn't the same money in track roadsters as there had been several years earlier, and the costs of racing outweighed the purses offered. Not able to sell it as a complete package, the roadster was parted out to various buyers across the country. Harold White bought the body and chassis, and drag raced it after installing a flathead V-8, before converting it back into a track roadster with a Hemi Chrysler to compete under the Ray Brown Automotive banner.

In 2002, Bill had the Spalding track roadster reproduced in miniature by the skilled model-maker Chuck Meschter of Hesperia, California. It took Chuck four months to build the intricately detailed model at a cost of $3,000.

CITY OF PASADENA STREAMLINERS

In the late 1940s, racing enthusiast Marvin Lee built a fairly radical open-wheeled streamliner for the lakes. The car featured torsion bar suspension front and back, a six-cylinder Chevrolet engine in the midsection of the car, and the driver sitting up front in an enclosed cockpit. The 248-ci 1942 Chevy ran a Wayne 12-port head. The Spalding brothers supplied the camshaft and ignition system, and

Marvin experimented with both multiple carburetion and Hilborn fuel injection.

When the streamliner was taken up to Harper Dry Lake for its maiden run, Bill, who had worked on the car, volunteered to be the test pilot. It was officially clocked at 153 miles per hour, but Bill says that at the end of the run the tachometer indicated approximately 175 miles per hour; because of the poor condition of the lakebed, there were no further high-speed runs that day. Later on, the car set the class record for B/Streamliner with a two-way average of 153.54 miles per hour, which at the time was the fastest two-way speed for an SCTA dry lakes meet.

In 1950, Marvin arrived at the week-long Bonneville Nationals with a totally new *City of Pasadena II* design that had a fully streamlined fiberglass body. It was powered by a 273-ci, Wayne Horning–built, 12-port GMC equipped with a Spalding cam/ignition and a Hilborn fuel-injection system. With "Puffy" Puffer driving, the car averaged 195 miles per hour, but during another run, the poor aerodynamics of the design sent it into a self-destructive tumble, totally destroying the streamliner. Luckily, Puffy sustained only minor injuries. Lee's design was similar to the Spaldings' prewar streamliner.

FORD MOTOR COMPANY

Bill retired from the camshaft business on July 5, 1954, thanks to two fellows whom he was acquainted with from his dry lakes racing days: Charlie Camp and Lowell Lewis.

"Charlie Camp came up one day and said, 'Bill, you got to report to the Ford Motor Company next week on the fifth of July downtown in L.A.,' " Bill said. "And I said, 'What for?' And Charlie said, 'To go to work.' Because of what I'd done with the Ford motors, those two guys had gone to their boss and said that they had a guy to fill the service rep job."

Bill looked at what the job had to offer and realized that the security and benefits outweighed the uncertainty of grinding camshafts. Bill began his long career with Ford as an instructor/representative, traveling throughout Arizona to visit Ford Motor dealers' service departments. Later, he became the instructor at the district service school for two years, and then transferred to the Ford aircraft engine division in Chicago, where Ford manufactured more jet engines licensed from Pratt & Whitney than any other company in the world. It was Bill's job to call on the Strategic Air Command air force bases, as they used Ford-manufactured jet engines in Boeing B-52s, C-130 transports, and tanker aircraft. Bill returned to California in 1958 to the Los Angeles district office, and in 1964 was assigned to the heavy-truck merchandising department as a sales engineer until retiring in 1974 after 20 years with Ford.

ARROYO GRANDE

In 1988, Bill married his wife, Diane, and settled in at her home in Arroyo Grande, California, a stone's throw from Tom's house. Bill began constructing an archery range on the property in 1990. The layout consisted of seven targets with 14 assorted shots and shooting distances up to 97 yards. It wasn't long before there were weekly shooting tournaments on the Spalding Range. The course

Bill holds a replica of their famous bright-orange 1925 CRA track roadster. *Author photo*

record of 443 points was set by Californian and archery champion Frank Smith in December 1991 and stood for over four years.

After settling down in Arroyo Grande, Bill and Diane began to frequent Trader Nick's, an eatery that offered fine food and a great view of the ocean. The walls of the hallway leading into the dining area were covered with photographs of the local area. One old black and white photo that caught Bill's attention was of a man standing behind an ancient motorcycle. Upon closer examination, Bill realized that the man was his father! Back in 1911, his father was riding a 1910 Harley-Davidson en route to college in San Francisco, and while traveling through the Pismo Beach area was involved in an accident and taken to the Good Samaritan Hospital. Fortunately for Bill's father, he sustained only minor cuts and bruises, but what was really fortunate for him (and Bill) was that he met Effie Gould there, who would eventually become Mrs. Spalding. Without that long-forgotten motorcycle accident in 1911, there would be no story about the Spalding brothers.

Trader Nick's has since been sold and is under new management with a new name, but the photographs of Bill's father and his Harley still remain on the entrance wall.

ELECTRIC PICKUP TRUCK

After retirement, Tom Spalding needed something to keep himself stimulated, and he felt that building a vehicle with an alternative power source would do the job. He found a compact Mazda pickup truck that would work out perfect for what he had in mind, as it had plenty of room for the vehicle's power source.

The four-cylinder gasoline engine was removed to make room for an electric motor, which in turn was mated up to the Mazda's stock three-speed transmission using a homemade adapter. Initially, 12 car batteries were installed under the truck bed, hidden from view and allowing usage of the bed. Later on, the batteries were installed on top of the bed to allow easy access for maintenance. At first, Tom had problems with erratic starts due to the instant high-torque output of the electric motor, but he solved this issue by designing a control that applied the power smoothly to the transmission.

The emissions-free Mazda pickup was a common sight in and around the Arroyo Grande area for numerous years. He enjoyed many years of trouble-free, silent driving and then sold the vehicle to a neighbor, who in turn used the electric truck as his daily ride to the local high school where he taught.

CHAPTER 19

Wayne Manufacturing

WAYNE HORNING AND HARRY WARNER

In a time when the Ford flathead V-8 was the undisputed king of its peers, there were a few who sidestepped the popular vote and dared to pet the underdog: the Chevrolet six-cylinder. Innovators such as Chet Herbert, Frank McGurk, Nicson, Harry Warner, and Wayne Horning could see potential in the overhead-valve engine. The equipment these speed merchants produced allowed performance aficionados an alternative choice to the flathead that was competitive on the track.

W. F. HORNING

The story of Wayne Manufacturing plays out like a soap opera, with players coming and going, and name changes that no doubt confused a great many six-cylinder enthusiasts who were only interested in purchasing hop-up equipment for their engines. It all began with one Chevrolet six-cylinder devotee named Wayne F. Horning, who is credited with conceiving the 12-port head for a passenger automobile engine.

When Chevrolet introduced the newly renovated six-cylinder in 1937, it attracted the attention of several dry lakes racers who were looking for something other than Henry's V-8. GM's engineers originally designed the engine to be cost-efficient to manufacture and to provide basic reliable transportation for the consumer. It didn't present itself as a threat to the flathead's domination in racing circles, but the hop-up potential of the overhead-valve design over the L-head engine was appealing to some. Wayne F. Horning gave the engine more than a casual glance and liked most of what he saw, except for the intake and port layout of the head. He was concerned that the layout of the three intake ports and four exhaust ports on the same side didn't offer much in the way of performance possibilities. He knew that the ideal way to achieve real performance from an engine of that configuration was to have the exhaust on one side and the intake on the other—inline racing engines were always set up with this layout—but in all domestic inline engines, the intake and exhaust manifolds were on the same side.

At a time when V-8 and four-cylinder Fords literally ruled the dry lakes, racers look upon Horning and fellow Chevrolet enthusiast John Hartman as if they were trying to get a dead horse to pull a wagon. But Wayne was looking further into the engine than the others, and in 1939, he began working on drawings for a 12-port head that would place the exhaust on one side and the intake on the other side. It was also in 1939 that war was declared in Europe, which impacted Wayne's work as a mechanical engineer at the Lockheed aircraft factory. The head had to be put aside for another day, and it wouldn't be until after World War II ended that Horning would get back to his plans for the 12-port head.

Dry lakes racer and speed equipment merchant Barney Navarro recalled that Wayne Horning had bought a brand-new Chevy around 1938 or 1939 and had entered it in a stock car race in Oakland. During the race, he'd put the car through a retaining fence, damaging the grille and front fender. He was unable to report the damage to his insurance company and did not have enough money to repair the damage, so

Opposite: Dan Warner's personal 1947 Chevy was outfitted with a Wayne five-carb intake, valve cover, and cast exhaust headers installed on a 292 GMC. Harry Warner is seen tightening up the header bolts. *Courtesy Dan Warner*

A full-competition Wayne 12-port Chevrolet shows six short straight exhaust pipes. *Courtesy Dan Warner*

The exhaust side of a 12-port-equipped six-cylinder engine. *Courtesy Dan Warner*

he drove the car on the street for numerous months until he saved up the funds for the repairs.

12-PORT HEAD

After being discharged from the navy at the end of the hostilities in the South Pacific, Wayne Horning collaborated with Jim Borger, a machinist he'd worked with at Lockheed, in opening the Western Mechanical Development Company with the purpose of developing a 12-port head for the Chevrolet.

The cast-iron, Wayne 12-port was designed with six large, rectangle-shaped intake ports on the left side and six large, round exhaust ports on the right side of the head. The combustion chamber was a squat oval shape, modeled closely after that of Ed Winfield's Model A rocker-arm head combustion chamber. He used Buick rocker arms for strength and increased valve lift, special push rods, dual valve springs, and modified 1947 Cadillac valves. Wayne incorporated the services of Frank Venolia to assist in designing and manufacturing

special cast-aluminum pistons, as the pistons controlled the compression ratio in the 12-port. He even named them Venolia pistons.

Though strictly a Ford flathead man in the early days, Barney Navarro said of the 12-port, "When you make an overhead, you've got to have the know-how that Wayne Horning had when he made his Chevy. That head was made right; that's why he sloped the ports out; he's got very little turn."

Before the company really got going, Borger decided to follow other interests and opened up his own machine shop, leaving Wayne in need of a partner—and that's where Harry Warner comes in. Wayne and Harry had worked together at Lockheed before the war, and Harry helped Wayne out at the dry lakes with his race car. After the war, Warner had moved back to Illinois, where his family was originally from. In 1947, Horning wrote and asked Harry to come back west and go into business with him. No doubt the Los Angeles snow-free winters had some influence on his decision to relocate back to the West Coast.

WAYNE MANUFACTURING COMPANY

Over the winter months of 1947 and 1948, the partnership of Horning and Warner was formed, and the company's name changed from Western Mechanical to the Wayne Manufacturing Company, which was then located at 3206 Fletcher Drive in Los Angeles. The partners didn't waste any time developing parts and, in 1948, were advertising in *Hot Rod*, offering a complete line of speed equipment for the Chevrolet six-cylinder. In addition to advertising in *Hot Rod*, Wayne wrote an article titled "Overhead Valves," selling the virtues of the Chevrolet six-cylinder engine.

RACING

In order to get some publicity on the head and work out any bugs that might inhabit the design, Wayne and Borger realized they needed to test it out under actual racing conditions. For reasons unknown, the first Horning-built engine outfitted with a 12-port was installed in an E/Runabout called the *Saw-C-Su* rather than in a race car. After a little developmental work, the boat began to take its fair share of checkered flags at Marine Stadium in Long Beach, enough so that it attracted interested buyers. Once the 12-port proved itself on the water, a head was installed on the 248-ci 220-horsepower Chevy that powered the *Hartman Torsion Bar Special*. Hartman's track roadster competed in the popular CRA circuit as well as at El Mirage, where it set the B class record of 147 miles per hour at the 1948 SCTA meet.

Probably the second car in 1947 to be outfitted with a 12-port was the CRA track roadster that belonged to Wayne's longtime friend Nick Brajevich. When the two were talking about the 12-port, Nick mentioned that his roadster, with the talented Andy Linden driving, could have won the CRA's Little Indy 500 race at Carrell Speedway in 1947 if Andy hadn't run over a low guard post when coming into the infield during a pit stop. He also said that with Wayne's head, there was no lack of power, as the little Chevy had pulled into the lead and would have gone all the way, and would have been great advertising for Wayne Manufacturing if it had done so.

In the late 1940s, Marvin Lee built a radical, open-wheeled streamliner called the *City of Pasadena* that had torsion-bar suspension on both the front and rear of the car, a Horning 12-port '42 Chevy mounted in the midsection, and the driver up front sitting in an enclosed cockpit. The car set an average of 153.54 miles per hour, the fastest that was ever recorded at an SCTA dry lakes meet at that time. For the 1950 Bonneville Nationals, Marvin built a totally new *City of Pasadena II* featuring a fiberglass-bodied streamliner powered by a Horning-built GMC with a new 12-port head. Only the driver's helmet and windscreen broke up the car's clean lines. Regrettably, the streamliner's outline was very similar to that of the crosssection of an aircraft wing, and this shape no doubt led to a near-fatal accident. On the salt flats, driver "Puffy" Puffer had made several runs in the vehicle before the incident, with the best at 195.65 miles per hour.

Lou Senter of Ansen Auto was on hand to witness the horrific scene. Lou said, "The *City of Pasadena* streamliner at Bonneville in 1950 was a perfect airfoil. Unfortunately, the only thing to disrupt the lift was two exhaust pipes coming out the back of the car. Puffy Puffer was driving and was up over 200 miles per hour before it just took off like an airplane. It flipped and rolled, demolishing the car, and Puffy luckily ended up with a small cut on his ear and minor bruises—saved by a well-built frame. The heavy primer-gray fiberglass body just scattered."

After surviving the ordeal with only minor injuries, Puffer wrote an article about his exploits titled "On Your Head at 200 MPH!" that was published in the March 1951 issue of *Hot Rod*. He said that he figured the car could have reached at least 225 miles per hour with Horning's 285-horsepower GMC six. Before the crash, he recalled the tach read 4,700 rpm, which equated to approximately 197 miles per hour, and the last tach reading was 5,300 rpm before all hell let loose. After a series of flips and rolls, the remains landed on the wheels right-side up—Lady Luck and sound engineering were credited in saving his life. If it hadn't been for that ill-timed accident, and if Puffy had broken the record, the publicity the 12-port GMC Horning head would have received would have been phenomenal. Puffy was estimated to be traveling about 210 miles per hour when it all let go, and he no doubt would have bested the So-Cal streamliner high speed that day of 209 miles per hour.

THE SPLIT

Even though sales were up and business was very good, the Warner and Horning partnership was just two years old when the men decided to go their separate ways. At that point, it got confusing for those six-cylinder enthusiasts who were interested in dealing with what once had been the Wayne Manufacturing Company—it was almost as if the company had a split personality. In the course of the breakup, Harry Warner bought Wayne Manufacturing, along with the patterns to manufacture the Chevrolet 12-port head, and he relocated the business to 3517 Encinal Avenue in La Crescenta, California. Wayne Horning remained at the original Fletcher Drive address under the new name of the Wayne F. Horning Engine Company.

The news of the split was officially released by an ad in *Hot Rod*'s July 1950 issue in which Harry advertised that "Wayne Mfg. Co." had moved lock, stock, and barrel to new facilities and would

The exhaust side of a Wayne 12-port engine shows the huge round ports that accommodated a lot of volume. Note the attractive finned cast-aluminum Wayne side-cover plate. *Courtesy Dan Warner*

specialize in Chevrolet and GMC equipment as well as furnish complete performance engines. Wayne's ad in the same issue, under "Wayne F. Horning," also advertised Chevy and GMC parts and competition engines. It appeared that neither business was in the position to produce 12-port heads at the time.

Although both fellows advertised that they specialized in Chevrolet and GMC equipment and engines, it was Harry Warner who first advertised that the Chevrolet 12-port was back in production later on in 1950. A month or two later, Wayne Horning introduced his new, cast-iron, GMC 12-port head, just in time to try it out in Marvin Lee's ill-fated *City of Pasadena II* at the Bonneville Nationals. Not to be outdone by his old business partner, Harry soon introduced his own version of a 12-port head for the GMC six.

Wayne Horning's GMC 12-Port
Wayne Horning chose to manufacture his latest GMC 12-port head in cast iron, and its internal configuration differed than that of his Chevrolet 12-port design. He simplified the port layout by altering the factory valve design, exchanging the exhaust valves at each end with intake valves, and two exhaust valves sat back to back in the center of the head. The head contained a round combustion chamber with vertical valves and large water cavities in the casting. Like the Chevrolet 12-port head, the Jimmy utilized as much of the stock valvetrain as possible, and again, regrettably, like his previous design, Wayne Horning stayed with the vertical valve layout, restricting the valve size. The main drawback to this head was the added expense that the engine builder encountered in having to buy a specially ground billet camshaft to match the altered valve layout. But anyone working on the head would be pleased to see that the two-piece cast-aluminum valve cover permitted the top half to be removed without any oil leakage, which was convenient when adjusting the valves. Wayne was not just developing the head but a complete racing engine, as Don Francisco reported in his two-part article on the Horning GMC in *Hot Rod* in 1951. The story was a closeup on the all-out racing engine built by Wayne that had propelled Marvin Lee's unlucky *City of Pasadena* streamliner across the Bonneville Salt Flats the previous year.

Many years down the road, Nick Arias had an opportunity to talk to Wayne Horning about the GMC head that he'd designed. Nick recalled, "I said, 'Wayne, answer me a question that's been bugging me for 50 years. When you did your head for the Jimmy, how come you put a 90-degree bend in the intake instead of 45 like the Chevy?' He looked at me and said, 'Dumb!' " Nick said, "Howard was smart; when Howard copied [Wayne's head], he used the 45-degree entry."

Horning produced an estimated 12 cast-iron, 12-port, GMC heads before bowing out of the speed equipment business altogether in late 1951. He sold off the GMC head patterns to another six-cylinder specialist named "California" Bill Fisher, and the carburetor manifolds, piston patterns, and related equipment were sold to McGurk Engineering. Wayne moved from manufacturing automotive parts to manufacturing specialized equipment for the aerospace industry, but old habits and interests are hard to bury, years later he decided to give a hand in designing a novel powerplant for boats using an automobile engine.

Harry Warner's Wayne GMC 12-Port

The idea for a 12-port head must have been on the back burner prior to the breakup, because as Wayne was introducing his newest creation, so was Harry, although the heads did differ internally. The Wayne cast-iron, 12-port, GMC head (later cast in aluminum) was unique in that it didn't have the combustion chamber in the head but rather in the area above the piston at TDC and the block deck surface. The engine builder could purchase a particular set of Wayne pistons that would give him the compression ratio he needed. Harry advertised that the combustion chamber and valve location were very similar to that of the Rolls-Royce Merlin engine. He also mentioned that the head was designed so that the person building up an engine could use the maximum number of stock parts to reduce costs and a special billet camshaft was not required. Unfortunately, a drawback to the head was the layout of the vertical valves, which resulted in the engine bore limiting the diameter of the valves that might be used; if they'd been placed on an incline, larger valves could have been used with better flow characteristics.

WAYNE PRODUCTS

After several years on Encinal Avenue in La Crescenta, the Wayne Manufacturing shop was relocated to East Broadway in Glendale and then in 1954 to South Victory Boulevard in Burbank. Even though he was casting and machining from 10 to 12 Chevy 12-port heads monthly, Harry began to introduce other items the six-cylinder aficionado would need to build anything from a hot street engine to the ultimate racing job. With the introduction of his GMC 12-port, the Wayne catalog included crankshaft kits, pistons, main caps, bearings and rings, GMC rods, Spalding ignitions and cams, cast exhaust manifolds, and multiple-carburetor intake manifolds for both engines. For those enthusiasts who couldn't afford a 12-port, Harry offered stock Chevrolet heads that had been filled and milled with compression ratios up to 10:1 at $80 exchange. He even came out with a transmission conversion kit to adapt the Chevrolet or GMC block to fit the popular Ford transmission.

Not to miss out on a business opportunity, Wayne Manufacturing began to offer complete, ready-to-run, performance Chevrolet and GMC sixes; the company would also build a custom engine to whatever specifications the customer required. The basic Wayne engines were hot street jobs equipped with reworked stock heads and produced anywhere from 135 to 175 horsepower. Next, there were 12-port-equipped engines for those with deep pockets who wanted a true racing engine. For powerboat racers, Harry offered a 244-ci 240-horsepower marine engine and a 248-ci track engine pumping out 245 horsepower. These Wayne ready-to-run engines ranged from $500 to $1,150.

Although the majority of his business was conducted all across the United States, Wayne-built racing engines did find themselves in South America, where they were used for stock car road racing. The internationally famous driver Juan Fangio won the Buenos Aires Grand Prix in 1950 with a Wayne Chevrolet–powered car.

When General Motors had released its Chevrolet V-8 to the public in 1955, Harry could see that the market was about to change. In keeping with the times, he introduced cast-aluminum Chevrolet V-8 valve covers that gave the appearance of a dual-overhead-cam engine. Not entirely giving up on the Chevy six, he also came out with a four-barrel intake manifold that provided a 16-horsepower increase over the stock job.

Bob Toros and Nick Arias had been renting shop space from Harry. In late 1957, Bob relocated across the street to his new location, and Harry decided to move on to other interests, selling the complete Wayne Chevrolet 12-port package to Toros. Bob then sold the 12-ports under the Toros Equipment Company name. Why he didn't also purchase Harry's GMC 12-port is unknown; someone obviously did, but it was never put into production. Harry estimated that the total production of his Wayne Chevy and GMC 12-ports amounted to around 200 units, including those built when he and Horning were still working together.

A side view of an all-out Wayne-equipped GMC with Hilborn fuel injection. *Courtesy Dan Warner*

Compression Risers

Though he wasn't into flathead equipment, Harry did observe one small glitch in the L-head design that could be improved upon with little expense to the engine owner. To circumnavigate the expense of buying high-compression aluminum cylinder heads, a lot of flathead owners opted for the fill process. The stock, cast-iron heads were heated and the combustion chambers were filled with welding rod to take up excess volume, followed by the labor-intensive and time-consuming job of grinding the weld into a suitable shape. In 1950, Wayne Manufacturing came out with cast-iron head inserts to replace the filling process. With Harry's inserts, the buyer could choose what compression ratio was needed and simply arc weld the insert in place, as compression ratios were available up to 8.5:1 for street-driven engines and the inserts were not advised for all-out racing engines.

Wayne DOHC Six-Cylinder

Sometimes the timing is never right, as was the case with Harry and an experimental engine he was designing. This engine was based on an inline, GM six-cylinder with a DOHC 12-port head containing 12 valves (with a 24-valve 12-port in the works). Harry's son, Dan, said that his dad was fascinated with the Mercedes 300 SL DOHC six-cylinder engine and that was what he modeled his version on. It's been reported that Harry had a prototype DOHC engine that had seen time on a testbed, and a photograph shows an uncompleted DOHC engine equipped with a Hilborn injection system. But this is where bad timing killed the project, or so it is believed. In 1955, Chevrolet unleashed an uncomplicated, light-weight V-8 engine that had loads of performance potential. Harry could see the writing on the wall, and not letting his ego get in the way of clear thinking, he shelved the DOHC idea for good.

Chevrolet's introduction of its groundbreaking V-8 engine foreshadowed the fall of the six-cylinder. As the popularity of GM's V-8 grew along with the engine's cubic inches, the demand for six-cylinder speed equipment fell off, especially for an expensive 12-port head. Harry manufactured equipment for the six-cylinder until 1957, when he sold out and went into doing machine shop work. After relocating his shop to Saugus, California, Harry was bit by the karting craze of the early 1960s, and he manufactured live-axle kits, sprockets, manifolds, and more for the little chainsaw engine–powered speed demons. Besides the karting stuff, Harry did custom machine shop work and produced work for the Jet Propulsion Laboratory in Pasadena until he finally closed the doors of Wayne Machine Shop Service in 1973.

DAN WARNER

Growing up in the midst of the family business, Dan Warner spent a great deal of his teenage years working in the shop after school and on weekends. It was only natural that he also would be partial to the inline six and had his '47 Chevy equipped with Wayne equipment for power to get him to school on time. Dan described how his dad got into manufacturing speed equipment: "It was while Dad was working at the Lockheed plant as a pattern-maker and machinist that he first met Wayne Horning. My dad had moved out to Los

Angeles in the late 1930s to work at the Lockheed aircraft plant and after the war returned to Illinois to run the family business.

"After the war, Wayne Horning and Jim Borger worked on designing a 12-port cylinder head for the six-cylinder Chevrolet. Wayne called my dad to come back out to California to go into partnership with him after Borger left the business. About 1947 or '48 the two entered into a partnership to start up a business and changed the company's name from Western Mechanical Development to Wayne Manufacturing. Whether it was person-ality differences or who knows what, but several years later the partnership broke up, with Dad keeping the 'Wayne' name along

Harry, right, talks to Argentinean Grand Prix driver Jorge Daponte. They're discussing the *Wayne Manufacturing Special* that was entered at the Indianapolis 500 in 1953. The car was motivated by a 12-port 268-ci GMC six. The engine was built by Nick Arias Jr. (Arias Pistons) and Bob Toros (Venolia Pistons), both of whom were employed at the Wayne shop. *Courtesy Dan Warner*

with the Chevy head pattern, while Horning went solo and came out with a 12-port GMC six-cylinder head.

"My dad was enamored with the mid-1950s Mercedes 300 SL. When he designed a dual-overhead camshaft head for the GMC six, it was along the same lines as the Mercedes head, but unfortunately the head was never completed. He was going to incorporate desmodromic valves in the heads design, and what did exist of the castings, patterns, and blueprints just disappeared into oblivion.

"While attending high school, I worked part-time for my dad and recall the time I helped ready three new cars for the Pan American Road Race. Wayne Manufacturing was contracted by a client to buy three 1953 Chevrolets that were to be run in the Pan-Am race, and I helped in the preparation of the cars; whether it's fact or not, I kind of remember that all three cars never made it to the finish line. It seems that as soon as they were across the border into Mexico, the Chevrolets were pulled from the race and quickly shipped to South America to be sold for a high profit. Apparently, the owner just wanted to get them across the border duty-free." Now there's a bit of entrepreneurial spirit.

Sometimes a little ingenuity helps out all around, as was the case when Dan's mother found a way to assemble the company's catalog and help out her Cub Scout pack. Dan said, "She was a Cub Scout den leader and got the young lads to lay out the catalog pages in order, and she would staple the finished product together, and the junior scouts earned a badge and a little financial remuneration for their efforts."

HARRY WARNER'S ROADSTER

When it came to building a hot rod in the prewar days, it seems 99.9 percent of the cars built were based a Ford product. In reality, the percentage wasn't that high, but it sure does look like it from all the old photos. Similarly, the engine of choice was usually one of Ford's four- or eight-cylinder jobs. Harry Warner followed the norm when he first built his street rod in 1940.

His '33 Ford roadster was a complete frameup rebuild. The frame joints were welded for added strength, a two-speed Columbia rearend and an up-to-date hydraulic braking system were installed, the windshield was cut down 2 inches and the steering wheel lowered 2 inches, and the seat was lowered and moved back 2 inches—a lot of engineering and cutting just to get that certain look. For motivation, a '39 Merc V-8 was hopped up and installed under the engine hood.

Everything was fine until Harry bought out Wayne Horning's half of the company. It didn't exactly look good to be driving around in a street rod powered by an engine opposite to what you were manufacturing speed equipment for. If you aren't going to run your own stuff, why should anyone else? Out came the flathead, and in went a '46 Chevy six. To reduce the expense of the transformation, Harry machined his own engine adapter to mate up to the Ford clutch assembly. The Chevy was outfitted with a 12-port head, cast headers, three carburetors, a Spalding ignition, and a Winfield camshaft. When all the nuts and bolts were on and tightened, he took the roadster over to Nicson Engineering

The record-setting 1937 Chevrolet coupe of Nick Arias Jr. and Bob Toros as seen at an unidentified hot rod show. In 1954 the pair traveled to Bonneville where the car set a B/Coupe class record of 138.41 miles per hour powered by a Wayne 12-port Chevy six; it took C/Coupe with a Wayne 12-port GMC six. *Courtesy Dan Warner*

and ran the car on Nicson's chassis dynamometer. There was approximately 162 horsepower at the rear wheels, and the car could turn a respectable 90 miles per hour at the drag strip, which wasn't too shabby for a daily driver.

One of the unique features of this street rod was the way Harry designed the exhaust system. Normally, a six-cylinder engine used one exhaust pipe out the rear of the car; Harry's had two, but not with the usual low rumble of a flathead. After the exhaust left the dual Wayne cast headers, the pipes ran into a common butterfly valve, which split the exhaust. Under daily driving conditions, the exhaust was routed through a muffler and out the tailpipe, but when the need arose for a little more power, Harry activated the solenoid-controlled valve from the driver's seat. This valve allowed the exhaust gases to flow freely out the rear of the car via a straight pipe, no doubt surprising all within hearing distance at the crackle of an inline six over the deep, throaty rumble of a flathead. Nothing ever stays the same, and eventually the six got bounced in favor of Chevy V-8.

INDY 500

Since the Brickyard reopened in 1946, there have been a variety of challengers for the checkered flag at Indianapolis. Usually, any attempt to displace the mighty Offenhauser came from thoroughbred racing engines such as the Novi or Maserati, not from a pushrod six-cylinder domestic job.

But in 1951, there were two inline sixes entered, one a Chevrolet and the other a GMC. The *Johnson Special* ran a Wayne-equipped Chevrolet, and even with 265 horsepower on straight methanol and turning a respectable 125 miles per hour, it failed to qualify for the race. The Jimmy was collaboration between Wayne

Horning and John Koehnle with a 12-port Horning-equipped GMC running in Koehnle's homemade chassis. Originally, the race car was to be sponsored by *Hot Rod*, but the name "Hot Rod" was not allowed to appear on a race car due to existing AAA regulations at the time. The name was changed to the *Motor Trend Special*, but it also failed to make the show.

For the 1953 Memorial Day Classic, Wayne Manufacturing supplied two entries with racing engines. Wayne built a 2-port GMC for George Wilson and Gabe Sacco of Pennsylvania; the cost of the engine was a bargain at $1,500 when compared to a race-proven $7,000 Offenhauser engine. The total cost of the Wilson and Sacco entry, including engine, was under $6,000—$1,000 less than an Offy engine alone. Unfortunately, the fellows couldn't get the car up to speed to qualify for the race; apparently, the extra thousand bucks did make a difference!

The other entry was the underfunded Jorge Daponte race car, which came all the way from Argentina to Los Angeles to have Harry install one of his Chevrolet engines in the chassis prior to setting off for the Brickyard. Serious racing costs money, and regrettably, this hopeful just missed making the show by a reported 1 mile per hour. Nick Arias said that if he and Bob Toros had been able to work as the pit crew for Daponte's *Wayne Manufacturing Special*, they might have squeaked him into the race with a little nitro. Unfortunately, close only counts in slow dancing and hand grenades, and even though neither of these assembly-lines engines actually made the show, they were capable.

FISHER GMC 12-PORT

When Wayne Horning decided that it was time to get out of the speed equipment business in the late 1951, "California" Bill Fisher stepped in and purchased the GMC 12-port patterns, parts, and manufacturing rights. At the time, Bill was involved with Chevy and GMC sixes. Under the name of Fisher Automotive of Los Angeles, he kept the Horning-Fisher alive by having three or four new heads cast in iron. Once those were sold, he changed over to having the heads cast in aluminum, producing a weight savings of 32 pounds per head. In switching to aluminum, he designed cast-iron valve seats in the shape of a figure eight, which were installed when the head was being cast to ensure a secure fit. He retained Horning's valve configuration and had to utilize the specially ground camshaft to suit this layout. Once all of the Wayne Horning two-piece valve covers were used up, Bill came out with the same valve cover but with "Fisher-GMC" cast on the top cover.

A Fisher Automotive Engineering ad in 1953 offered the Fisher-GMC 12-port in a complete kit form that included a Howard steel-billet camshaft, complete valvetrain, intake manifold, and racing pistons, all for $495. The ad went on to say that all the buyer needed was a 270-ci GMC short block and Hilborn fuel injection for a guaranteed 1 horsepower per cubic inch on methanol. Besides manufacturing the 12-port, Bill also offered the Fisher Dual-Coil conversion kit for Chevy and GMC distributors and put out a booklet entitled *GMC Speed Manual* to assist hot rodders in building up a Jimmy six-cylinder. (Bill had previously published how-to-hop-up booklets on the Chevy six and flathead V-8 Ford.)

During the time Bill offered the Fisher-GMC 12-port for sale, he produced an estimated 15 to 20 aluminum heads. In total, there were approximately 25 to 30 Wayne Horning/Fisher 12-port heads manufactured, including both cast-iron and aluminum. There was a good writeup about both the Wayne Chevrolet and Fisher-Horning GMC 12-port heads in the December 1954 issue of *Car Craft*.

Eventually, Bill moved on to other interests and sold off the Fisher 12-port to Hoy Stevens from Fredericktown, Ohio. Stevens had purchased a 12-port head from Bill in 1956 for his GMC-powered sprint car, with which he competed in the All American Racing Club (AARC) racing circuit. Once the patterns were in his possession, Stevens made some alterations to the combustion chamber and had four heads cast. In turn, he sold the 12-port patterns to another interested buyer.

Not removing himself completely from the automotive field, in 1965, Bill Fisher became the president of HP Books, which published automotive books on everything from carburetors to turbochargers.

ARIAS-BIGELOW-TOROS

Today, the Arias name is associated with high-quality performance pistons and exotic engines. But it wasn't always so. Like the majority of speed equipment manufacturers, Nick Arias started off as a teenager in love with hot rodding, and in the late 1940s, he joined the Photons car club with his buddies, Kenny Bigelow and Bob Toros. His activity at the dry lakes and the drag strip earned Nick the handle, "The Spy," as his keen eye observed the little speed nuances other engine builders were secretly using.

While stationed in Korea, Nick received the sad news that his longtime friend Kenny Bigelow was killed in a crash while racing at the dry lakes in 1951. After receiving the news, Nick and another friend sent money to Kenny's mom to buy the remnants of the wrecked '37 Chevrolet coupe. Apparently, Bigelow had been attempting to better Bob Pierson's RTA A/Coupe record.

Nick said, "Kenny's coupe was a street rod and was even outfitted with push button windows. He'd take out the seat to go racing at El Mirage and had two blocks of wood that he'd bolt to the floor and then attach a bucket seat to the blocks. He installed the seat-belt bolts at ninety degrees rather than at a forty-five-degree angle that would have held him back into the seat in case of an accident. When he crashed, he slid downward out of the seat and died in the accident." Kenny Bigelow's fatal crash occurred on the last day of the RTA 1951 Season Finals meet at El Mirage; it was the first RTA fatality since 1948.

After the service, Nick teamed up with Bob Toros around 1952 and bought a '37 Chevrolet coupe to race at the dry lakes. They wanted to go after and claim the class record in memory of their deceased friend, Kenny Bigelow. The coupe was to be an all-out race car, and they made it as safe as possible. The interior was completely gutted, a full roll cage was installed, and the stock rearend was replaced with a Ford unit coupled up to a quick-change. Kenny's Chevy six had survived the fatal crash and was updated with a Chet Herbert roller camshaft. At Bonneville, they ran the Chevy in A/Coupe class at 138 miles per hour with a 12-port Wayne Chevy head and then in B/Coupe at 150 miles per hour with a 12-port GMC engine at same meet. Bob Toros still has the original Bigelow Chevrolet engine.

In a rather strange twist of events, while rebuilding Bigelow's engine, Nick went over to Wayne Manufacturing to buy a set of new pushrods. After a long conversation with Nick, Harry was impressed enough with the young fellow that he offered Nick a job to run the shop. At the time, Nick was working for Sharp Engineering, machining and drilling cylinder heads and intake manifolds. If it hadn't been for the unfortunate demise of his good friend, Nick wouldn't have been rebuilding an engine to run in his memory, and Nick wouldn't have been over at Wayne's buying pushrods and ending up with a job. Nick's and Bob's futures were both heavily influenced by that fatal crash on the dry lakes.

A good-looking Wayne-equipped GMC six outfitted with triple Stromberg 97s, intake, valve cover, and cast exhaust headers. The 292-ci engine put out 175 horsepower at the rear wheels on a chassis dyno. *Courtesy Dan Warner*

A Wayne-equipped and modified six-cylinder installed in a Siata sports car. Note the lengthy carburetor linkage. *Courtesy Dan Warner*

At the Wayne shop, Nick got hands-on experience with everything from hopping up engines to porting cylinder heads, and after several months, when they were busy enough to hire another employee, Nick got Harry to hire Bob Toros. While working at Warner's shop, Nick had the opportunity to build a Chevy six-cylinder that would power an entrant for the 1953 Indianapolis 500. Jorge Daponte commissioned Wayne Manufacturing to prepare an engine for his car to be entered in the Memorial Day Classic. Nick recalled that they picked up Daponte and his race car at the Los Angeles harbor dockyards and got the car ready for Indy back at the Wayne shop. Regrettably, Daponte had barely sufficient funds to get himself and his car to the track in Indiana, let alone both Nick and Bob to whom he offered the chance to pit crew. To add to their misery, neither one had any extra money to take off work and pay his own expenses to Indianapolis. Nick believed that if they'd been there, they could have livened up the engine enough with a little nitro to have helped Daponte make the show.

VENOLIA PISTON COMPANY

Frank Venolia owned a house on the corner of San Fernando Road and Fletcher Drive in Los Angeles and had built a machine shop in his backyard that faced onto Fletcher. He was a mold-maker for High Duty Pistons in Los Angeles and rented out his shop space to Wayne Horning and Harry Warner for Wayne Manufacturing.

Venolia was never in the piston business himself, although he owned a piston grinder and a turret lathe and could have easily manufactured pistons. He did, however, make the piston die for Wayne Horning that was designed to use a GMC rod in a Chevrolet. Frank had hired Charlie Robins of Robins Pistons in east Los Angeles to cast the pistons, and Frank machined them for Horning. After the split between Harry and Wayne, Harry ended up with the Wayne

Chevrolet head patterns and moved the operation into a garage behind his own home. Horning stayed on at Venolia's shop and designed his 12-port GMC head until selling out to Bill Fisher.

Later on, Nick wanted Frank to make him a piston mold for the newly introduced Chevrolet 265-ci V-8 engine. He remembered Venolia as an old, one-legged, eccentric grouch who wanted nothing else but to retire. Nick said, "If Venolia got to dislike you, he called you a bozo, and all of a sudden Toros and I were bozos." Nick and Bob paid Harry Warner to buy Frank's machine shop and then moved the equipment into a spot they'd rented in Harry's shop at 432 South Victory Boulevard in Burbank, staying there until the partnership dissolved in 1957.

Nick and Bob created the Venolia Piston Company in 1956, using Frank's name because it was well known locally and the two entrepreneurs decided to capitalize on its popularity. Until the piston venture took off, the pair did general machine work to help pay the bills. Once married and in need of a steady paycheck, Nick sold out in 1957.

The Wayne 12-port head was designed for the Chevy 235-ci six, and since Chevrolet had come out with a 261-ci engine, Bob had to update the patterns to fit the newer engine before going into production. From late 1957 to 1960, he sold 26 of the revised cast-iron heads.

As the forged piston began to make itself known in the high-performance marketplace, Nick Arias and Joe Pisano formed a partnership with Bob in 1963 to go into the piston business. Nick left the partnership in 1969, when he bought the Ansen Piston line from Lou Senter of Ansen Automotive and started and Arias Pistons with three employees. Because he was starting off with a proven product, it didn't long for Nick's new venture to become one of the leaders in the specialty piston business. In 1972, Nick branched out into manufacturing a hemi-head for the Chevrolet V-8 and proceeded to design complete performance engines that have powered everything from race boats to monster trucks.

Hard work and dedication does pay off, as Nick Arias was inducted into the Dry Lakes Hall of Fame in 1999 and was recognized as the Man of the Year by the Bonneville 200-Mile-Per-Hour Club, also in 1999.

The successful *Tatum Engineering Special* sports car from Stockton, California, competed with a Wayne 12-port 292-ci GMC with three Zenith side-draft carburetors. *Courtesy Dan Warner*

Harry Warner adjusts the carburetors on the powerboat *Saw-C-Su* that competed in the E/Runabout class at Marine Stadium in Long Beach. Wayne Horning is looking into the cockpit on the far side of the boat. *Courtesy Dan Warner*

CHAPTER 20

Weber Racing Cams

HARRY WEBER

The Weber Tool Company can trace its origins back to 1925, when Alexander Weber opened a machine shop at 4200 Whiteside Street in Los Angeles. It began as a general machine shop that swiftly developed a reputation for high-quality work and carrying a first-class line of precision machine tools. Eventually, Alex ventured into a profitable sideline business of designing and manufacturing his own line of precision tools under the Weber trademark. He had a knack for inventing tools that would simplify jobs that a skilled machinist would need a fair length of time to complete.

One such tool was the Weber crankshaft turner. This precision tool could be used on any metal lathe that could swing a crankshaft between its centers. The device could turn any crankshaft from 1 to 18 inches in diameter and was advertised as being easy to operate. Another Weber-designed specialty item was a portable crankshaft grinder. This tool was especially useful in commercial boat repairs, where removing a heavy-duty crankshaft from a large marine engine meant high costs and downtime for the boat owner. With the Weber portable grinder, the crank journals could be ground without removing the crankshaft from the engine, enabling repairs at a fraction of the normal cost.

Johnny Ryan of Taylor & Ryan Engine Rebuilding recalled the time as a teenager when he ran into problems with a Model B engine he was building. He couldn't find anyone to grind and balance the crankshaft because the counterweights were welded onto the crank.

"You just couldn't turn it and grind it; no one had the proper facility to do it," Johnny said. "I took the crank to a commercial crankshaft company in downtown Los Angeles, only to be told that there was only one outfit that could possibly grind it: the Weber Tool Company." John's Model B crankshaft was similar to the large marine crankshafts that had welded counterweights, and Weber's crankshaft grinder did the job for him.

THE WEBER BROTHERS

Bill and Harry Weber received a formal education in the workings of a machine shop at an early age. Bill and the younger Harry were schooled in the art of skillful craftsmanship under the tutelage of their mechanical-perfectionist father. Growing up in City Terrace in east Los Angeles, Bill attended Montebello High School, where he majored in machine shop practices. Being four years older than Harry, he was already working for their father when Harry graduated from Lincoln High in 1936. Although Alexander's shop wasn't automotive-oriented, his sons were entrenched in the sport.

Of the two brothers, Bill Weber was the original hot rodder. In 1935, he acquired one of Ford's flathead V-8s, an engine that was still waiting to be discovered by the four-cylinder racing fraternity. After studying the layout of the engine, he decided to try something quite radical for the time. According to Johnny Ryan, Bill designed a reverse-flow camshaft, where the intake ports become the exhaust ports and vice versa. Bill had rigged up a grinding fixture on one of his father's lathes to grind the cam. Years later, Tucker Cams of Los Angeles came out with a similar camshaft for the flathead that ran with some

Opposite: Harry Weber, standing at far right, hands a camshaft to an attractive woman at a hot rod show in San Francisco in 1948. The engine in the picture was built on-site by the Hubbard Auto Parts crew. Harry donated the camshaft as a prize. *Eric Rickman photo*

This is part of the early Weber Tool Company's machine shop that Harry and Bill Weber practically lived in as kids.
Courtesy John Ryan

degree of success. Ryan mentioned that the engine was built, but the results must not have been up to Bill's expectations, because it wasn't long before he was experimenting with Model A and B cam profiles for friends and some dry lakes racers.

When he was old enough to have a driver's license, Bill joined the Gophers car club, and it was this interest in hot rods that influenced younger brother Harry. The two brothers often slept in a converted loft above their father's machine shop on weekends, which allowed them and their friends easy access to whatever they needed in the shop for their hot rods. As soon as he was of legal driving age, Harry purchased a '29 Model A roadster and joined the ranks of the Gophers. The club's roster included Johnny Ryan, Nellie Taylor, Bill Zaring, Eddie Riddle, Johnny Price, Ulrich Regus, Russ Synder, Don Lenk, Roland Mays, and many more; there were at times close to 20 members in the club. Johnny Price would later on become the shop foreman for Weber Cams.

The Gophers were fairly active at the dry lakes races, and Bill's roadster won its fair share of trophies at these meets. On April 30, 1939, he set top speed at 116 miles per hour at the newly formed Western Timing Association's first sanctioned meet held on Rosamond Dry Lake. In October of the same year, he took the roadster class at a sanctioned SCTA meet with a speed of 107 miles per hour.

By the late 1930s, the Weber Tool Company was donating engine machine work as prizes to the racers at the Muroc Dry Lake speed trials.

THE WATERMELON CAPER

As long as there have been farmers' fields and orchards, there have been a few adventurous lads with enough nerve to make a midnight sortie for a free bag of produce. Farm dogs, irate farmers, and rock salt–filled shotguns were minor obstacles that were easily overcome. When the boys had a beach or house party coming up, the main staples (besides girls) were beer and watermelons. The Gophers had developed their own rather unique method of obtaining watermelons without even having to venture out into farm country.

Heavily laden farm trucks delivering produce to Los Angeles wholesale grocers would slowly edge their way over the steep inclined road of Coyote Pass during the night to avoid daytime traffic. Under the darkness of night, with headlights out, the Gophers were able to pull up to the rear of an unsuspecting truck, and as the overloaded truck began to bog down in a low-gear crawl, it became an easy target for the enterprising troop. The boys would pull a roadster up to the tail end of the truck, and one of the members would climb over the car's windshield and toward the front. From there, he'd hop onto the truck bed, and another member would move to the front with another fellow behind him. As soon as the human watermelon chain was ready, a half-dozen or more melons were quickly hoisted off the truck. Johnny Ryan said that he can't ever remember any of them getting caught during a melon run.

A scene from 1938 finds Bill Weber sitting in his stripped down Model B–powered T-bucket. Note the straight exhaust that most likely contained no baffles to keep the racket down. *Courtesy John Ryan*

A couple of Gopher car club members ham it up for the camera. Harry Weber, right, holds a very large wrench, while Nellie Taylor holds a rod and piston. That's Nellie's roadster. *Courtesy John Ryan*

TRAGEDY

The war in Europe was well underway, and Bill was anxious to help save the world from the invading Huns. He had a private pilot's license, was an accomplished flyer, and, in 1941, wrote and passed all the requirements for admission into the Royal Air Force in England. While waiting for confirmation from Canadian authorities acting on England's behalf, Bill decided to visit the dry lakes one last time before going off to war. He rented an airplane from Nagle Airport in Los Angeles and flew up to El Mirage for the August 1st race meet. While using the plane to time a race car, a mishap occurred, resulting in Bill's death and that of his passenger, James Bischoff. The front page of the August 7, 1941, issue of the *Montebello News* reported, "The crash was witnessed by 400 spectators at the 'jalopy' races held on the dry lake. The plane was said to be about 200 feet above the ground when it slide-slipped and nosed down with a terrific crash. Bischoff died shortly after he was pulled from the wreckage, and Weber passed away Monday morning at the hospital in San Bernardino."

As a consequence of that tragic accident, Harry would eventually take over the family machine shop business. One brother's demise would help direct the other brother into a lifelong career as a successful speed equipment manufacturer.

WEBER CAMS

After the sad loss of his brother, Harry continued working at the family machine shop and only reground cams when asked by friends and racers. One of the first flathead V-8 cams he ground that proved successful was for Phil Weiand's Merc-powered '40 Ford coupe.

As the United States entered the war, the Weber shop came under contract to the military, machining aircraft parts for the Northrop Aircraft Company and other priority work. Harry was deemed essential to the war effort as a machinist and spent the duration of the war at the shop.

The postwar boom in auto racing and subsequent demand for speed equipment was great for any company involved in manufacturing the stuff, as Harry began to experience with inquiries for camshafts. In order to keep up with the orders, he set up a proper cam grinder and did more developmental work on camshaft profiles. The hard work paid off, and by the late 1940s, a fair number of record-setting cars at the dry lakes and oval tracks were equipped with Weber cams. By 1948, his influence as a cam grinder was impressive enough that the fledgling *Hot Rod* had him pen an article titled "Choosing a Cam."

Even though the company was into cams and flywheels, Weber Tool did continue to offer general machine shop services to the public into the 1950s, until there was sufficient business in manufacturing speed equipment to discontinue those services.

WEBER PRODUCTS

The shop managed to manufacture its fair share of out-of-the-ordinary speed equipment for engines that weren't exactly heading any popularity lists. With the camshaft business well under way, Harry branched out. In 1948, he introduced a high-compression head for the Studebaker flathead six-cylinder engine. This venture into the performance head business must have been short lived, as the only information available on the subject is a short blurb about it in *Hot Rod*. That same year, Harry got into the aluminum flywheel business, which would prove to be very popular and profitable. The following year, Weber Tool went after young performance-minded enthusiasts by offering high-compression heads for the Whizzer motor bike and the Cushman motor scooter.

In the early 1950s, the business expanded into manufacturing Lincoln bell housing adapters for converting the Lincoln V-12 over to the Lincoln Cosmo V-8 for extra power and better fuel economy. This adapter wasn't exactly a hot sales item, but Weber eventually offered adapter housings for the majority of the early OHV V-8 engines to mate up to Ford transmissions.

Besides manufacturing, the company also carried several products to complement its own line, including distributors and oil additives. Weber Tool was the West Coast distributor for the Lucas Company, which manufactured a performance Ford ignition distributor, and for Liqui Moly, a molybdenum disulfide–based lubricant.

In 1952, Weber Tool came out with a stroker kit for the short-lived Crosley engine, which was one of the smallest but probably one of the most technically advanced American automobile engines built in that period. The SOHC engine's 44-ci displacement made it ideal for certain boat and automotive racing classes. Weber manufactured a cast-iron 3/16 stroker crankshaft to bring the Crosley up to almost 48 ci with a compression ratio of 10:1 using stock pistons.

When GM introduced its ill-fated Corvair, Harry came out with several stroker kits for the opposed flat six. He was so taken with the Corvair that he purchased his own to street-test equipment. Weber was also one of first manufacturers to offer stroker kits for the VW and was quite busy in the VW cam department, grinding cams in lots of 100 at a time. The company was also heavy into sports car and motorcycle performance camshafts and offered a 180-degree crankshaft for the small-block Chevrolet V-8. The only drawback to the 180 crank was that it was also necessary to run a special Weber steel-billet camshaft, making it a rather expensive package for the engine builder.

WEBER DAYS

Though Harry's company may not have been as aggressive in the camshaft advertising department as some of his competitors, his equipment was out there and did get the job done, as evidenced by a writeup from the September 1960 issue of *Drag News*. The race results for August 28 from the Half Moon Bay drag strip were reported as "Weber Day" at the strip. The story reported that Weber-equipped cars took Top Fuel time, Top Gas time, Top Eliminator, Top Gas Eliminator, and set low ET. Other class wins included B/Gas, C/Gas, F/Gas, TAX, A/SR, B/MR, B/A, A/D, D/D, C/OG, and H/PU—all the winning cars were Weber equipped. No doubt Harry was very pleased to see these results.

TAYLOR & RYAN ENGINE REBUILDING

From their prewar days as members of the Gophers car club, Harry, Nelson "Nellie" Taylor, and Johnny Ryan remained lifelong friends. After the war and a short stint at Evans Speed Equipment, Nellie and John opened Taylor & Ryan Engine Rebuilding in Whittier, California. Their primary business was building custom engines, anything from mild to wild, whatever a customer requested. Not only did they build the stuff, both fellows were very active in racing at the dry lakes, and Nellie was elected acting president of the Russetta Timing Association in 1948.

Before Harry had his own dynamometer facility, he would send his latest prototype cam profiles over to the Taylor & Ryan shop for evaluation. He'd receive an unbiased test report on the camshaft's performance, which usually decided if the cam went into production or back to the drawing board. The boys continued to run his cams when they performed engine dyno tests until Harry finally got his own dynamometer in 1953. Remembering Harry Weber after the many years of friendship and business dealings, John said, "He was a great guy and would never be mean to anyone—a real gentleman."

KARL PAYNE AND MICKEY THOMPSON

Karl Payne was one of the machinists employed at Weber Cams in the early 1950s. He remembered the shop as, "having two employees, plus Harry's wife working in the front office, with five machinists in the shop. There were two Norton camshaft grinders at the time, operated by Ruddy Castill and me. John Pierce was the shop foreman at the time. Pierce had lost an eye from enemy anti-aircraft flak while flying a P-38 aircraft in Europe during

A photo shot in the back lot of the Weber Tool Company in 1938 shows the lineup of Gopher car club hot rods. Notice that they're all four-banger roadsters. *Courtesy John Ryan*

World War II." Karl recalled the time when John gave the boys a good laugh one day, when the fairly good-looking secretary from the office strode through the shop. "She distracted poor Pierce to the point to where he walked into and knocked over a stack of aluminum flywheels."

"A young hot rodder by the name of Mickey Thompson would visit the shop," said Karl. "It seems that Mickey was in competition with a neighbor over who had the fastest riding lawnmower. Thompson had our shop massage the mower's Briggs & Stratton camshaft and mill the head, and the last time I heard, Mickey was feeding small doses of nitro to the engine."

Payne said he received a considerable amount of knowledge of machine shop practices from Harry and was given plenty of hands-on projects, including helping to build the Weber hydraulic-brake dynamometer. To compete against Isky's infamous 404 grind, Harry introduced the F-7 camshaft, a fast valve-action cam that also used radius lifters. Karl was on the grinder that ground the concave-flanked F-7 cam lobes and drew up the installation instructions for the special keyed-radius lifters that came with that particular camshaft. Though the F-7 didn't get ink like

CAMS FOR ALL CARS

The first Weber Tool Company speed equipment catalog came out in 1950. The selection of cams was limited mainly to flathead Ford V-8s, but there were offerings for other models as well. Also listed were Lucas ignitions, Ford aluminum flywheels, and for some reason or other, Lincoln bell housings. *Courtesy John Ryan*

Isky's 404 and Potvin's 425, Harry's cam held its own in competition. In 1963, Ron Roseberry was sponsored by Harry and ran an F-7 radius cam and stroker crankshaft assembly for his flathead V-8 D/Dragster. Ron won his class at the 1963 Winternationals and later that same year was runner-up at the Smokers meet in Bakersfield.

From grinding camshafts, the shop moved Payne over to balancing the aluminum flywheels that were a big sales ticket for the company. Originally, Karl balanced the wheels by supporting them on a shaft through the flywheel and placed on the lathe, letting the wheel rotate freely. The low spot on the wheel was then drilled until it didn't rotate any more. Not very high-tech, recalled Karl, but it did the trick until an electronic balancing machine took over that job.

One of the most popular hot rodders to ever climb the ladder of success, who set numerous speed records along the way, built a specialty parts manufacturing empire, and accomplished more in his short lifetime than most of us can imagine, was Mickey Thompson. Before his climb to fame, Mickey was a frequent visitor to the Weber shop. At Bonneville in 1952, Mickey drove a radically modified '31 Austin powered by two inline Merc engines running Weber cams to claim the D/Competition Coupe class with a very respectable speed of 194.34 miles per hour. With the record in his back pocket, Mickey had no problem enticing Harry to sponsor him the following year.

Ever an innovator, Mickey replaced one of the flatheads with a Chrysler—a very abstract combination of engines. The normally aspirated Merc was equipped with the F-7 camshaft, while the Hemi ran an experimental roller cam. The 4-71 GMC-supercharged Chrysler Hemi was fed a fuel mix through five carburetors mounted on a sheetmetal intake manifold fabricated by Mickey. It pulled a strong 400 horsepower on the Weber dynamometer. Mickey claimed that it was the first Chrysler ever to have a top-mounted GMC blower. Unfortunately, the car wasn't as successful as expected, but it ran a decent 164 miles per hour for the class win before the Chrysler blew. Clearly, the engine choice didn't work out for Mickey, and any possible advertising value to Harry was lost when the car didn't set any outlandish speed records.

WEBCO SPEED & POWER

When Bob Hughes was discharged from the military after serving in the Korean War, he went back to his old job at the Offenhauser Equipment Corporation. Another Offenhauser employee named Tom Heininger became good friends with Bob, and both had a comparable dream of opening his own business.

Harry Weber was a good friend of Fred Offenhauser and was often at the shop, where he got to know Tom and Bob, and once he'd learned of their interest in opening a performance business, he made them an offer they couldn't refuse. Harry had a dormant corporation called Webco and said that he would give them this unused corporation to save Bob and Tom the $200 it'd cost to start a new corporation. Besides being a silent partner, Harry would also provide the financial backing.

The innovative Mickey Thompson showed up at the 1952 Bonneville Nationals with an Austin D/Competition Coupe equipped with two Merc V-8s. The Weber-cammed car set a 194.34-mile-per-hour record and a one-way run of 196.72. *Leslie Long collection*

In 1953, Webco Speed & Power opened for business at 4773 Valley Road in Los Angeles. The company provided an ideal retail sales outlet for Weber products, and in Webco's advertising, it was mentioned that it was a division of the Weber Tool Company.

In short order, Bob and Tom were manufacturing their own performance products and had the full use of the Weber Tool Company's machine shop facilities during Weber's off hours and on weekends. As a silent partner, Harry sold out his interests to the two partners in 1957. Bob said, "It was such an amicable parting of the ways that Harry still allowed us the use of his machine shop facilities."

Neil Holt worked at Offenhauser part-time while in high school and had gotten to know Bob and Tom fairly well. After graduating from college, he went to work for Webco as its general manager. Webco would eventually buy out the motorcycle camshaft division of Harman & Collins Cams in the early 1960s, as Webco was by then heavily into motorcycle products.

PETER VAN IDERSTINE REMEMBERS

Peter Van Iderstine first became acquainted with Harry at a specialty-equipment trade show in New Jersey. As the owner of several speed shops under the "Van Iderstine Racing Equipment" banner, he attended trade shows in search of new equipment lines for his growing businesses. Through carrying the Weber product line, he developed a strong friendship with Harry. After selling off the speed shops, Pete and his wife looked west to California for an idyllic location to settle down in semiretirement, and once settled, they became even closer friends of the Webers. Pete is the proprietor of the Early Wheel Company, a specialty wheel business in Solvang.

Pete remembered Harry telling him how, as newlyweds, he and Barbara would deliver re-bored Model A blocks to their customers from the rumble seat of their '32 roadster. On one occasion, Pete was at Harry's shop and saw large wood crates of used VW camshafts. At the time, Weber Cams couldn't keep up with the demand for reground VW cams because new blank cam cores were unavailable. Apparently, there was an outfit in Texas that supplied used VW cams by the crateful and would ship Weber 300 to 400 used cams, still covered in grease and oil, just as they'd been pulled from the engine blocks.

Pete mentioned that Harry was an astute businessman with good knowledge of machinery, and that Harry never missed an opportunity to buy a used piece if it was a good deal. On many occasions, while on business trips throughout the country, Harry would go through the yellow pages in search of used machinery dealers. He had built up a fairly decent sideline business of shipping machinery back to Los Angeles for resale, and he was shrewd enough to invest the profits from Weber Cams wisely, purchasing commercial real estate.

Pete recalled that Harry also never missed the opportunity to provide quick and satisfactory service to a customer. "Many times a customer would walk in and place a cam on the counter

Harry runs a test on a flywheel to check balance prior to shipping. *Courtesy John Ryan*

to be reground. Harry would tell the customer to go for a coffee and return within the hour, and the cam would be ready for him," Pete said.

THE WEBER LEGACY

The number of camshaft companies far outnumbered the companies offering performance clutches and flywheels, and it didn't go unnoticed by Harry. The Los Angeles area alone had its share of cam grinders, and just to keep up with the competition was an ongoing job. Although he was heavily involved in grinding camshafts, Harry could see a business opportunity where the competition wasn't as fierce, and he began to place more emphasis on manufacturing performance clutches and flywheels, leaving Iskenderian, Engle, Howards, and others to fight over the rights to camshaft supremacy.

By the early 1970s, Harry had put in a solid 30-plus years of long days working in the performance industry. When Echlin approached him with an offer in 1974, he went for it. The Echlin outfit was buying into the specialty manufacturing market, purchasing small but profitable businesses to incorporate into its portfolio, and Weber looked good to the accountants.

It didn't take too many years for Echlin to begin selling off specialty businesses that were deemed unsuitable for corporate interests, including Harry's camshaft shop. In 1981, a Weber employee named Steve Story and a partner bought the camshaft division and moved the contents to Riverside, California, operating under the name of Web-Cam. Today, Steve and new partner, Laurie Dunlap, operate a modern machine shop, grinding camshafts for the latest automobile engines, foreign and domestic alike. They excel in motorcycle cams—their performance bike cams can be found in many of the quickest motorcycles on the racing circuit.

The profitable Weber clutch department was relocated to Chatsworth, California, and then again to Columbus, Kansas, operating under the roof of the Ace Electric Company; it remained there until 1980, when it was returned to California. Eventually, the corporation decided that the flywheel-clutch division didn't fit into its product line any longer and put it up for sale, strangely enough also selling out to a former Weber employee. P. G. "Red" Roberts went to work for Harry around 1970 as the head of the clutch department and wound up buying the operation. Today, the company is known as McLeod.

Roberts refers to Harry as one of the three founding fathers in the clutch business, along with Bill Hays and Paul Schiefer. He worked for both Harry and Hays and was a good friend of Schiefer's, and over time he purchased the Weber clutch division and Schiefer Clutches; Mr. Gasket picked up the Hays Company. Today, Red retains the name Weber Performance Products, which offers a complete line of clutches and flywheels for the nostalgic market.

When speaking to Red about his time spent at the Weber shop, he recalled watching Harry personally grind motorcycle cams on a small grinder that was set up specifically for that purpose. Evidently, when Harry wasn't concerned with pressing business matters in the front office, he could be found contentedly standing in front of that grinding machine, putting a jewel-like finish on a motorcycle cam.

Retirement is not suitable for some people, and Harry was one of those who didn't take to sitting around and doing nothing. He went back into the field of his first love—camshafts—and with the assistance of his son, Jeff, opened Weber Cams & Products in Costa Mesa, California. He kept this new venture on the small side, but it was still a progressive outfit in its own right. Besides offering the usual performance cams for the majority of engines, including antique automobiles, in 1993 the company developed a new style of hydraulic mushroom valve lifter. In his ads, Harry always mentioned that this company was not to be confused with Web-Cam.

When Harry died on December 24, 1997, his cam business closed its doors for good, bringing to an end a family legacy that began with Alexander Weber in 1925 and lasted some 72 years.

CHAPTER 21

Weiand Power & Racing

PHIL WEIAND

The Phil Weiand story can be best described as illustration of an astute individual's dogged determination to overcome a circumstance that was not of his own doing. Like Chet Herbert, who overcame the adversity of being wheelchair bound, the situation that Phil found himself in after an unfortunate accident in no way hindered his aspirations to better himself. Phil did not waste time dwelling in self-pity or thinking about what might have been.

He was born in Los Angeles in 1913 to parents who were both professional tailors in the manufacture of men's business suits. While attending John Marshall High School in Pasadena, Phil began to lean toward hot rods, enough so that at the age of 14 he gave up any aspirations of becoming a musician and traded his mandolin for a 1922 Model T Touring automobile. The Touring body was eventually discarded for a sporty-looking '24 T-bucket that served him well throughout his days at John Marshall. In shop class, Phil first became acquainted with speed equipment when he fabricated a custom exhaust header and straight pipe combination, as well as a downdraft carburetor intake manifold for his street rod. However, any serious engine modifications and competition at the dry lakes would have to wait until he finished school and got a job. By 1933, his roadster was ready for Muroc.

TRACK T

After graduating and getting out into the workforce, he had the time and resources to concentrate on racing, and fortunately there was a fairly decent supply of used speed equipment for the T engine. Henry Ford's fabulous little four-cylinder has seen service in everything from race cars to powerboats and homebuilt aircraft. Through wheeling and dealing, Phil ended up with an engine outfitted with a Rajo overhead-valve conversion activated by a Laurel racing cam, a modified Stutz automobile dual ignition, lightweight pistons, a single downdraft carburetor perched on his own manifold, and Buffalo wire wheels and tires. Everything that was nonessential on the car was removed, and power from the engine was transmitted to the rear wheels via a two-speed Ruckstell rearend.

In those early days, Lee Chapel's wrecking yard/speed shop and Eastern Auto Supply were two good sources for used speed equipment.

MUROC DRY LAKE

Weiand's first outing on the dry lakes was in May 1933 at a sanctioned Muroc Dry Lake Racing Association event. For his $1 entry fee, Phil got the roadster up to a respectable speed of 91.80 miles per hour. Looking to go faster, the Model T frame was replaced with a more suitable 1926 Chevrolet chassis along with a Franklin front axle and two of Ed Winfield's downdraft carburetors on a Weiand-designed manifold. Possibly through the assistance of DeWinter's Garage, Phil was able to transform his roadster into a competitive race car. Some sources suggest that he was working at the automotive repair shop as an apprentice mechanic at the time.

Opposite: A wheelchair didn't keep Phil Weiand out of the shop. Here he helps Bruce Robinson bolt a polished triple-carburetor manifold to a flathead V 8. *Courtesy Joan Weiand*

At the following dry lakes meet, his roadster was clocked at 102 miles per hour, then 109 miles per hour, and before the season was over, it reached a blistering 116 miles per hour; it set fast time for that show. Remembering that safety equipment in the early 1930s consisted of a leather flying helmet and a pair of old aviator's goggles to peer through the dust, it took a lot of guts to sit in an open tin can with questionable rubber on the wheels and push the accelerator pedal to the floor.

THE ACCIDENT

For Phil, his first season racing at the dry lakes had been successful and a learning experience. When the season came to a close, the engine and car were overhauled and modified wherever needed. Nothing was overlooked, and even little things, such as covering the frame horns with formed sheet metal, were done to improve the airflow at the front of the car. Photographs show that the engine was outfitted with one large Winfield downdraft carburetor in place of the smaller duals.

During the winter months, the lakes are normally flooded with runoff and rainfall from the surrounding mountains, making them inaccessible to the racers. Not wanting to wait until the lakebed was ready, Phil decided to take the car out to the deserted roads around the sparsely populated Mines Field area (now Los Angeles International Airport) for a road test. Mines Field contained a 2-mile dirt race-track facility, and the area was even large enough that it held aircraft races on the property.

On January 21, 1934, Phil, his cousin, and a group of friends ventured out to Lennox Boulevard with the roadster, sporting his sponsor's name, DeWinter's Garage. As these tests were just shakedown runs, Phil made the error of taking a passenger along with him on a high-speed run.

The writeup in a local newspaper mentioned that, "Phil was catapulted from the car at 110 miles per hour as it skidded and then turtled at a turn in the road. The accident occurred at Mines Field." The report went on to say. "He suffered from a fractured spine, and when he arrived at the hospital, the surgeons didn't feel that he had much of a chance of recovery."

Phil was approaching a bend in the road and wasn't too concerned about negotiating the curve, but his terrified passenger madly grabbed the centrally located emergency brake handle to slow the speeding car down. The sudden jerk on the brake threw the roadster into a skid, and the car then tumbled over a series of times, coming to rest upside down as a mangled wreck. Regrettably, Phil had been thrown from the roadster. Thinking that they were doing the right thing by getting him to the hospital as quickly as possible and not waiting for the ambulance, his cousin and friends loaded Phil into their station wagon. They put him in the vehicle in a sitting position and drove off to the hospital, not realizing that this was very detrimental to his condition. Some felt their actions may have added to the already aggravated state of his injury. Strange as it seems, the passenger who lost his nerve and caused this misfortune suffered only minor cuts and bruises.

When this tragic accident occurred, Phil was only 20 years old and found himself confined to a wheelchair. At first, he tried everything to regain the use of his legs, but eventually he had to face the fact that he was going to spend the rest of his life as a paraplegic. It took some getting used to for someone accustomed to having the freedom to drive a car to now have to depend on others for transportation. That lasted for two years, until 1936, when Phil purchased a 1929 Ford coupe and converted it to hand controls. It took a bit of engineering, but he had his freedom back once more. No doubt it surprised a lot of his friends when they saw Phil pull up in the coupe, as this type of conversion was fairly uncommon in those days. The Ford provided him with a dependable means of transportation, but like any young guy, the four-

This shot was taken on January 21, 1934, just prior to what would be a life-altering accident. Phil and helpers had taken his roadster out to Lennox Boulevard (today's LAX) for practice runs. Note the front airfoil between the frame horns to assist in streamlining, and his new sponsor, DeWinters Garage, lettered on the front cowl. At the time, Phil was running a single carburetor on the Rajo-equipped Model B engine. *Courtesy Joan Weiand*

The remnants of Phil's 1927 T roadster after the devastating crash on Lennox Boulevard. Onlookers marvel at the mechanical wreckage. *Courtesy Joan Weiand*

The original Weiand shop on San Fernando Road was built in front of Phil's mother's house. The picture shows the ground in front of the original garage being readied for the building of new facilities. *Courtesy Joan Weiand*

cylinder just didn't have it, and in 1938, he moved up to a flathead V-8–powered '34 Ford coupe.

He was still faced with some major decisions about what he was going to do with the rest of his life. Phil possessed a strong desire to be around cars but obviously was limited in what he could do in that field. Around the same time, everybody from moonshine runners to stock car racers and hot rodders was discovering the benefits of Ford's side-valve V-8. Even the notorious bank-robbing duo of Bonnie and Clyde had nothing but praise for the speed of Henry's V-8 and wrote a letter to Ford extolling its attributes. This engine created a market for speed equipment manufactured by prewar companies, such as Roof, Morrison, Thickstun, Meyer, Edmunds, Winfield, and a variety of others. In those days, probably the easiest method for the average performance enthusiast to create a little more horsepower with the flathead was to increase the amount of fuel delivery to the engine by adding more carburetion and to have the stock heads milled. Of the commercial intake manifolds available at the time, the one that caught Phil's attention was Jack Henry's two-carburetor setup, based on the open plenum chamber of the '32 Ford V-8 aluminum manifold. Henry cleverly transformed the factory intake into a dual manifold by adding high-rise runners to the stock manifold. Phil liked the simplicity of the Henry design but saw where improvements could be made and paid Vic Edelbrock Sr. a visit to learn his take on the subject. At the time, Vic was selling Thickstun manifolds out of his auto repair garage and was in the middle of developing his own manifold design, as he was convinced that the Thickstun manifold could also be improved upon.

This discovery left Phil to make his own decision on what course he should take. Phil never considered that going into the aftermarket manifold business would end up the way it did; the endeavor was intended to be something to tide him over until he could land something permanent with a solid future.

HIGH WEIAND MANIFOLD

With a $250 loan from his mother, Phil approached a pattern-maker named Herman Husbey to make a wood pattern and core box for a dual-carburetor manifold. Husbey had already produced manifold patterns for Thickstun and newcomer Vic Edelbrock.

Barney Navarro was working as a machinist for the Heidrich Tool & Die shop at the time and would play a role in machining the first-ever run of manifolds ordered by Phil in his new venture. This business enterprise wasn't without a bit of intrigue, as Barney Navarro related: "Around 1941, Phil went to Husbey and asked to make him a manifold pattern. He agreed and the price would be $200 for a wood pattern and core box. Weiand had specified high risers so he could run the generator on the front and big passages in the base like Edelbrock's [slingshot manifold]. Weiand went back there about three weeks later, and here's a manifold that looks like a mixture of Thickstun's and Edelbrock's. Weiand says, 'Don't you think those two guys will be unhappy?' Husbey says, 'Oh no, we'll put a filet here and gusset there; they'll never know the difference.' Well, that never got to happen. Edelbrock dropped into the shop and saw the pattern and wouldn't leave until he personally took a hammer and broke it up. So now Husbey was stuck in making a cheap [cost-wise] manifold for Weiand."

After ordering a run of 10 manifolds from the aluminum foundry, Phil still had to overcome the problem of having the raw castings machined and drilled before he had a viable product to sell. His borrowed money was tied up in the manifold pattern and 10 castings, and he had purchased a Sears, Roebuck drill press on credit (Joan Weiand still has the original drill press). As luck would have it, Phil was introduced to Barney Navarro through some members of the Glendale Stokers car club, of which Barney was a member. They figured that maybe Phil and Barney could work something out, knowing that Barney was looking for a dual intake for his own engine and that he had access to machine shop facilities. Phil needed the castings machined and access to some sort of drill jig that would enable him to drill the manifolds. The two young hot rodders struck a deal in which Barney would machine the 10 castings and make a drill jig in return for one of the manifolds. Barney rented Heidrich's shop on a Saturday

A highly polished example of the manifold that got Phil started in the speed equipment manufacturing business: the Weiand high-rise dual-carburetor intake. *Courtesy Joan Weiand*

afternoon to do this. By performing these services, Barney became Phil Weiand's first customer and the first to install and run his manifold in a car. It's a little ironic that later on Phil and Barney would be competitors in business.

Phil had set up a work area in the small shed at his mother's house, and with Barney's drill jig, he could drill and tap the remaining nine manifolds. Unbeknownst to Phil and others in those prewar days, the manifold's high-rise runner design gave the manifold a tunnel-ram effect.

It was one thing making manifolds, but finding customers to buy them was another obstacle, and being confined to a wheelchair made the task that much more difficult. The only racing periodicals of any significance that carried advertising were the SCTA newsletter and *Throttle* (publication ended with the outbreak of World War II). Phil pondered the situation for a while and then loaded up his manifold inventory in the trunk of the '34 coupe and visited such speed shops as Douglas Muffler, Karl Orr's Speed Shop, Bell Auto Parts, and Eastern Auto Supply. After selling what he could to the speed shops, there were still manifolds left over, so he drove around to the local drive-in burger joints where the hot rodders hung out. There, he'd watch and wait as two cars would pair up for a runoff and observe which one ended up as the loser—now there was a potential customer. Phil chose to try and sell the loser a manifold to help him regain his dignity rather than going after the victor, because his car was doing all right as it was.

Phil began to sell more manifolds than he'd originally anticipated, and it looked as if he might have his future right in front of him. Even his mother could see that her son had something going as she moved the family to a home at 2733 San Fernando Road with a large garage out front where Phil could operate his business. As more manifolds were cast, he farmed out the machining to Cook's

Machine Works, but he continued the drilling and tapping process in his own shop. Things were really looking up, as he was getting more phone calls inquiring about the "high Weiand" manifold, but then the war came along, shutting down Muroc for good and forcing the racers to run on several other dry lakes in the area until racing ceased altogether.

Given the small size of his shop, Phil wasn't able to land any military contracts, so he continued to produce manifolds if the aluminum was available. Prospective customers would bring in everything from pots and pans to bits of salvaged scrap aluminum in hopes of getting enough metal together to have a manifold made for them. This method continued on until the end of the hostilities, when aluminum was freed up from military usage.

As the war came to a close, the demand for speed equipment mushroomed, and Phil needed more manufacturing space. His existing garage shop couldn't handle the workload, so he had a brick building extended from the old shop out to the sidewalk. Eventually, the need for even larger facilities moved Phil to purchase the house next door to his shop, where he erected a 5,000-square-foot warehouse facility and offices that became the company's headquarters. By 1974 the company, now called Weiand Automotive Industries, had approximately 125 employees working in 100,000 square feet of manufacturing space and producing 3,000 pieces of speed equipment monthly.

1940 FORD COUPE

Phil's '34 coupe had served him well, but in 1942, when the chance to acquire an almost new but slightly damaged vehicle came around, Phil jumped at it. It was a 1940 Ford Deluxe coupe that had been involved in a fire, so the price was right. After a trip to a body shop, the car looked as if it had just come out of the showroom. Of course, there was no sense in selling speed equipment and driving

An interior view of Weiand's busy machine shop in the late 1940s shows three workers machining heads and intake manifolds. Fumio Okamura, left, and Ken Minkey, center, machine heads, while Yam Okamura, right, domes cylinder heads. *Courtesy Joan Weiand*

a car with a stock engine, so Phil had a 1942 Mercury V-8 installed with one of his dual manifolds and a hot cam, a ported and relieved block, and milled cast-iron heads. Over time, the coupe evolved into a street rod that even sported fender skirts. Barney Navarro recalled Phil pulling into his laneway with the '40 and said that Phil had a cable hooked up so he could release the trunk lid from inside the car when he was out selling manifolds.

After the war, the Russetta Timing Association became the home to anyone who wished to run at the dry lakes. The SCTA organization was for roadsters and streamliners only, thus everyone else had to look elsewhere, giving the RTA and smaller racing associations a leg up. In 1946, the Weiand '40 coupe ran 112 miles per hour, which was pretty respectable for a daily driver. Phil held on to the Ford until 1953, when he felt that it would be a lot easier to drive with an automatic transmission. He traded in the '40 coupe for a 1951 Ford equipped with an auto tranny.

CALIFORNIA ROADSTER ASSOCIATION

At the end of World War II, a hot rodder named Babe Ouse and some fellow racing enthusiasts put together a racing organization called the California Roadster Association. It was originally set up for amateur drivers and their stripped-down street rods. The inaugural race for these street-legal roadsters was held on Labor Day 1946 at the just-completed Gardena Bowl, a half-mile dirt track in Gardena. (This race track would later be known as Carrell Speedway.) There was no scarcity of entries for these races, and within a year, most of the once semi-street-legal roadsters were transformed into highly competitive all-out race cars. As the popularity grew with the fans, so did the involvement of speed equipment manufacturers, which either fielded cars or sponsored them.

Phil saw the benefits of running in such a circuit and put together a high-dollar, ultra-clean 1927 track T roadster powered by a '42 Merc V-8 (possibly the same engine from the '40 coupe). He didn't spare the coin with the race car, which was outfitted with Kinmont disc brakes, center steering, and lots of chrome. The gold/bronze No. 4 Weiand roadster had its share of wins with great drivers such as Jack McGrath, Slim Mathis, Bud Van Mannen, and the Rathmann brothers. Being a hands-on race car owner, Phil could usually be found with his crew in the pits at the race track.

In 1946, Bud Van Mannen drove the Weiand roadster to a record speed of 124.82 miles per hour at the dry lakes, making it the fastest roadster ever to run in an RTA event at the time.

Besides having his own roadster run at the dry lakes, Phil sponsored a car belonging to an employee named Bruce Robinson. Bruce's roadster competed in the B/Roadster class at RTA events as a member of the Glendale Coupe and Roadster Club and in A/Roadster at SCTA events as a member of the Sidewinders club. The car turned a record-setting 152.54 miles per hour at El Mirage and was used as a testbed for any new Weiand flathead V-8 products.

SPEED EQUIPMENT

Phil's original high-rise dual intake sold very well, but after the war there were a lot of new kids on the block, and competition began to get tough. New innovations in manifold design were appearing on the market, and to keep up, he had to add new products to the Weiand line. In addition to the high-rise, Phil introduced a low-style dual intake designed for racing. Because he was fielding a race car powered by a flathead V-8, he needed to either run with modified cast-iron factory heads or come out with his own. Being involved in racing basically forced him to manufacture aluminum high-compression heads and a triple-carburetor manifold. From there, he branched out into V8-60 equipment and even had enough faith in the underpowered Studebaker flathead six-cylinder to come out with a high-compression head for that engine.

A price list from 1947 stated that Phil's foundry cost for a set of aluminum heads was $10. To sandblast the heads cost 25 cents, the machining of the heads was $4, and polishing the heads cost $1. The high-rise dual intake manifold set him back $10, with an additional $7.50 for machining and $4 for polishing. The racing low-profile intake casting was $7.25. The machine work was another $2.25, and polishing cost $2.25. The heads retailed for $76, while the high Weiand was $44.50, and the low-profile model was $46.

The introduction of *Hot Rod* by Robert Lindsay and Bob Petersen proved to be the catalyst for the development of the speed equipment industry. Before its introduction in 1948, there was little in the way of national racing automotive magazines or other media where companies could place advertisements to reach prospective customers throughout the country. Suddenly, this magazine appeared nationwide to spread the gospel of the California hot rodding scene to the masses.

As far as the majority of racing aficionados were concerned, anything made in California had to be the latest in hot rodding design and racing technology. *Hot Rod* proved to be a lifeline that saved a lot of manufacturers who were otherwise on a financial edge, having to depend on the local market for survival. The huge responses manufacturers received from advertising in this magazine provided the incentive to expand their operations.

As the speed equipment industry grew, so did Weiand Power & Racing. By 1950, it manufactured a complete line of speed equipment for the popular engines of the day and offered custom flathead engine-building services to suit any need. As Oldsmobile, Cadillac, and Chrysler introduced overhead-valve V-8s, Weiand kept pace by developing equipment for these engines; those companies that didn't eventually fell by the wayside.

The early 1950s car magazine *Hop Up* did an article on Phil for its series, "Meet the Advertiser." The article came out in a 1952 edition and described how Phil got started in 1941 with his dual-intake manifold and grew into one of the leading manifold manufacturers of the day.

SPONSORED RACERS

Sponsorships are much like betting on horses—sometimes they come in, and sometimes they don't. The safer bet was to sponsor a racer with a proven track record, such as Don Garlits. The Big Daddy was a formidable drag racing opponent from early on, which didn't go unnoticed by Phil. In the mid-1950s, he and Isky co-sponsored Garlits' Chrysler-powered dragster, which was known as the

The Weiand CRA track roadster powered by a modified '42 Merc V-8. Even though it was very competitive on the track, the bronze-colored car was also show-car quality. It ran 148 miles per hour on alky and 131 on gas at the dry lakes. *Courtesy Joan Weiand*

Isky-Weiand Special. It was equipped with Phil's eight-carburetor cast-aluminum Drag Star log manifold. When Don switched over to a GMC blower, he ran a Weiand eight-carburetor manifold that sat on top of the Jimmy blower until it was eventually dropped in favor of a Hilborn fuel-injector system.

As the GMC blower began to get noticed by engine builders searching for ultimate power, Phil quickly got on the bandwagon and came out with a manifold for the supercharger. In order to get some advertising ink, he sponsored the well-known Robert "Jocko" Johnson and his rear-engined streamliner dragster and gave him the first Weiand blower manifold to try out. Johnson was the proprietor of Jocko's Porting Service in Los Angeles and performed head porting on some of the nation's top-running cars. Jocko was also talented with aluminum sheet metal, which he molded into a beautiful streamlined body for his dragster. It was powered by a blown Chrysler and was driven by "Jazzy" Jim Nelson.

As with the Garlits car that was co-sponsored by Weiand and Iskenderian, Phil teamed up with Howards Cams on several successful cars, including the rear-engined Tucson *Speed Sport* roadster, the twin-engined *Bustle Bomb* dragster, which was the first car to exceed 150 miles per hour, and the *Money Olds Special* dragster, which was the first to break 140 on gasoline. These three winning race cars all ran carburetion and were equipped with the Drag Star log manifold.

FOUNDRIES

Any company that makes a product requiring metal casting is dependent on a foundry. It has no control over the casting quality, pricing, or even when the item will be ready.

Business was flourishing for the Weiand shop, and the time came when Phil felt owning his own aluminum foundry warranted the expense in relation to what it would provide in the long run. His shop classes back in high school included an in-depth study on foundry work, so he had a fairly good idea what he was getting into. In 1958, he started up the All-Aluminum Foundry on Medford Street in east L.A. and now had complete control of every step in manufacturing his products. At the time, Weiand Power & Racing was the only speed parts manufacturer to own a metal casting foundry, and it cast products for other manufacturers, even for the competition. In 1971, Phil opened a larger, modern foundry just down the street from his original operation.

SCCMA AND SEMA

By 1958, speed shops were springing up all over the country, which spelled prosperity for equipment manufacturers but also brought out some unscrupulous business operators. The manufacturers formed an organization called the Southern California Credit Managers Association to combat the problem. Weiand and other manufacturers, including Ansen, B&M Racing & Performance Products, and Offenhauser, held monthly meetings at the White Elephant Restaurant in L.A. to review credit ratings of various warehouse distributors from coast to coast. It kept the manufacturers abreast of any speed shops that were deemed a bad credit risk.

In 1963, this same group, with the addition of more specialty outfits, founded the Speed Equipment Manufacturers Association, and Phil was on the board of directors. In 1975, he was inducted into the SEMA Hall of Fame, and in 1995, his wife, Joan, was also inducted into the Hall of Fame, thus becoming the first husband and wife to be inducted. As a note of interest, the original SEMA logo is credited to Weiand's artist, who came up with the design.

BUSINESS

As the technology of racing equipment improved, so did the quality and sophistication of race cars. Constant advancement in the field of performance camshafts, manifolds, exhaust systems, and the like were coupled with very noticeable improvements in the design and safety of the cars. As a result, speeds dramatically increased.

To keep abreast in a business that was constantly changing, and to deal with the performance claims made by his competitors, Phil enlisted the skilled services of Warren Brownfield from Air Flow Research of Van Nuys, California. Air Flow Research specialized in flow design, using the latest in high-velocity flow equipment to come up with workable runner designs for intake manifolds used in a variety of different applications. In 1972, the company developed a 360-degree, single-plane, open-plenum manifold called the X-Terminator that was suitable for the street. This intake had all the characteristics of high fuel and airflow velocity needed for performance without hampering the engine at slow speeds. It was known as the Weiand X-Terminator single four-barrel intake manifold. Keeping with the "X" theme, several years later Phil introduced the X-CELerator manifold.

As with any performance-enhancing engine part, the only way to really prove its worth was with a dynamometer, so Phil

One of Phil's early sponsored racers was Don "Big Daddy" Garlits, shown here wrenching the head on a Chrysler engine topped off with a Weiand Drag Star cast-aluminum eight-carb log manifold. *Courtesy Joan Weiand*

On June 1, 1935, Phil stands next to his '34 Ford coupe that he modified to allow him to drive with hand controls. Note the spotlight and radio antenna. *Courtesy Joan Weiand*

opened his own research and development facility. In 1977, Dick Davis was brought on board to head the test lab, which was responsible for the development of performance manifold designs for street-driven vehicles, with the aim of lowering exhaust emissions. The center housed a Clayton chassis dyno purchased from Ford and an 800-horsepower engine dyno, both to be used for product development. For all-out racing equipment testing, Phil had a 1,000-horsepower Heenan & Froude dyno installed at another facility.

In 1978, Weiand began to market the very successful G-Team line of manifolds. This performance design was the result of the combined efforts of Bill "Grumpy" Jenkins, Andy Krumm, Art Chrisman, Gene Adams, and Bill Brooks. These performance-savvy gentlemen, working out of the dyno facilities at Grace Industries, created a serious performance manifold. Fortunately for Phil, Grace lost interest in the project and Weiand picked it up.

Phil also teamed up with Henry Bechtloff to open a crankshaft specialty business, with Henry managing the affair. Henry began his career at an early age with L.A. Crankshaft. He and Phil bought out C&T Automotive and renamed it "Hank the Crank." The company provided performance crankshaft assemblies for NASCAR, Mercury Marine, drag racers, and engine builders.

In order to stand out from the crowd, sometimes a company will adopt a distinctive, highly recognizable color, as well as a logo, to assist in identifying its product. Every piece of Weiand equipment was packaged and shipped in bright yellow boxes with its renowned slogan, "Say Why-And." During a SEMA trade show at the Disney Hotel in Anaheim, a major competitor's sales rep, whose display was situated directly across from Phil's, jokingly referred to the Weiand display as the "yellow-box outfit"; obviously, the color was working.

Phil's long and successful career in the speed equipment business could be said to have been a direction taken out of necessity, not of design. Obviously, if he hadn't been involved in an accident that left him a paraplegic, it's hard to say in what direction he would have set his sights. Regardless of the direction, however, individuals such as Phil have that one special ingredient that brings them success in whatever endeavor they choose in life.

Once he came to the realization that he could make a living manufacturing engine manifolds, he embraced the idea totally. What originally began with 10 aluminum manifold castings, a drill press bought on credit, and a shed for a workshop was in time transformed into a multimillion-dollar empire, but not without years of hard, dedicated work.

Phil never lost interest in what originally attracted him to cars, and he began to collect Model T memorabilia. At the time of his passing, he was in the process of completing a duplicate of his original 1924 race car. He had several Model T cars in his collection, including an original coupe in mint condition. Besides the Ts, Phil had an original showroom-condition 1940 Ford coupe that still contained the opera seats.

At the fairly young age of 65, Phil Weiand passed away in September 1978, leaving the company in the hands of his wife, Joan, who had to contend with a business sector that was predominately run by men. Clearly, Joan was more than competent in running Weiand Automotive, as it continued to expand and hold its share of the marketplace. In respect to her late husband, and to give something back to the industry, she instituted a Phil Weiand Scholarship program that became part of SEMA's scholarship fund. Joan continued to manage the company for another 20 years, and in 1998, Weiand Automotive Industries was sold to the Holley Corporation.

CHAPTER 22

Dempsey Wilson Racing Cams

DEMPSEY WILSON

In the days before our dependency on computers and heavily automated business practices, it was a hard road for any individual to follow more than one time-intensive vocation and to be successful in each endeavor. Dempsey Wilson was one of those who had the right stuff. He loved racing and was successful at it; at the same time, he started a business with next to nothing and made it grow into a flourishing company. In both his racing career and in his camshaft business, Dempsey was confronted with and overcame many adversities that would have made many throw in the towel.

He was born on March 11, 1927, in Los Angeles and grew up in a family of five siblings. Dempsey's mother passed away when he was five years old, leaving his father and two grandparents to raise the children during the Great Depression.

APPLE-BOX RACER

The seed of competition that was planted in Dempsey began to sprout at a very early age. It began when his father built him a racer from an old, discarded apple box, some scrap wood, and roller-skate wheels, just like the one in the *Our Gang* movies. This simple, homemade racer sparked the six-year-old's desire for speed and competition.

"He would challenge anything with wheels on it," Dempsey's wife, Manon, said. "One day, while out alone with his racer, a kid rode by on a bicycle outfitted with a noisy toy motor. Dempsey took off hard after the bike and chased it long enough to find himself lost in a strange neighborhood. The fact that he was lost didn't bother him as much as that he didn't get a chance to race that bicycle."

Dempsey's academics began to slide after he learned how to drive at a fairly young age. "His father received a phone call one day from the [junior high] school's principal asking him if he knew that Dempsey had the family car at school and that obviously he was too young to drive," Manon said. "His dad replied that he didn't know that Dempsey had the car and promised that this wouldn't happen again. After retrieving the car at the school, his father handed Dempsey the car keys and told him not to park in front of the school again."

Dempsey continued to stray from his studies, choosing instead to work on his friends' cars and souped-up hot rods. Like a lot of kids his age, he did his fair share of street racing.

PRESCOTT

In his late teens, Dempsey and his brother, Rex, moved to Prescott, Arizona, to live with their grandmother. It was only fitting that Dempsey entertained the idea of becoming a mechanic, as he spent most of his waking hours under the hood of an automobile. He entered into an apprenticeship program at the local Ford dealership, and by age 19, he'd earned his "Doctor of Motors" certificate. When not working on cars at the dealership, he was fine-tuning his own hot rod.

He received his first taste of organized competition at Prescott's Yavapai County Fairgrounds dirt track in 1946. In Prescott, he developed his driving skills on rut-laden tracks and met a girl named

Opposite: Dempsey Wilson won the 150-lap midget race at Gardena in April 16, 1955, driving the Billy Graham Offy. Talk about Lady Luck—note Dempsey's right hand on the rear tire with a huge chunk of rubber missing. J. C. Agajanian, in the white hat, is presenting the trophy. *Dave Ward collection*

The corrugated-steel Wilson Racing Cams shop before the cement-block building was erected in front of it. *Courtesy Manon Wilson*

Manon, who would one day become his wife. A high school student from San Diego who was visiting relatives in Prescott, she was totally awestruck by the dashing, young race car driver.

Although Rex Wilson didn't possess the racer's spirit like his brother, he did go on to be instrumental in developing the four-track tape player for the automobile, which was eventually introduced to the marketplace by the famous Earl "Madman" Muntz.

CRA'S LITTLE INDIANAPOLIS 500

The annual Memorial Day Classic 500 race in Indianapolis has always been the Grand Prix of racing in America, and the California Roadster Association members felt that they should have their own, smaller version of the 500 in Southern California. It was held at Carrell Speedway in Gardena during the Memorial Day weekend in 1948, and was the longest race in the history of the CRA up to that date. The race would be 500 laps on the half-mile dirt oval for a total of 250 miles, and like the big 500, there would be 33 cars in the starting field. The winner's purse would be a princely sum of $7,680, which was the biggest payout by the CRA at that time.

Tony Gonzales, Nick Arias, and Walt Mahoney had built a track roadster for the big race, but being a little short in the financial department, they'd installed Walt's lightly modified '34 Ford V-8 engine from his street roadster in the race car. None of the fellows were astute race car drivers, so they contacted Dempsey to see if he was interested in the job.

Tony and Walt had been friends with Dempsey since their school days, while Nick, being a bit younger than his companions, had teamed up with Tony and Walt after Dempsey had left Los Angeles for Prescott.

The huge cash purse that the CRA was offering to the winner of the Little 500 was enough to attract some serious competitors. It didn't leave much hope for anyone running a street engine. Disaster struck during the time trials when Walt's engine blew, but it was not before Dempsey had landed the car in the race, qualifying 17th. Providence stepped in when Pat Flaherty, driving Howard Johansen's track roadster, hit the retaining wall during time trials and caused enough damage to put the car out of the race. The boys were good friends with Johansen, having spent a great deal of time

hanging out at Howards Cams, and with one team lacking an engine and the other team lacking a car, it didn't take long to install Howard's strong-running Mercury V-8 in their roadster.

With a sellout crowd of 17,000 watching, Don Freeland started the race in pole position, only to spin out on the first lap. Andy Linden, driving Nick Brajevich's Chevy six-cylinder roadster, took over the lead from Roy Prosser several laps into the race and might have run away with it, but he took out the bottom end of the car after running over a support post on his way to the pit. By lap 208, Dempsey had worked his way up through the pack to take the lead, and he held on for the checkered flag 292 laps later.

Due to the length of the race, the roughness of the dirt track, and the fact that these roadsters contained the very basics for comfort and safety, a large majority of the cars had relief drivers. Dempsey drove all 500 laps of the race himself, only pitting twice to refuel. The second- and third-place winners had relief drivers, and out of the 33 entrants, only 18 cars finished the grueling race.

RACE RESULTS

Winning the CRA 500 would prove to be a turning point in Dempsey's life. The win paved the way to a career as a race car driver, eventually taking him to his beloved Indianapolis 500. It also enabled him to marry his sweetheart, Manon, and that milestone indirectly led to a successful camshaft-grinding business.

Since their first meeting in Arizona, he'd kept up the relationship with Manon in hopes of someday marrying her. Before her parents would even entertain the idea of marriage, however, Dempsey first had to have at least $500 in his bank account. Little did they realize the determination of their future son-in-law; the Little Indy victory was the beginning of the Wilson family.

Dempsey left for San Diego right after winning the race to propose to Manon and visit his future in-laws. He was 21, and she was 16. After the wedding, the young couple bought a bungalow on Freeman Avenue in Lawndale, California. When not racing, Dempsey did general auto repairs in their backyard and salvaged camshafts from junk motors at the local scrap yards, which he sold for 50 cents each to Howards Cams to be reground for the performance market.

DEMPSEY WILSON RACING CAMS

Misfortune has a peculiar way of redirecting one's future. One day in 1951, while out in the backyard doing an engine tune-up, Dempsey had the owner of the car slowly pour a trickle of gasoline into the carburetor as he was working on the stubborn engine. Suddenly, it backfired through the carb, igniting the can, which was quickly dropped onto Dempsey. Suffering burns to the side of his head, his hands, and his chest, Dempsey was rushed to Torrance Hospital, where Lou Senter's brother was his attending doctor. Luckily for Dempsey, the burns weren't life-threatening, and he was able to return home after about a week in the hospital.

The accident made him realize that he needed to do something more than simple repair cars in the backyard. He needed a job that would support his growing family and, if possible, allow him to go racing once he was back on his feet. Having spent a lot of time over at the Howards Cams shop, he'd seen firsthand that the performance business was growing at a tremendous pace.

Given Dempsey's lack of a formal education, he had to work to understand the fundamentals, for example, of a cam grind. Nick Arias remembered Dempsey going down to the public library and spending a week just reading and studying everything he could find on camshaft fundamentals, grinding, and design. The rest was self-taught by trial and error, basically following the same road as his competition. Steve Wilson said that his dad told him Leo Goosen had advised Dempsey on certain camshaft theories and fundamentals.

With a little bit of knowledge and a whole lot of determination, Dempsey ventured into the camshaft business. Because there were no commercial grinders readily available, he made a copy of Johansen's cam grinder. But there was nowhere to put it; without a garage and with no money to rent a shop, the only suitable spot was his son's bedroom. The young couple moved the baby crib into their bedroom, and the baby-blue bedroom became the new home of Dempsey Wilson Racing Cams. In order to get cashflow, he took on a contract regrinding camshafts for Fenton Industries. His business quickly outgrew the tiny bedroom, so he moved the grinder to the backyard and installed it on a trailer. Manon recalled that by the time the machine was moved outside, the pretty blue wall behind the grinder was coated in black metal dust from the camshaft grinding.

Dempsey still hadn't fully recuperated from the accident, so his father would arrive at daybreak to help out, and they would start grinding cams before the family had gotten out of bed. As a youngster, Dave Ward was the neighborhood paperboy and remembered seeing a high-tension electrical cord running along the ground from the house to the monstrous machine sitting on the trailer. To show just how enterprising Dempsey could be in solving what confronted him, he purchased a large, wooden, surplus, aircraft storage container, about 12 by 15 feet in size, and turned it into a shop. This shelter got the grinder out of the weather and reduced the noise, much to the relief of the neighbors.

By 1955, Dempsey needed more room and considered building a suitable shop if he could pick up some properly zoned property. As luck would have it, Manon was driving along Roscrans Avenue in Hawthorne when she noticed a small "for sale" sign on a vacant piece of property. Dempsey purchased it from the owner on a contract with $250 down and $25 monthly payments.

Once he had the lot, he still needed a shop. He noticed a vacant frame building that had once served as a two-bay service station in Manhattan Beach, not far from his property. The old station was about to be demolished, so he made a deal and removed it from the site. He and his father manually leveled the building, and after dismantling and hauling the service station by trailer to the new site, they reassembled it all by hand. Dempsey erected the structure well back from the roadway, a decision that would prove very beneficial in years to come.

Manon said that few obstacles ever stopped or distracted her husband from what he set his mind to, and in those early years, his sheer determination usually overcame any financial shortcomings.

WILSON MOVING COMPANY

Once the cam business was up and running, Dempsey was able to go racing again, and he signed up with a sprint car team to run in the eastern circuit. He decided to combine racing out east with a little holiday for Manon and their son, Steve. That way, the family could enjoy several weeks of sightseeing before he sent them home and continued on with the racing team. His father agreed to manage the camshaft business until Manon returned. Alas, by the time they hit Chicago, Dempsey had a falling out with the team owners, and he was forced to look for other means to get his family back home.

Dempsey had always heard that Detroit auto companies sold off outdated engine-manufacturing machinery at rock-bottom prices, so he decided to find out what was available before heading back home. But first, the family needed transportation, so he bought a 1938 Buick from a used-car dealer for $90. Manon remembered that it didn't have third gear. Once Dempsey sorted out the transmission problems, they were off to Detroit in search of a camshaft grinder. They didn't have any problem in locating a cam grinder at a surplus machinery dealer—this particular one had been used by Ford—the problem was how to get it back home economically. Dempsey made a visit to a local scrap dealer, where he purchased a Model A phaeton, minus its engine. He borrowed a welder to beef up the undercarriage, made a tow bar, gutted the car's interior, and presto—he had a trailer to haul the grinder back to California.

Manon recalled the 2,500-mile trip home was very slow, hot, and tiring, and every 50 miles or so a tire would blow. She fondly remembered the generosity of strangers when they were stuck in the middle of New Mexico with a blown tire and no spares, and a '36 Ford coupe stopped to lend assistance. The couple asked if they could help and, seeing the Wilsons' predicament, gave them their own spare tire.

A scene from the interior of Wilson Racing Cams finds Dempsey pulling tests on his dynamometer. *Courtesy Manon Wilson*

EXPANSION

Times were improving, and as the business grew so did the need for expansion. Having a keen eye for a bargain paid off again for Dempsey, as the Pollard-Carrell Chevrolet dealership in Van Nuys was replacing its body shop and offered the building to him for free if he removed it.

In order to remain competitive in a business that was constantly growing through technical advances, Dempsey purchased a 1,000-horsepower Clayton dynamometer from a diesel plant in Los Angeles to assist in camshaft research. Several more years went by, and business was still booming; again, there was a need for more room to house the five camshaft grinders, the dynamometer, and a new retail speed shop. This time, Dempsey had a two-story cement block addition built at the front of the property. The second floor was for storage and offices, which allowed Manon to run the business away from the noise of the machinery, and the main floor space was divided into a speed shop outlet and an area to work on race cars. The retail speed shop allowed Wilson Racing Cams to offer the customer everything from a single part to a complete, coordinated, engine-assembly package.

STORIES FROM DAVE WARD

Dave Ward was a longtime friend of the Wilson family and worked at Wilson Racing Cams for a time. He left Dempsey's shop to work in construction, then later on went to work for Frank McGurk, and ended up running that business after it was sold to Iskenderian Racing Cams.

This story begins when Dave first noticed the goings-on in the backyard of a house on Freeman Avenue while delivering newspapers. It the early 1950s, he began hanging out at the Wilsons' because of all the race cars that came and went. He watched with fascination as they ground cams in the repurposed packing crate out back. Dempsey figured that if the kid was going to hang around the shop, he may as well do some work. He offered Dave a part-time job relieving camshafts at 75 cents a cam. Dave made

A customer's Plymouth drag car sits in front of the shop, waiting to have the engine installed. *Courtesy Manon Wilson*

the mistake of getting too good at it and was up to four cams an hour before Dempsey lowered his pay rate.

Upon graduating from high school, Dave started in full-time at the Wilson shop, operating one of the two homemade cam grinders. The bread and butter of cam grinding in those days was the flathead V-8 and Model A/B cams.

Ward usually accompanied Dempsey to the races as a crewmember, and Dave recalled the time in 1958 when they were loading up to go to Gardena Speedway. "Manon was debating on whether to go or not to the races with us," Dave said. "Dempsey was driving the Graham Offy, which was a pretty good Kurtis midget from out in the valley. Manon decided to stay with the kids at home, and Dempsey ended up winning the 150-lap feature. When we arrived home, Dempsey entered his house with the huge first place, winning trophy, and Manon began to cry her eyes out. 'What's wrong with you?' he asked, and Manon replied, 'If I'd known you were going to win, I'd have gone.' Dempsey came back with, '[chuckling]I'm always trying to win.' "

Dave said, "Dempsey's driving ability was better than the equipment he had." This statement was the consensus of many who knew Dempsey.

LOGO

Over the years, there were two different Dempsey Wilson Racing Cams logos, and both originated from Winston Beaumont. The first logo was the Indy roadster and the latter a crest shape.

Dempsey wasn't in a position to sponsor a flock of Top Fuel dragsters, but he did have some cars that raced with distinction wearing the Wilson Racing Cams logo. One of the oddest and best known was the *Widow Maker* motorcycle of E. J. Potter, known as the "Michigan Madman." Potter ran a chain-driven, fuel-injected, Chevy V-8 mounted sideways in a motorcycle frame and performed full, quarter-mile, tire-burning runs in the 160-plus-mile-per-hour range as an exhibition stunt—a show one doesn't forget!

Another memorable drag racer under the Wilson Racing Cams banner was Frank Pedregon, the "Flamin' Mexican." Frank drove the world's fastest AA/FC Fiat coupe with a blown, fuel-burning Chrysler that occasionally erupted into flames. Lions PR man Ralph Guldahl Jr. recalled that Frank's car would get about 50 yards down the strip before the exhaust flames from the zoomies would ignite the bits of rubber that had been flung from the slicks and collected around the wheelwells of the coupe. Frank's legacy to drag racing was to have two sons who followed in his footsteps successfully.

RACE CAR DRIVER

After returning to Los Angeles in 1948 and winning the CRA 500, Dempsey continued to drive as often as time and expenses would allow. The following year, he held the 1-lap, 3-lap, and 25-lap track records at Carrell Speedway in the jalopy class. In doing so, he competed alongside many future notables, including Parnelli Jones and Troy Ruttman. The jalopy class allowed up-and-coming drivers to hone their driving skills and still pocket some prize money.

Dempsey nearly won the last race that promoter Bill White held on the quarter-mile board track at the L.A. Coliseum. The 40-lap feature for the old board track was hotly contested between the eventual winner, Sam Hanks, and Dempsey, who came in a close second. The legendary Sam Hanks had a celebrated racing career at Indianapolis that spanned from 1940 to his last race in 1957, which he won.

In the early 1950s, drag racing was coming into its own, and Dave Ward remembered seeing a yellow '27 T powered by a hopped-up Buick straight eight behind the house on Freeman Avenue. Like Frank McGurk, Dempsey was a circle-track racer at heart, but he gave the quarter-mile a try and was successful in taking the B/Roadster class with a speed of 121 miles per hour at Santa Ana in February 1954. This race was one of the few times, if not the only time, that he ventured out onto a drag strip.

Dempsey felt most at home on the oval, and in the early 1950s, he got to drive Bill Krech's Offenhauser-powered midget. He quickly became a regular winner at the Gardena Speedway; in 1955, he set the one-lap and three-lap track records during at race at Bonelli Stadium in Saugus, California, and placed second behind Troy Ruttman in the 200-lap USAC-sponsored stock car race on the 1/3-mile paved oval track. The following year, he was in the driver's seat of the *Joe Hunt Magneto Special*, competing on the 1956 USAC Championship Trail. Dempsey was getting many rides, but the chance to drive at Indy still eluded him.

NEW STOCK CAR

The only new car that Dempsey ever bought was a 1956 Chevrolet, and the only reason for the purchase was to make a stock car out of it. Those were the good old days when stock cars were basically stock, bearing little resemblance to the highly sophisticated NASCAR jobs of today. In Dempsey's case, he left the factory front seat and radio in place and told Dave Ward that he occasionally listened to the radio while racing. The Wilson Racing Cams Chevy started off with the No. 44 for several races, but when he signed up to race under the USAC banner in the western circuit, he was given No. 56.

In that year, three stock cars ran out of the Wilson shop—a '56 Ford driven by Cecil Chambers, Ray Crawford's '56 Dodge, and Dempsey's '56 Chevrolet—all competing against the heavily financed factory teams. Dempsey was just as much at home behind the steering wheel in a full-size sedan as he was in a champ car. He placed second behind Troy Ruttman in the USAC National Stock Car short-track point standings that year.

Race car owner and promoter J. C. "Aggie" Agajanian put on a USAC stock car race at Saugus Speedway in 1957 and announced that Sam Hanks, winner of that year's Indy 500, would be competing in the event. Hanks was running with the Mercury factory-sponsored racing team, but just prior the Saugus race, Mercury pulled out. Aggie was in a panic and made a deal with Dempsey to let Hanks use his Chevrolet for the race. Sam drove the Chevy to the third fastest overall time, won the dash, and came in fourth in the main feature, competing against the big-dollar factory teams. After the race was over, Dave Ward heard Hanks say it was the best-handling stock car he'd ever driven in his life.

Jim Hurtubise had a very long and successful career at Indianapolis, but while climbing the ladder of success, Jim worked part-time at Wilson Racing Cams welding hard-face overlay camshafts. To keep racing expenses affordable, Jim and Dempsey ended up sharing the '56 Chevy stock car. Dempsey ran USAC, while Jim drove NASCAR, as the rulebook prohibited a driver from running in both camps.

Dave Ward remembered the time Jim had a NASCAR race over at Gardena Speedway, not far from the Wilson shop. Dave watched as they loaded the jack, toolbox, and spares into the car and drove it over to the track. Hurtubise had said, "I don't see no need to put the tow bar on that thing when we can just go over to 130th Street and sneak down there."

Dave said, "They left the Roscrans shop and just drove normally over to the speedway and into the pit gates as if they were out on a Sunday drive."

A FATHER FIRST

Steve Wilson recalled the time he watched his dad race at Ascot in a Turkey Nite Shootout with Parnelli Jones and other prominent drivers: "I watched my dad running in third place coming out of turn two and noticed that there was an opening under the leaders, but he didn't take it. After coming in third, I asked him why he didn't go for the opening. Dad's reply was, 'The reason I didn't was cause I wanted to come home and see you guys.' He ran hard and safe and didn't want to jeopardize his or anyone else's life; he had respect for the race car and what a foolish mistake could do. This struck me, making me realize that Dad wasn't out there just to put on a show but took this racing seriously."

Even though Dempsey loved racing above most things, it didn't come before his family. Manon told of the time of when he raced at Indy and was due to compete in Milwaukee the following weekend. Driving night and day back to Los Angeles, he picked up her and the kids, turned around, and drove back in time for the

Dempsey powers a Dodge stock car around the Pomona Fairgrounds course in 1958. Note how clean the car is. Dempsey was either not trying hard enough or was following the pack. *Dave Ward collection*

Dempsey with his fuel-injected Chevrolet powered Halibrand Shrike racecar at Las Vegas Speedway. *Courtesy Manon Wilson*

race in Milwaukee. He wanted to show his boys the Museum of Science and Industry in Chicago after the race.

THE ROAD TO INDY

To compete at the fabled Brickyard has been viewed by many drivers as the pinnacle of a racing career, and Dempsey's view was no different. Just after he'd received his Indy driver's license, Dempsey told Manon about the first time he saw Indy. "It was 1946, the war was over, and the five hundred was again running at Indy," Manon said. "There was a Wilson family reunion back in Illinois about the same time the Memorial Day race was to be held. Both he and his grandmother saved up gas money for the trip, and when the time came, they set off in Dempsey's '36 Ford coupe. They cooked their meals over an open fire and camped along the side of the road until arriving in Indianapolis. Dempsey said that he watched the race from the infield with his face pressed up against the wire fence, dreaming of driving there one day."

She went on to say that her husband's greatest desire was to race cars and ultimately make it to the Indianapolis 500. Once Wilson Racing Cams was well established, it provided Dempsey the financial means to take several months off in the summer to race out east, leaving Manon to run the business and Chris Neilson to manage the machine shop. Neilson worked full-time from 1964 to 1968 and then went over to Iskenderian's shop, eventually opening his own camshaft-grinding business in Farmington, Utah.

Dempsey and Dave Ward used an Airstream trailer in a trailer park on Georgetown Road next to the Indianapolis Speedway as their home base of operations. Before the factory and high-dollar teams came onto the racing scene, car owners and drivers showed up for a USAC Championship meet towing their race cars on open trailers. Dempsey hauled his car behind a 1958 Oldsmobile station wagon loaded with spares. In between races, he and Dave worked on the car in Lysle Greenman's leased garage in Gasoline Alley, where Greenman kept his Indy car.

DRIVER'S LICENSE

The years of struggling and dedication finally paid off in 1956, when Dempsey got to try out for his Indy license. To qualify, he had to pass a driving test on the track. The only car Dempsey could locate for the tryout was an outdated, 15-year-old dinosaur that hadn't seen any serious action since the late 1940s. It was a car that "Curly" Wetteroth built in 1941, and it would be lucky to reach the speeds needed to pass the test.

Dempsey managed to get the tired old beast up to 131 miles per hour, leaving the astounded officials in disbelief that the car was capable of those speeds, so they asked Freddy Agabashian to test it out. After lapping the track several times, a concerned Agabashian brought the car back into the pits and said, "I don't know how Wilson got it up to 131 miles per hour; I couldn't, and it scared me."

Things seemed to be coming together at last for the aspiring driver that year: he got his license and was offered a ride in the *Martin Brothers' Special*. It may have been Dempsey's inexperience, or maybe the car just didn't have it, but the car couldn't get up to qualifying speed. Again in 1957 he tried to place the same car in the 500 with a lap speed of 139 miles per hour, but he was less than 1-mile-per-hour from making the cut.

THE BRICKYARD AT LAST

The 1958 Memorial Day Classic was looking better, as Dempsey squeaked the *Hall-Mar Special* into the show with a marginal qualifying speed. All seemed safe until the second-to-last day of qualifying, when Dempsey was bumped by Freddy Agabashian. The rules stated that if a driver hadn't qualified his car for the show, on the last day of qualifying he was a free agent and could offer his services to another team.

Among the cars trying to qualify for the race that year was the *Sorensen Special*, an ex-Agajanian Kuzma race car that no one had ever been able to qualify for the race. Aggie, out of desperation, sold it in 1958 to Bob Sorensen, the owner of an auto salvage yard in Los Angeles. Several drivers tried it, but the best anyone could push the car to was about three miles per hour below qualifying speed.

Dempsey went over to Sorensen's garage, studied the car for a while, and said, "I can fix that." He'd noticed that the tie rod had been rubbing up against the radiator saddle at one point, so someone had taken a torch and heated one of the steering arms to bend it for clearance, but this resulted in uneven steering geometry. Dempsey and Dave Ward worked quickly to have the radiator saddle reshaped, moved it back a little, replaced the steering arms, and with about a half-hour left on the last day of qualifying, Dempsey got in with a 143.2-mile-per-hour run and started the car in the 32nd spot. Maybe it was just as well he didn't start closer to the front, because in turn three on the opening lap the two lead cars mixed it up and caused a 15-car pileup. The carnage resulted in the tragic death of fifth-place starter Pat O'Connor, and eight cars were put out of the race.

Once the race restarted, Dempsey's laps were among the fastest on the track, and he moved up to seventh place when he came in for his first pit stop. By the second pit stop, he was in fourth place, but the third stop was disastrous. Oil had leaked into the belly pan and caught on fire while Dempsey was in the pits. It was extinguished quickly, and Dempsey continued on until lap 151, when the car developed clutch-pedal problems that put him out of the race. Dave said that the Sorensen team was so low-budget that after Dempsey made a pit stop for tires, the crew had to run over to the Firestone trailer to have new tires mounted on the only spare wheels they had—enough for one pit stop.

Dempsey finished the 1958 Indy 500 in 15th position, one spot ahead of another rookie, A. J. Foyt. Dave said that at the next year's race, Dempsey took Foyt a shoebox full of Continental racing camshafts for his kid's quarter-midget race cars.

NOVI

After his success at Indy, Dempsey received many inquiries from car owners. In late 1958, Norman Delmer called for Dempsey, who happened to be out of town. When Dempsey returned and heard the message, he said that it was too late, as he'd already signed up to drive the notorious Novi. Dave Ward was more than a little disappointed with the choice and always felt that the decision to drive the Novi had repercussions on his racing career. The car that Delmer offered Dempsey to drive had placed second at Indy in 1958 with a rookie behind the wheel, and in 1959 it carried Paul Goldsmith to fifth place.

RACING AT THE SPEEDWAY

After his lack of success in the Novi and a couple other middling years at the Speedway, Dempsey failed to make the field with his first ride for the 1963 event but was given the opportunity to qualify another car. It would be the only time that he ever completed the full 200 laps, and it would be his last time competing in the 500. He qualified the *Vita Fresh Orange Juice Special* in the 30th spot and finished 11th. The Vita Fresh car owners were pleased with his performance and had him back in the driver's seat the following year, but he spun out and wrecked the car during qualifying with no hopes of getting it ready for the race.

The 1967 race was Dempsey's last attempt to complete an unfulfilled dream, and he attempted it in his own car, the *Dempsey Wilson Racing Cams Special*. The rulebook permitted 305 ci for an unblown stock block compared to a 255-ci engine like the Offy. A stock block with a blower was limited to 221 ci, and a blown Offenhauser-type engine was down to 183 ci. Dempsey sleeved and de-stroked a 265-ci Chevy V-8 down to 220 ci, added a turbocharger with three side-draft carburetors in lieu of fuel injection, and dropped the 550-horsepower package into his Halibrand Shrike. Providence once again turned a blind eye to his valiant and underfunded endeavor, as Dempsey encountered unsolvable clutch problems during a qualifying run.

REMEMBERING DEMPSEY WILSON

It's hard to say whether Dempsey Wilson is best remembered as a race car driver or a specialty equipment manufacturer. He was a man with two very active careers who was successful in both fields.

It may have been his strong self-reliance that prevented him

Dempsey sits patiently in his Halibrand Shrike, sidelined with fuel-delivery problems as his crew attempts to sort out the situation. *Dave Ward collection*

from tying up with a top-end race car team. "Dempsey wasn't really a team player who'd play politics in order to get a ride," Manon said. "It ran against the stubborn, independent streak in him."

Whatever it was that shaped Dempsey's outlook on life; it wasn't a lack of effort or raw talent. If he'd been given the opportunity to drive for a first-class team, the name Dempsey Wilson might have been up there alongside A. J. Foyt and Parnelli Jones in the annals of racing.

After battling a rare form of cancer for four years, Dempsey Wilson passed away in 1971 at the age of 44, leaving behind his wife, Manon, sons Steve, Bart, and Jon, and daughters Marilyn and Lana. It wasn't an easy task for Steve, who was 18 and the eldest son, to take over the reins of the business. The following year, the performance market began to weaken, as the gas crunch descended upon America. Steve recalled that a large portion of the camshaft business leaned toward street rods and muscle cars, and when that market softened, the family decided that it was best to close the doors of Dempsey Wilson Racing Cams.

The renowned Smokey Yunick once said that Dempsey Wilson was in his list of a very special class of humans. "Just because you never heard of Dempsey Wilson doesn't mean he wasn't a good driver," Smokey said. He went on to tell of the time he had four of the top Indy drivers try out his race car—Tony Bettenhauser, Paul Russo, A. J. Foyt, and Dick Rathmann—and they all said no to driving it. Dempsey came along and asked to give the car a try.

"He jumped in her cold and drove it 'til he was completely exhausted," Smokey said. "No complaints. If I don't know anything else about Dempsey Wilson, he was a strong mother and had plenty of balls."

Afterword

Today, hot rodding has its eye on the future as well as the past. We look now to the third generation to keep the pulse strong. And they are out there, doing it well, much to the delight and gratitude of the 1920s–1940s kids who started this pandemic.

We could start a list now of the carriers-on and see 50 years from now where it led and who's still passing it along to the fourth and fifth generations. Another romanticist, like Paul Smith, will venture along and fall victim to the siren of the passion that began so many years past and we'll wonder what call it was they heard.

The accelerative for the yen to gain speed was a studied knowledge of physics and of thorough testing and restarting. Of runs and more runs. Patience and dedication. Some of these young men in oily whites and jeans and blackened fingernails were capable of intellectually conquering any dream they had wanted, but in those days money was key, and what they accomplished by trading, borrowing, scraping, and scrounging was awesome. Things were different then. Honor was alive and individuals counted. It was true fellowship among those dry lakes racers—and, look, it's actually still alive, flickering perhaps, for our dwindling heroes, but, the heart of it still beating.

The resurgence of the flathead and the manufacturing sophistication of speed equipment today makes one realize just how much heart those "hop-up" boys had back in the 1920s, '30s, and '40s. The question is, can the new merchants carrying the torches of the "oldies" keep the romance going and for how long? Excellence will always eventually shine through the throng. The shale will erode, but the rock will stand long after. There will always be the climbers skinning the knees and pounding their pitons. So, let's continue to strive for excellence in product and follow the beacon that fired competition so many years ago.

—*Donna Navarro*

Photo taken by Ed Iskenderian on Jefferson Boulevard in 1941. Ahead of the famous Isky roadster is the roadster belonging to the Camfather's lifelong buddy, John Athan. *Courtesy Ed Iskenderian*

Acknowledgments

The time spent researching and writing this book has been lengthy, and over that period of time, sadly, several of the fellows profiled within have passed away. I got to know some better than others, and was quite fortunate to spend considerable amounts of time with the likes of Ed Iskenderian, John Athan, Barney Navarro, and Lou Senter. The generosity shown by all the gentlemen I interviewed can only be described as unbelievable and very rewarding. Jack Underwood, for example, openly shared his filing cabinets full of racing history, and Dennis Webb offered encouragement when it was sorely needed. Leslie Long's vast photo archive and uncanny memory were also immensely helpful. But above all, it was a pleasure to sit and listen to men whose brilliant minds contained more technical knowledge than most text books.

The following individuals assisted in the research for *Merchants of Speed* and their contributions are greatly valued. There were others whose names, unfortunately, have escaped me, but whose help was no less appreciated:

Nick Arias Jr.; John Athan; Tony Baron; Fred Blanchard; Nick Brajevich; Fred Carrillo; Stan Chersky; Harvey J. Crane Jr.; Mark Cravens; Randy Cummins; Chuck Daigh; Harold Daigh; Jim Davis; Walt Diederich; Laurie Dunlap; Vic Edelbrock Jr.; Dimitri Elgin; Gene Ellis; Jack Engle; Ted Frye; Jaime Gonzales; Tony Gonzales; Ralph Gudahl Jr.; George Hale; Doug Hartelt; Chet Herbert; Stuart Hilborn; Bob Hughes; Dick Hughes; Ed Iskenderian; Bill Jenks; Bob Johansen; Don Johansen; Frank Kloss; Bruce Larmer; Rod Larmer; Rodger LeCroix; Leslie Long; Bud Meyer; Roy Miersch; Jim Miller; Lloyd Menveg; Ollie Morris; Bob Morton; Don Nairn; Barney Navarro; Donna Navarro; Chris Nielson; Fred Offenhauser Jr.; Gene Ohly; Joe Panek; Karl Payne; Kevin Perciado; Gary Richards; Eric Rickman; Ron Roseberry; Mike Russel; Johnny Ryan; Mel Scott; Lou Senter; Al Sharp; Zane Shubert; Jerry Silberstein; Ron Soll; Bill Spalding; Diane Spalding; Steve Story; Don Turner; Jack Underwood; Pete Van Iderstine; Dave Ward; Dan Warner; Don Weaver; Dennis Webb; Joan Weiand; Manon Wilson; Sherry Woods.

Index